The Politics of Religious Party Change

The Politics of Religious Party Change examines the ideological change and secularization of religious political parties and asks: when and why do religious parties become less anti-system? In a comparative analysis, the book traces the striking similarities in the historical origins of Islamist and Catholic parties in the Middle East and Western Europe, chronicles their conflicts with existing religious authorities, and analyzes the subsequently divergent trajectories of Islamist and Catholic parties. In examining how religious institutional structures affect the actions of religious parties in electoral politics, the book finds that centralized and hierarchical religious authority structures – such as the Vatican – incentivize religious parties to move in more pro-system, secular, and democratic directions. By contrast, less-centralized religious authority structures – such as in Sunni Islam – create more permissive environments for religious parties to be anti-system and more prone to freely formed parties and hybrid party movements.

A.Kadir Yildirim is a Fellow for the Middle East at Rice University's Baker Institute for Public Policy. He holds a Ph.D. in political science from the Ohio State University.

Cambridge Studies in Social Theory, Religion, and Politics

Editors
David E. Campbell, University of Notre Dame
Anna M. Grzymala-Busse, Stanford University
Kenneth D. Wald, University of Florida, Gainesville
Richard L. Wood, University of New Mexico

Founding Editors
David C. Leege, University of Notre Dame

In societies around the world, dynamic changes are occurring at the intersection of religion and politics. In some settings, these changes are driven by internal shifts within religions; in others, by shifting political structures, institutional contexts, or by war or other upheavals. *Cambridge Studies in Social Theory, Religion, and Politics* publishes books that seek to understand and explain these changes to a wide audience, drawing on insight from social theory and original empirical analysis. We welcome work built on strong theoretical framing, careful research design, and rigorous methods using any social scientific method(s) appropriate to the study. The series examines the relationship of religion and politics broadly understood, including directly political behavior, action in civil society and in the mediating institutions that undergird politics, and the ways religion shapes the cultural dynamics underlying political and civil society.

A.Kadir Yildirim *The Politics of Religious Party Change: Islamist and Catholic Parties in Comparative Perspective*
Taylor C. Boas *Evangelicals and Electoral Politics in Latin America: A Kingdom of This World*
David E. Campbell, Geoffrey C. Layman, and John C. Green *Secular Surge: A New Fault Line in American Politics*
Ramazan Kılınç, *Alien Citizens: The State and Religious Minorities in Turkey and France*
Gary J. Adler Jr., *Empathy Beyond US Borders: The Challenges of Transnational Civic Engagement*
Amy Erica Smith *Religion and Brazilian Democracy: Mobilizing the People of God*
Kenneth D. Wald, *The Foundations of American Jewish Liberalism*
J. Christopher Soper and Joel. S Fetzer *Religion and Nationalism in Global Perspective*
Mirjam Kunkler, John Madeley, and Shylashri Shankar, editors, *A Secular Age Beyond the West: Religion, Law and the State in Asia, the Middle East and North Africa*
Andrew R. Lewis, *The Rights Turn in Conservative Christian Politics: How Abortion Transformed the Culture Wars*
Darren W. Davis and Donald Pope-Davis, *Perseverance in the Parish? Religious Attitudes from a Black Catholic Perspective*
Mikhail A. Alexseev and Sufian N. Zhemukhov, *Mass Religious Ritual and Intergroup Tolerance: The Muslim Pilgrims' Paradox*
Sadia Saeed, *Politics of Desecularization: Law and the Minority Question in Pakistan*
Damon Mayrl, *Secular Conversions: Political Institutions and Religious Education in the United States and Australia, 1800–2000*
David T. Smith, *Religious Persecution and Political Order in the United States*
Jeremy Menchik, *Islam and Democracy in Indonesia: Tolerance without Liberalism*

Ryan L. Claassen, *Godless Democrats and Pious Republicans? Party Activists, Party Capture, and the "God Gap"*

Jonathan Fox, *Political Secularism, Religion, and the State: A Time Series Analysis of Worldwide Data*

François Foret, *Religion and Politics in the European Union: The Secular Canopy*

Luke Bretherton, *Resurrecting Democracy: Faith, Citizenship, and the Politics of a Common Life*

Amy Reynolds, *Free Trade and Faithful Globalization: Saving the Market*

David E. Campbell, John C. Green, and J. Quin Monson, *Seeking the Promised Land: Mormons and American Politics*

Karrie J. Koesel, *Religion and Authoritarianism: Cooperation, Conflict, and the Consequences*

Peter Stamatov, *The Origins of Global Humanitarianism: Religion, Empires, and Advocacy*

Pippa Norris and Ronald Inglehart, *Sacred and Secular: Religion and Politics Worldwide* Second Edition

Brian J. Grim and Roger Finke, *The Price of Freedom Denied: Religious Persecution and Conflict in the 21st Century*

Ahmet T. Kuru, *Secularism and State Policies toward Religion: The United States, France, and Turkey*

Kees van Kersbergen and Philip Manow, editors, *Religion, Class Coalitions, and Welfare States*

Paul A. Djupe and Christopher P. Gilbert, *The Political Influence of Churches*

Jonathan Fox, *A World Survey of Religion and the State*

Anthony Gill, *The Political Origins of Religious Liberty*

Joel S. Fetzer and J. Christopher Soper, *Muslims and the State in Britain, France, and Germany*

Pippa Norris and Ronald Inglehart, *Sacred and Secular: Religion and Politics Worldwide*

The Politics of Religious Party Change

*Islamist and Catholic Parties
in Comparative Perspective*

A. KADIR YILDIRIM

Rice University's Baker Institute for Public Policy

Shaftesbury Road, Cambridge CB2 8EA, United Kingdom

One Liberty Plaza, 20th Floor, New York, NY 10006, USA

477 Williamstown Road, Port Melbourne, VIC 3207, Australia

314–321, 3rd Floor, Plot 3, Splendor Forum, Jasola District Centre, New Delhi – 110025, India

103 Penang Road, #05–06/07, Visioncrest Commercial, Singapore 238467

Cambridge University Press is part of Cambridge University Press & Assessment, a department of the University of Cambridge.

We share the University's mission to contribute to society through the pursuit of education, learning and research at the highest international levels of excellence.

www.cambridge.org
Information on this title: www.cambridge.org/9781009170741

DOI: 10.1017/9781009170734

© A.Kadir Yildirim 2023

This publication is in copyright. Subject to statutory exception and to the provisions of relevant collective licensing agreements, no reproduction of any part may take place without the written permission of Cambridge University Press & Assessment.

First published 2023

A catalogue record for this publication is available from the British Library.

ISBN 978-1-009-17074-1 Hardback

Cambridge University Press & Assessment has no responsibility for the persistence or accuracy of URLs for external or third-party internet websites referred to in this publication and does not guarantee that any content on such websites is, or will remain, accurate or appropriate.

Contents

List of Figures		*page* ix
List of Tables		xi
Acknowledgments		xiii
Introduction		1
	What Are Anti-System Parties?	8
	Contributions and Significance	10
	Methods and Data	11
	Cases	14
	Organization	17
1	Explaining Religious Party Change	21
	An Institutional Theory of Religious Party Change	31
	Religious Institutions	35
	Main Actors	44
	Catholic Parties versus Islamist Parties	46
2	Catholic and Islamic Religious Institutions	51
	Hierarchical Organization in the Catholic Church	52
	Decentralized and Nonhierarchical Structure	
	of Religious Authority in Sunni Islam	62
	The Break and the New Equilibrium	67
	Criticism of the Ulama	71
	Invoking Islamic Concepts	74
	A New Public	78
	Ulama's Response	82
	Conclusion	85

viii
Contents

3 Anticlericalism, Religious Revival, and the
Rise of Religious Political Identities 86
  Political Identity Formation 88
  Waves of Anticlerical and Anti-Ulama Attacks 89
  Religious Revivalism 103

4 The Origins of Religiopolitical Identity 110
  The Egyptian Muslim Brotherhood 114
    The Origins of the Movement 115
    Creating the Brotherhood Brand 119
    Early Years of the Brotherhood 127
    Political Activism and Growing Tensions 130
  Tunisian Ennahdha Movement 132
  The National Outlook Movement of Turkey 138
    The Rise of the National Outlook Movement 140
    The Early Years: Party–Movement Relationship 146
    The Welfare Party 149
  Center Party in Germany 152
    Rise of the Catholic Mass Movement 155
    Brewing Intra-Catholic Conflict 156
  Popular Party in Italy 164
    The Rise of Catholic Action 167
    Catholic Political Activism 172
  Catholic Party of Belgium 177
    Anticlericalism in Belgium 177
    The Rise of the Catholic Mass Movement 181

5 Intraparty Conflict 190
  The Muslim Brotherhood in Egypt 193
    The 2011 Revolution and the Nonevolution of the Brotherhood 196
  Ennahdha Movement in Tunisia 204
    Specialization Policy 205
  The Justice and Development Party in Turkey 222
    The AKP and Religious Discourse 227
  The Rise of the Center Party 233
  _The Formation of PPI and the Catholic Church's Response
  in Italy_ 247
  The Rise of the Catholic Party in Belgium 253

Conclusion: Looking Ahead – The Challenge of Islamist
  Organizational Reform 261

Bibliography 269
List of Interviews 297
Index 301

Figures

2.1	Development of the Islamic religious sciences	*page* 65
2.2	Mean primary enrollment rations in developing regions	81
5.1	Religion–governance relationship in Tunisia	214

Tables

2.1 Adult literacy and primary school enrollment (%)   *page* 80
2.2 National primary enrollment ratios (%)   80

Acknowledgments

I first began working on this book in 2014. Stathis Kalyvas' *The Rise of Christian Democracy in Europe* served as a key inspiration for me. *The Rise of Christian Democracy* was well argued and well researched; it was, and still is, one of the best books on politics and religion. Yet, to me – as someone who works in a different regional context – the book felt incomplete, but not because it has any glaring shortcomings. I was intrigued by how the theory might travel in the Middle Eastern context where Islamist parties were the dominant religious parties. I wondered if there were systematic differences between Catholic and Islamist parties, in particular from an institutional point of view and using political economic approach to the study of religious politics. *The Rise of Christian Democracy*, however, was not meant to answer these questions. Fortunately, it motivated me to take up the task and examine the two sets of religious political parties in a comparative framework.

I am indebted to many individuals in the writing of this book. Without their support, the book would certainly not have come to fruition. I want to thank all of them for their support and help. First and foremost, I thank my colleagues at the Edward P. Djerejian Center for Middle East at the Baker Institute. Kelsey Norman, Mohammad Tabaar, and Kristian Ulrichsen have been excellent colleagues and friends, offering support every step of the way. I can't imagine having better colleagues.

Many friends and colleagues graciously offered their feedback and criticisms on the draft of the book. They were generous with their time in reading drafts of the manuscript, engaging in discussions, and overall putting up with my inferior work. Jillian Schwedler, Nathan Brown, and Anthony Gill offered tremendously helpful feedback in my book workshop. Their feedback helped clarify the argument, improve the organization, and better connect the argument and the empirical evidence. The workshop served as a critical step in completing the book. Over the years, I benefitted from feedback by Abdullah

xiii

Acknowledgments

Aydogan, Matt Buehler, Kristin Fabbe, Courtney Freer, Sharan Grewal, Lisel Hintz, Amaney Jamal, Ekrem Karakoc, Ramazan Kilinc, Esen Kirdis, Ahmet Kuru, Mirjam Künkler, Jonathan Laurence, Avital Livny, Marc Lynch, Peter Mandaville, Tarek Masoud, Rich Nielsen, Irfan Nooruddin, Annelle Sheline, Hakki Tas, and Scott Williamson.

I received the Smith Richardson Foundation's Strategy & Policy Fellows grant in support of this book. The grant supported the fieldwork and allowed me an opportunity to draft the manuscript. I am grateful for their support.

Baker Institute leadership and staff have offered unyielding support in the writing of this book. Ambassador Edward Djerejian consistently encouraged me and offered policy-based feedback. Lianne Hart in the editorial team, Shawn O'Neill in the graphics team, and Lisa Winfrey in the development team have all provided excellent assistance at different stages.

Cambridge University Press editorial team have been outstanding since the start of the review process. Sara Doskow and Rachel Blaifeder have been excellent editors to work with. Jadyn Fauconier-Henry provided superb editorial assistance. Becky Jackaman oversaw the production process admirably. I also thank the series editors of the Cambridge Studies in Social Theory, Religion and Politics. In particular, I want to single out Anna Grzymala-Busse for her exceptional feedback on the manuscript during the review process. I also thank the anonymous reviewers for their criticisms and feedback.

I feel extremely fortunate to have had excellent research assistance over the years. I am grateful to Colton Cox, Makenzie Drukker, Marie Lawrence, Jack McCall, Meredith McCain, Mason Reece, Sarah Smati, and Elaine Zhang for their assistance. I also want to thank Safa Belghith for her help with fieldwork in Tunisia.

Last but not least, I want to acknowledge an unlikely source of motivation. In my years dedicated to writing this book, I encountered many challenges, including but not limited to uncertainty about the direction of the book, the pressure of working on multiple projects simultaneously, and the extant haze. Under similar conditions, many seek external sources of motivation to get back on track and refocus on occasion. In my case, hip-hop music offered a way out of the occasional rut I might have found myself stuck in. The Wu-Tang Clan deserves distinct recognition here. Wu-Tang's grimy beats, raw sound, defiant lyrics, and extensive use of self-aggrandizement drew me in. The dynamics of hip hop music, in certain ways, evoke pre-modern Sufi poetry. Despite the seeming contrast in their arts, contemporary hip-hop and pre-modern Sufi-inspired poetry have much in common. Poetry represented one of the highest forms of art in many pre-modern Muslim societies. The poets of the day were excellent in rhyming; yet, it was their ability to relate to the social and political issues of their time and the extent to which they could engage with their contemporaries in their craft that characterized and ultimately perfected their art. At a time when music might feel like a largely sanitized enterprise, the social and political undertones of the Wu-Tang beats certainly struck a chord. As

Acknowledgments   xv

cliché as it may sound, there is more to Wu-Tang than the iconic sword sounds and the lines the group liked sampling from kung fu flicks. Wu-Tang's grit and intrepidity have been inspirational in resetting my focus and reorienting my mind toward tasks ahead. Timeless Wu-Tang is forever.

Despite all the help and support I received over the years, the book almost certainly falls short of reflecting the generosity and brilliance of this support. If the book has achieved any of its stated objectives, it is due to the support I received.

Introduction

On June 30, 2017, the German parliament passed a bill legalizing same-sex marriage in the country. It was Germany's Catholic party, the Christian Democratic Union (CDU), that paved the way for this progressive reform as the party leader and German Chancellor Angela Merkel deemed the issue a "question of conscience," permitting individual members of her party to vote their personal preferences.[1] Roman Catholic bishops of Germany campaigned against the legislation on doctrinal grounds.[2] Same-sex marriage fundamentally differs from how the Catholic Church conceives marriage; the Church classifies same-sex relationships as a major sin. Many Catholics take their cue from the Church's official position and oppose it as they believe same-sex marriage to be "unnatural." Party officials, however, justified the legislation on the basis of citizenship. Frank Henseler, the CDU leader in Bonn, argued that the decision was overdue and that the party should "completely accept that there are also ways of life different from those that the CDU always promoted."[3] CDU's deputy finance minister Jens Spahn hailed the decision as a "logical" step for conservatives because it is "a value that we as Christian Democrats should cherish."[4]

---

[1] "Germany Approves Same-Sex Marriage, Bringing It in Line with Much of Western Europe," *Washington Post*, June 30, 2017. Available at: www.washingtonpost.com/world/germanys-parliament-legalizes-same-sex-marriage-bringing-it-in-line-with-most-neighbors/2017/06/30/55033686-5d09-11e7-aa69-3964a7d55207_story.html

[2] Tom Heneghan, "In Germany, Catholic Church Grapples with Blessings for Gay Marriage," *National Catholic Reporter*, January 24, 2018. Available at: www.ncronline.org/news/world/germany-catholic-church-grapples-blessings-gay-marriage (accessed August 9, 2020)

[3] "CDU Reconsiders Stance on Gay Marriage," *DW*, March 4, 2013. Available at: www.dw.com/en/cdu-reconsiders-stance-on-gay-marriage/a-16642949

[4] "Christian Politicians Are Trying to Stop Same-Sex Weddings in Germany," *Newsweek*, March 7, 2017. Available at: www.newsweek.com/same-sex-marriage-marriage-laws-angela-merkel-csu-germany-631258

For Merkel, the decision boiled down to introducing "more social cohesion and peace" in Germany.[5]

By contrast, on August 26, 2018, Tunisia's Ennahdha Party – deemed one of the most progressive and moderate Islamist parties in the Muslim world – opposed the proposal to change the Personal Status Code from the 1950s and grant women equal inheritance. Provisions of the traditional Islamic law allot women an unequal share of the inheritance, typically one half of men's share.[6] The Tunisian Personal Status Code faithfully mirrors religious law and gives women half of men's share in inheritance.[7] The Code is viewed as one of the major impediments to establishing gender equality in Tunisia.[8] Importantly, Ennahdha justified its opposition to the proposal on the grounds that the issue of inheritance is well established in the Qur'an.[9] Abdelkarim al-Harouni, Ennahdha Shura Council leader at the time, stated that Tunisia is a "civil state for Muslim people, committed to the constitution and the teachings of Islam" and that Ennahdha would reject "any law that goes against the Qur'an and the constitution," which refers to Islam as the religion of the Tunisian state in Article 1.[10]

This contrast between the CDU and Ennahdha is not exceptional; rather, it exemplifies the differences between today's Islamist parties in the Middle East and Catholic parties in Western Europe. Yet, this polarity was not a historically foregone conclusion. Christianity and Islam experienced remarkably similar phases of religiopolitical mobilization dating back to the nineteenth and early twentieth centuries.[11] Political Catholicism and political Islam both emerged in reaction to increasing secularization in state policies and a perceived threat to the traditional influence of religion and religious institutions in public life. Both quickly gained significant traction in countries across Europe and the Middle East, respectively. When these religiopolitical movements did finally emerge, the similarity in political discourse and activism between the two was unmistakable. Both espoused anti-system discourses that emphasized religious education, a social and political order grounded in

---

[5] "German Lawmakers Approve Same-Sex Marriage in Landmark Vote," *Reuters*, June 30, 2017. Available at: www.reuters.com/article/us-germany-gay-marriage/german-lawmakers-approve-same-sex-marriage-in-landmark-vote-idUSKBN19L0PQ

[6] Esposito and DeLong-Bas 2001, 37.

[7] Sharan Grewal, "Can Tunisia Find a Compromise on Equal Inheritance?" *Brookings Institution* (September 25, 2018). Available at: www.brookings.edu/blog/order-from-chaos/2018/09/25/can-tunisia-find-a-compromise-on-equal-inheritance/

[8] "Women's Rights Reforms in Tunisia Offer Hope," *Council on Foreign Relations*, December 4, 2017. Available at: www.cfr.org/blog/womens-rights-reforms-tunisia-offer-hope

[9] "The Closing Statement of the 21st Session of Ennahdha Movement Shura Council," August 26, 2018. Available at: www.ennahdha.tn/البيان-الختامي-للدورة-21-لمجلس-شورى-حركة-النهضة

[10] "Tunisia's Ennahda Rejects Proposal to Enshrine Secular Inheritance into Law," *Middle East Eye*, August 27, 2018. Available at: www.middleeasteye.net/news/tunisias-ennahda-rejects-proposal-enshrine-secular-inheritance-law

[11] Altinordu 2010.

Introduction

moral and patriarchal principles, rejection of secularism and pluralism, and enforcement of social hierarchy.[12] Democracy did not belong to either political agenda. Catholic mass movements emphasized the creation of a "Christian society" where supreme authority would be held by religious leaders: "By creating a distinct Catholic society (or subculture) within the secular society, a real country that is hostile and opposed to the legal country, it sought to build a *societas christiana* (Christian society) that was based on restrictions of individual freedom, organicist conceptions of representation, and fusion of state and church. Supreme authority would be wielded by spiritual leaders, and all ideological or religious projects contrary to Catholic dogma would be forbidden."[13] Likewise, Islamist movements expressed their keen interest in creating an "Islamic" state and society that would be ruled on the grounds of religious law.[14] Egyptian Muslim Brotherhood's founder Hassan Al-Banna, for example, encouraged legal reforms to conform to "Islamic legislation," surveillance of all public employees' personal conduct, harsh penalties for moral transgressions, gender segregation, extensive control over media and arts, a national dress code, and religious instruction.[15] Religious mobilization and mass religious movements defined the social and political activism of these actors while creating distinct Catholic and Islamic *political* identities and parties.[16] The core issue that religious political parties face deals with reconciling two conflicting imperatives. On one hand, they want to guide humanity toward "otherworldly salvation" in the sociopolitical arena as an extension of their "spiritual mission"; on the other hand, they must come to terms with the idea that modernity requires separation between the religious and political spheres and that the state cannot serve as an instrument for religious parties to fulfill their "spiritual mission."[17]

Despite these striking similarities in origin, Catholic parties were able to make a definitive transition to adopt secular and democratic ideas, shed their anti-system character, and frame their political discourse accordingly early in their evolution. Unlike Catholic parties of Europe, Islamist parties of the Middle East never got over their "confessional dilemma" – the conflict between the unique political identity religious parties want to develop and the constraints imposed on them by their religious origins – and have largely been unable to transform themselves in the same manner.[18] This book asks, what explains the diverging trajectories of Catholic and Islamist parties? More broadly, when

---

[12] Brown 2012.
[13] Kalyvas 1998, 297.
[14] Hallaq 2012.
[15] Wendell 1978.
[16] Kalyvas 1996; Kirdiş 2011.
[17] Accetti 2019, 170.
[18] See Kalyvas (1996, 222) for a greater discussion of the implications of the notion of confessional dilemma in the Catholic context.

4 *The Politics of Religious Party Change*

and why do religious parties become less anti-system? At a time when religious actors are gaining political significance across the world, religious party change away from an anti-system posture constitutes a critical component of stable and prospering democratic governance.[19]

My answer to the question of when and why religious parties[20] move away from anti-system positions rests on religious institutions. Informed by the historically divergent trajectories of confessional parties in Western Europe (the Zentrum Party in Germany, Popular Party in Italy, and Conservative Party in Belgium) and Islamist parties in the Middle East (the Muslim Brotherhood in Egypt, Ennahdha Party in Tunisia, and the Justice and Development Party in Turkey), I systematically analyze the institutional context in which religious parties operate. I argue that religious institutions and religious competition are central to the process of religious party change. Studying the creation of Catholic and Islamic political identities in the early modernization periods in Western Europe and the Middle East reveals how institutions shaped the divergent trajectories of religious parties in their respective contexts. While embracing virtually identical religious visions for the society and the state at the time of their emergence in the modern period – a *societas christiana* versus an Islamic state and society – Catholic and Islamist parties gradually carved out divergent paths as they faced distinct religious institutional contexts. As a result, only one was able to overcome its confessional dilemma.

Religious parties are embedded in distinct *religious* institutional structures that deeply influence their actions as they chart their paths in electoral politics. As part of these religious structures, religious parties compete with other religious actors for religious authority and political power. As such, religious party change is a story of competition over political and religious power. This religious competition is embedded within the existing religious institutional structure. The existing structure of religious authority affects emerging religious parties in two distinct ways. Externally, the level of institutionalization and hierarchical organization within a religious tradition conditions religious parties' ability to absorb authority and compete with other religious actors. Whether authority is centralized or decentralized shapes religious party

---

[19] Toft, Philpott, and Shah 2011; Brocker and Künkler 2013; Ozzano and Cavatorta 2013; Driessen 2014.

[20] In this book, I adopt Brocker and Künkler's definition of what a religious party is: "We use the concept of 'religious parties' as encompassing parties that hold an ideology or a worldview based on religion (having, thus, a cross-class appeal) and mobilize support on the basis of the citizens' religious identity ... religious parties, it should be noted, can also become identity and preference shapers when religious identities are rather fluid than fixed" (2013, 175). These parties can utilize religious terminology, religious symbols, or religious rituals in their names or party programs. What sets apart religious parties from nonreligious parties is not the mere use of religious symbols. As Brocker and Künkler state, "Nonreligious parties may naturally also use or refer to religious ideas, terminology, goals, and symbols (as, for instance, the Republican Party in the United States does). For religious parties, however, these are *central* [emphasis added]" (2013, 176).

Introduction

strategy on whether to contest religious authority and to what extent. In cases where a centralized, hierarchically organized, and autonomous religious institution – for example, the Vatican – defines the parameters of the religious sphere, religious parties have a harder time breaking free from the monopoly of this centralized religious institution, ultimately weakening their claim on religious and moral authority. This centralized religious institution typically controls the religious discourse and wields religious and moral authority.[21] In cases where a centralized religious institution does not exist – for example, Sunni Islam – religiopolitical movements seek to justify their political legitimacy by claiming religious authority and authenticity. Counterintuitively, I argue that the more centralized and hierarchical religious authority structure is, the less incentive and freedom a religious party has to function as anti-system. In turn, religious parties in this religious institutional context will move in a more pro-system, secular, and democratic direction. By contrast, the less institutionalized religious authority is, the more incentive and freedom a religious party has to operate as anti-system. Religious authority structure demarcates the limits of political discourse that religious parties can engage with.

Internally, the religious institutional structure shapes the organizational structure of religious parties and conflict between the religious and political elements of the party. Religious parties typically evolve out of mass religious movements.[22] The nature of the organizational relationship between the religious party and their parent religious movement adds another layer of institutional constraint to what the party can or cannot do in the political arena.[23] The conflict between religious and political factions of religious parties fundamentally alters the political landscape and the meaning of electoral politics for religious parties, with major ramifications for ideological rigidity.[24] Centralized religious institutional structures lead to a sharp separation between the religious and political factions, forcing religious movements to a choice between the centralized religious authority structure and the bourgeoning religious party. By contrast, decentralized religious institutional structures do not force a choice, which empowers religious factions and allows religious parties to maintain their hybrid organizational structures.

---

[21] Lakoff 1995; Campbell 2007; Grzymala-Busse 2015.

[22] Wegner 2011, XXXVII; Ozzano and Cavatorta 2013.

[23] The significance of the relationship between the movement and the political party goes beyond religious parties. Communist, socialist, green, and populist right parties had similar relationships with social movements that gave rise to these parties at various points in time, particularly in Western Europe (Papadakis 1984, 13–17 & 174–86; Kuechler and Dalton 1990; Betz and Immerfall 1998; Kitschelt 1989). Importantly, new political parties in emerging or transitional democracies can also hail from a social movement (Zollner 2019, 3).

[24] A similar dynamic is at work in other types of parties that hail from social movements. For example, see Offe (1990) for an analysis of the German Green Party.

Religious parties prefer the party-movement hybrid organization structure for two primary reasons. First, this hybrid structure allows religiopolitical movements to operate as encompassing organizations with a wide range of goals that are religious, educational, missionary, political, social, and health-care-oriented in nature. This structure aligns well with the broad-based religious transformation they envision in the state and society. Religion, in this vision, cannot be excluded from specific spheres of life, thereby necessitating religiopolitical activism to encompass politics, welfare, education, and healthcare. Second, this hybrid structure enables religious parties to sustain anti-system discourse by claiming religious legitimacy and harnessing it for electoral advantage. It is in this organic relationship between the party and the movement that we find religious parties vying for religious and moral authority. While some argue that the blurred boundaries between a social movement and the political party that hails from the movement might lead to pluralism and an open political system,[25] this relationship between the party and the movement, in fact, facilitates the anti-system character of these parties by obfuscating the distinction between the movement's membership (to which the religious movement appeals to) and the broader electorate (to which the party aims to win over). The focus on religious institutional structures helps make a vital distinction between religiopolitical movements and organized religion, emphasizing that the two need not be the same.[26] Although the party-movement relationship constitutes one of the most vital institutional factors that religious parties operate within, it is striking to note that beyond occasional casual references to it,[27] little systematic research exists on this topic.

In order to establish a theoretical framework that can be applied in multiple contexts, a systematic and comparative inquiry into the question of religious party change from the perspective of religious institutions requires a set of cases that meet several criteria. The cases should display similarities in their origins as religiopolitical movements, possess similar anti-system ideological orientations at the time of their foundations (especially in regard to democracy, pluralism, secularism, and the role of religion in society), and yet have divergent trajectories over time. Catholic parties of Western Europe and Islamist parties of the Middle East meet these criteria and offer the optimal case of analytical equivalency in order to employ the most similar systems design.[28] Relying on the historically divergent trajectories of these two groups of religious parties in Western Europe and the Middle East, this book theorizes that the role of religious institutions on religious party change carries significant weight.

---

[25] Goldstone 2003, 2.

[26] Kalyvas 2003, 296.

[27] Rosenblum 2003; Mohseni and Wilcox 2009; Wegner 2011; Brown 2012; Clark 2012; White 2012; Ozzano 2013; Ozzano and Cavatorta 2013; Spiegel 2015; Wuthrich and Ciftci 2020.

[28] Nielsen 2016.

Introduction

What religious institutions do is constrain religious parties in ways that other kinds of political parties do not experience. Religious parties in the Middle East and Western Europe, in this regard, were met with two distinct environments. On one hand, like other political parties, they were subject to the constraints and opportunities presented by the political environment. Politically, religious parties in both contexts encountered an environment ripe for their religiopolitical activism. On the other hand, religious parties faced constraints in a religious environment, unlike other political parties. This religious environment was permissive in the case of Islamist parties, while it worked against Catholic parties in Western Europe. Confronted with a centralized and hierarchical religious authority, Catholic parties constructed their political discourse and organizational structure around this religious institution. Catholic parties in Western Europe operated purely as political parties and universally transitioned to become mainstream, pro-system parties coexistent with democracy and secularism and often play critical roles in democratic consolidation.[29] By contrast, Islamist parties did not encounter a dominant religious actor that challenged them at their inception, allowing Islamist parties the freedom to shape and structure their discourse and organizations as they deemed fit. As a result, Islamist parties universally embraced hybrid party-movement organizations and operated as bulwarks of anti-system politics, impeding the progress of democracy in their respective societies.[30]

The question of religious party change remains relevant for both policy and scholarly audiences. In recent years, religion and religious actors have assumed an ever-more critical role on a global scale. These parties have taken on governmental roles in various parts of the world (PJD in Morocco, AKP in Turkey, BJP in India, Ennahdha in Tunisia, Muslim Brotherhood in Egypt, CDU in Germany, and The Jewish Home in Israel), drawing attention to heightened tensions surrounding the religion-democracy nexus. In contexts where democratic politics is still being negotiated and the religion-secularism conflict constitutes a key component of ongoing struggles, religious party change is a topic of critical importance. As such, this book is not solely a historical comparison or a scholarly exercise but also lends itself to current policy discussions.

All major religions have "the power to delegitimize a democratic government, and religious political movements have often played the part of regime destabilizer," as Driessen notes.[31] The subject of this book thus deserves a great deal of scholarly attention because Islamist parties have become staples of the political space in one of the most democracy-resistant regions of the world. Religious parties' move away from being anti-system parties underlies broader democratization processes worldwide despite the prevalence of the "secularization paradigm" utilized to understand – *and* to dismiss – religious parties until

---

[29] Driessen 2014.
[30] Jamal 2013.
[31] Driessen 2014, 7.

8 *The Politics of Religious Party Change*

recently.[32] The focus on religious parties is vital because political parties tend to be "the most important carriers and shapers of normative attitudes toward democracy."[33] Ultimately, this book seeks to understand the mechanisms through which religious parties evolve over time and the institutional arrangements that facilitate the best ways to engage religious parties. These concepts, I argue, are crucial elements in the design of a successful regional policy that could remedy the paucity of democracy in the contemporary Middle East.

WHAT ARE ANTI-SYSTEM PARTIES?

I want to explain and define my usage of the term anti-system because it is so central to my argument. Studying religious parties in comparative perspective necessitates value-neutral language, particularly when examining changes in these parties. In this regard, I avoid referring to religious parties with the frequently used term "moderation" for several reasons. First, the notion of moderation carries an inherently subjective connotation. "Moderation" of religious parties implies a preference for the direction of change in religious parties. While there may be numerous reasons why religious parties might prefer a more moderate platform, I am not interested in allowing any of these considerations to compromise the scholarly objectivity of this book.[34]

Second, the concept of moderation does not easily lend itself to comparative analysis; any attempt to conceptualize it is bound to feel incomplete. What is included in the definition of moderation and what is left out varies from one particular political context to the other. This potential issue with the poor traveling of the concept is true not only in cross-regional or cross-religious contexts but even within the same region or religion. For example, a review of the literature on Islamist parties' moderation reveals a myriad of ways in which such parties' moderation is conceived by scholars.[35] A further complication in this book involves temporal differences between Catholic and Islamist parties' emergence and the policy issues that were prominent in each period. Such issues are likely to show great variation across countries and, as such, do not lend themselves to a sound comparative analysis.[36]

---

[32] Künkler and Leininger 2009; Ozzano and Cavatorta 2013. See Jeremy Menchik's (2016) insightful analysis of Indonesian Islamic organizations for how these groups negotiate the relationship between democracy and Islam. Similarly, Amr Hamzawy and Nathan Brown (2008) examine Islamist movements' relationship to the democratization processes in the Arab world.

[33] Mainwaring and Anibal Perez-Linan 2013, 57.

[34] For example, Sheline (2020) examines how the label "moderate" remains far from reflecting the true nature of certain political systems in the Middle East; instead, the label is used as a "reputational strategy."

[35] Karakaya and Yildirim 2013.

[36] I encountered this difficulty in my own work (Yildirim 2016). In analyzing the effects of distinct economic liberalization processes over Islamist party platforms and their societal base, I examined platforms of Islamist parties in three different Middle Eastern countries in order to

Introduction

Instead, this book will focus on the evolution of religious parties from being anti-system to pro-system. I use anti-system to describe any political party that fundamentally challenges the "values of the political order within which it operates" and seeks to change not the government "but the very system of government."[37] The underlying assumption here is that the current system of government is neutral and constitutes the yardstick with which to evaluate alternative positions and ideologies – that is, anti-system parties.[38] This conception of the political system typically entails an implicit recognition of democracy as the baseline from which to evaluate a party's anti-systemness. In the case of religious parties, secularism accompanies democracy to form the core tenets of the political system. However, the inherent attributes of a political system need not always be self-evident; they may be contested.[39] A key advantage of the term anti-system, in this regard, lies in the fact that it is relative and does not require an assumption about the nature of the government system – that is, democratic or authoritarian – that the anti-system parties challenge. Islamist and Catholic parties accordingly faced different political systems at the time of their formations, yet both sets of parties were united in their oppositions to the existing systems of government.

This approach to religious parties concerns itself with ideology less by focusing on the "content" of party ideology and more on the party's "ideological difference." In particular, anti-systemness is relational in two distinct ways. On one hand, it refers to the party's ideological distance from the regime's parameters. A large distance between the two suggests that the party will be more likely to be categorized as anti-system. This makes sense – anti-system parties consider the entire political system illegitimate and seek to replace it. The further away a political party is from the ideological center, the higher the tension with the regime is. On the other hand, it indicates the party's ideological distance from other parties in the political system.[40] Such distance from other political parties in the system typically creates additional challenges for the anti-system party, including exclusion from coalition governments and inability to affect policy. This relational conception of anti-systemness also implies that other actors' perception of anti-system parties (in this case religious parties) as a threat to the existing political system can lead to their stigmatization and encounter with obstacles in their political participation.[41]

---

chronicle the change in their ideologies and how their platforms transformed over time. One of the challenges in this exercise was establishing the conceptual distinction between an Islamist and a Muslim democratic platform in regard to the public role of Islam as envisioned by these two sets of different parties in three different countries.

[37] Sartori 1976, 132–33.
[38] Zulianello 2017.
[39] Altinordu 2016, 153.
[40] Capoccia 2002, 14.
[41] Altinordu 2016, 149–50.

The roots of the anti-system nature of religious parties lie in their extensive opposition to modernity, secular society, and the idea of secular governance. For these parties, their very existence stems from the religious vision they conceive for the state and society. Anti-system religious parties regard democratic politics as a means of seizing power to transform societies and states to allow religion to dictate all aspects of life.[42] Their opposition to the system of government is deeply steeped in this normative stance. I am therefore interested in understanding what causes religious parties to change their normative stance against the system; their position on specific policy issues is not of primary concern.

My focus is on the evolution of these parties. The reference to the evolution of religious parties aims to capture the process that leads to the foundation of such parties in the first place and their early histories. This process begins with an anti-system platform in the embryonic phase when Catholic and Islamic political identities were first created and evolves to take different shapes in response to institutional constraints. While the main parameters of such an evolution are outlined and discussed by reference to the religious institutional structures, I do not lay down a particular timeline regarding how long such an evolutionary process might take. Likewise, I do not focus on the particulars of these parties' platforms. Such an exercise runs counter to the reasoning behind the focus on anti-system characters of religious parties in this book.

CONTRIBUTIONS AND SIGNIFICANCE

I do not aim to fully account for the question of religious party evolution or change in different religious contexts. Such a tall task is beyond the scope of this book. Instead, my aim is more modest. I examine how religious institutions and authority structures affect the evolution of such parties across different religious contexts, focusing particularly on their anti-system characters.

This book makes an original and important contribution to the study of religious parties by bringing together literatures that developed largely independent of each other and failed to engage in a meaningful and fruitful conversation. Their engagement here works to further enhance our understanding of religious parties in different religious and regional contexts. Such a contribution is critical to conceptualizing both the formation of religious parties from a cross-religious perspective and how religion and religious institutions can mold the process of religious party formation and ideological development. In this regard, the remarkable similarity in the emergence and early phases of Catholic and Islamist parties' existence challenges conventional wisdom that these two sets of political parties are fundamentally different.

Despite these similarities, however, the religious institutional structures pose constraints that religious parties – irrespective of the faith tradition they identify

---

[42] Ozzano 2013, 11.

Introduction

with – must navigate, ultimately pushing them in divergent trajectories. In this regard, the primary goal of this book is to examine the underlying dynamics of these divergent paths that religious parties take once I establish key similarities among religious parties across different religions. Religious parties are subject to constraints that other parties do not face; religious parties strive to serve two distinct constituencies, they have access to religious discourse, and can utilize religious authority as a political resource. Organizationally, religious parties can – and oftentimes do – serve multiple functions with a complicated organizational structure that goes beyond being merely a political party.

In doing so, however, this book does not suggest that religion is the only factor shaping the actions and ideology of religious parties. Religious parties do, in fact, respond to the political environment around them in the same way that nonreligious political parties do. Shifts in the electorate or constraints imposed by the state factor into religious parties' organizational and ideological policies. This is a particularly critical observation for Islamist parties. Looking ahead, organizational reform, i.e., separation between the religious and political activism, has been gaining greater prominence as the key dynamic to impel Islamist parties toward more democratic platforms and leave behind anti-system postures. This book's close examination of how organizational reform comprised a vital element of the Tunisian Ennahdha's and Turkish AKP's paths to ideological change carries important policy implications, especially in the context of recent efforts to steer Islamist parties in a more pro-democracy direction.

The comparative framework for the study of religious parties in this book speaks to literatures such as religion and politics, political parties, and regional studies. Its primary original contribution, in this regard, is not so much in its individual case studies and analyses; many other scholars examined various religious parties or groups of parties in their own right. Such contributions are invaluable and constitute the foundation of my understanding of religious parties. Instead, this book brings together such disparate works in different contexts and presents a coherent and systematic analysis of religious parties and how they are influenced by religious institutional structures. While a wealth of detailed information on various cases will be lost in the comparative analysis I present here, I am convinced that analytical gains make up for, if not outweigh, such losses.

METHODS AND DATA

The primary method of analysis in this book is process tracing. Following Collier, I define process tracing as "an analytic tool for drawing descriptive and causal inferences from diagnostic pieces of evidence – often understood as part of a temporal sequence of events or phenomena." Careful and thorough description of "trajectories of change and causation" underlie this method. What sets process tracing apart from other methods is the centrality of "sequences of independent, dependent, and intervening variables" in the analysis,[43] in the absence of which it is merely a collection of descriptive facts. In order to present a full account of the causal mechanism at work and the sequence of events, my analysis will offer a detailed descriptive narrative of the unfolding events and change over time.

I use process tracing to gain new insight into the causal role of religious institutions over religious parties and identify the causal mechanisms at play. It is not merely the exact moment of change in religious parties where my interest lies; instead, I examine and describe how religious institutions affect the evolution of religious parties step-by-step and subsequently the change in these parties at decisive junctures. As such, there are no "logical holes" in associating the cause to an effect in the "causal story." In doing so, I employ a systems understanding of process tracing, whereby I "unpack" the causal process at work and track down the relationship between religious institutions and religious party change away from anti-system postures.[44] By describing in detail the activities that the actors engage in through specific religious institutional structures, I account for the causal mechanisms at work.

The choice of the process tracing method reflects the comparative advantage it offers in drawing causal mechanisms using "detailed, within-case empirical analysis." Process tracing can be instrumental in obtaining a thorough understanding of "causal dynamics" at play that produce a particular outcome of interest in one single case. It can also help within a group of cases that operate on the basis of the same causal dynamics that link the causes and the outcomes under identical contextual conditions.[45] Process tracing is a particularly powerful tool when combined with the most similar systems design, which I do here. Process tracing can help minimize the limitations of the most similar systems design by providing the latter with a sharp focus on the factors that might have causal impact.[46] More specifically, the most important advantage of combining process tracing with the most similar case analysis is that "rather than contending with all potential alternative causes through process tracing, the analyst must only contend with those not addressed at the matching style."[47] The most similar systems design, in other words, allows me to eliminate a series of potential causes through matching cases in the design stage by selecting cases that have similar characteristics but vary on a potential causal factor. While the most similar systems design can control for various possible causal factors, it does not eliminate all. Process tracing complements the matching design and enables me to consider a very small number of potential alternative causes throughout the analysis that have not been accounted for in the matching stage. In this regard, this book is an attempt at theory-building;

---

[43] Collier 2011, 823–24.
[44] Beach 2017, 5.
[45] Beach 2017, 4.
[46] George and Bennett 2005, 215.
[47] Nielsen 2016, 574–75.

Introduction

defining key concepts in the potential causal mechanism at work is followed by an extensive descriptive narrative of how the causal dynamics lead to the outcome of interest. While this approach falls short of offering a complete and satisfying test of the theoretical argument developed in this book, it nonetheless serves as a "smoking-gun" test where the evidence offers strong support for the causal argument but does not entirely dismiss competing hypotheses.[48]

The key religious institution I focus on has clear observable implications as to which direction a religious party should lean when faced with these institutional constraints. Greater levels of centralization of religious authority push religious parties toward pro-system positions while decentralized religious authority structures trap these parties in anti-system postures. Ideally, therefore, the theoretical argument developed here should apply to religious parties irrespective of region or religion. Yet, in order to more clearly trace the effect of religious institutions, I choose to focus on religious parties from opposing ends of the religious institutionalization spectrum. On one end, Catholicism represents the most centralized and hierarchical institutional framework; Catholic parties operate within the limits of this religious structure. On the other end, Sunni Islam offers one of the most deregulated, noncentralized, and nonhierarchical institutional structures. Islamist parties feel minimal constraints as they forge their paths in electoral politics.[49]

I draw empirical evidence from various sources. For Catholic parties, I rely on secondary sources that analyze Catholic mass movements and confessional parties of Western Europe in the nineteenth and the early twentieth centuries. The rich literature on Catholicism and politics in the modern period offers the best opportunity to examine the history of the institutional relationships between the Catholic Church, Catholic mass movements, and Catholic parties. My analysis of Islamist parties relies on a more diverse set of resources. While I employ primary and secondary sources to study the early history of Islamist movements, I turn to personal interviews with party and movement officials to discuss the recent organizational and ideological changes taking place within these parties. I conducted extensive fieldwork on the Islamist parties examined in this book primarily in the form of face-to-face interviews with party and movement officials. The

---

[48] Bennett 2010.

[49] Yet, it is crucial to note that the dynamics of religious party change do not neatly cut across religious lines, which might have raised the specter of essentialism. It is not always the case that the existence of a hierarchical structure ensures the rise of a pro-system Catholic party, as the failure of such a party to rise in France illustrates. Likewise, the conflict between the Qum-based ulama and the Islamist movement in Iran (Roy 1998; Kurzman 2003) and the ability of some Islamist parties to dominate their movements, such as in Morocco (Spiegel 2015) and Turkey, are noteworthy examples of the significance of agency and the strategic calculations by religious parties. Endogeneity of religious institutions and the agency of actors such as religious parties play critical roles in determining these outcomes. To reiterate, religious institutions offer only part of the variation as to why religious parties change and embrace a pro-system character, and my goal in this book is to demonstrate how such effect comes about.

interviews are the main instruments for exploring the motivations of key decisionmakers in these religious parties and movements, as well as understanding the religious and moral authority they claim. These interviews offer complementary evidence for the conceptualization of the party-movement relationships and the claims on religious authority by religious parties. By conducting a comparative analysis of religious parties in different contexts, I demonstrate the shared theoretical basis for explaining change in both Catholic and Islamist parties. This book goes beyond region- or religion-specific analyses of religious parties by focusing on the common dynamics that exist across different cases, regions, and religious contexts and avoids getting bogged down in minute differences.[50]

CASES

I examine three Islamist parties in the Middle East and three Catholic parties from Western Europe: the Muslim Brotherhood in Egypt, Ennahdha in Tunisia, the AKP in Turkey, the Center Party in Germany, Popular Party in Italy, and Conservative Party in Belgium. Because my goal is not to explain religious party formation, I select cases that are successful instances of religious party formation.[51] The case selection reflects a number of important methodological considerations. First, the cases offer variation on the main independent variable of interest – the structure of religious institutions and the nature of religious authority – across Catholic and Sunni Islamic contexts. Moreover, Catholic and Islamist cases also show variation within themselves. In the case of Catholic parties, the extent to which they were beset by the Church's opposition varies significantly across the three parties, where the influence is greatest in Italy and the least in Germany. The Italian Popular Party, as a result, was quick to distinguish itself from the Church and underscore its independence even before it was formally established. By comparison, German and Belgian Catholic parties forged their independent paths as they gradually made their way into the political system. While the same variation cannot be established for the Islamist parties due to the decentralized nature of religious authority, the level of competition in the religious field, alternatively, exhibits variation. In Turkey, and to some degree in Egypt, religiopolitical activism had a large presence at the time of Islamist parties' rise. In both cases, burgeoning movements carefully distinguished themselves from other religious actors to ensure the legitimacy of their organizations and discourse. In Tunisia, Ennahdha encountered a relative void of religious activism; therefore, the movement spent less time engaging other religious actors and devoted its energies to taking on the secular regime.

[50] Schwedler (2011) chronicles such differences in various works on Islamist parties in extraordinary detail in a review article.

[51] For thorough studies of religious party formation in the Catholic and Islamic contexts, see Kalyvas' (1996) and Kirdiş' (2019) excellent analyses.

Introduction 15

Second, among a large group of religious parties in both contexts, I elected to focus on the largest and electorally most important ones. For any theory of religious party change to have validity, the larger religious parties must be part of the theory-building exercise. If the argument developed here does not apply to the most crucial cases,[52] then there is reason to suspect how far the theory can travel, ultimately weakening it considerably. In addition, the larger parties can also act as pioneers and set examples for how other religious parties might determine their course of action in the political arena. Indeed, the leadership of many of these parties interact and follow closely what other parties do. Lastly, the Islamist parties studied here vary in their relationships with Islamist movements. This provides an extraordinary opportunity to analyze in real time the motivation behind some Islamist parties' decisions to de-couple the movement and the party, such as in the case of Ennahdha in Tunisia and the AKP in Turkey. This focus on how some Islamist parties respond to shifting political conditions carries crucial policy implications as Islamist parties continue to constitute a major element of democratization prospects in the Muslim Middle East.

Established in 1928 by Hassan Al-Banna, the Muslim Brotherhood is one of the oldest religious mass movements in the Muslim world. Despite its humble origins, the movement took Egypt by storm and grew into a religious and political powerhouse in the 1930s and the 1940s. Although the Brotherhood did not establish a formal political party until after the 2011 Revolution, political activism has been a staple of the movement. The Brotherhood's hybrid model of religiopolitical activism served as the pivotal pillar of its organizational existence and ensured the religious faction's dominance over the political one, even after the formation of the Brotherhood's political party – the Freedom and Justice Party – as a separate entity. This hybrid religiopolitical model quickly became the norm among Islamist activists and diffused throughout the Middle East, either as a branch of the Brotherhood or inspiring other nonaffiliated Islamist groups.

Ennahdha is Tunisia's premier Islamist movement, taking on a nebulous form in the late 1960s. Like the Egyptian Brotherhood, Ennahdha sought to combat secular modernity and secularization of the state and society; its eventual goal was restoring Islam to its rightful place among Tunisians. Ennahdha embraced the hybrid movement-party structure and embarked on religiopolitical activism within a singular organizational entity. While there were some attempts in the 1980s to formally establish a separate political party, those efforts did not come to fruition. In the postrevolutionary period, Ennahdha's political faction successfully reignited discussions about the relationship between the religious movement and the political party. In a remarkable move, Ennahdha adopted the Specialization Policy in 2016, which set up Ennahdha to officially cease its religious activism and operate solely as a political party.

---

[52] Gerring 2007.

This unusual act to relinquish its claim to religious authority sets Ennahdha apart from most other Islamist parties and deserves closer examination.

The Justice and Development Party (AKP) in Turkey has captured the imagination of many inside and outside the country since its formation in 2001. Underlying this interest are the party's ideological transformation and success in economic policymaking and democratization reforms in its early years in government. However, intrigue quickly turned into shock as the party switched gears and embarked on a path of authoritarian politics, repression, and widespread corruption. The AKP grew out of the National Outlook Movement, Turkey's primary Islamist group. Established in the late 1960s, the movement aimed to undo the policies of the secular Turkish Republic and rectify the ills of the modern age through a return to religion. Like other religious parties, they embraced the hybrid model that envisions overlapping spheres of activity across religious and political fields. Unlike the Egyptian Brotherhood and Tunisian Ennahdha, the National Outlook Movement created a separate entity to function as the movement's political party that remained subordinate to the movement. Fighting the Turkish state's wrath over the years, a group of younger, reform-minded members of the movement's political faction decided to break away and establish the AKP in 2001. The case of the AKP offers noteworthy insights into the utility of religion, religious discourse, and religious legitimacy for political parties.

Stuck between an anti-Catholic German state and an overbearing and ultramontane Catholic Church, the origins of the Center Party lie in the mid-nineteenth century waves of anticlericalism. Despite the insistence of middle-class German Catholics to embody more decisive political activism by way of a separate political party, the Catholic Church resisted these efforts for fear of losing its control and power over the Catholic laity. When the Center Party finally emerged during the 1870s in response to the Kültürkampf, it was only as a secular party that took inspiration from Catholicism rather than a political outfit of the Church. In fact, the Catholic Church opposed the party and discouraged the clergy and laymen from supporting it. While the Center Party stood against the suppression of the Catholic Church and its faithful, the party did so independent of the Church. Indeed, party leaders fiercely defended their independence from the Church and resisted pressure from the Church hierarchy to fall in line with the Church's position on important policy decisions.

Among all fledgling Catholic parties of Western Europe, the Popular Party (PPI) in Italy faced the most pressure from the Catholic Church due to its geographical proximity to the Vatican. The PPI emerged from the Catholic mass movement in Italy under Don Luigi Sturzo's leadership in 1919. Italian Catholics first organized into the Opera dei Congressi and subsequently Catholic Action to fight against the forces of modernity and the secular state, with the goal of bringing Catholicism and the Church back into its rightful place in the modern era. The Italian Catholic mass movement operated largely under the Catholic Church's control, mirroring its ecclesiastical structure.

Introduction

The Church hierarchy was careful to limit the freedom of movement leaders because of potential competition for its power over the Catholic faithful. When Sturzo failed to convince the Catholic Church that a separate Catholic party under the Church's supervision could improve the Church's interests vis-à-vis the Italian state and socialist threat, he ultimately decided to form the PPI as a secular party independent of the Church.

Compared to other Catholic parties, the Belgian Catholic Party took a different route in its formation. The party morphed into existence on the heels of the 1884 electoral victory of Conservative Catholic politicians in the Belgian parliament. Belgian Catholics began organizing in response to the anticlerical policies of the Belgian government starting in the 1850s, particularly in education. The Catholic mass movement grew in various directions in Belgium, appealing to different socioeconomic segments of Catholics in the country. The Federation, Boerenbond, and Belgian Democratic League spoke to the middle class, farmers, and workers, respectively. The Catholic Party was originally dominated by the Federation and the ultramontanes in its early years, hewing the Church's line. However, the Belgian Democratic League gradually took over the party leadership and solidified its position with the expansion of suffrage in the 1890s.

ORGANIZATION

In Chapter 1, I lay the theoretical groundwork for the empirical analyses in the rest of the book. I begin with a review of the existing literature on the difference between Catholic and Islamist parties and dynamics of religious party change. Previous research on the topic underscored the role of religious doctrine in explaining the difference between Catholic and Islamist parties, how inclusive political structures can encourage ideological change of religious parties through the inclusion-moderation mechanism, and the way institutional structures can facilitate credible commitment to ideological change among religious parties. I show that the existing literature, while contributing to our understanding of religious party politics, falls short in some important ways. It is highly context-specific (that is, lacking comparative perspective), fails to incorporate the dynamic nature of religion into the analysis of religious institutional structures, and omits the agency of religious actors and their ability to alter the institutional structure that constrains their actions. Next, I lay out my alternative theory to account for religious party change by examining the distinct religious institutional structures in which religious parties are embedded. How do these institutions constrain and mediate religious parties' actions, as well as provide new opportunities? These religious institutions shape religious party organizational structures and discourse as they chart their paths in electoral politics. In discussing the key actors, their interests, and strategies, I adhere to a political economic approach and discuss how religious party change reflects the competition between religious actors over religious authority and political power.

Chapter 2 provides a thorough historical account of how religious institutional structures evolved in Catholicism and Sunni Islam. This discussion is instrumental in setting the stage for the subsequent analysis of the political implications of the conflict over religious authority in the modern period. The nature of religious authority takes many forms. On one extreme, such authority can be highly centralized. Religious authority is conferred upon religious actors according to its place within this hierarchy. The Catholic Church is the epitome of this ideal type. In Catholicism, the early development and ensuing institutionalization of the church structure enabled a centralized and hierarchical institutional framework to oversee religious doctrine and practice among Catholics worldwide. This strict hierarchy affords the Church an advantage that other religious actors lack: the legitimate authority to speak on behalf of the religion and the concomitant legitimacy in representing the religion and its adherents in various platforms, including the political arena. The Church, consequently, has been averse to competition in its religiopolitical authority and fiercely territorial in protecting its hegemony; it challenges all actors who lay claim on the Church's religious authority. All political, social, and religious activism in the name of Catholicism is deemed illegitimate unless graced by the Church. The Church is the ultimate authority on whether an action, organization, or attitude is in line with religious doctrine. The case of Islamic religious authority sits on the other extreme. The low level of institutionalization entails no hierarchical religious entity, with the corollary that religious authority is utterly decentralized, creating a free market of religion and religious authority. At times, states attempted to control religion within their polity by establishing religious agencies; such attempts fell short of being encompassing or long-lasting and typically did not enjoy broad legitimacy. At other times, the ulama (the class of religious scholars) functioned as the main religious body. Widespread recognition of the *ulama*'s religious authority notwithstanding, it lacked hierarchy and a centralized structure, paving the way for fierce competition among religious actors. Following the demise of the ulama class in the early twentieth century, this competition intensified. By thoroughly analyzing the constraints that religious institutions present for political action, Chapter 2 lays the foundation for examining the distinct ways that religious authority shapes religious party politics. This examination carries through following chapters and analyzes why and how the notion of religious authority is deeply infused within the political activism of religious political actors. The creation of a *religious* political identity in the nineteenth and twentieth centuries, a hitherto nonexistent phenomenon, interacts with the prevailing structure of religious institutions and religious authority to usher religious parties on distinct paths.

Chapter 3 builds on the historical analysis in Chapter 2 and analyzes the origins of the Catholic and Islamist political identities. By utilizing Katznelson's theory of political identity formation, this chapter examines how the Catholic Church and Islamist actors have created respective religious political identities

Introduction

in response to the rise of modernity, secularism, and the brewing anti-religion sentiment in Western Europe and the Middle East. In the nineteenth and the early twentieth centuries, anticlerical attacks, secularization of public education, and adoption of secularism as a principle of government generated a strong reaction from the Church in Western Europe and religious leaders throughout the Middle East. Chapter 3 shows how religious actors mobilized around the idea that no part of human existence lays outside the scope of religion. This chapter also examines the ways religious authority might offer religious actors a valuable *political* resource that is not available to other actors. Religious authority offers credibility and legitimacy for religious actors' political discourse; likewise, it affords religious actors the ability to mobilize the electorate around a religious identity.

Chapters 4 and 5 lay out the strategies adopted by religious mass movements as they embark upon establishing new religious parties. It explains how the distinctive institutional environments and corresponding ramifications on religious authority drive religious movements to adopt different strategies in creating religious parties. In addition to chronicling the conflict over religious authority and the distinct trajectories of Catholic and Islamist parties, these chapters focus on the implications of distinct organizational paths for the electorate. If organizational structures truly matter *and* religious authority plays a decisive role in how religious parties craft their discourse, then we should observe that Catholic and Islamist parties target different audiences in their respective political discourses. Indeed, while Catholic parties sought to forge broad-based electoral coalitions and were not constrained by the demands of a particular religious movement, Islamist parties had to simultaneously maintain their core support base in Islamist movements *and* appeal to the general electorate. Chapter 4 examines the dynamics that gave rise to the emergence of a religiopolitical identity in the modern period. The chapter analyzes the rise of religious movements in the six cases as a novel phenomenon and sheds light on the discussions behind the formation of religious movements, their organizational structures, their relationship to religious authority structures, and ideological and power conflicts within these movements. As such, it builds on the analysis of the emerging religious political identity in Chapter 3. The emergence of Islamist movements during this period represents the materialization of the religious pushback against anti-ulama and anti-religion attacks. In the twentieth century, Islamist movements found themselves competing with other religious and nonreligious actors for power. They relied heavily on religious authority for leverage in the absence of a significant challenge to their claim for moral authority. These movements actively undermined existing holders of religious authority and effectively utilized religious terminology that was previously the exclusive purview of the ulama class. The rise of Catholic mass movements as independent actors who could claim religious authority put them on a collision course with the Catholic Church, the traditional wielder of this same authority. This chapter illustrates the strategies that the Catholic Church utilized in its opposition to the Catholic mass movements' political activism and their use of the Church's authority to this end.

Chapter 5 reviews the eventual emergence of religious parties from within religious movements, focusing on the conflict between the religious and political factions within the religious movements. Each faction's relationship to the religious authority structure shapes the specific organizational structure that the party takes and its relationship to the movement. Islamist movements, unopposed by a hierarchical religious authority, found the liberty to pursue hybrid organizational structures. This carte blanche to assume religious authority enabled Islamist movements to operate both as a religious movement that serves in religious, social, and educational areas *and* as a religious party in the political arena. Unlike Catholic parties, contemporary Islamist parties' evolutionary trajectories are very much still in flux. Evidence shows that the Church hierarchy forced Catholic mass movement leaders to choose between expulsion and avoiding political activism in the name of Catholicism. Catholic political activists largely responded to this challenge by formally parting ways with mass movements and creating their own Catholic parties without the blessing of the Church, ultimately depriving them of the ability to rely on religious authority in their political ventures. This chapter examines the other constraints that Islamist parties face today, particularly shifts in the electoral landscape and state repression of Islamist parties. I overview the strategies that contemporary Islamist parties utilize to meet the challenges posed by these factors and reconfigure the hybrid movement-party structure. In regard to the movement-party relationship, the sharp contrast between Tunisia's Ennahdha and Turkey's AKP, on one hand, and the Egyptian Muslim Brotherhood on the other, illustrates the extent of the agency possessed by Islamist parties. This chapter provides evidence for these parties' internal deliberations on the advantages and disadvantages of changing organizational structures in response to shifts in the political landscape. Of particular interest in this chapter is the recent specialization policy adopted by Ennahdha that deals with separating the political and missionary facets of the party organization.

The Conclusion summarizes the theoretical argument of this book and reviews the empirical analysis in Chapters 1–5. One critical implication of the research in this book pertains to the role of institutions and institutional design in shaping religious parties' democratization. Looking forward, this chapter evaluates whether Islamist parties can pursue a trajectory similar to that of Christian parties in Western Europe by creating the requisite institutional structures through internal or external incentives. The role of Islamist parties continues to be one of the most pressing issues in the post-Arab Uprisings period. The Conclusion, therefore, helps examine the prospects of change for Islamist parties in the near future and relevant policy implications.

I

Explaining Religious Party Change

Research on religious parties in different geographic and religious contexts has greatly enhanced our understanding of the underlying dynamics of religious party change. These significant contributions notwithstanding, one fundamental area in which the literature falls short is that most research on religious parties has developed disparately. In particular, the literatures on Catholic and Islamist parties grew virtually independent of each other, focusing on entirely different sets of questions or factors that explain change in these parties. As a result, to echo Bellin, the literature collectively failed to "coalesce around a common question or overarching agenda" and was unable to "build ambitious theoretical stands."[1] The existing literature offers three major explanations for the divergence we observe in Catholic and Islamist parties' trajectories and for why religious parties change or moderate[2]: religious, political, and institutional explanations.

An extensive literature attributes a slew of political outcomes such as democratization, religious ideology, and religious politicization to fundamental differences in religious doctrines of Islam and Christianity.[3] Theologies of Islam and Christianity differ remarkably in their political visions, according to this religious argument; it naturally follows that the trajectories of Islamist and Catholic parties differ as well. After all, these parties merely mirror their religious doctrines and truthfully represent such doctrines in the political arena. Whether this has to do with patriarchy,[4]

---

[1] Bellin 2008, 345.

[2] While my analytical focus will be on the change in anti-system characters of religious parties, my review of the literature will include the moderation literature because the bulk of the literature on religious parties, particularly comparative analyses or the ones on Islamist parties, make the notion of moderation the center of their analyses.

[3] Kedourie 1992; Huntington 1996; Lewis 1996; Fish 2002; Donno and Russett 2004; Cook 2014; Rubin 2017, 2019.

[4] Fish 2002; Inglehart and Norris 2003.

21

The Politics of Religious Party Change

the importance of God's absolute sovereignty and the role of hierarchy in religion,[5] or "the nature of Islam itself,"[6] this argument emphasizes Islamic doctrine as the root cause of its political problems. Some argue that Islam stresses the importance of God's absolute sovereignty above all else. In this regard, the divine nature of Islamic law puts it on a collision course with democratic forms of governance. Michael Cook (2014) analyzes why Islam is a highly politicized religion in comparison to its Hindu and Christian counterparts. Cook focuses on religious doctrine and textual sources to account for Islam's exceptionalism in the modern age, especially regarding political Islam.[7] The inability to separate between the religious and the secular in Islam, thus, underlies Islamists' political ventures. Along the same lines, Samuel Huntington famously declared in *The Third Wave*,

Islam, however, also rejects any distinction between the religious community and the political community. Hence there is no equipoise between Caesar and God, and political participation is linked to religious affiliation. Fundamentalist Islam [i.e., Islamists] demands that in a Muslim country the political rulers should be practicing Muslims, shari'a should be the basic law, and ulema should have a decisive vote in articulating, or at least reviewing and ratifying, all governmental policy. To the extent that governmental legitimacy and policy flow from religious doctrine and religious expertise, Islamic concepts of politics differ from and contradict the premises of democratic politics.[8]

Yet, irony is not dead. The same faith that seemingly dictates the lack of separation between the religious and the secular commands blind obedience to leaders without regard for their religious observation. Huntington declares that "The political history of Islam is one of almost unrelieved autocracy" and ties the prevalence of authoritarianism in Muslim-majority countries to religious doctrines that command Muslims to obey sovereign rulers irrespective of those rulers' adherence to Islamic norms and values:

There are no parliaments or representative assemblies of any kind, no councils or communes, no chambers of nobility or estates, no municipalities in the history of Islam; nothing but the sovereign power, to which the subject owed complete and unwavering obedience as a religious duty imposed by the Holy Law .... For the last thousand years, the political thinking of Islam has been dominated by such maxims as "tyranny is better than anarchy" and "whose power is established, obedience to him is incumbent."[9]

By contrast, a correlate of this argument underscores the moderating quality of Catholicism that channeled Catholic parties into adopting platforms that were not anti-system.[10] Critically, the religion referenced here concerns "pure

---

[5] Fox and Sandler 2005, 319.
[6] Rowley and Smith 2009, 298.
[7] Cook 2014.
[8] Huntington 1993, 307.
[9] Lewis 1958, 318.
[10] Mergel 1996, 161.

Explaining Religious Party Change

religion" that is tolerant and nonviolent as told by Jesus and other prophets. For example, the Catholic social teaching in the nineteenth century was a good reflection of this religious mindset, teaching "to be credible to people of good will, and to have a proper understanding of the role and limits of the hierarchical magisterium."[11] This teaching acted as a moderating agent, preventing extremism in political discourse.[12]

While this literature takes religion seriously and engages in a *religious* explanation of political outcomes, these arguments often invoke concerns about delving into essentialism. There are three fundamental issues in theological and doctrinal arguments that undermine their value to better understand religious parties. The first one is methodological in nature. Simply put, an unvarying factor (religious doctrine) is used to account for change in a variable outcome. This is a common and frequently examined problem in religious explanations, as Gill (2008) underscores; I will not go into much detail here. Second, religion is critical to understanding political outcomes, but the true variation across religions occurs at the institutional level and on the "human side" of religion.[13] Absent focus on institutional variation, it becomes impossible to explain the divergence in the development of Catholic and Islamic religious parties, especially in light of the functionally identical responses that Catholicism and Islam produced when faced with modernity and secularism in the nineteenth and twentieth centuries.

Lastly and empirically, a review of the literature reveals a broader array of similarities between Islam and Catholicism than is usually assumed, bringing into question the utility of doctrinal perspectives to account for differences in religious parties. Historically, both religions have been similarly inclined to support autocracies. Until the nineteenth and twentieth centuries, backing autocracy was the norm in Christian Europe,[14] and the historical relationship between Islam and

---

[11] Curran 2002, 223.

[12] Meral (2018) shows that religion–violence relationship can be complicated and violence can shape religion just as religion can affect violence.

[13] Stark and Finke 2000.

[14] The most damaging implications against the Church and democracy were the Church's initial attempts to obstruct democracy. All the way up until the dawn of World War II, the Church appeared to be entrenching itself on the side of totalitarian rule (Sigmund 1987, 541). A great example of the Church's support for authoritarianism was the Vatican's forced disbandment of Luigi Sturzo's Partito Populare after Mussolini's electoral victory in 1926 (Sigmund 1987, 537). Soon after the dissolution of a democratic presence in Italy, the Vatican signed the Lateran Treaty (1929) with Mussolini and the Concordat Agreement (1933) with Hitler, which further cemented their political position (Sigmund 1987, 538). If that were not enough, the German authorization of the Vichy regime (a pro-Catholic government) in France during the early stages of World War II sealed what side the Church was on for many French. Some reason for this willingness to support despots came from the ease with which the Church secured deals with monarchies, as opposed to the drawn-out process of rewrites and revisions that parliaments tended to make use of (Diamant 1957, 620; Sigmund 1987, 534; Glenn and Stack 2000, 7). Anton Orel, the successor to Vogelsang in his respective antidemocratic school of thought,

24 The Politics of Religious Party Change

autocratic rule runs very deep.[15] Likewise, Catholic doctrine is viewed as inherently antidemocratic. The belief in God's absolute sovereignty, much like among many Muslims and Islamists, is a key argument to this effect. For example, Acts 5:29 is usually presented to support this position: "We must obey God rather than men." Because God is the only rightful ruler, any divergence from this doctrine in the form of a set of laws created by humans poses theological problems.[16] Religions contain large swaths of doctrines that can be construed in democratic or authoritarian ways.[17] As Laurence states, "there are so many strains of religious interpretation and historical cases from which to choose that the notion of compatibility with the secular rule can appear selective and ad hoc."[18] Selective arguments about Islam's aversion to secularism can be regarded as a "trope of orientalist discussion"[19]; historically, the Islamic tradition incorporated elements of secularism to a larger degree than we are typically led to believe, underscoring another similarity with Catholicism.[20] A different approach that takes religion seriously but moves beyond theology and essentialism to bring out the fundamentally *political* character of religious politics is necessary.

The second major argument for the difference in Catholic and Islamist parties' trajectories is more political in nature. Religious parties, in this literature, are stripped of their religious elements and treated purely in political terms. There are two main variations of this approach. The first approach focuses on the political environment. That Catholic parties arose in a political environment where democracy, electoral politics, and secularism reigned while Islamist parties hail primarily from authoritarian settings explains why the former adopted prosystem discourses, whereas the latter embraced anti-system ones. The fact that free elections and democratic politics were available in Western Europe facilitated

---

believed that authoritarian feudalism was the only social organization based on Christian Universalism. He argued that autocracy was the best form of government to support the Christian faith (Diamant 1957, 627). The relationship between authoritarianism and Islam was especially strengthened by the concept of divine rule, a notion shared by the Muslim nations with their Christian European counterparts (El Fadl 2007, 257).

[15] Binder 1998, 41; Momayesi 2000, 2; Hefner 2001, 497; Kuru 2019.
[16] Diamant 1957, 611; Sigmund 1987, 537. The release of two papal encyclicals by Pope Leo XIII in 1885 (*Immortale Dei* and *Libertas Humana*) informed its audience of Catholicism's stance on various corporeal matters. These encyclicals featured attacks on liberal nationalists and accused them of trying to make the state an "absolute and omnipotent" body. At the core of these attacks lay the belief that liberals desired for people to live without God (Sigmund 1987, 537). The denial of God's sovereignty meant that law was at the arbitrary disposal of the masses, and no longer was there a "superior and morally binding law" that could ground people in virtue (Diamant 1957, 617; Glenn and Stack 2000, 8). The belief that democracy would have a morally detrimental impact on Catholicism reveals itself in another way. God's absolute sovereignty coupled with the Church's role as the hand of God on earth requires the faithful Catholics to be responsible to the Vatican before the state, according to this argument.
[17] Abou El Fadl 2007; Hashemi 2009; March 2011; Kuru 2019; Ciftci 2021.
[18] Laurence 2021, 10.
[19] Lapidus 1996, 3.
[20] Rabasa et al. 2007, 123.

Explaining Religious Party Change

Catholic parties' peace with the system. Likewise, increased levels of secularization are viewed as a significant factor behind Catholic parties' secularization, especially in the post–World War II period.[21] By contrast, the lack of access to such politics led Islamist parties to stake out anti-system platforms. A derivative of this argument, inclusion-moderation, focuses primarily on Islamist parties. The inclusion-moderation theory emerged in recent decades as one of the most compelling explanations for change in Islamist parties. The argument has its origins in non-Islamic contexts, dating back to democratic transitions and socialism, and European communist parties' integration into democratic political systems.[22] While it comes in varying forms, the core of the inclusion-moderation theory holds that more inclusive and accommodating state policies toward Islamist parties tend to cultivate moderate political discourses on the part of Islamist parties.[23] As a result, political inclusion – or, more broadly, favorable changes in political opportunity structures – pushes Islamists into adopting more moderate behavior and/or ideologies.[24] Variations of this theory emphasize political learning,[25] Western experience,[26] political context,[27] internal party debates,[28] and cooperation with non-Islamists.[29] Just as some scholars claim that it is the Islamists' willingness to take stock of the political opening – that is, "carrot" – that results in moderation,[30] other scholars observe that what is crucial for Islamist parties is the "stick" – that is, state repression of conservative and radical Islamist parties.[31] Further, a more recent argument offers greater nuance and suggests that creating an environment conducive to ideological moderation is more important than whether inclusion or exclusion leads to moderation as such.[32]

A variation of this political argument focuses on how religious parties – particularly Islamist parties – respond to socioeconomic factors. This literature argues that what makes Islamist parties politically relevant is not their roots in religion but the economic positions they take and the social classes they speak to.[33]

---

[21] Boswell 1993; Hanley 1994.

[22] Przeworski and Sprague 1986; Bermeo 1997; Herzog 2006; Berman 2008.

[23] Buehler (2013) flips the causal direction and finds that the Moroccan Party for Justice and Development threatened the regime with turning "un-moderate" to gain leverage vis-à-vis the regime at the time of Arab Spring protests in the country.

[24] Schwedler 2011; Brocker and Kunkler 2013.

[25] Wickham 2004; Cavatorta 2006.

[26] Grewal 2020.

[27] Yadav 2010; Gurses 2014.

[28] Schwedler 2006.

[29] Clark 2006.

[30] Brooks 2002.

[31] Willis 2004; Somer 2007; Cizre 2009; Cavatorta and Merone 2013; Hamid 2014. Matesan, by contrast, argues that repression by the state can lead to violence on the part of Islamist parties. See Matesan 2020.

[32] Storm 2020.

[33] One notable exception here is a recent experimental study by Grewal et al. (2019) on how Islamist parties' religious discourse can be more appealing to those who experience economic hardship in anticipation of "divine compensation."

Such socioeconomic considerations deeply relate to the electoral consider-ations of such parties.[34] The distinct socioeconomic origins of Islamist parties push them into adopting a particular set of policy positions that dispropor-tionately cater to the lower and lower-middle classes in the Muslim societ-ies of the Middle East,[35] although others have also pointed out middle- and upper-middle-class support for Islamists.[36] Clientelism, likewise, has been associated with Islamist parties' electoral success.[37] In a recent study, Brooke and Ketchley found that the Egyptian Muslim Brotherhood's organizational growth was facilitated by factors such as higher literacy rates and better infrastructure (i.e., connection to the railway network)[38]; this finding rein-forces the idea that Islamist parties enjoy significant support among middle and upper-middle classes. Severe economic inequality, widespread poverty, corruption,[39] and pervasive underdevelopment constitute key elements of Islamist discourse across the region.[40] For Tarek Masoud, it was not the Brotherhood's stance on religion or Islamic law but rather its ability to appeal to the middle classes that underlaid the group's electoral success. The middle class is not "poor enough to be captured" by the regime's clientelism nor "wealthy enough" to benefit from the corruption facilitated by the regime.[41] Secular regimes' failure to deliver on these socioeconomic issues constitutes, for Islamists, a major point of electoral mobilization. The secular parties by and large were not well positioned to grab the electoral opportunities created by decades of poor economic policies, which advantaged Islamists. When economic and social conditions change, Islamist parties' platforms adapt and absorb the changing socioeconomic dynamics. Supporting this conclusion, Wegner and Cavatorta find that in a series of surveys across the Arab world, supporters of Islamist and secular parties display no notable difference in their economic attitudes.[42] A related body of literature examines other demand-side dynamics of Islamist moderation. In some cases, it is the pursuit of electoral success pushing these parties into adoption of moderate platforms[43]; in others, Islamists aim to remain politically relevant.[44]

[34] Yildirim and Lancaster 2015.
[35] Harik 1996; Ismail 2001; Woltering 2002.
[36] Waltz 1986; Woltering 2002; Clark 2004; Pellicer and Wegner 2012; Masoud 2014; Brooke 2019.
[37] Marschall, Aydogan, and Bulut 2016.
[38] Brooke and Ketchley 2018.
[39] Tessler 1997.
[40] Masoud 2014.
[41] Masoud 2014, 98.
[42] Wegner and Cavatorta 2019. Using expert survey data, Abdullah Aydogan (2020) finds, in contrast, that the economic left–right divide complements the religious–secular cleavage in the Middle East and North Africa region.
[43] Sanchez-Cuenca 2004.
[44] Cavatorta and Merone 2013; Freer 2018.

Explaining Religious Party Change

Exogenous explanations such as electoral politics, democracy, and secularization undoubtedly play an important role in defining the scope of actions a party can take, including religious parties. Several factors, however, call into question whether electoral politics or democracy can sufficiently explain religious party change. First, religious parties face additional incentives and constraints that other kinds of political parties do not. Such constraints arise due to these parties' distinctive relationship with a faith tradition; an exclusive focus on political institutions thus fails to provide a satisfactory explanation. Second, although political regimes in nineteenth-century Western Europe were admittedly more democratic than most, if not all, of the twentieth-century Middle East, European democracies were still in their infancy then and could be characterized as emerging democracies. Likewise, many Middle Eastern countries that were formed in the twentieth century had limited experience with electoral politics; yet important electoral openings allowed Islamist parties to be part of these processes and respond to political constraints in ways that are similar to the nineteenth-century Catholic parties in Europe. Third, because this book's focus is on the anti-system character of religious parties rather than specific components of their discourse or their moderation, the effect of regime type or the level of democratic politics is less a concern for the argument developed here. Likewise, the argument about secularization paving the way for Catholic parties' secularization and democratization does not hold up to scrutiny. The secularization of Catholic societies in Western Europe did not precede the secularization of Catholic parties but followed it. As importantly, the secularization process followed an uneven path across Muslim societies of the Middle East. In countries such as Tunisia and Turkey where wide-ranging secularization efforts occurred, Islamist parties took these secularization processes as opportunities to mobilize and recruit in order to reach a broader segment of the population with their anti-secular ideologies, rather than adjust and recalibrate their political stances. Without proper context as to which segments of society experienced secularization and what the religious institutional environment was for religious parties, it is impossible to conceptualize the role played by societal secularization.

A third approach introduces a political economic perspective to understanding religious parties. Analyzing the formation of Catholic parties in Western Europe, Kalyvas argues that the secularization of Catholic parties is the outcome of "a process endogenous to these parties that took place during and right after their formation."[45] Catholic parties "moved away" from their dependence on the Church and determined "their identity in a way that both deemphasized and reinterpreted religion." While religious institutions and competing religious actors are in Kalyvas' analysis, it is a story about confessional parties and their agency to use religion to define their identity and

---

[45] Kalyvas 1996, 222.

"redefine Catholicism."[46] Yet, as Kalyvas' analysis in the earlier part of his book exceptionally shows, the nature of religious institutions and competition with other religious actors are essential to understanding Catholic parties and how they use their agency to determine the direction of the party. Lacking a comparative basis, it is unclear from Kalyvas' argument how a confessional party in a different religious institutional setting, that is, under a decentralized religious authority structure, might forge its relationship to religion.

In a subsequent analysis, Kalyvas takes a different approach and ascribes greater influence to religious authority structures. In his analysis of the roles played by religious institutions and parties in the democratization processes of nineteenth-century Belgium and twentieth-century Algeria, Kalyvas argues that centralized religious institutions allow religious parties to commit to democratic politics "by credibly signaling future compliance." The Belgian Catholic party could commit to democracy in the nineteenth century because the Church's existence facilitated "public denunciation of its central ideological planks and the purge of prominent radicals" from the party.[47] By contrast, the Algerian Islamist party, Front Islamique du Salut (Islamic Salvation Front), suffered from internal divisions and an inability to signal commitment to democracy when radicals undermined moderates' public messages within the party; the absence of a centralized religious structure was vital to this outcome. For Kalyvas, centralized religious hierarchy helps religious parties overcome their "commitment problem."[48] Schwedler rightly criticizes Kalyvas' focus on commitment by arguing that "in any case, credibility is ultimately in the eye of the beholder, so the burden is not entirely on the messenger."[49] In contemporary Muslim-majority societies, there is hardly anything that Islamists could do to convince seculars in these societies that Islamists can credibly commit to democracy. Reducing religious party politics to a commitment problem reinforces the idea that religious parties are fundamentally different, untrustworthy, and duplicitous because their primary loyalties lie elsewhere. Moreover, this argument is contingent upon the existence of sharp divisions within a religious party between radicals and moderates – a distinction that may not always exist. In cases where they do, focusing on the divide between radicals and moderates disregards the dynamics that led to such a split in the first place.

Yet, at its core, the real issue is not a credibility problem nor convincing others that religious parties have changed; rather, it is about the constraints imposed by religious institutional structures and the level of ideological and political flexibility it affords. Despite the role that religious institutions may play in solving commitment problems, the gravity of such institutions far

[46] Kalyvas 1996, 255.
[47] Kalyvas 2000, 381.
[48] Kalyvas 2000, 390.
[49] Schwedler 2011, 354.

Explaining Religious Party Change

exceeds that ability. Religious institutions first and foremost create the incentive structures that underlie the politicization of religion in the modern era, thereby facilitating the divisions among religious actors with different religiopolitical visions. Religious institutions shape the kinds of actors that will emerge, create the incentives and disincentives they will face in their relations with other religious actors, and determine how conflict among religious actors will be resolved. Therefore, it is imperative to take a step back to better conceptualize religious institutions' effect on religious parties.

Despite the abundance of studies on religious parties, existing scholarship fails to offer a satisfactory comparative account of religious party change. There are three fundamental shortcomings of the existing literature, which I aim to address in this book. First, religion barely enters as an independent variable.[50] In particular, religious institutions are conspicuously absent; the role of *religious* institutions in explaining important political outcomes is largely bracketed in favor of other factors.[51] This lack of focus on religion matters because religious parties do not operate in a vacuum. By virtue of their special (or "fundamental") relationship with a faith tradition that other parties do not have, they are constrained by religion, that is, religious institutions and conceptions of religious authority, in distinctive ways.[52] This "associational nexus" with religious institutions and authority is crucial to the creation and functioning of the party and the mobilization of voters.[53] What they can and cannot say as a party, what policy positions they can take, how much they can commit to democratic and secular politics, and their very existence rests on the nature of this special relationship with religious institutions.[54] The rise of religious parties induces competition over religious (and political) power and authority. As new entrants to the political space with an eye toward reshaping institutions, they challenge existing actors and their religious authority as well as threaten the institutional structure. Therefore, while constraining and shaping the behavior of religious parties, religious institutions are also being challenged and redefined by the very same actors.

---

[50] Bellin 2008, 345.

[51] Altinordu 2010. In recent years, some important works increasingly focus on the role of religious institutions on a range of outcomes. For example, Laurence (2021) examines the role of religious institutions in mediating the Catholic and Muslim worlds' relationship with the modern state. Mecham (2017) examines how religious and political institutions affect Islamist mobilization. Other important works include Kalyvas' (2000) comparative analysis of Belgian and Algerian parties, Toft's (2007) use of jihad as an Islamic institutional factor to explain the prevalence of civil war in the Muslim world, Philpott's (2007) emphasis on the level of "mutual autonomy" between the state and religious institutions in explaining democracy and political violence, and Künkler and Leininger's (2009) analysis of the organizational structures of religious actors and their ability to influence political outcomes and the democratization process.

[52] Gorski and Altinordu 2008; Grzymala-Busse 2012.

[53] Ozzano and Cavatorta 2013.

[54] Cary 1996; Grew 2003; Driessen 2014.

A different but closely related problem limiting research on religious parties is the absence of agency. Religious parties have long been treated as passive political actors whose actions simply reflect the constraints of the underlying institutional, theological, political, and socioeconomic structures within their national contexts.[55] It implies that we can understand religious parties only by looking at factors beyond these parties. If we assume that religious parties are rational actors, we cannot ignore the actions which religious parties themselves carry out. Consequently, our understanding of how religious parties create their paths, interact with the institutional structure in which they operate, and the conflicts they wage against other actors over institutions and power will rest on taking the agency of religious parties and their leaders seriously. This book sets out to correct such missing considerations.

Lastly, there is a growing need to marry literatures that analyze religious party change in different contexts. Various scholars have emphasized the lack of comparative analysis on religious parties in Europe, the Middle East, and elsewhere.[56] Such comparative analysis merits greater attention. On one hand, it helps avoid essentialism by portraying religious parties as rational actors that respond to a broad array of incentives, rather than entities hopelessly crippled by religious scriptures. While limiting empirical focus to a single religious context does not necessarily entail essentialism, it makes it more difficult to isolate culture- or context-specific factors. On the other hand, cross-regional analyses allow for exploring longitudinal changes across different contexts and highlighting similar dynamics at work. Such analyses are likewise instrumental in controlling for alternative explanations. Overall, a comparative framework facilitates efforts to generalize about religious parties and more broadly to theorize about religious party dynamics.

In summary, this book builds on past research on religious parties and tackles three important shortcomings in the existing literature in doing so. Specifically, it draws on religion – i.e., religious competition and religious institutions – as the primary causal factor, emphasizes the agency of religious actors in shaping political outcomes and institutions, and brings together two distinct sets of religious parties: Islamist parties of the Middle East and Catholic parties of Western Europe. In the following section, I will lay out my argument to explain religious party change. I will first discuss my overall approach to the question of religious party change by applying a political economic perspective to the study of religion; next, I outline the effect of institutions on political behavior, and in particular how religious institutions affect political behavior and religious parties. Then, I overview the major actors in my theory before concluding with a comparative assessment of how Islamist and Catholic parties fit into my theory.

---

[55] Kirdiş 2019.
[56] Kalyvas and Kersbergen 2010; Brown 2012; Driessen 2014. Helmy (2006) is a notable contribution to the literature with its comparative framework.

Explaining Religious Party Change

AN INSTITUTIONAL THEORY OF RELIGIOUS PARTY CHANGE

I argue that religious institutions play a critical role in why some religious parties are able to shed their confessional dilemmas and become pro-system, whereas others sustain anti-system stances. Religious institutions define the parameters of the environments that religious parties operate within. They also shape the meaning of electoral politics for religious parties and the factional conflict within them, as these parties compete with other religious actors for religious authority and political power.[57] Externally, greater levels of centralization and hierarchical organization of religious authority give a religious institution monopolistic control of the religious marketplace. This undermines a religious party's ability to break free, making religion an unviable option for political mobilization. By contrast, greater levels of decentralization allow religious parties more space to claim moral authority in a larger field of religious competition. Internally, greater religious centralization tends to sharpen the religious and political factions within the hybrid organizational structures of religious parties, ultimately leading to a rupture between the religious movement that gives rise to the religious party and the party itself. Religious decentralization, in contrast, blurs the lines between the religious movement and the party, empowers the religious faction over the political one, and sustains the hybrid party-movement structure. As a result, higher levels of centralization and hierarchical organization in a religion provide a religious party *less* incentive and freedom to operate as an anti-system party. Conversely, low levels of centralization and institutionalization offer a religious party *greater* incentive and freedom as an anti-system party. In what follows, I will define some key concepts, discuss my approach in examining religious parties in this book, and gradually build my theory.

I take the "religion" in religious parties seriously for two related but seemingly conflicting reasons. On one hand, religion provides these parties with a valuable political resource that is not readily available to other political actors.[58] Religious parties can mold a distinct religious political identity, mobilize the electorate, and reshape policy discussions around cultural and identity issues.[59] On the other hand, religion carries innate constraints for religious parties in the political arena. While religious actors have great leverage in how they can shape religious discourse for political ends, such autonomy is limited by doctrinal pillars,[60] the rigidity of which provides the core of religious legitimacy for many faithful. Likewise, the religion's institutional structure puts additional checks on what kinds of actions religious actors can take or determine their place in the religious pecking order. My focus on religious institutions reflects

[57] Mecham 2017.
[58] Grewal et al. 2019.
[59] Livny 2020.
[60] Tabaar and Yildirim 2020.

the ways in which religion affects a religious party's broad political orientation. Institutions provide the setting where religious actors pursue their goals. Given the specific array of resources and abilities at their disposal, religious actors must navigate the constraints posed by these institutions.

Although I take religion as a decisive factor in explaining political outcomes, my method departs from more conventional approaches. These approaches pay outsized attention to the variation in doctrine and theology to see how such differences across religions explain variations in the political behavior of each religion's adherents.[61] Religious doctrine and theology certainly hold central roles in shaping the lives and behavior of believers; many devout and nondevout believers follow religious doctrines at least to some degree. Yet, while religious doctrines help set broad goals for believers, such goals are usually accompanied by flexibility in terms of how believers can attain them. This broad focus on religious doctrine also carries another disadvantage. Religious doctrines apply universally and do not change frequently by their nature. As such, when doctrines are used to explain political variation across a large space, they inevitably fail to explain such variation. A focus on religious doctrines tends to veil differences across countries and regions instead of explaining them. Lastly, religions are amalgams of many doctrines that might conflict with each other. Because religious doctrines were created centuries or even millennia ago (and certainly not with contemporary political consequences in mind), contemporary observers are bound to notice doctrinal inconsistencies on modern political issues such as democracy, pluralism, and tolerance. Ultimately, it is political conflict that determines which doctrine emerges victorious.

One potential criticism here is whether the focus on religious institutions as the causal variable offers an advantage over religious doctrine insofar as avoiding essentialism is concerned. I disagree with this criticism for three reasons. First, doctrinal arguments constrain religion to a divine sphere where humans have limited, if any, roles in how religion dictates the faithful's behavior. Religion, as such, functions primarily as a divine enterprise. Focus on religious institutions as the principal force behind change in religious actors shifts the conversation away from the divine realm into the temporal realm. Second, the focus on doctrine reinforces a sense of permanence and inflexibility, whereas institutions – although inherently meant to be durable – can more easily adapt to changing circumstances, in part because their roots are firmly entrenched in the mortal realm rather than the sacred. Lastly, deviation from religious doctrine implies heterodoxy by nature, and therefore conflict with religion. Yet, because doctrinal arguments leave little room for heterodoxy or intra-religious conflict about doctrine, they are inherently homogenizing. Religious institutions can offer a mechanism in which intrareligious conflict and heterodoxy

---

[61] Cook 2014; Rubin 2017, 2019. See Leininger's (2016) account of the democratization process in Mali and how institutional structure rather than theology was the key factor.

Explaining Religious Party Change

can be understood as an integral part of religiopolitical life and help better conceptualize religious actors and their behavior.

I examine religious parties from a political economy of religion perspective. I rely on rational choice theory, placing maximizing behavior and cost–benefit calculation at the core of my analysis and applying "microeconomic theory and techniques to explain patterns of religious behavior among individuals, groups, and cultures."[62] While initially counterintuitive, the fundamental insight of this approach rests on the assumption that religious actors operate on self-interest just as secular actors do; religious actors' behavior constitutes "an instance of rational choice rather than an exception to it." These actors are constrained by market forces in the same way that nonreligious actors are: monopoly, regulation, and competition provide them with various kinds of opportunities and constraints on their behavior.[63] Religious market conditions and competition with other religious actors, therefore, constitute critical tools of analysis in this approach. A fundamental insight of the political economic approach to the study of religion is that the behavior of religious actors varies across different religious environments.[64] This is the key reason why I prefer using this approach to examine how religious institutional structures shape religious parties. A growing literature examines various aspects of the religion–politics relationship through the political economic perspective.[65]

Religious beliefs adopted by individual believers must be distinguished from the actions of religious actors and institutions. While personal religious beliefs may be considered beyond concerns of rationality, the actions of religious actors and institutions "are subject to the many of the same concerns and constraints as their secular counterparts (e.g., politicians, labor leaders)". As Anthony Gill explains, their actions are shaped by their efforts to make the best of limited resources at their disposal to attain institutional goals: "No matter how divinely inspired clergy may be, a church exists in this world of scarcity and can thrive only to the extent that its leaders use resources efficiently. The conditions that cause secular actors to modify their behavior in defense of their institutionally determined goals will likewise apply to leaders of religious institutions".[66]

An important assumption I make is that all religions, without exception, are open to multiple interpretations. Without this flexibility in interpretation, religious actors would lack the ability to adjust their discourses in line with

---

[62] Iannaccone 1998, 1465.
[63] Iannaccone 1998, 1478.
[64] Jelen 2003.
[65] Kalyvas 1996, 2000; Gill 1998, 2001, 2019; Stark and Finke 2000; Warner 2000; Iannaccone and Berman 2006; Witham 2010; Driessen 2014; Koesel 2014; Achilov and Shaykhutdinov 2014; Grzymala-Busse 2015; Kilinc and Warner 2015; ; Spiegel 2015; Warner et al. 2015; Feuer 2017; Nielsen 2017; Rubin 2017, 2019; Sandal 2017; Tabaar 2018; Brooke 2019; Kilinc 2019; Kuru 2019.
[66] Gill 1998, 11.

34   *The Politics of Religious Party Change*

changes in religious competition. The possibility of multiple interpretations allows religious actors to pick those elements of religion that will further their interests and leave behind those that do not serve them well.[67] Yet, this flexibility is not limitless and entails a risk; any new interpretation or modification must "be engineered in such a way that they do not undermine the very legitimacy upon which their moral authority rests in the first place.... The perceived 'rigidity' in the doctrine may provide its very legitimacy."[68] This economic approach to studying religious actors and their behavior challenges fundamental principles of the secularization thesis: that religious commitment and behavior are irrational and that religion is a relic of humanity's ancient past.[69] As developments since the 1960s have demonstrated, religion has revitalized and "wreaked savage revenge" on secularization.[70]

To explain change in religious parties, my core argument rests on the idea of religious competition. What is religious competition? It is competition by religious actors to achieve influence and power through religion. Multiple religious actors pursue similar goals and engage in "obstructing behavior" to attain their goals.[71] Religious actors vie for greater religious authority and influence as the most prized political resource because it facilitates greater effect and support base for various political, social, and economic goals these actors pursue. In this regard, religious parties' rise intensifies competition among religious actors. Specifically, the rise of religious parties sets up conflicts at two different levels. At the national level, as new entrants into the religiopolitical arena, religious parties clash with existing religious actors. At the organizational level, an intraparty clash unfolds between the religious party and the movement that gave birth to it. Neither of these conflicts, however, is about ideology; these different religious actors share similar worldviews and aim to achieve similar goals at the time of religious parties' rise. The conflict, instead, is about securing greater political and religious power and influence; change in religious parties is an incidental outcome of these conflicts.

Lastly, I draw a critical distinction between what might be regarded as the divine and human components of religion. All major religions include some theological and doctrinal elements that are regarded as sacred irrespective of the authenticity of their divinity. Such components are rarely, if ever, subject to change. Believers are expected to adhere to these doctrines with little room for human interpretation. The "human side" of religion, by contrast, is typically open to varying, and usually conflicting, human interpretation.[72] Different

---

[67] See, for example, Shahab Ahmed's (2016) analysis on Islam and the inherent multiplicity of interpretation of what Islam means.

[68] Ensminger 1994, 752.

[69] Iannaccone 1998, 1468.

[70] Gill 1998, 3.

[71] Olson 2003, 140.

[72] Stark and Finke 2000.

Explaining Religious Party Change

religious actors vie for greater influence over religion. It is within this human dimension of religion that politics play a major role. Therefore, shifting the discussion from the doctrinal and divine components of religion to the nondivine is imperative to better understand politicization of religion.

RELIGIOUS INSTITUTIONS

What are institutions – religious and nonreligious – and how do they affect political behavior? Definitions of institutions span from the very broad to the very narrow. Peters, for example, defines an institution merely as a persistent structural feature that affects individual behavior and provides a shared sense of values. Institutions are literally formal administrative units such as bureaucratic or civil service agencies and governmental structures such as legislatures, courts, and election procedures.[73] Others, however, consider both formal and informal rules and norms as institutions.[74] March and Olsen conceive institutions as a "relatively enduring collection of rules and organized practices, embedded in structures of meaning and resources that are relatively invariant in the face of turnover of individuals and changing external circumstances."[75] In this regard, Greif and Laitin consider societal cleavages as institutions due to their "salience," using Kalyvas' explanation of religious cleavages in Western Europe as an example.[76]

Autonomy, strength, and persistence are major features of institutions. Institutions must also entail some temporal dimension; otherwise, they would be unable to affect political behavior. As such, institutions are the "foundation of all political behavior" because they are the basis on which society is able to operate politically.[77] Most importantly, regardless of how broad or narrow one's conception of "institution" is, one trait common to all is that institutions act to both empower and constrain individual and group behavior and sanction noncompliance.[78] In this regard, institutions exist because human interaction necessarily leads to uncertainties. Institutions provide a structure that ensures interactions are prudent and efficient.[79] According to Steinmo, institutions can structure politics because they determine who can participate in the political space, affect strategies of political actors, and define the realm of what is politically possible.[80]

What are *religious* institutions and how do they affect political outcomes? Almost all religions are associated with religious institutions, which may

---

[73] Peters et al. 2005.
[74] Aspinwall and Schneider 2000; Steinmo 2001.
[75] March and Olsen 2008, 8.
[76] Greif and Laitin 2004.
[77] Steinmo 2001.
[78] North 1990; March and Olsen 2005; Schmidt 2010.
[79] North 1990; March and Olsen 2005.
[80] Steinmo 2001.

play disparate roles based on contextual differences as well as the level of institutionalization in a religion. A religious institution may be as large and influential as the Catholic Church or as small as a prayer group for a Korean Presbyterian immigrant community. Sunni Islam, for example, is a religion of relatively low institutionalization. There is not, and has never been, the equivalent of a priesthood or otherwise strict hierarchical structure in the religion. Recently, in a comparative analysis of the effects of Catholic and Islamic institutions on Catholic and Muslim worlds' relationship to the modern nation-state, Laurence argues that "Sunni Islam was far more centralized under the Ottoman Caliphate than is generally acknowledged"[81] and draws an analogy between the Vatican in Catholicism and the caliphate in Sunni Islam as "unified religious-political" hierarchical religious institutions.[82] While religion was certainly centralized in the Ottoman Empire, it reflected the Ottomans' obsession with bureaucratization and can be better understood as an effort at imposing state control over the religious sphere. It does not indicate the Ottoman caliphate's deep and hierarchical reach across the Sunni populations of the empire. The caliphate in Sunni Islam was merely a political institution despite its contemporary reincarnations as a religious one.[83] It symbolized the political unity of the Muslim world; irrespective of the emotions it might have evoked, the historical institution of the caliphate was by no means the equivalent of the Vatican in Catholicism as far as dictating and upholding religious orthodoxy and orthopraxy. In the absence of a centralized and hierarchical religious institutional structure in the Islamic context, the religious authority structure is more diffused. The ulama – the collective body of religious scholars – are a religious institution and served a function akin to clergy in Catholicism until the turn of the twentieth century. Small Sufi orders in rural Pakistan or community mosques in the United States can also be deemed religious institutions in the Islamic context.

A religion's level of institutionalization is partially indicative of its role in society; that is, how much or how little strength it has in the face of other institutions, namely the state, and in many cases, secularism.[84] It is also indicative of the role that religion plays in the lives of individuals. The church, or more generally institutionalized religion, acts as a "mediating structure" between state and society.[85] However, this not need always be the case. Religious institutions may be on par with the state, coopted by (and thus subordinate to) the state, or at odds with the state. As such, religious institutions' actions may supplement those of the state, replace them, or supply that which the state does not or cannot supply. For example, religion cannot be a mediator when it has been coopted by the state and thus used for political ends.

---

[81] Laurence 2021, 13.
[82] Laurence 2021, 13.
[83] Keddie 1972.
[84] Soper and Fetzer 2007.
[85] Durham and Dushku 1993.

Explaining Religious Party Change

What are the different ways that religious institutions affect societies, interact with the state, or shape political behavior? First, religious institutions can act as a control mechanism that supplements state or political control.[86] This occurs due to religion's reinforcement of moral norms. The form of control afforded by religious institutions is unique among the various social control mechanisms in that it is based solely upon personal acceptance.[87] In other words, an individual has the ability to choose to come under the control of a religion, whereas one may or may not have such a choice in regard to traditional state control. It should be noted, however, that one's decision to submit to religious control is not always entirely free; in many cases, a state's dominant religion can affect social and political norms. Saudi Arabia's Committee for the Promotion of Virtue and the Prevention of Vice offers an example of a religious institution enforcing public morality with the state's support.[88] As such, even those not subscribing to the religion may still be submitted to the moral requirements it preaches. For example, Rose (2000), in a quantitative study of Chicago neighborhoods, finds that communities with high levels of involvement in religious institutions generally have lower crime rates, which speaks to the ability of religion to subvert criminal tendencies and instill morality.

A second potential role of religious institutions is that of state legitimation, nation-building, and antigovernment threat subversion.[89] Particularly in the modern era, states can rely on religious institutions and their authority to implement modernization and secularization reforms. States expect the broad legitimacy enjoyed by religious institutions to translate into support for state modernization reforms when such reforms may not always enjoy popular appeal. Kristin Fabbe's excellent analysis shows how post-Ottoman states' diverging interactions with domestic religious establishments resulted in a variety of state–religion power configurations. While in some cases, religious elites and institutions furthered state policies, in other cases, constraints proved more difficult to overcome.[90] The Egyptian state's relationship with Al-Azhar University – perhaps the most influential institution of religious education in the Sunni Muslim world – offers key insights into this process of state legitimation. Under President Gamal Abdel Nasser (1954–70), the Egyptian state began to bring mosques, Al-Azhar, and other religious schools under state control. Nasser then secured fatwas from Al-Azhar in order to lend support and legitimacy to the regime's policies; of particular interest to the government was legitimizing land reform policy. Thus, major religious institutions became

---

[86] For example, Sezgin and Künkler (2014) demonstrate how judicialization and bureaucratization of religion, as two different strategies to manage religion, have led to two fundamentally different outcomes in state–religion relationship in India and Indonesia.

[87] Eister 1957.

[88] Ochsenwald 1981, 275.

[89] Sheline 2019.

[90] Fabbe 2019.

38   *The Politics of Religious Party Change*

instruments to legitimize official state policy. Further, the government's co-optation of these religious institutions meant that imams could only preach that which was sanctioned by the state. Since mosques convene a large group of congregants on a weekly basis and have significant influence over individuals, the government had thus subverted the potential threat of antigovernment activity and religious radicalization developing from religious institutions.[91] One perverse effect of the Egyptian state co-opting religious institutions was that Islamists such as the Muslim Brotherhood began asserting that the ulama were illegitimate representatives of Islam, as they were required to submit to official state ideology. Thus, the state's attempt at co-optation simultaneously shifted the dynamics of religious authority.

Third, religious institutions and religion are subject to change from states' actions and policies. In the modern era in particular, religious institutions and actors can be deemed representatives of the traditional order, thereby blocking states' modernization efforts. States can choose to suppress or eliminate these potential sources of opposition. In the face of pressure from the state, religious institutions and actors may temper their opposition to state policies or limit their claims to power and influence, albeit falling short of embracing state policies. Alternatively, states can co-opt religious actors and institutions by either purchasing their loyalty through access to material benefits, providing them voice in the policy making process, or integrating them into the state. In certain contexts, such as the broader Middle East region, states emerged as major actors in the religious landscape due to this process of co-optation. States began commanding a vast swath of religious powers including control over places of worship, the power to determine "correct" religious discourse, and the power to hire and fire personnel for the new state religious agencies.

Finally, religious institutions may be the cause of, or deterrent to, conflict. Before many Western European countries established official state churches, religious conflict was relatively rampant. With the advent of secularism – an institution in and of itself – such conflicts have become less common.[92] However, just as religious institutions may be easily able to organize protests and thus encourage conflict, they can likewise inhibit mobilization and conflict through the moral authority they possess as Koesel (2014) shows in a recent study of how authoritarian regimes in Russia and China conflict and cooperate with religious institutions over money, power, and prestige. Sandal (2017) likewise shows religious leaders' ability to mediate and transform conflict. Similarly, due to their authority, religious institutions can legitimize social movements they advocate for or are sympathetic toward. By contrast, they may also delegitimize those of which they disapprove.[93]

---

[91] Moustafa 2000.
[92] Soper and Fetzer 2007.
[93] Fox 1999.

Explaining Religious Party Change

As the discussion thus far illustrates, religious institutions can affect or be affected by the political sphere in various ways. In this book, I focus on one consequential religious institution that deeply shapes how religious parties evolve ideologically: structures of religious authority, i.e., institutionalization and hierarchical organization within a religious tradition. The choice of this particular religious institution reflects my focus on locating the mechanisms through which religion influences religious parties. This effect on the evolutionary trajectories of religious parties comes in two specific forms. Externally, the structure of religious authority shapes the nature and intensity of religious competition that nascent religious parties will face in their efforts to incorporate religion into their platforms. Internally, the organizational form that religious parties will take – with critical implications for the party's audience and ideological flexibility – rests on the broader religious institutional setup.

The structure of religious authority constitutes one of the most critical institutions through which religion can exert influence over the political behavior and actions of religious actors. What is religious authority? Religious authority is a form of authority that is based on the threat of "psychic coercion" as opposed to the "threatened use of physical coercion" by political authority. In this regard, a religious authority structure refers to "a social structure that attempts to enforce its order and reach its ends by controlling the access of individuals to some desired goods, where the legitimation of that control includes some supernatural component, however weak. Religious authority, like other forms of authority, has a staff capable of withholding access to something individuals want. When that withholding is legitimated by reference to the supernatural, authority is religious."[94] Thus, religious authority's coercive power is rooted in a nonreal threat to which individuals voluntarily subject themselves. While religious authority is uniquely legitimated by a divine source, it also draws on societal roles, norms, and beliefs to reinforce this authority.[95] Often, it involves the use of "god-talk."[96] Historically, however, the state – that is, political authority – often colluded with religious authority, and as such, the two had a monopoly on the use of power; this implies that religion could have forcibly been imposed on the populace.[97]

The institutionalization of religious authority varies greatly across different religions, sects, time, and space. Hence, it necessitates a focus on hierarchal power structures.[98] Such structures can exist either on the micro level – that is, state-wide, community-wide – or transnationally as in the case of the Vatican in Catholicism. Transnational religious authorities have the power to potentially undermine state political authority.[99] In Sunni Islam, by contrast, there

---

[94] Chaves 1994, 755–56.
[95] Campbell 2007.
[96] Chaves 1994.
[97] Jurgensmeyer 2007.
[98] Campbell 2007.
[99] Nexon 2009.

is a low level of institutionalism and thus religious authority is more diffused; it often lies with imams, "muftis, preachers, and intellectuals."[100] Religious authority, in other words, is often equated with religious leadership. Further, in Islam, as well as in Judaism, there are not usually formal initiations into the "priesthood" or religious leadership, as is the case in both Protestantism and Catholicism. Thus, the religious authority rests largely on individual choice to follow specific religious teachers that the individual finds knowledgeable and worthy of respect. Respect is earned, in this regard, rather than conferred.[101]

It is also common in less centralized traditions for texts to be considered religious authorities. This is especially the case among the more conservative or fundamentalist traditions.[102] For example, many Protestants consider the Bible to be a key religious authority.[103] More moderate or liberal traditions tend to place themselves more directly in line with societal norms and morality rather than in literalistic readings of texts.[104] In more recent years, online preachers outside official channels of religion can hold significant authority: "The Internet helps religious actors who construct authority through popularity, media visibility, charisma, and lay engagement – precisely the sources of authority that differentiate many independent Salafi religious authorities from the traditional religious elite in Islam."[105] That being said, it is not uncommon for individuals to hold opinions that differ from those of their religious authorities. As such, religious authorities do not necessarily hold moral authority.[106] Often, however, religious leaders tend to hold moral authority among those whom they lead.[107] This is also the argument of Durkheimians, who assert that "religion refers to a set of collective representations providing moral unity to a society."[108] By contrast, for many French Muslims, French Islamic authorities are often regarded as having less moral and religious authority than those in the Middle East, even if the French authorities hail from Arab backgrounds. This is because it is assumed that authorities in France are "watered-down" or "secularized" Muslims.[109] Other than religious leaders, texts and institutions can also hold moral authority.[110]

Political parties can develop a relationship with religious authorities or assert religious authority themselves, thereby directly interjecting themselves into the field of religious competition. The historical development of Catholic and

[100] Peter 2006.
[101] Turner 2007.
[102] Sherkat and Ellison 1999.
[103] Probst 1989.
[104] Sherkat and Ellison 1999.
[105] Nielsen 2020.
[106] Hamil-Luker and Smith 1998.
[107] Djupe and Grant 2001.
[108] Chaves 1994, 750.
[109] Bowen 2004.
[110] Lakoff 1995.

Explaining Religious Party Change

Islamic political identities and political parties testifies to the close relationship between religious authority and political activism.[111] Like other religious actors, religious parties value religion and religious authority because of its utility as a political resource. For example, Grzymala-Busse explains religion's political benefit for the church as follows: "Moral authority is a political resource. All churches wield authority over religious matters and morality – where religious and national identity are fused, such churches also gain a particular, *political*, moral authority a voice in policy debates and a reputation as defenders of broad societal interests, above secular partisanship and petty politicking."[112] There are three main ways that incorporating religious authority can help religious parties. First, religious authority increases party identification. In societies where the religion–secularism divide is prominent, authoritative representation of a religious identity enhances political identification, especially among constituencies identifying with the faith that the religious party claims to represent. Second and relatedly, speaking for a religion and community of the faithful helps legitimize a religious political party's discourse.[113] In particular, the faithful are more likely to attribute greater credibility to the party's stance on various policy issues when issues are couched in religious terms. Such legitimacy, in turn, boosts party identification among the faithful. Finally, religion helps religious parties mobilize voters more effectively, especially on issue areas that are social- or identity-based in nature. Religious parties, as political actors, aim to mobilize as many voters as possible in order to best position themselves for electoral gain. Whether the goal is to achieve policy changes or secure power, electoral mobilization remains critical to achieving the party's objectives.

Religious parties are mass-based parties that draw significant support on the grounds of religious identity in addition to ethnicity, clientelism, social services, or anti-elite backlash. These parties often arise from a political opening to represent disenfranchised, religious populations. While some contend that religious doctrines define the limits of compatibility between religious parties and various democratic and political notions,[114] I disagree with this perspective. As discussed previously, religious parties do have the agency to modify their religious ideology in line with their political objectives.[115] As such, religious parties come in different varieties, as they comprise a vast ideological and organizational spectrum. While all religious parties base their ideologies and policies on their respective religions in some fashion, some are more pluralistic about religious tenets than others.[116]

---

[111] Van Kersbergen 1994; Kalyvas 1996; Altinordu 2010; Kalyvas and van Kersbergen 2010; Grzymala-Busse 2012.

[112] Grzymala-Busse 2015, 8.

[113] Grewal et al. 2019.

[114] Tepe 2012, 467.

[115] Tabaar and Yildirim 2020.

[116] The more democratically inclined are often center or center-right due to their somewhat leftist economic disposition coupled with their conservative social preferences. Gunther and Diamond

In this regard, the organizational structures of religious parties matter a great deal for their political journeys because they allow an easier path "to reach out to voters through these institutions than their secular rivals," as Masoud explains.[117] Kirdiş suggests that different Islamist parties have "differing organisational needs."[118] Having a social service arm, for example, could enable a religious party to overcome "certain structural disadvantages" in its bid to achieve political goals.[119] Likewise, religious parties can frequently face suppression or pressure from the state; being part of a broader movement enables these parties to continue their existence in "abeyance" in "nonreceptive political climates."[120] Religious parties usually evolve out of religious mass movements.[121] The early stages of religious party formation are marked by a hybrid party-movement organizational structure. These movements operate as large organizational networks that provide a variety of services such as missionary activism, healthcare, education, and charity work. They also include, however, arms or wings that operate as a political party. In some cases, the political arms of these movements remain within the broader body without having a distinct organizational existence. In others, religious parties leave the movement and operate as separate political parties yet remain firmly subservient to the movement's organizational hierarchy regarding finances, decision-making, personnel, and policies. Furthermore, other parties claim complete organizational independence from the religious movement. For example, in explaining the rationale for organizational change among some Islamist movements, Brown, Hamzawy, and Ottaway suggest the following: "Movements that combine missionary and political activities in one institutional structure take particularly ambiguous stances for fear of undermining their credibility with either their religious followers or their political constituents. Conscious of the danger of pursuing two conflicting agendas simultaneously, the Moroccan PJD

---

identify two broad types of religious parties. The first one is more "pluralist, democratic and tolerant" (denominational-mass party); the second type is more fundamentalist in its orientation (religious fundamentalist party): "The principal difference between this [religious fundamentalist party] and the denominational-mass party is that the fundamentalist party seeks to reorganize state and society around a strict reading of religious doctrinal principles, while denominational-mass parties are pluralist and incremental in their agenda" (2003, 182). More recently, Ozzano (2013) introduced a more encompassing typology for "religiously-oriented parties." According to this typology, religious parties are categorized on the basis of six criteria: organizational model, ideology, relationship with interest groups, social base, goals, and pluralism. As a result, Ozzano comes up with five different types of religious parties: conservative, progressive, nationalist, fundamentalist, and camp. While this typology is more fine-grained and helps conceptualize Islamist parties in greater detail, for the purposes of this book I mainly distinguish between anti-system and pro-system religious parties.

[117] Masoud 2014, 168.
[118] Kirdiş 2019, 18.
[119] Brooke 2019, 69.
[120] Taylor 1989, 761.
[121] See, for example, Wegner's (2011) discussion on Islamist parties' origins.

Explaining Religious Party Change

and the Jordanian Islamic Action Front became purely political organizations, leaving religious activities to the Moroccan Reform and Renewal Movement and the Muslim Brotherhood in Morocco and Jordan respectively."[122] The hybrid party-movement organization of religious parties often leads to strictly hierarchical power dynamics within the party; in some cases, hierarchical and authoritarian structures within the party may lead to secrecy and a "conspiratorial cell structure."[123]

Most contemporary analyses of religious parties disproportionately focus on parties' ideologies, activism, and intraparty conflicts while their organizational structures receive relatively scant attention despite their political relevance. This is problematic for several reasons. First, as rational actors religious parties spend time on how to effectively organize, reach out to their audiences, and achieve their policy or political goals. Therefore, their preferred organizational structure greatly informs how these parties deliberate and operate. Second, the organizational structure of political parties might have major implications for their discourse and ideologies.[124] This is a more significant issue for religious parties due to their "divided loyalties".[125] Religious parties typically vacillate between audiences and allegiances such as a hierarchical religious organization (i.e., a national church or the Vatican), the electorate, and religious doctrines. Religious parties' organizational structures, in this regard, can act as impediments to or facilitators of these parties.[126] One direct effect of such variation in organizational structures is the party's inability to shape its own ideology independent of the religious movement from which it hails.[127] As Abedi and Lundeberg explain, whether or not anti-system parties are office-seeking can have a major effect on their organizational structures.[128] If religious parties as anti-system parties do not seek office and electoral success, there exists little incentive for them to undertake change in their organizational structures. By contrast, if they want to win power, organizational change enters the realm of possibility, as illustrated by Tunisia's Ennahdha and Turkey's AKP.

What ultimately defines the character of such parties is how they navigate different loyalties and audiences. The specific configuration of the party's allegiances across different audiences determines the ideological flexibility and the organizational structure of the party.[129] Hence, it is critical to conceptualize how such divided loyalties might play out in varying organizational structures for these parties. As Tarrow argues, organizational changes in social

---

[122] Brown, Hamzawy, and Ottaway 2006, 7.
[123] Gunther and Diamond 2003, 179 & 183.
[124] Wegner 2011, XL.
[125] Warner 2012.
[126] Wuthrich and Ciftci 2020.
[127] Gunther and Diamond 2003, 182.
[128] Abedi and Lundberg 2009.
[129] Wegner 2011, XXXIX.

movements can be instrumental in undertaking ideological changes.[130] Lastly, if distinct organizational structures affect the ideology and political activism of religious parties in different ways, it begs the question of how organizational change among religious parties occurs in the first place. Religious parties do not remain faithful to the same organizational structure throughout their lifetime; instead, they adopt changes proactively in their political journeys. The Moroccan PJD, Turkish AKP, and most recently Tunisian Ennahdha are good examples of such transitions.

MAIN ACTORS

There are three main actors in my analysis. The *existing, or traditional, holders of religious authority* are the religious actors that wield religious authority at the time of religious parties' emergence. On one extreme, the Vatican or national church can act as the sole existing religious actor, as in Western Europe when religious authority is hierarchically organized and centralized. The hierarchical structure of the Catholic Church, in this sense, paves the way for monopoly in religious authority and "tends to mute internal conflict."[131] On the other extreme, there might be numerous holders of religious authority, as in the case of Sunni Islam when religious authority lacks hierarchy and is decentralized. Between these two ideal types, existing religious actors can take many forms based on the nature of the religious market. States can also thrust themselves into the religious field and operate as religious authorities by incorporating traditional religious authorities into the state apparatus.

While the structures of religious markets may vary, the core interests of the existing religious authority holders remain the same across contexts: upholding their institutional interests. In this case, interests correspond to protecting their privileged position in relation to religious authority and the ability to represent and speak on behalf of the religion. As such, they aim to limit competition for religious authority. These actors do not enjoy new religious actors' entry into the fray and claims for a share of their religious authority. The existing religious actors have a wide range of tools at their disposal to undercut the new actors' overtures. Such tools include formal religious indoctrination, informal religious gatherings, publications, and religious education.

Where these existing holders of religious authority differ is the extent of their ability to challenge new entrants in their claims for religious authority; this variation affects the strategies they use to deprive the new actors of religious authority and to secure their own. Those actors that wield greater control over religious authority (akin to a monopoly) can utilize a wide range of options in thwarting the new religious actors and their claims. They can deny legitimacy to the new religious actors by preventing access to resources,

[130] Tarrow 1994, 217.
[131] Gill 1998, 8.

Explaining Religious Party Change

limiting the extent of religious doctrines or discourse that could be employed, forcing clergy to disassociate from these new actors, and publicly claiming that the new actors do not speak for the religion. By contrast, in contexts where religious authority is diffused and not hierarchically organized, existing religious authorities lack the resources to credibly denounce the legitimacy of new religious actors. Because they lack the broad legitimacy enjoyed in hierarchically organized religious contexts, their strategy is based on undermining the legitimacy of the new actors by claiming that their interpretation is not the "correct" interpretation of religion.

Another group of actors is *religious movements*. These are the mass movements from which religious parties originate. They arise in response to the perceived backslide in the religious life of a society. Religious movements can be defined as "social movements that wish to cause or prevent change in a system of beliefs, values, symbols and practices concerned with providing supernaturally-based general compensators."[132] Unlike their secular counterparts, these movements claim "to represent the truths and values" of a religious tradition; their legitimacy can be questioned if religious movements diverge "too far outside the boundaries and precedents of the tradition."[133] Religious movements are encompassing organizations that serve in various capacities and issue areas to help revive religious life, including missionary activities, education, healthcare, and charity work. The core interest of religious movements is to establish, and later sustain, themselves as actors in the new religious revival efforts. Unless they can secure their positions as such, the efforts to revitalize religion in the society will be in vain. This prospect potentially puts religious movements on a collision course with the existing holders of authority.

Because their efforts are societal and aim to reach as many faithful as possible, grassroots mobilization is the preferred strategy for religious movements. Such mobilization requires not only provision of various social services but also a source of legitimacy. Efforts to convince prospective members of the movement necessitate appealing to their religious convictions; hence, these religious movements must incorporate religious authority in order to credibly claim religious legitimacy. Lacking religious credentials not only opens them up for criticisms and attacks from different groups but also undermines these movements in their conflict with other religious actors. Absent religious authority, religious movements would face a major handicap in the religious competition. Religious movements approach institutional political participation with caution as it might compromise their identity and undermine their anti-system character.[134] In this sense, religious political activism through the formation of a political party offers both advantages and disadvantages.

---

[132] Stark and Bainbridge 1979, 124; Stark and Bainbridge 1985, 23.
[133] Kautzer 2012, 23.
[134] Offe 1990, 240.

46 *The Politics of Religious Party Change*

Religious parties are the other major actors. These parties typically hail from religious mass movements with which they share very close organizational ties as well as a religious vision. While they share this religious vision and hope to erect a religious state and society, realizing this vision requires obtaining political power – which is religious parties' main interest – in order to secure this vision. Yet, the quest for political power puts religious parties in a predicament. Political parties appeal to the electorate and, when necessary, adjust their political ideologies to boost their electoral prospects. However, religious parties do not solely address the broader electorate; they must also account for the movement's membership as they deliberate political discourse. Religious parties' political strategy rests on balancing the two distinct components of their base: the electorate and the movement members. For example, as religious parties attempt to maximize their votes, they might be required to revise or soften their discourse; the broader electorate may not find "restrictive morals" or nonspecific policies as proposed by the movement appealing. By contrast, any deviation in the party's ideological makeup from that of the movement can be labeled as a "betrayal" by the movement base.[135] The organizational structure of the party and the movement-party relationship shape the party's strategy to obtain its goal. While the party and the movement might have identical visions for the state and society, their strategies to attain this vision might show notable variation, depending on the nature of the party-movement relationship. Unlike the movement, which prefers an intransigent religious discourse that primarily caters to its own membership, religious parties might prefer a more flexible political stance that is open to compromise. Such an approach works to align the system with their vision through gaining greater power and influence in the political arena. This incongruence in strategies between the two sets up a conflict in how the party acts in the political arena. How does this theoretical framework apply to the cases of Catholic and Islamist parties? I will be discussing this next.

CATHOLIC PARTIES VERSUS ISLAMIST PARTIES

Catholic parties' transformation into secular-democratic political parties was facilitated by Catholicism's centralized and hierarchical religious structure. At the national level, the presence of a centralized religious authority such as the national church pitted confessional parties of Western Europe against this institution over the political representation of Catholic identity. At the organizational level, the existence of a centralized religious institution wielding religious authority undercut Catholic mass movements' overtures to overtaking the Church's authority in the political arena. Indeed, the Church emphatically sent the message that the Church and "Catholic interests was the business

---

[135] Wegner 2011, XL.

Explaining Religious Party Change

of bishops," not laymen, and "no one can defend such a power without its recognition and authorization." The Church disciplined Catholic mass organizations early on by increasing levels of "clericalization".[136] Importantly, the Church was highly territorial about its religious authority not because of ideology – that is, the nature of the vision for the state and the society – but due to the organizational and political threat from Catholic mass organizations and confessional parties. This threat perception waxed and waned in response to the Church's strength in a given context. In countries where the Church had significant political influence such as Italy, the Church's threat perception from religious parties was amplified. By contrast, when anticlerical attacks weakened the Church, its perception of Catholic political parties was relatively less threatening.

The conflict between the two led to an eventual institutional separation between the confessional party and the Catholic mass movement from which it hailed, enabling the party to access a wider audience. The confessional party's political space was no longer demarcated by the ideological rigidity imposed by the movement and its moral authority, or the requisite anti-system features. This religious institutional structure granted greater independence to Catholic parties in the political arena. Taking part in politics, therefore, alluded to a choice between remaining firmly within the Church's control as an anti-system entity, on one hand, and the "implied acceptance" of the system, democratic governance, and state institutions, on the other hand, for confessional parties.[137] The conflict and eventual break from the Church offered Catholic parties the freedom to experiment with alternative policy positions in their efforts to achieve electoral success and gain political power, and ultimately, greater agency. Crucially, this independence and freedom to determine policy positions allowed confessional parties to make peace with the system. By endorsing democratic and secular platforms to appeal to wider constituencies and leaving behind their anti-system orientations, they moved from being parliamentary Catholics who were "permanently constrained by the representation of a confessionally defined constituency and the defense of religion and of the church" to Catholic parliamentarians who did not shoulder such a burden and could act freely.[138] In other words, what led these parties to ultimately renounce their anti-system stance and embrace the system was the opportunity to act independent of religious institutional constraints.

By contrast, Sunni Islam lacks a comparable centralized, authoritative, *and* independent religious institutional body at the national or transnational level. As such, political Islam's rise was, in part, facilitated by the reality that Islamists faced a religious environment marked by a fragmented religious field. As Mecham rightly observes, Islamists as political entrepreneurs tend to have ample

---

[136] Kalyvas 1996, 60–68, 174–75.
[137] Brown 2012.
[138] Kalyvas 1996, 55.

48   *The Politics of Religious Party Change*

opportunities to successfully politicize religion in environments of fragmented religious authority where they "cannot be effectively policed by religious superiors."[139] Devoid of a dominant religious authority and facing fewer obstacles in their search for religious and moral authority, Islamists capitalized on the political utility of religious discourse. The ulama (Islamic scholars) were the *de facto* holders of religious authority between the eleventh and the nineteenth centuries. This was by virtue of their scholarship; their "competent human agency to discover God's law" and the fact that they largely stood for the "best interests" of their community as "Guardians of Religion" legitimized their claim.[140] This class functioned as a proto-religious institution, wielding great religious and moral authority, in part as a direct outcome of the state-ulama alliance struck in the eleventh and twelfth centuries.[141] Nonetheless, the ulama were in no way the only holders of religious authority, nor was their authority centralized or hierarchically organized. At the turn of the twentieth century, however, there emerged a clear vacuum of religious authority as the ulama's power waned for various reasons; Islamist movements and others aspired to fill this void.[142] The ulama further lost its vitality and authority due to Islamist reprisal in the face of growing weakness of the ulama.[143] Indeed, the criticisms leveled against the Church and clergymen in regard to their inadequacy in addressing the needs of Catholicism in the nineteenth century were nearly identical to the ones raised by Islamists against the ulama, demonstrating the extent of the similarities in the early trajectories of the two religious political identities.[144]

Islamist movements were unique organizations in that they claimed religious authority while engaging in political activism. In a clear break from the Catholic experience, Islamist movements were not pressured to limit themselves to religious activism, which led to hybrid religiopolitical organizations that took on strong religious and political characters. Unchecked and unchallenged by a universal religious authority such as the Vatican in Catholicism, Islamist movements were free to both claim religious authority and represent the faith and the faithful in electoral politics. The outcome was the absence of incentives for Islamist parties to move beyond Islamism; instead of becoming Muslim parliamentarians, they emerged *and* remained as parliamentary Muslims who were constrained to representing and defending Islam and a confessional constituency within the political system.

---

[139] Mecham 2017, 7.

[140] Hallaq 2003; Zaman 2012; Nawas 2013.

[141] Kuru 2019.

[142] Kersten and Olsson 2013.

[143] The only contemporary example of the ulama institution is the Qum-based ulama class in Iran which, until the 1979 revolution, fulfilled a function similar to that of the national church in the Western European context. However, after the 1979 Revolution, the ulama in Iran lost their autonomy when they came under Islamist state control and now largely operate as a state functionary (Roy 1998; Kurzman 2003).

[144] Ayoob 2004; Soage 2008; Zaman 2009.

Explaining Religious Party Change

Similarly, critical to the evolution of religious politics in the Middle East is the absence of separation between Islamist political parties and the religious movements from which they originate. Islamist political parties have often maintained an organic co-existence with these religious movements through overlapping organizational and decision-making structures. In this institutional arrangement, Islamist parties have usually assumed a subservient role within the movement's broader organizational structure. Political Islam lacks a defining moment comparable to Catholic parties' struggle for independence from the Church. Compared to Catholic parties, Islamist parties faced minimal institutional constraints in establishing themselves in the political arena. As a result, the line between religious discourse and political discourse remains blurred at best. A key outcome of this heterogeneous institutional design is that most Islamist parties cannot operate as mere political parties; rather, they are party-movement hybrids. Unlike Catholic parties, Islamist parties have historically lacked the room to maneuver in experimenting with alternative policy positions, courting different constituencies along the way, and submitting to electoral dynamics. Hence, despite occasional lip service, Islamist parties largely failed to fully commit to being pro-system and seriously entertain notions of secularism and democracy. If Islamist parties are to change and become pro-system, their evolution will require "not only ideological changes but organizational ones as well."[145]

Despite the vast array of similarities in the early trajectories of Catholic and Islamist parties, scholars have not explored this fruitful area of research from a *comparative* perspective. A comparative analysis of Islamist parties of the Middle East and the confessional parties of Western Europe is not merely an interesting exercise but an analytically imperative endeavor to better understand religious party evolution. The perception has been, and largely remains, that these are two inherently different kinds of political parties. One obvious drawback of this assumption is that it compartmentalizes the religion–politics relationship in differing religious contexts, thereby essentializing religious parties. Consequently, it undermines our ability to account for longitudinal change in either set of religious parties, leading instead to static comparisons. This book presents one of the first examples of truly comparative cross-national empirical research into religious parties' evolution across time and space. Such a comparative framework provides a valuable opportunity to take stock of extensive past research into Catholic parties of Europe and compare the insights of this body of work to the contemporary case of Islamist parties.[146] Likewise, a comparison between contemporary religious parties in the Middle East and the historical experiences of Western nations offers a distinct advantage in the analysis of religious parties by ensuring similar political, economic, and societal conditions between the two contexts.[147] By focusing on the origins and early histories of both sets of parties, this study can establish analytical

---

[145] Brown 2012, 34.
[146] Casanova 2005; Altinordu 2010; Brown 2012; Driessen 2014.
[147] Tilly 1964.

equivalence for a sound analysis. In the absence of such equivalence, we not only fail to control for various contextual factors that might affect the evolutions of these parties but also risk reinforcing essentialism.

Lastly, I want to briefly discuss Protestantism and Shiite Islam in this context. Protestantism has a more decentralized religious authority structure compared to Catholicism, which should facilitate the rise of religious parties that are closer to the dynamics faced by Islamist parties. Yet, we do not observe the emergence of Protestant parties in a fashion similar to Islamist or Catholic political parties. The Church's relationship with the state constitutes a key reason why Protestant parties failed to emerge in most cases in Western Europe. In cases where Protestant churches developed dependence on the state, Protestant parties are unlikely to emerge. Similarly, fragmented and decentralized denominational structures have been pointed out among the causes of the failure of Protestant parties to rise.[148] Shiite Islam notably differs from Sunni Islam in how religious authority is structured. Unlike Sunni Muslims, Shiite Muslims have a more interwoven vision of religious and political leadership. For Shiites, the Prophet's death did not necessarily suggest the end of "the need to guide humans and to explain the contents of the divine teaching"; rather, this function fell upon the Twelve Imams who traced their lineage to the Prophet.[149] Most Shiites belong to the Twelver or Imami denomination, believing that the religious and political leadership of the Muslim community belongs to the Twelve Imams who are the male descendants of Ali – the cousin and son-in-law of the Prophet and through whom the Prophet's lineage lives on. While the Imams are not prophets, they are divinely inspired and interpret God's will. This position granted them unparalleled status and authority.[150] The occultation of the twelfth Imam serves as the turning point for Shiite Islam. As the Imam's presence gradually faded, Twelver Shiite doctrine evolved to delegate the religious authority and duties of the occulted Imam to other religious actors, the majority of them being scholars. It was only after the 1970s that there was a major shift in how this authority was reinterpreted, endowing Shiite clergy with outright political power. Ayatollah Khomeini's twist to the Shiite doctrine in the form of velayat-e faqih (guardianship of the jurist) rendered Shiite clergy the uncontested religious and political authority in Iran and beyond. The fact that the origins of the Sunni–Shiite separation were strictly political notwithstanding, doctrinal differentiation ensued, leading importantly to vital differences in how religious authority is conceived and structured. Compared to Sunni Islam's decentralized authority structure, Shiite Islam is characterized by a decidedly more hierarchical authority structure around the institution of Imamate, clergy, and more recently velayat-e faqih.

---

[148] Kalyvas 1996, 3; Freston 2017.
[149] Hughes 2013, 125.
[150] Esposito 2002, 40.

2

Catholic and Islamic Religious Institutions

What do the religious institutional structures look like in Catholicism and Sunni Islam? In order to trace how religious institutional structures may shape the early evolutions of religious parties, this chapter explores the historical development of structures of religious authority and how they looked when religious parties arose. The focus of the analysis for each religion varies to reflect the historical trajectories of their religious institutions and what such different trajectories mean for the analytical narrative of this book. The analysis proceeds in chronological order and begins with Catholicism to be followed by Sunni Islam. In the case of Catholicism, the focus is less on the evolution of religious institutions and more on how divergence from orthodoxy and orthopraxy are handled within the Catholic Church. As the religious authority in Catholicism, the Church's handling of divergences is key to understanding how it dealt with the rise of Catholic parties. In the case of Sunni Islam, I focus more on the historical evolution of religious authority, paying close attention to the parameters of major shifts in the eleventh and early twentieth centuries.

This analysis of the religious institutional structures and religious authority in Catholicism and Sunni Islam goes beyond mere description of religious institutions and authority in both religions; it examines how religious authority is maintained and the conditions under which it changes. This discussion is instrumental in setting the stage for analyzing the political implications of the conflict over religious authority between various religious actors in the modern period. In Catholicism, the early development and ensuing institutionalization of the church structure enabled a centralized and hierarchical institutional framework to ensure orthodoxy in religious doctrine and praxis among Catholics worldwide. Strict hierarchy affords the Church an advantage other religious actors lack: the legitimate authority to speak on behalf of the religion and concomitant legitimacy to represent the religion and its adherents in various platforms, including the political arena. The Church, consequently, has been averse to competition for its religiopolitical authority.

By contrast, Sunni Islam has historically lacked a comparable institutional structure. At times, states attempted to control religion within their polity by establishing religious agencies; such attempts fell short of being encompassing or long-lasting and typically did not enjoy broad legitimacy. At other times, the ulama (the class of religious scholars) functioned as the main religious body. Widespread recognition of its religious authority notwithstanding, the ulama lacked hierarchy and a centralized structure, paving the way for fierce competition among religious actors. This competition intensified following the demise of the ulama class in the early twentieth century. By thoroughly analyzing the constraints that religious institutions present for political action, this chapter lays the foundation for examining the distinct ways that religious authority shapes religious party politics in Chapters 3–5.

HIERARCHICAL ORGANIZATION IN THE CATHOLIC CHURCH

The Roman Catholic Church represents the "Mystical Body of Christ." Formed as a hierarchical society to rule over believers, this hierarchy reflects the Church's desire and is independent of the sociopolitical conditions, according to Council of Trent and Vatican I. Missions or parishes are the smallest organizational unit of the Church, each led by a priest. A bishop oversees a specific geographical area that is constituted by several parishes in that area, forming a diocese. Ascending in the hierarchy, several dioceses make up an archdiocese, overseen by an archbishop. Cardinals come next in the hierarchy, followed by the pope who is the "bishop of Rome, the primate or chief bishop of Italy, the patriarch of the West, the absolute monarch of the Vatican City State, and the head of the college of bishops and of the Catholic church."[1] By and large, state churches have maintained a strong connection to the Vatican even under the most challenging political contexts.[2]

The Protestant Reformation was a consequential event for the history of the Catholic Church in many ways. Two specific changes concern us here. First, Western Christianity was divided into Lutheranism, Reformed Protestantism (Calvinism), and Catholicism. The Catholic Church was no longer the only confession, but one of three separate faiths. Such a division undercut the Vatican's religious influence across Europe. The Reformation challenged the spiritual influence of the Catholic Church by calling into question the necessity of the episcopate and the entire system of clergy. When Lutheranism became a prominent force in German territories, it displayed "subserviency of the church to the central secular authority."[3] Protestantism did not accept the Catholic norm that the religious authority of a church should also imply temporal authority as a governing body.

[1] Reese 1996, 10.
[2] Vallier 1971, 494.
[3] Hall 1913, 230.

Catholic and Islamic Religious Institutions

The Augsburg Confession of 1530 was critical to the rise and spread of Lutheranism and Protestantism. Authored by German reformer Philipp Melanchthon, a friend of Martin Luther, it consisted of 28 articles that were considered common doctrine among Lutheran communions. The document was notable in understanding Protestantism's approach to religious institutions and authority because it constitutes Protestants' first collective declaration on doctrine. What is particularly significant about the Augsburg Confession is that its components found acceptance among the followers of Reformed Protestant leaders, such as Huldrych Zwingli and John Calvin.[4] Even though Zwingli and Calvin maintained important objections to Lutheran doctrines regarding eucharistic practice, it is significant that the Augsburg Confession seemed to lay the groundwork for Protestant communions to declare their newly proclaimed beliefs against the authority of the Catholic Church.

Calvinism, the most notable of the denominations in Reformed Protestantism, also posed new challenges to the religious and political authority of the Catholic Church. With the rise of Calvinism, Catholics started to feel that monarchy "threaten[ed] their religion and traditional authority of the pope."[5] While European monarchs had traditionally allowed the Church to carry on its presence and religious authority in their territories, the rise of Lutheranism and Reformed Protestantism in Europe allowed certain monarchs to adopt a new state religion and thus break free from the temporal influence of the Catholic Church. Although this was not the only factor, the post-Reformation spread of Protestantism was due in part to some monarchs' belief in the advantage of adopting a faith that would be subservient to their political interests; this could not be guaranteed in a political alliance with the Catholic Church.

The second way the Protestant Reformation shaped the Catholic Church concerned how the entire process of Counter-Reformation – by which Catholics tried to regain influence in Europe following Luther's movement and codify key Catholic beliefs – was in many ways founded on an effort to re-clarify the influence of bishops within the Catholic Church.[6] Around the time of the Council of Trent (1545–63), the papacy abandoned its traditional apprehension of the episcopate. Against the rise of Lutheranism and Calvinism and their rejection of episcopal authority, the Church abandoned their long-held fear that a powerful episcopate could diminish the pope's influence. Instead, the Church proclaimed that influential bishops, who at times held political power as well as spiritual authority, were absolutely central to the mission of the Catholic Church. The Council of Trent became a turning point in that "Catholics surrendered the hope for reconciliation with Protestants and sought to draw a clear border with them." The Council of Trent laid out a new role for bishops and pastors such that they "were

---

[4] Steinmetz 2010, 170.
[5] Reinhard 1989, 386.
[6] Bergin 1999.

54 *The Politics of Religious Party Change*

not chiefly benefice-holders but shepherds who resided with their flocks and preached to them regularly."[7]

As a result of this shift, the Catholic Church underwent a process of restructuring by the rise of "territorial churches." This structure has two distinct features. First, the entire world is divided into "mutually exclusive" territorial units under the Catholic Church's authority. Second, these territorial units of the Church are tied in "a vertical system of authority and administration to the transnational center of the church, the Holy See" with the pope as the bishop of the Holy See.[8] By virtue of creating additional layers of hierarchy, the Vatican's religious authority was restructured in ways that expanded the reach of the Catholic Church throughout the continent. Despite the emergence of these national churches, the Catholic Church was able to sustain its administrative autonomy over institutional structures and personnel decisions.[9]

The popes of the past four centuries have been both reigning over the universal Catholic Church and governing the Papal State as "absolute monarch of the Vatican City State."[10] The term Papal States refers to the sovereign control exercised by pontiffs over varying parts of the Italian Peninsula between the eighth century and 1870.[11] The pope's civil power waxed and waned over time but was consistently significant around Rome and Italy. Even during the disintegration of the Papal States, the Vatican maintained and solidified its religious control over Catholics worldwide. The power to control the organizational structure and personnel has been the key element of this change in the Vatican. In the words of Casanova, "The Vatican's unchallenged control over the process of nomination of bishops through the papal nuncios has proven to be the single most important factor in papal control of the transnational Catholic Church."[12]

In principle, all Catholics fall under the Catholic Church's religious authority as a reflection of the Church's hierarchical institutional structure. Such centralized and hierarchical authority furnishes the Church with various tools to ensure believers' compliance with church authority, doctrine, and policies.

The doctrine of the Catholic pope's infallibility first took written shape at Vatican Council I in 1870. While the concept had long existed in the Catholic Church, the codification of papal infallibility put into definite terms the ultimate spiritual authority of the Roman Pontiff.[13] Vatican Council I declared that the Catholic Church was "unblemished by any error" and was blessed with "the gift of truth and never-failing faith." Vatican Council I decreed:

---

[7] Bireley 2009, 237.
[8] Vallier 1971, 480.
[9] Gorski 2000, 151.
[10] Reese 1996, 10.
[11] Woods 1921, 2.
[12] Casanova 2005, 2.
[13] Tierney 1972, 3

Catholic and Islamic Religious Institutions

Therefore, faithfully adhering to the tradition received from the beginning of the Christian faith, to the glory of God our savior, for the exaltation of the Catholic religion and for the salvation of the Christian people, with the approval of the Sacred Council, we teach and define as a divinely revealed dogma that when the Roman Pontiff speaks ex cathedra, that is, when, in the exercise of his office as shepherd and teacher of all Christians, in virtue of his supreme apostolic authority, he defines a doctrine concerning faith or morals to be held by the whole Church, he possesses, by the divine assistance promised to him in blessed Peter, that infallibility which the divine Redeemer willed his Church to enjoy in defining doctrine concerning faith or morals. Therefore, such definitions of the Roman Pontiff are of themselves, and not by the consent of the Church, irreformable.[14]

Vatican Council II (1962–65) echoed the doctrine of 1870, with some minor differences.[15] Lumen gentium, or the "Dogmatic Constitution on the Church" was one of the primary documents of Vatican II, and declares (Chapter 3, Section 25) the infallibility of the pope, in addition to the infallibility of bishops when proclaiming the word of the pope: "The infallibility promised to the Church resides also in the body of Bishops, when that body exercises the supreme magisterium with the successor of Peter."[16] The original decree on papal infallibility in 1870 enshrined the authority of the pope over that of a general ecumenical counsel, while the Lumen gentium refers to a "college" of bishops having supreme authority over the Church, subject to the pope's power. This is perhaps the most significant difference between the doctrine of infallibility in the first and second Vatican Councils; however, a *Nota praevia* was added to the Lumen gentium before its approval to reaffirm that the authority of the college of bishops is subordinate to that of the pope.[17]

As it stands post-Vatican II, papal infallibility still ensures the hierarchical and even monarchical structure of the Catholic Church. The pope is the ultimate source of wisdom – an infallible teacher who transmits and interprets the word of God for the good of the people.[18] Even though Vatican II liberalized certain Catholic doctrines to make the Church more accessible, such as a more lenient stance on non-Catholic churches, the pope and his teachings reign supreme.

By contrast, Protestantism has no concept identical to papal infallibility. Most Protestant sects do not have as structured of a hierarchy or a supreme leader like the Catholic Church. A notable exception is the Church of England, which is symbolically led by the British monarch, who serves as the de facto Supreme Governor of the Church of England and "Defender of the Faith."[19] Perhaps the closest Protestant parallel to papal infallibility is the doctrine of biblical inerrancy, under which some conservative Protestants uphold the

---

[14] Vatican Council I, First Dogmatic Constitution on the Church of Christ, 1870.
[15] Tierney 1972, 5.
[16] Vatican Council II, Dogmatic Constitution on the Church, 1964.
[17] Hastings 1990, 88.
[18] Powell 2009, 3.
[19] Preface to the Thirty-Nine Articles of the Church of England.

entire Bible as absolute truth and offer "ingenious explanations for the purported errors and contradictions in scripture."[20] According to these Protestants, those who question the inerrancy of the Bible risk rejecting the entirety of the Christian religion, similar to how Catholics who question the Pope's authority are rebuffing God's will. However, Protestant sects lack a centralized, all-powerful, infallible religious authority, which has always been one of the primary differentiators between Catholicism and Protestantism. Thus, papal infallibility is a uniquely Catholic concept whose historical roots and modern conception form the foundation of the Catholic faith.

The Magisterium is another key concept in understanding the Catholic Church's institutional and authority structures. It refers to the ability of the body of bishops within the Church to pronounce authoritative doctrine. For Catholics, magisterial authority has always existed within the Church. At its core, the Magisterium rests on the conception that "revealed truth" is not solely confined to scripture. Rather, the teaching authority of Christ's apostles has been passed down for centuries to all Catholic bishops, who have a divine authority to expound on teachings to guide the entire Church – a doctrine known as "apostolic succession." As the magisterial authority began with Christ himself, Catholics believe that this authority will endure eternally. Pope John XXIII emphasized in Vatican Council II that the Magisterium "is unfailing and endures until the end of time."[21]

The word "magisterium" itself means "the status or function of a master," and refers to "the traditional and authentic Catholic doctrine that final authority in matters of doctrine, the final judgment where there is controversy, is the responsibility and right of the pope and bishops."[22] This form of authority is different from outright "teaching," in the sense that Catholics are free to learn from theologians and others who are not themselves bishops or the pope. That bishops are endowed with magisterial authority does not mean that they are the only ones who can compose authoritative teaching. Instead, the idea of "magisterium" refers to how popes and bishops of the Catholic Church are able to give final judgment on which teachings are or are not authoritative: "In the world of law there is a hierarchy of courts: lower courts, higher courts, courts of first instance, courts of appeal, supreme courts, and courts of final resort. Now in the Catholic Church, the final judgment from which there is no further appeal lies with the pope. And we have the guarantee that his final and formal ex cathedra judgment in matters of faith and morals is infallible – precisely because it is the final judgment of the Church, which he supremely represents and in whose infallibility in such circumstances he participates."[23] The term "Magisterium" usually refers to the fact that Church teachings are

[20] Powell 2009, 2.
[21] Bennett 2016, 37.
[22] Hill 1989, 67.
[23] Hill 1989, 71.

Catholic and Islamic Religious Institutions

generally authoritative due to the work of the Holy Spirit within the Church; this general level of authority does not mean that the beliefs cannot sometimes be questioned by laymen and clergy.

The magisterial authority in the Catholic Church was a major reason why the Church held such political dominance up until the Protestant Reformation. For Luther, giving primacy to the Church's teaching authority over what he saw as the Gospel truth was sinful, and thus Luther accepted the political consequences that would occur when new Protestant churches sprung up. The prominent Catholic priest Desiderius Erasmus attributed the rise of religious conflicts in post-Reformation Europe to Luther's rejection of the magisterium: "[Erasmus] believe[d] that the confusion and the revolts following in the aftermath of the Early Reformation have caused more damage than good to the gospel and to the common people in Europe. He point[ed] at the call to follow the church, its magisterial authority, and the unity of tradition."[24]

Because the Magisterium is not an institutional body as much as it is an institutional feature of the Catholic Church, the Magisterium can be said to have been acting at any point when bishops or popes have ruled on political matters. The Magisterium's main role was traditionally ensuring doctrinal cohesion within the Church, which, by its nature, carried political ramifications.

Knight writes, "the authority of the living magisterium of the Church [...] is the way in which Catholics demonstrate to Protestants that there should be and that there are in fact Divine traditions not contained in Holy Writ."[25] There is no comparable "magisterium" institution in Protestantism. *Sola scriptura* – the belief that there is no divine truth outside of what is contained in the Bible – was a founding doctrine of Protestantism. As such, Luther's doctrine meant that "no longer would papal pronouncements or the decisions of Church councils matter."[26] *Sola scriptura* meant that Lutheranism and subsequent Protestant churches that grew out of the Reformation would reject the idea that any clergy structure could form or sanction any new traditions not found in Scripture. It does not mean that Protestant churches rejected the institution of clergy altogether; rather, Protestants rejected the aforementioned idea of "apostolic succession" and did not believe that their own clergymen carried the same teaching authority that Christ's apostles had.

The tools at the Catholic Church's disposal apply not only to lay followers of the faith but to clergymen as well. Bishops and priests can also be formally removed from their positions or asked to resign for teaching incorrect doctrines. Even in cases where it may be justifiable for clergy to formally break with the Church (in order to break church law for a moral necessity), excommunication is a serious possibility. Archbishop Lefebvre's case is instructive.[27]

---

[24] Mjaaland 2013, 158.
[25] Knight 2017, 7.
[26] Pelz 2016, 20.
[27] Reese 1996, 248.

With the establishment of the Vatican Council II, some dissatisfaction surfaced in French seminaries in the 1970s where young seminarians were unhappy with the modernist ideals of Vatican II, including "weekly liturgical experiments, seminarians concocting their own liturgies, seminarians going out at night, bad theology courses, no rule of life, no cassocks, no Latin, no discipline, contempt for Tradition, total collapse."[28] In order to address these concerns, Archbishop Lefebvre founded his own House of Studies, which soon evolved into both a seminary and his Priestly Society of St. Pius X for traditional Catholics against the newly evolving religion. Archbishop Lefebvre became the center of controversy due to his continued use of the Tridentine Mass, the traditional form of Latin mass. By 1974, the controversy had become so immense that Lefebvre publicly called into question the validity and orthodoxy of the Second Vatican Council.

Pope Paul VI suppressed Lefebvre's seminary after this declaration. Ignoring the canonical suppression, Lefebvre began illicitly ordaining his seminarians to holy orders, an action that soon led to the suspension of his faculties. In 1976, Pope Paul VI suspended the archbishop from priestly functions and prohibited him from celebrating Mass and giving the sacraments. The archbishop ignored the penalty and continued ordaining priests. Over the next 13 years, he continued to operate unlawfully and expand his seminary.

On June 30, 1988, Archbishop Lefebvre proceeded with his plan to consecrate bishops without Rome's permission, directly violating canon law and incurring an automatic excommunication. The following day, Cardinal Bernadin Gantin of the Congregation of Bishops formally announced Lefebvre's and the illegitimate bishops' excommunication, while Pope John Paul II confirmed his excommunication for schism and having consecrated bishops despite the holy warnings not to do so. Archbishop Lefebvre lambasted Pope John Paul II and other Vatican officials for pursuing changes in church doctrine and practice adopted in the 1960s: "They are in the process of destroying the church."[29] He repeatedly said that "such changes as saying Mass in the vernacular rather than in Latin and reconciling Catholicism with other religions were 'heretical' acts that distanced the church from its roots."[30] The Vatican's chief spokesman, Joaquin Navarro-Valls, read a statement on the day of the excommunications saying that the consecrations "have been carried out expressly against the Pope's will" and that Archbishop Lefebvre "openly refused submission to the Holy Father and communion with the members of the church under his jurisdiction."[31]

---

[28] Tissier de Mallerais 2004, 215.
[29] Steven Greenhouse, "Rebel Archbishop Anoints 4 Bishops," *The New York Times*, 1988.
[30] Steven Greenhouse, "Archbishop Lefebvre, 85, Dies; Traditionalist Defied the Vatican," *The New York Times*, 1991.
[31] Steven Greenhouse, "Archbishop Lefebvre, 85, Dies; Traditionalist Defied the Vatican," *The New York Times*, 1991.

Catholic and Islamic Religious Institutions

59

The tradition of establishing religious orthodoxy began very early in the Church, dating back to Pope Clement I's reign in the first century. Reese summarizes the development of this tradition as follows: "Rome became a court of appeals to deal with disputes in local communities and disputes between bishops. Heretics were condemned, and a tradition of church teaching developed ... These practices have continued into the twentieth century when the Vatican has suppressed theologians who are out of step with the papacy, first during the Modernist period (around 1907) and even more so today. Theologians who disagree with the pope on birth control, married clergy, and women priests have been removed from teaching positions in seminaries and Catholic faculties."[32]

The Church's control over religion extends to personnel decisions. Popes can appoint bishops or other clergy members whom they know would agree with them. As a result, the Church substantially diminishes the odds of dissent and opposition within its institutional structure. It is "the monopoly on authority by the Church" that minimizes "the possibility of dissent" either by the clergy or lay followers.[33]

One particular outcome of modernization has been augmenting the Church's power among Catholics. In the early modernization period, states assumed greater religious power in some cases. In France, the state made the Catholic clergy state employees and thrust itself into the process of church appointments: "The archbishops and bishops were appointed by the government with the sanction of the pope. The bishops in turn appointed priests, but only after consultation with the government."[34] In Spain, the state similarly attempted to control religion and the national church, banning church taxes and seizing approximately 90 percent of church property.[35] As states increasingly adopted secularization policies (i.e., state–church separation), national churches and the Vatican saw less competition from political leaders for their authority: "Without Catholic kings to oppose it, the papacy's power and influence in the European and Latin American church continued to grow throughout the nineteenth and twentieth centuries."[36] Indeed, the changes taking place in the political arena ushered in a new era in which new policies and reforms undertaken by the Church would face "little contestation from below" in enforcing such policies and further contribute to the "remarkable global homogenization of Catholic culture at least among the elites."[37] This point is particularly critical to understanding the dominance and singularity of the Church's religious authority. Diotallevi convincingly shows the extent of this authority for

---

[32] Reese 1996, 26.
[33] Blancarte 2000, 592.
[34] Guerlac 1908, 260.
[35] Moran 1995, 535–36.
[36] Reese 1996, 28.
[37] Casanova 2005, 9.

contemporary Italian society: "This is why Italian Catholicism can be spoken of as just one church ... Every Italian Catholic religious firm strongly refers to the same religious authority. But it is impossible to find any organized or organizable connection that unites all these Catholic religious firms."[38]

When Catholic laity or clergy deviate from the authority of the Catholic Church, there are multiple courses of action which the Church may take. Since the Church tells its members "what they ought to believe and how they ought to behave," it views formal discipline as a way "to guide [the members'] footsteps so that each may be fully aware of the spiritual import of his or her action" and to achieve three interrelated goals: "punishment of the offender, protection of the common good, and reformation of the transgressor."[39] Violations of church authority are divided into two broad categories: infractions that are punishable (or used to be punishable) both by secular law and the Church, such as suicide and abortion, and those infractions that are punishable solely under ecclesiastical law.[40] The misdemeanors that fall under the latter are extensive, ranging from heresy and apostasy to "profanation of the Holy Species" and violation of the Sovereign Pontiff.

Church punishments for offenses cover a broad range but usually fall under one of two categories. The first is "vindictive" penalties, which are of a fixed duration and designed to punish the offender; these include withholding a Christian burial, imprisonment in a monastery, and pecuniary punishments.[41] The more common category of offenses is "medicinal penalties" or censures that aim to reform the transgressor.[42] These include excommunication, suspension, and interdict. Excommunication is the most frequent penalty and can occur either immediately after an offense (*latae sententiae*) or after a judgment by the Church (*ferendae sententiae*). *Latae sententiae* excommunication results from direct offenses such as abortion, apostasy, heresy, or schism, while penalties *ferendae sententiae*, which are rarely imposed on the laity today, stem from rarer circumstances.[43] Excommunicates are barred from participating in the ministry, receiving Holy Communion, or exercising any ecclesiastical functions; they may only be absolved and permitted to partake in these activities by amending their wrongdoing or repenting. An interdict is a lesser penalty than excommunication, as the offender may still hold ecclesiastical office. Suspension applies solely to clerics and prohibits "either all or some" powers, actions, and rights attached to their office.[44]

Numerous prominent figures throughout history have been excommunicated, interdicted, or suspended. In 1809, Napoleon I was excommunicated by Pope Pius VII after ordering the invasion of Rome and continually giving

[38] Diotallevi 2002, 148.
[39] Rahner 1968, 411.
[40] Rahner 1968, 412.
[41] Rahner 1968, 413.
[42] Peters 2014.
[43] Rahner 1968, 415.
[44] Code of Cannon Law 1983, Title IV, Chapter I.

Catholic and Islamic Religious Institutions

anti-papal orders.[45] Other notable excommunications of the nineteenth century include King Victor Emmanuel II of Italy, Stephen Kaminski (bishop of the Polish National Catholic Church), Charles Loyson (a Carmelite who protested Vatican I), and Colombian writer José María Vargas Vila. A more recent high-profile excommunication is that of French Archbishop Marcel Lefebvre, who was excommunicated in 1988 for consecrating four priests without the permission of the Church, as previously discussed. Father Roy Bourgeois was excommunicated in 2012 for ordaining a woman in 2008 and refusing to recant to the Vatican.[46] Pope Francis also excommunicated and defrocked an Argentinian priest who was convicted on five counts of child molestation.[47]

Prior to the full canonization of Catholic law, all baptized Christians, "even non-Catholics, [were] in principle subject to the laws of the Church," including censures like excommunication.[48] Protestantism's approach to deviation from church authority differs from that of Catholicism. John Calvin argues that censure by the church is reversible and is intended to encourage repentance and restoration to communion.[49] Accordingly, many Protestant sects used to or still have provisions to discipline wayward members. Certain divisions of the Lutheran Church practice excommunication, but it must be voted upon by the congregation in a democratic process.[50] The Church of England, while not having an explicit excommunication process, may deny proper burial rites to those who "have been declared excommunicate for some grievous and notorious crime and no man to testify to his repentance."[51] In the Church of Jesus Christ of Latter-day Saints, members can be "disfellowshipped" or excommunicated after going before a disciplinary council. Disfellowshipment is less serious and does not result in removal from the church; excommunication, on the other hand, is for the most severe of sins, including murder, adultery, homosexual acts, or open criticism of church leaders.[52] Thus, certain Protestant sects have discipline procedures for those who violate the church's teachings or authority; however, they can scarcely compare to the layers of complexity in the Catholic procedures of discipline for laity and clergy. In this regard, the Catholic Church's hierarchical structure headed by a pontiff "whose supreme authority is recognised by the faithful in every country" sets it apart from other Christian sects.[53]

The centralized and hierarchical development of the religious authority structure in Catholicism has historically helped reinforce orthodoxy and orthopraxy among Catholics. This centralization of religious authority, in turn, monopolized

---

[45] Napoleon, Gourgaud, and Tristan 1823, 331.
[46] Goodstein 2012.
[47] San Martin 2014.
[48] Herbermann 1910, 64.
[49] Calvin 1536, IV.12.10.
[50] "The Role of the Congregation in Excommunication."
[51] "Canons of the Church of England," Section B38.
[52] Hafen 1992.
[53] Knippenberg 2006, 259.

power within the Church and minimized religious competition. A direct result of the institutional development of Catholicism is the difficulty of challenging the Church as the legitimate representative of Catholics. Any Catholic actor who claimed to speak on behalf of Catholics and Catholicism had to confront the Church and its monopoly on representing Catholics. Such a centralized religious institutional structure in Catholicism contrasts sharply with the more open and competitive religious authority structures in Sunni Islam, which I discuss next.

DECENTRALIZED AND NONHIERARCHICAL STRUCTURE OF RELIGIOUS AUTHORITY IN SUNNI ISLAM

Compared to Catholicism and other Christian denominations, Islam is a more heterogenous religion characterized by the absence of an authoritative body similar to the pope or a national church. In this regard, Islam lacks centralized and hierarchical religious institutions that "define and enforce" official religious doctrines.[54] Likewise, Islam does not envision an intervening agency or "intermediary figures" such as an official clergy class to mediate the relationship between God and the believer.[55] The Islamic religious institutions that we observe today are created by states for various political purposes, chiefly for control and manipulation of religious discourse and activism. As such, institutionalization in Islam is largely external.[56]

Islam differs from many other faith traditions in two important ways as it relates to the notion of religious authority and its institutional structure: the centrality of the text and absence of a centralized hierarchical religious institution. God and the Prophet have always constituted the "authoritative center" in Islam.[57] Yet, God does not speak to humans directly and the Prophet is no longer alive; God speaks via the Qur'an and the Prophet through volumes of prophetic narrations. Hence, it is through texts that God and the Prophet's authority are represented. Both texts (the Qur'an and hadith), however, have distinct features. Muslims accept the Qur'an as the verbatim word of God; this authenticity underlies the centrality of the Qur'an among Muslims and the respect it draws. The Prophetic traditions, by contrast, do not command the absolute authenticity of the Qur'an; nonetheless, a consistent methodological tradition evolved to create standards for classifying Prophetic traditions on the basis of their authenticity.[58] Muslims of all backgrounds have historically considered the text as a primary religious authority. This is not a uniquely Islamic notion. It is common in less centralized traditions for texts to be considered religious authorities, especially so in more conservative or fundamentalist

[54] Casanova 2005, 9.
[55] Tibi 1980, 211.
[56] Silvestri 2007, 171.
[57] El Fadl 2001, 11.
[58] Hallaq 1999.

Catholic and Islamic Religious Institutions

traditions. Many Protestants, for example, consider the Bible to be a predominant religious authority.[59]

Here, Muslims face a major conundrum. Islam does not have a centralized hierarchical institution to establish orthodoxy for adherents of the religion. The fundamental religious texts need interpreters who wield authority, which is why we frequently hear of "right" or "wrong" interpretations of the Qur'an, especially in relation to extremist fringes.[60] Various Islamists continually reference the Qur'an and the hadith to justify their political positions and wield religious authority in support of their political campaigns.

Thus, the primary question is who can interpret the Qur'an *with* authority in Islam? At its core, this is not a religious question but a *political* one. Without clear parameters for determining the rightful owners of such interpretation, politics assume a primary role. Conflicts over the right to interpret the holy text or its "correct" interpretation have shaped parts of early Islamic history. Indeed, the political and religious authority split occurred very early in the Sunni tradition, shortly after the Prophet's death.[61] The fourth caliph Ali's conflict with Kharijites and Umayyad caliph al-Ma'mun's *mihna* ordeal are examples of such religious conflicts that were *political* in nature.[62] The absence of a centralized hierarchical institution complicates matters in another way. Following a religious authority in Islam is a voluntary and personal decision; Muslims cannot be compelled to accept the religious authority of a person, body, or institution.[63] As such, the question of religious authority in Islam is a political matter and its evolution, as I discuss next, carries major political ramifications.

Until the turn of the twentieth century, ulama largely possessed the religious authority in Islam by virtue of their scholarship. Their "competent human agency to discover God's law" and the fact that they largely stood for the "best interests" of their community as "Guardians of Religion" legitimized their claim.[64] While Islam does not have an official clergy class, the ulama acted in the capacity of clerics.[65] They organized themselves into corporations, creating "an institutional order built upon feelings of collective belonging (shared knowledge, representations, references, rites of initiation, and so on)." As such, the ulama operated as a "collective actor" who determined orthodoxy and orthopraxy.[66] Historically, however, the lack of a central religious body and

---

[59] Probst 1989.

[60] See, for example, the exchange on ISIS between Graeme Wood ("What ISIS Really Wants") and Caner Dagli ("The Phony Islam of ISIS") in the *Atlantic*: Available at: www.theatlantic.com/magazine/archive/2015/03/what-isis-really-wants/384980/; www.theatlantic.com/international/archive/2015/02/what-muslims-really-want-isis-atlantic/386156/

[61] Crone and Hinds 1986; Dabashi 1989.

[62] Crone and Hinds 1986.

[63] Kersten and Olsson 2013, 8.

[64] Hallaq 2003, 252–58.

[65] Seyit 2006, 55.

[66] Mouline 2014, 2.

64   *The Politics of Religious Party Change*

primacy of the text sparked conflicts over who should hold religious authority. The inquisition (*mihna*) undertaken by three Abbasid caliphs between 833 and 849 encouraged the ulama to institutionalize their religious authority.

Mihna was an effort initiated by the Abbasid caliph Al-Ma'mun to force support among ulama for a theological doctrine he proposed in 827, namely that the Qur'an was created as opposed to being eternal. The substance of this theological debate was epiphenomenal.[67] Al-Ma'mun was bent on "curb[ing] the growing influence of the 'ulama' by attempting to make the caliph and the caliphal institution, rather than the 'ulama', the religious authority in Islam."[68] *Mihna*, as such, served to hold the ulama of the time to a "test" in which the caliph pitted his religious authority against "the authority of those men who saw themselves – not the caliph – as the legitimate repository of religious knowledge and heritage and the authentic transmitters of such knowledge."[69] While many ulama appear to have given their consent to the caliph, the inquisition eventually died off around 849 and caliphs' attempts to monopolize religious authority failed.[70] The most important legacy of *mihna*, in this regard, was transforming the ulama from "a loose grouping of devout followers of the Prophet" into a "societal group" that cohered around the education and promotion of law within the institutional confines of madrasa. Put differently, *mihna* "confirmed the sole and exclusive authority of the 'ulama' in their capacity as 'heirs to the prophets' or the 'people that bind and unbind'."[71]

The Ulama Project undergirds the claim about the transformation of the ulama during this period with data on Muslim scholars and their fields of expertise in various Islamic sciences. Project data covers the period between the seventh and eleventh centuries, an era that best demonstrates the shift in ulama's expertise around *mihna*. The data shows a clear shift in expertise of Islamic sciences (Figure 2.1). Specifically, the focus in early periods was largely on Hadith, which implies a desire "to know more about God and his revelation" and it was "quenched" by learning more about the Prophet and his way of life.[72] Over time, this "informal search of information" to know more about the Prophet gradually gave way to a committed interest in Fiqh (Islamic jurisprudence) and other fields of study: "At the outset the founding fathers of Islamic law and their direct associates at the moment collected 'juridical' information and started to define how they conceived a specific legal matter. As time progressed and as Islam's belief system evolved it gradually became more and more juridical."[73]

---

[67] See footnote 8 in Nawas (2013) and Mouline (2014, 21–27) for a detailed discussion of the theological dimension of the issue.

[68] Nawas 2013, 15.

[69] Nawas 2013, 22.

[70] Eickelman and Piscatori 1996, 47.

[71] Krämer and Schmidtke 2006, 11.

[72] Nawas 2013, 24.

[73] Nawas 2013, 24.

Catholic and Islamic Religious Institutions

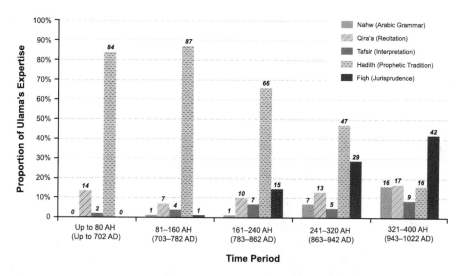

FIGURE 2.1 Development of the Islamic religious sciences, early and classical age of Islam ($n = 1,049$)
Source: Nawas (2013).

Thus, the process of "juridisation" facilitated greater focus on law, which the madrasas primarily taught. The ulama embedded themselves at the core of Islam as *the* cardinal religious authority through the process of juridisation of the entire belief system. This process throughout the ninth and tenth centuries entrenched "professionalization" of the ulama and institutionalized their religious authority for many centuries to come. To use Mouline's terms, the ulama were able to construct a form of ideological authority for themselves. This is a form of authority that is "based on the symbolic power of an enunciator – in general, a collective actor – to produce and transform beliefs inspired by a first reference (revelation, instruction, ideology, and so on)."[74]

Over the next millennium (tenth to twentieth century), the institution of ulama evolved from a highly autonomous enterprise into one that was decidedly dependent, ineffective, and increasingly irrelevant. Early periods of the ulama's dominance in religious authority showed little governmental interference. Following the fallout from the *mihna*, the relations between the ulama and the political elite were defined by countervailing dynamics. The ulama perceived the ruling elite with great suspicion, equating political power with "vice and corruption,"[75] but also viewed this class as the principal mechanism through which to uphold Islamic law and control rulers' personal and political ambitions.[76] For the ruling elite, the ulama offered the most convenient path to securing political

[74] Mouline 2014, 5.
[75] Hallaq 2009, 42.
[76] Winter 2009.

66 *The Politics of Religious Party Change*

legitimacy; by committing themselves to upholding application of Islamic law in their predominantly Muslim societies, they ensured the support of the ulama and political legitimacy. Of note, this pact between the ulama and the ruling elite maintained the distinctive institutional structures of the state and the religion: "States were officially committed to the defense and patronage of Muslim worship, but they were not inherently Islamic institutions."[77]

The pact between the ulama and the ruling elite also carried a major religious implication. Despite the absence of an official clergy to mediate between God and the believer, the ulama began operating in a clergy-like capacity during this period, in great part due to the pact between the religious and political elite.[78] The ulama lacked a centralized or hierarchical structure to regulate their Islamic authority, yet they operated in a pluralistic jurisprudential and theological framework that successfully excluded outsiders (i.e., non-ulama) and virtually monopolized religious authority for the ulama.

While madrasas – the early Islamic institutions of learning that taught both religious and nonreligious curricula[79] – functioned as the key channel allowing the ulama to institutionalize their religious authority, their constant need of financial support also posed a salient vulnerability. The operating expenses of madrasas and student- and professor- (i.e., ulama) related expenses such as shelter, food, and salaries were conventionally met by waqfs – religious endowments or charitable donations typically undertaken for the benefit of the poor and for education. The strong association between madrasas and waqfs after the eleventh century derived from several distinct advantages that waqfs offered. Most importantly, establishing a waqf was permanent. Legally, it was a peremptory act; since "the ownership passed from the individual to God," the status of the waqf, or the property associated with it, could not be changed.[80]

Although the establishment of a waqf was open to anyone, their expensive nature advantaged the ruling elite. Initially, the contributions of the ruling elite accounted for only a small share of waqf resources. Over time, as the *political* utility of supporting madrasas through waqfs became more apparent, a greater proportion of madrasas came to be directly supported by the ruling elite.[81] The search for legitimacy was the most acute need of the political elite and what ultimately motivated this process. Why exactly did the ruling elite need political legitimacy and why did they seek it outside of the political arena? The answer lies in the nature of the relationship between the ruling elite and the society. Typically, rulers lacked both the "bureaucratic organization" that characterizes modern states and the systematic control over their societies,

---

[77] Lapidus 1992, 5; Kuru 2019.
[78] Tibi 1980.
[79] Makdisi 1981.
[80] Hallaq 2009, 47–48.
[81] See Timur Kuran's (2016) analysis of how waqfs served as a crucial legal and institutional instrument of the authoritarian rule in the Middle East.

Catholic and Islamic Religious Institutions

resulting in largely ineffective administration. Recourse to the ulama helped the ruling elite govern with a heightened sense of rule of law and obtain legitimacy by upholding the religious law overseen by the ulama.[82] Also, the ulama embodied stability and enabled a sense of continuity even during periods of major disruptions.[83]

By the seventeenth century, the state firmly controlled the ulama class by bringing them under state payroll and through greater financing of the waqf institution. This extensive state control and the ulama's evolution "from a highly independent legal enterprise into a markedly subordinate one," however, hardly undermined the ulama's religious authority because the basic structure that gave rise to institutionalizing this authority remained intact.[84] The ulama managed to speak for Islam and "bind and unbind" despite their co-optation by the state. By the mid-nineteenth century, the ulama maintained its "special position" within society. In Egypt, al-Jabarti's 1820 chronicle listed the ulama among the most virtuous of humankind as "the depositors of truth in this world and the elite of mankind" who were "the heirs and the successors of the prophets."[85] Moreover, the profession of Islamic scholarship potentially represented one of the rare avenues of "social mobility" for individuals in the lower socioeconomic classes, owing in part to ulama's control over tax farms (iltizams) and the assets held by waqfs under ulama's trust.[86]

The Break and the New Equilibrium

The break in this religious structure arose following early European colonization efforts in the Muslim world and extensive Western influence over Muslim societies with multiple factors at play. First, European powers such as the British and the Dutch who controlled these territories sought to reform the legal system via codification of law. For the British, Islamic law was "unsystematic, inconsistent and mostly arbitrary." Moreover, it was "irregular, lacking in efficacy and 'founded on the most lenient principles and on an abhorrence of bloodshed'."[87] Likewise, the conventional legal system lay beyond state control, contradicting the emerging modern state's monopolistic claim on the use of power within a given territory. Second, modernization efforts in the Middle East, primarily in the Ottoman Empire, Egypt, and subsequently in other parts of the region, were focused on centralization of state administration and legal reforms. Ottoman Sultan Mahmud II broke the "administrative autonomy"

[82] Hallaq 2009, 50.
[83] Marsot 1972, 159.
[84] Hallaq 2009, 38.
[85] Marsot 1972, 149.
[86] Crecelius 1972, 172; Marsot 1972, 156–58. As other avenues of social mobility began to emerge in the modern period, being a member of the ulama class lost part of its allure (Keddie 1972, 47).
[87] Hallaq 2009, 86–87.

68   *The Politics of Religious Party Change*

that the ulama and the religious establishment enjoyed by "bureaucratizing" the religious establishment.[88]

In this spirit, the Ottoman reforms evinced "highly modern notions of discipline, law, inspection, and incarceration."[89] Waqfs especially became targets of modernization efforts in the Middle East during the late nineteenth century because they held the key to bringing the entire legal profession under state control, a crucial component of modernizing the state apparatus. Thirdly, at a time when states were in dire need of finances, the waqfs' control of a vast array of inert and unproductive property provided a chance to develop the economy and strengthen the military.[90] In Egypt, waqfs controlled close to one-fifth of all cultivable land and a greater share of real estate property.[91]

While this process was largely a gradual one between the end of the nineteenth and the early twentieth centuries, the effects were decisive.[92] It was nothing short of an institutional transformation, and the anchors of the system that rested on the ulama were unhinged. Shariah law, or Islamic law, possessed both content and process. While the reforms of the late nineteenth and early twentieth centuries made an effort to remain faithful to the *substance* of shariah law, its *process* was virtually undone. The institutions of the "shariah system weakened or died out or [were] abandoned"[93]; shariah was turned into positive law.[94] A good example of the codification of Islamic law was that of Majalla al-Ahkam al-'Adliyya in the Ottoman Empire, or Majalla for short. The law, based on the Hanafi school, was compiled between 1869 and 1876 and consisted of 16 volumes.[95]

Waqfs that supported madrasas, ulama, and their students were disrupted. A great many ulama involved in the traditional Islamic scholarship and shariah law were hired in the state legal bureaucracy as part of this transition.[96] Judges were now being trained in modern institutions instead of madrasas, and the judicial system was brought entirely under state control. Hence, the legal reforms of the period "fundamentally" altered the dynamics of the legal system. Ayata summarizes the Turkish case as follows: "By placing legislation, education, and the judicial system under secular control, religion was kept out of governmental processes. Institutional Islam was disestablished in its entirety by the dismantling of such powerful institutions as the Sultanate, the Caliphate, the ulama (religious scholars), and Sufi religious orders."[97]

---

[88] Chambers 1972, 35.
[89] Hallaq 2009, 98.
[90] Chambers 1972, 36. Timur Kuran's (2001) analysis of the waqf system offers insights into why waqfs were crucial resources for the modernization efforts during this period.
[91] Marsot 1972, 153.
[92] Brown 1997.
[93] Brown 1997, 368.
[94] Skovgaard-Petersen 1997, 37.
[95] Chambers 1972, 45.
[96] Bein 2011, 4.
[97] Ayata 1996, 42.

Catholic and Islamic Religious Institutions

To summarize, two developments helped seal this watershed moment in the gradual evolution of the ulama from an autonomous body to a decidedly subordinate one, creating a void in Islamic religious authority. On one hand, changes in the legal institutional structure disrupted the intimate connection between law and religion, where the critical casualty was the ulama and their religious authority. The ulama acquired its distinct and historically dominant religious authority from its (exclusive) ability to legitimately derive Islamic law from foundational texts, that is, the Qur'an and the hadith. Now that the ulama no longer commanded the inside track to exclusive religious authority, the field became wide open for challengers to emerge and contest the ulama, inducing "fragmentation" of religious authority.[98] This new equilibrium in the structure of Islamic religious authority can be defined as "a growing crisis of authority" since the early twentieth century.[99] On the other hand, new secular and mass forms of education (in conjunction with the introduction of the print press) created a society with a more skeptical approach to religion and religious authority, which eventually resulted in the "objectification" of Islam.[100] These developments collectively shaped the early course of Islamist parties in the Middle East.

Historically, the ulama persistently faced competition in their religious authority; challenges are not unique to the modern age. Their authority was challenged by political leaders, as in the case of Abbasid caliph Ma'mun and his successors, and nonpolitical figures such as "preachers and storytellers," Sufis, and philosophers. The challenges we observe in modern times, nonetheless, differ from historical cases in "scale and severity" and substance; they were "unparalleled."[101]

The *new* challengers to religious authority came from various backgrounds and commanded audiences larger than the old challengers could ever imagine. Such competitors included the state, new religious intellectuals, reformist ulama, Muslim modernists, and Islamists. Even when such contenders are traditionally trained ulama, they act not as part of a corporate identity but as loners. For example, a person like Yusuf al-Qaradawi who commanded superstar status among contemporary scholars is exceptional in that his influence was individual, not emanating from being part of a distinct class.[102] Al-Qaradawi expanded his influence by way of various institutional bodies *he* led and through media.[103]

The state emerged as an important actor amid this current of change. The key motivation for Middle Eastern states to increasingly venture into the religious sphere has been the quest to acquire greater control of religion and religious discourse. As the modern state emerged, states pursued various strategies

---

[98] Eickelman and Piscatori 1996.
[99] Robinson 2009, 339.
[100] Eickelman and Piscatori 1996.
[101] Zaman 2009, 209–21.
[102] Krämer 2006.
[103] Zaman 2012.

70 — The Politics of Religious Party Change

to convince or compel other religious actors to cede their religious authority. For the Ottoman Empire, this involved pushing heterodox religious groups such as the Shiites toward the fringes of the empire, formalizing religious education, and incentivizing the ulama to join the state bureaucracy by way of a state-created judicial hierarchy.[104] In the postindependence period, the Directorate of Religious Affairs (Diyanet) was established "to control and domesticate Islam in accordance with the needs of the state" in Turkey.[105] In Egypt, al-Azhar underwent administrative reform and was brought under complete state control in 1961. This shift allowed the new Egyptian regime to rely on al-Azhar to increase its religious legitimacy and moderate the content of religious knowledge produced in the country.[106] The Saudi monarchy chose to strike an alliance with the Wahhabi family that traded political influence for religious legitimacy. Despite its appearance of a strict religious regime, the Saudi regime conveniently used the Wahhabi clergy to support various policies and actions such as the modernization reforms in the 1920s, the response to storming of the Grand Mosque in Mecca in 1979, stationing of American troops in the country during the Desert Storm operation in 1991, and crackdown on Islamist dissidents in 1993.[107]

Among the new challengers, this chapter focuses primarily on Islamists and proto-Islamists (or, early Islamists) in the period around the turn of the twentieth century, also referred to as "Islamic intellectuals"[108] or "new intellectuals."[109] Islamists were overwhelmingly educated in new secular schools and employed in nonreligious fields such as the state bureaucracy as "administrators, teachers, lawyers." What defined them as Islamists was their "deep commitment to the Islamic character of the state and society."[110] Islamists were those Muslims "whose consciousness has been objectified ... and who are committed to implementing their vision of Islam as a corrective to current 'un-Islamic' practices."[111]

The rise of political Islam, proto-Islamists, and Salafism during this period in Muslim history is no coincidence. Contemporary politics motivated these actors to act; their answers to fundamentally political questions of the time – i.e., Western colonialism and modernization – were religious in character – a variation of "Islam is the solution." If Islam can deliver answers to Muslims' problems such as colonialism and backwardness, then the key reason Islam had not done so in the past lay in the failures of those who wielded religious authority. Hence, Islamists' critique of the ulama was in a way a critique of Islam's status.

---

[104] Mardin 1981, 193; Lapidus 1996, 16–17.
[105] Yavuz 2000, 29.
[106] Zeghal 1999, 373–74.
[107] Nevo 1998, 41–42.
[108] Bein 2011.
[109] Eickelman and Piscatori 1996.
[110] Bein 2011, 24.
[111] Eickelman and Piscatori 1996, 44.

Catholic and Islamic Religious Institutions

Islamists assisted in the fragmentation of religious authority and objectification of Islam, and ultimately claimed religious authority. They pursued two interrelated but distinct routes to carve a niche for themselves: criticizing of the ulama and invoking Islamic concepts. While the former enabled the undoing of the existing religious establishment and undermining of its legitimacy, the latter legitimized Islamists' actions to supplant the ulama as the new religious authority.

Criticism of the Ulama

Islamists directed their criticisms at the ulama on two grounds: material underdevelopment of Muslim societies and undue Western influence. The ulama class was typically criticized for being self-interested, bent on upholding its religious authority, and failing to prioritize the interests of the Muslim community over its own corporate interests. This dim view rested partially on the "anachronistic traditions" and "antiquated methods" of the ulama.[112] In Islamists' view, the Muslim world desperately needed guidance and leadership as its material development lagged significantly behind the West. The ulama failed to understand the "momentous changes around them" and had "little relevance to contemporary needs" of Muslims.[113] Hassan Al-Banna in Egypt was disillusioned by the ulama's "inability to oppose the state and its colonial wire-pullers" and charged al-Azhar with producing "religious literates ... not spiritual guides"[114] just as Rashid Rida bemoaned al-Azhar's "total failure to defend Islam against the European colonial powers" in Libya, Algeria, Egypt, Palestine, and Syria.[115] This was an important attack because al-Azhar historically acted as "the guardian of religious tradition" in Egypt.[116] By contrast, authority for al-Banna's Muslim Brotherhood lies solely with God and power lies solely with the umma, which is represented by the Muslim Brotherhood itself.[117]

In particular, reformists and proto-Islamists such as Jamal ad-Din al-Afghani, Sayyid Ahmad, Muhammad Abduh, and Rashid Rida underscored the "intellectual sterility" of the ulama. They charged that the ulama's adherence to blind imitation of traditions and failure to cut superstitions made them outdated and inadequate to deal with questions of modernity. The ulama class was accused of "traditionalism, obscurantism, and antiscientific tendencies," which set back progress in Muslim societies. According to Islamists, the ulama and the religious establishment not only failed to grasp the nature of change in their age but also stood as major obstacles to other reform efforts in

---

[112] Ayoob 2004, 29; Zaman 2012, 6.
[113] Zaman 2012, 6.
[114] Skovgaard-Petersen 1997, 156–57.
[115] Brunner 2009, 126–27.
[116] Scott 2012, 141.
[117] Mozaffari and Vale 1986, 61.

72 The Politics of Religious Party Change

society and acted as "bastions of obsolete orthodoxy in need of comprehensive reforms." In one such case, Mehmed Arif Bey – a former Ottoman bureaucrat with some madrasa education and a hadith commentary to his name – claimed in the 1890s that the ulama knew nothing beyond "how to recite past traditions" and that "in our age those who are labeled the ulama (scholars) of Islam all appear as if they were manufactured in the same factory, have graduated from the same school, and had been educated in the same manner."[118] This view reverberated loudly among Ottoman bureaucrats and intellectuals in the early twentieth century as the term ulama became synonymous with "fanaticism, reactionism, medievalism, and scholasticism" and stood as "the essential 'other' to a modernized and Westernized new elite."[119]

The ulama and the religious establishment were also criticized for the increasing Western influence over Muslim societies. In some cases, such influence took the form of material domination and colonization of Muslim lands by the West. Critics blamed outdated methods and traditions of the ulama for such domination. For example, al-Afghani's call for the ulama to depose the Shah in Iran, whom he saw as a collaborator with Western powers, fell on deaf ears.[120] Ayatollah Khomeini mirrored al-Afghani's call on the scholars in late twentieth century: "The scholars of Islam have a duty to struggle against all attempts by the oppressors to establish a monopoly over the sources of wealth or to make illicit use of them."[121] Often times, the ulama were challenged to prove their "usefulness" by actively partaking in anti-colonial efforts.[122] A statement from Egyptian Muslim Brotherhood founder Hassan Al-Banna epitomizes such criticisms:

One of the excuses adopted by some of those who have followed the path taken by the West was that they had become aware of the course taken by the Muslim religious authorities, in view of their hostile attitude towards nationalist revival, their activities against the nationalists and their alliance with the occupiers, their choice of selfish interests and worldly ambitions over the welfare of the country and the nation. If true, this was a flaw within the religious establishment itself, not in the religion as such. Does the religion command such things? Or are they dictated by the lives of the most virtuous and illustrious ulama of the Islamic umma, who used to burst in upon kings and princes, past their gates and walls, censuring them, forbidding them, rejecting their gifts, declaring what the truth was before them, and bringing them the demands of the nation? Nay, they even took up arms in the face of tyranny and injustice![123]

Like Al-Banna, Muhammad Abduh yearned for a more activist ulama to be in charge of "morality" and "to make preachers .... aware of the city and

[118] Bein 2011, 24–25.
[119] Bein 2011, 1, 7–12.
[120] Black 2001, 302.
[121] Khomeini 2000, 258.
[122] Zaman 2009, 224.
[123] Al-Banna 2009, 71.

Catholic and Islamic Religious Institutions

household policies and of what constitutes a happy city and a happy household."[124] The Indian-Pakistani author Maududi in the mid-twentieth century cautioned against "western domination" in his religious reform calls.[125]

In other cases, the diffusion of secularism and secularization from the West constituted the most significant threat to the Muslim world. Not only secular-educated Islamists but also some (reformist) ulama criticized the religious establishment and the ulama. For them, the threat of secularization was too real. The most scathing criticism of the ulama in this vein was that the ulama and the religious establishment formed a clergy class in Islam akin to priesthood in Christianity; conservative ulama in particular were accused of "scholasticism" that typically characterized Catholic priests. An early Islamist and former Ottoman Grand Vizier Said Halim Pasha argued in 1918 that the ulama class "degenerated into an ecclesiastical organization" that concerned itself only with the personal and corporate interests of the religious establishment.[126] Islamists also accused the ulama of aiding the "antireligious camp" and being their "helpless victims" – a potent charge because secularism connoted being anti-religion. Bein explains: "In fact, these critics often criticized the religious establishment for inadvertently strengthening the antireligious camp through the ulama's inaptitude, excessive traditionalism, and self-interest, just as the clergy in Europe helped bring about the spread of secularism and atheism."[127] Filibeli Ahmed Hilmi, an important Islamic writer of this period, made this point unequivocally by suggesting that "For centuries, those who profess religion [as a vocation] did all they could to implement their ideal of steering the Islamic community in opposition to history and the changing times ... They are unconnected with and opposed to contemporary mentality and knowledge. Consequently, they force the Muslims to adopt one of two awkward and deplorable options: either the acceptance of naturalism, skepticism, and atheist philosophies and moving away from their religion and national attributes; or the development of distaste for science and knowledge, and a consequent persistence of ignorance."[128]

At its core, this was ultimately more of a *political* than a religious challenge to the ulama. This conservatism of the ulama brought their religious authority under greater scrutiny. Musa Kazim Efendi – a reformist ulama who served as Sheyhulislam – argued that the ulama did not possess modern theological ideological tools to confront "antireligious ideas" of the time, requiring a thorough reconsideration of the "edifice of the ulama's claim to religious authority."[129]

[124] Abduh 2000, 48–49.
[125] Maududi 2000, 209.
[126] Bein 2011, 23–24.
[127] Bein 2011, 22.
[128] Bein 2011, 27–28.
[129] Bein 2011, 31–32.

Invoking Islamic Concepts

Unlike pre-modern challengers to the ulama's religious authority, Islamists did not merely seek to underscore the political vulnerability of the ulama, which would have left the ulama's authority and legitimacy intact while carving a niche for the new challengers. Rather, Islamists problematized the very nature of authority and the ulama's monopolistic claim to speak for Islam.[130] Islamists held that the ulama did not wield monopoly over "interpretative authority" and challenged that religious knowledge was not the exclusive domain of the ulama.[131] In fact, in a conscious effort to confront the ulama, new religious intellectuals "expound[ed] on all matters Islamic for their own readers and listeners,"[132] akin to fulfilling the role of "new priesthood."[133] Two Islamic concepts in particular proved instrumental for Islamists in this effort: Ijtihad and fatwa.

Ijtihad

The response of early Islamist figures like al-Afghani, Abduh, and Rida to the ulama's perceived failure to meet the challenges of modernity was rooted in their championship of ijtihad and rejection of taqlid. Ijtihad traditionally stood for legal reasoning by scholars to reach a ruling, on the basis of the Qur'an and the Sunnah. Despite its infrequent use until the turn of the twentieth century, it became a buzzword for reformists, new intellectuals, and Islamists. Noticeably, they downplayed the conventional understanding that ijtihad be undertaken by scholars well versed in Islamic disciplines and aimed at reaching "a ruling (hukm) in accordance with the principles of fiqh." Instead, Islamists bestowed every Muslim with the right to individual ijtihad, which can be likened to a "protestantic" approach.[134] By contrast, taqlid, which traditionally refers to "the acceptance and faithful following of the teaching of the madhhab [legal school]," is cast as the uncritical acceptance and imitation of ideas and authority with the implication that the ulama "cop[ied] the words of the masters without ever considering their relevance, or even meaning."[135]

This Islamist approach prescribes a largely literalist interpretation of religious texts since the Qur'an and the hadith are easily accessible and do not require intermediaries. Because the Qur'an does not conflict with reason, Muslims' endowment with individual interpretation (ijtihad) should pave the way for Islam's adaptation to modern society.[136] This fundamental challenge against the ulama not only encouraged Muslims to engage with the foundational texts themselves but also rejected most Islamic tradition, accumulated

---

[130] Kamali 2001, 460.
[131] Kersten and Olsson 2013, 12.
[132] Zaman 2009, 212.
[133] Hatina 2009b, 249.
[134] Hatina 2009a, 2.
[135] Skovgaard-Petersen 1997, 66.
[136] Soage 2008, 4–6.

Catholic and Islamic Religious Institutions

knowledge, and schools of thought that emerged after the end of the Golden Age. The solution was the return to an unadulterated version of Islam centered around "original holy principles."[137] Yet, the outcome was a selective reconstruction of Islamic history.

In a scathing critique of the conservative ulama and their taqlid, Tatar scholar Musa Jarullah Bilgiyev accused them of "following existing traditions blindly and of reprehensible fetishism for centuries-old books, similar to the ways of the clergy in Christianity and the priesthood in past pagan civilizations" and lamented their "disinterest in discovering and teaching the genuine truths of Islam."[138] In 1928, Mustafa al-Maraghi, a reform-minded Shaykh al-Azhar and student of Abduh, attributed the "miserable condition" of Egypt to the ulama's desertion of ijtihad: "It was they [the ulama] who had removed themselves from the matters of the world, denying ijtihad and declining to learn the new disciplines, so that Islam had been bereft of defenders at a time when it most needed them."[139] Ultimately, taqlid impeded a return to the roots of Islam, or the Golden Age, during which reason was celebrated and irrational imitation was discouraged.[140]

Abduh called for a return to the "original teachings" of Islam in order to "rescue Muslim societies from backwardness and superstition, which they saw as consequences of un-Islamic accretions introduced in the later centuries of Islam."[141] Islam, for him, had become so laden with backwardness and bogged down in traditions that it was no longer capable of adaptation. By returning to Islam's roots, Abduh hoped to return to rationality and scientific positivism and foster a "general spirit of intellectual rejuvenation inspired by the model of the Prophet's early companions."[142] The ulama were the problem. For Rida, the ulama were "practicing and preaching a fossilized form of Islam"[143] and Muslims needed to "consult the Koran and sunna" themselves: "The great Imams were masters, but not necessarily infallible or valid for all times ... it is quite apparent that the traditional teachings of the madhahib [schools of jurisprudence] are insufficient to meet the demands of the age..."[144] Similarly, Al-Banna broadened the scope of religious authority to include all Muslims without exception: "Is it not more productive for a nation to reform its religious authorities and to reconcile with them, rather than adopt an oppressive attitude towards them? Even if these expressions which have crept into our language by way of imitation, like 'religious authorities', do not accord with our own usage – because this one is peculiar to the West, in the sense of 'clergy' – it

[137] Abduh 2000, 47.
[138] Bein 2011, 42.
[139] Skovgaard-Petersen 1997, 148.
[140] Strindberg and Wärn 2011, 75.
[141] Ayoob 2008, 7.
[142] Mandaville 2007, 52.
[143] Ayoob 2008, 27.
[144] Skovgaard-Petersen 1997, 74.

76 *The Politics of Religious Party Change*

includes every Muslim, according to the Islamic usage, for all Muslims from the least to the most outstanding of them, are 'religious authorities'."[145]

Abduh, expectedly, faced the traditional ulama's resistance because of his call for a rationalist interpretation of Islam.[146] Likewise, al-Afghani had a contentious relationship with the ulama whom he sternly criticized. When al-Afghani proposed to reinterpret the Qur'an to adapt to modernity, he became disillusioned with the ulama and was "frustrated by their ignorance and rigidity and accused them of abandoning believers in a state of fragmentation and illegitimate innovations."[147] Ubeydullah Efendi of the Ottoman Empire, who was heavily criticized for proposing the translation of the Qur'an for non-Arab Muslims, charged the ulama with being determined to "keep the Muslims ignorant in order to maintain their own monopoly over the interpretation of the holy book."[148]

The undercurrents of this debate about adapting Islam to modernity dealt with the question of who wielded authority and was therefore best suited to guide the Muslim community. As such, political Islam's enthusiasm for individual ijtihad and authority to interpret the text speaks more to their effort to undercut the ulama's traditional authority, which eventually led to "fragmentation of sacred authority."[149] Repeated Islamist efforts to undermine the ulama's legitimacy aimed to supersede them as the religious authority; Islamists "claimed to be attached to the authority of the Word of God alone and ... in public asserted the relative unimportance of all who claimed to come between God and the believer's conscience."[150] In more contemporary times, Hassan Al-Turabi, the leader of the Sudanese Muslim Brotherhood, expands on who counts as an Islamic scholar: "What do I mean by 'ulama'? The word, historically, has come to mean those versed in the legacy of religious (revealed) knowledge ('ilm'). However, 'ilm' does not mean that alone. It means anyone who knows anything well enough to relate it to God. Because all knowledge is divine and religious, a chemist, an engineer, an economist, or a jurist are all 'ulama'. So the 'ulama' in this broad sense, whether they are social or natural scientists, public leaders, or philosophers, should enlighten society."[151]

Islamists like the Muslim Brotherhood did not recognize the religious authority of the state or others; they had their own. For example, Rida viewed himself as one of the "good" ulama and was determined to "set the 'bad' ones right."[152] Rida envisioned a sort of papal model where he himself would preside over Muslims around the world in order to steer religious education, implement and redevelop shariah, and serve as a moral and spiritual

[145] Al-Banna 2009, 72–73.
[146] Soage 2008, 5.
[147] Soage 2008, 4.
[148] Bein 2011, 25.
[149] Eickelman and Piscatori 1996, 70–71.
[150] Lienhard in Eickelman and Piscatori 1996, 70.
[151] al-Turabi 1983, 245.
[152] Zaman 2012, 7.

Catholic and Islamic Religious Institutions

guide.[153] In the same vein, prominent works of Qur'anic exegesis by figures such as Abu-l-A'la Maududi and Sayyid Qutb captured the Muslim lay audience in the twentieth century. Much like fatwas and "religious advice," they amounted to a formidable challenge to the ulama on their own turf, allowing the new challengers to infuse credibility into their claims of religious authority. Ironically, Islamist invocation of religious and interpretative authority deems "their reasoning ... circular and closed, denying others a similar right to interpretation."[154]

Such emphasis on rejecting intermediaries, that is, the ulama, and yearning for the Golden Age put early Islamists squarely in the *salafiyya* camp.[155] More broadly, the term Salafi refers to "those who reject the authority of the medieval schools of law and insist on an unmediated access to the foundational texts as the source of all norms." For Abduh, "the example of the 'pious forebears'... lay in their demonstration to mankind of a divinely appointed, perfect intellectual balance."[156] Similar to Abduh's use, Rida called for an Islam grounded in the Qur'an, the hadith, and pious forbears' example, not one "'distorted' by centuries of legal, theological, and mystical debates, self-serving ulama, and despotic rulers."[157] Hence, they were (perhaps inadvertently) the inspiration for the *salafiyya* movement that took Abduh's encouragement to look back to Prophet Muhammad's time and concentrate on the first three generations of Islam.

Fatwa

Following a long hiatus, the notion of fatwa experienced a major "comeback" in the twentieth century alongside the idea of "religious advice."[158] Both fatwas and religious advice attest to the popularity and wide reach of non-ulama figures vying for religious authority. Fatwa refers to legal opinions from the Islamic law, the exclusive purview of the ulama in the pre-twentieth century period. It constitutes what Skovgaard-Petersen termed, "the most public part of traditional fiqh," allowing ordinary Muslims to enter a dialogue with the ulama.[159] This public nature of fatwas made them valuable tools in this time of "heightened competition for the mantle of authority."[160]

In this period, literacy rates increased, printing was widespread, and newspapers and magazines were easily accessible. Moreover, many Muslims were secular-educated, which stands in sharp contrast to previous periods when the ulama constituted "the majority of the educated Muslim population."[161] What would become of the *religious* education of these secular-educated masses lay

---

[153] Black 2001, 315.
[154] Eickelman and Piscatori 1996, 54.
[155] Brunner 2009.
[156] Strindberg and Wärn 2011, 75.
[157] Zaman 2012, 7.
[158] Krämer 2006, 182.
[159] Skovgaard-Petersen 1997, 72.
[160] Eickelman and Piscatori 1996, 71.
[161] Chambers 1972, 33.

78 The Politics of Religious Party Change

in the availability of print press and compilation of a *popular* Islamic literature because "most of the literary modes of the traditional ulama teachings ... were too specialized to be passed on to lay Muslims, given as they were by ulama to would-be ulama."[162] The timing of this emphasis on fatwas was also unmistakable, coming about just as the ulama increasingly faced alienation in fields they conventionally dominated: education and Islamic courts. Fatwa became the medium of choice for disseminating religious knowledge and messages to ordinary believers; it was the traditional and "ulama way" of doing so and its concise nature made it a convenient medium to convey Islamic positions to large segments of the Muslim population. Many early Islamist periodicals regularly published fatwas such as the influential al-Manar.

The unique social context of the late nineteenth and the early twentieth centuries in the Middle East made fatwas indispensable to the conflict over religious authority. Salafis and Islamists of the time argued that "their position was the truly Islamic [one], all referred to their authorities, and all had their muftis."[163] Hence, fatwas served not only to impart religious education on secular-educated Muslims but also expounded on "partisan" political positions to their audiences. On some occasions, the primary purpose of issuing a fatwa was to make a political statement or opine on Islam's role in this new age rather than answer an Islamic legal question per se. For example, the conflict between Rashid Rida and Yusuf ad-Dijwi (the anti-Salafi mufti of Nur al-Islam) was carried out on the pages of Rida's al-Manar and Nur al-Islam magazine of Egypt's Lajnat al-Fatwa. Rida regularly "issued fatwas in al-Manar to the opposite effect [of the ones by ad-Dijwi] ... clearly the two men detested each other. It is the continuation of the old competition between ulama and mufakkirun (intellectuals)."[164] Consequently, ardent opposition to fatwas issued by Dar al-Ifta and the conservative ulama was primarily undertaken by Islamists or reformist ulama.[165] After Rida's death in 1935, Hassan Al-Banna and the Muslim Brotherhood "inherited" al-Manar to continue publishing.[166]

A New Public

Without a new public that could read, discuss, and criticize religious ideas, Islamists would be frustrated in their aims to break the ulama's monopoly on religious discourse and authority. Changes in education and printing, however, facilitated such advantageous societal transformation. On one hand, rising levels of literacy and increases in secular public education broadened the potential audience for new claimants to religious authority. On the other

[162] Skovgaard-Petersen 1997, 71.
[163] Skovgaard-Petersen 1997, 28.
[164] Skovgaard-Petersen 1997, 153.
[165] Skovgaard-Petersen 1997, 29.
[166] Skovgaard-Petersen 1997, 156.

Catholic and Islamic Religious Institutions

hand, widespread use of the printing press allowed the new secular-educated public to partake in ongoing public discussions on religion, modernization, and sources of religious authority in the first half of the twentieth century.[167] Moreover, access to printed material was much easier and cheaper compared to traditional manuscripts.

Available data on mass education and literacy rates demonstrate a notable uptick in this period. In the first half of the nineteenth century, literacy rates hovered around 1–2 percent for the entire region[168] but Quataert estimates that literacy rates among Muslims within the Ottoman Empire climbed to around 15 percent by the end of the century. The last decades of the nineteenth century witnessed the emergence of a "state-sponsored educational system." Primary school enrollment rates saw a small-scale but sustained increase comparable to other regions of the world in the following decades (Tables 2.1 and 2.2). At the end of the nineteenth century, 650,000 students were enrolled in primary schools in the Ottoman Empire.[169] These rates are low not merely in comparison to the West but also to the non-Western world until the beginning of the twentieth century (Figure 2.2).[170] Yet, when literacy rates and educational attainment finally began to increase, the pace of change was "even greater" than the rest of the developing world.[171]

Despite lower rates, it is the upward trajectory of schooling and literacy rates that is most relevant. In tandem with the growth of print press during this period, the increase in literacy and educational attainment – regardless of its modesty – lent support to the idea of a "new public" in the region at this time. Historically, the art of writing was limited to the ulama and their close circles. Handwritten manuscripts (the primary mode of publication) were scarce, a fact also confirmed by the low literacy rates. Yet, beginning in the second half of the nineteenth century and especially in the last decades of the century, we observe a significant increase in print publications and readership. In 1880s Egypt, the circulation of satirical journal *Abu Nazzarah Zarqa* was estimated around 10,000 copies, while the daily *al-Mahrusah* published around 2,000 and weekly *al-Asr al-Jadid* around 800. *At-Tankit wa at-Tabkit*, an Egyptian political humor magazine was estimated to have a circulation of about 3,000; the combined circulation for 12 newspapers in Egypt was 24,000.[172] By 1928, the total newspaper circulation was estimated around 180,000. In Egypt, there were approximately 250 Arabic and 65 non-Arabic newspapers in 1937.[173] In 1914, Syria had 50 daily newspapers, 15 weeklies, and 20 monthlies/

[167] Brunner 2009, 111.
[168] Cole 1999, 115; Alam 2016, 142.
[169] Quataert 2005, 169.
[170] Issawi 1982.
[171] Limage 2005, 25.
[172] Cole 1999, 123.
[173] Shechter 2003, 49.

80 *The Politics of Religious Party Change*

TABLE 2.1 *Adult literacy and primary school enrollment (%)*

| | Adult illiteracy around 1950 | Primary school enrollment per 100 children 5–14 years old | |
		Around 1930	Around 1950
Algeria	82	11	17
Egypt	80	22	27
Turkey	68	15	33

Source: UNESCO (1957).

TABLE 2.2 *National primary enrollment ratios (%)*

	1880	1890	1900	1910	1920	1930	1935–1940
Algeria	6.2	8.9	9.9	10.5	9.3	10.0	13.2
Egypt	–	8.1	7.6	8.0	10.8	18.0	24.9
Iran	–	–	–	–	1.1	3.8	7.9
Iraq	–	–	1.4	2.6	1.1	3.8	9.5
Jordan	–	–	–	–	5.5	7.5	13.7
Kuwait	–	–	–	2.6	–	–	16.0
Lebanon	–	–	–	–	31.9	47.4	57.4
Morocco	–	–	–	–	1.7	3.3	3.6
Syria	–	–	6.1	9.4	–	14.4	17.7
Tunisia	–	–	3.8	7.2	7.6	12.0	13.3
Turkey	–	–	–	12.7	10.6	13.3	14.3

Source: Benavot and Riddle (1988).

quarterlies.[174] In the Ottoman Empire, two principal newspapers in Istanbul had circulation figures of 12,000 and 15,000 during Sultan Abdulhamid II's rule (1876–1909); the figures shot up to 40,000 and 60,000 after the Young Turks took power in 1909. Similarly, the total number of newspaper and magazine publications rose from 87 in 1875 to 548 in 1911.[175]

In terms of books published, Istanbul witnessed 11 book publications annually prior to 1840; the figure increased to 285 books in 1908. Another indicator of the sharp rise in the number of books published is the number of titles in print. Between 1729 and 1829, approximately 180 titles were in print. Between 1876 and 1892, the figure rose to 6,357 and between 1893 and 1907 it was 10,601.[176] To grasp the extent of the new media's reach during this period, one can consult readership estimates. Cole estimates between three

[174] Issawi 1988, 33.
[175] Quataert 2005, 172.
[176] Quataert 2005, 170.

Catholic and Islamic Religious Institutions

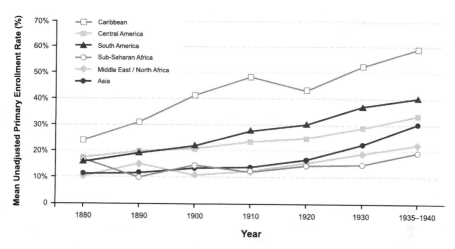

FIGURE 2.2 Mean primary enrollment rations in developing regions, 1880–1940
Note: Unadjusted enrollment rates refer to the number of pupils enrolled in primary schools divided by the 5- to 14-year-old population.
Source: Benavot and Riddle (1988).

and five readers per each copy of a newspaper or magazine.[177] This translates to about 72,000 newspaper readers in Egypt in the 1880s. *Al-Liwa* was estimated to have a readership of around 14,000 in Egypt between 1900 and 1908. In 1897, *al-Hilal* was estimated to have a readership of around 200,000 in Egypt.[178] In Istanbul, newspaper readership increased from 500 in the 1860s to 5,000 in the 1870s.[179] By 1909, daily readership for the best-selling newspapers in Istanbul was in the several hundreds of thousands.[180]

While these estimates are less than precise and might conflict with others, they nonetheless provide a reasonable approximation to evaluate the sharp shift in literacy rates and the number of printed materials, making a significant segment of the population part of the literate conversation. Islamists and the ulama were cognizant of what this new public and the widespread availability of print press implied: Books, magazines, and newspapers could disseminate Islamic ideas and visions. For Islamists, wider access to printed material meant that "more and more Muslims take it upon themselves to interpret the textual sources, classical or modern, of Islam,"[181] exactly the outcome expected of promoting the idea of ijtihad.[182] This would create the conditions to challenge the

[177] Cole 1999.
[178] Shechter 2003, 47.
[179] Cole 1999, 122.
[180] Quataert 2005, 172.
[181] Eickelman and Piscatori 1996, 43.
[182] Ayoob 2008, 27–28.

82 *The Politics of Religious Party Change*

"Order of the Text" where the ulama held monopolistic control over religious knowledge, restricted access to a small group of madrasa-educated scholars, and buttressed society's "moral education" via handwritten manuscripts.

For example, promoters of Salafi reform efforts welcomed the publication of Islamic dailies and magazines and imagined that their circulation would "further an ideology of a dynamic, self-conscious Muslim community, which ... should strive to rid itself of foreign influence and found a pious and just society ... [and] to achieve what the ulama had failed: the moral education of Egypt's Muslim population."[183] Indeed, Islamic books were popular because their "originality" and "unconventional" nature intrigued the public.[184] This new "literate" public "was eagerly buying, borrowing, reading, discussing and contributing to books and magazines on subjects Islamic."[185]

By contrast, the print press brought challenges for the ulama, the "learned" religious establishment.[186] First, it undermined the livelihood of many ulama involved in the manuscript tradition.[187] Second, printing presses expanded the potential reach of the ulama among believers. The conservative ulama in the Ottoman Empire recognized this as "the vehicle of choice" for their "image redo" in the face of increased criticisms.[188] Third, printing presses were bound to open the field to competition by the state and Islamists in their bids to "gain ascendancy as the arbiters of Islamic practice."[189] The long-term effect of this process was a reduction in "the authority of the ulama" due to the fact that Arabic was no longer the exclusive language of religion; local languages and dialects were increasingly being used as well.[190] Graduates of modern educational institutions were unwilling to support the state or the ulama in their bids for religious authority, favoring Islamist groups like the Muslim Brotherhood.[191] Because of this threat, the ulama criticized new print media for how it severed the link between text and author.[192]

Ulama's Response

The ulama's response to this adverse campaign illustrates the level of competition over religious authority between the ulama and Islamists, as well as the *political* nature of this conflict. The ulama were largely divided into two groups: the reformists and the conservatives. The reformist flank conceded that fundamental changes were needed among the ulama and the broader

---

[183] Skovgaard-Petersen 1997, 71.
[184] Eickelman and Piscatori 1996, 39.
[185] Skovgaard-Petersen 1997, 54.
[186] Repp 1972, 30.
[187] Keddie 1972.
[188] Bein 2011, 13.
[189] Eickelman and Piscatori 1996, 44.
[190] Robinson 1993, 245.
[191] Eickelman and Piscatori 1996, 72.
[192] Mitchell 1988, 90–92.

Catholic and Islamic Religious Institutions

religious establishment. The conservatives, by contrast, were furious at the criticisms directed toward them and the reforms undertaken by political authorities. They regarded themselves as the "steadfast defenders of cherished Islamic traditions," whereas the reformists were "useful idiots" who either failed to understand the true nature of the threat posed by Europe and secularism or acted as "unprincipled collaborators."[193] They rebuked criticisms by arguing that Europe-specific problems were being wrongly extrapolated to a Muslim context. Manastirli Ismail Hakki, a major preacher in Istanbul at the turn of the twentieth century, rejected the applicability of secularism in a Muslim country by arguing: "The priests became accustomed to live by way of corruption. They employed every vile deed to ensure their personal interests ... They forbade and allowed things at their whim ... Later, the Europeans were rescued from their influence by separating the temporal sphere [umur-i cismaniye] from the spiritual [umur-i ruhaniye]."[194] A future Sheyhulislam in the Ottoman Empire, Musa Kazim Efendi, acknowledged apparent contradictions between religion and science in this period but defied suggestions that such contradictions applied to Islam because "Islam and its qualified interpreters [the ulama] have never hindered scientific and civilizational progress."[195]

The political reverberations of reform suggestions lay at the core of the ulama's unease with Islamist criticisms.[196] The ulama strictly objected to the possibility of laypersons "with no background of traditional religious education to offer meaningful and worthy interpretations of Islamic texts and traditions." Moreover, scholars like Mustafa Sabri Efendi deemed it preposterous "that people who did not mater sufficient knowledge in theology (kalam), expertise in Islamic philosophy (hikma), training in logic (mantiq), and other required Islamic sciences were audacious enough to claim for themselves an interpretive authority."[197] Such statements directly tried to undermine the credibility of new, alternative sources of religious authority.

Rebuking the fitness of laymen to speak for Islam, the conservative ulama denounced criticisms of the ulama and the religious establishment as an affront to religion itself. An eminent religious scholar of the time, Muhammed Hamdi [Yazir] envisioned the ulama as the bulwark of Muslim faith in the face of European secularism. He charged critics with attempting "to detach Islam from the constitution, the Sheikh ul-Islam from the cabinet, and the title of caliph from the ruler [padisah]" which would eventually "weaken the religious establishment, diminish its status and importance, and marginalize the ulama as preliminary steps toward a European-like full-scale

---

[193] Bein 2011, 33.
[194] Bein 2011, 17.
[195] Bein 2011, 18.
[196] See Alaoudh (2018) for an analysis of recent efforts to reincorporate the ulama into the constitutional framework in several Muslim-majority countries.
[197] Bein 2011, 34.

secularization, both in its institutional meaning and in terms of decline of religious beliefs and practices."[198] As the conservative Mustafa Sabri Efendi later put it, attacks against the ulama aimed "to destroy religion" and were "part of a clandestine stage-by-stage plan to marginalize religion and eventually uproot it altogether."[199]

Essentially in this "unapologetic defense of the reputation and merits of the religious establishment," the ulama invoked religious loyalty and called on all Muslims to identify with them in all circumstances. Mustafa Sabri Efendi put it thusly: "…that even if it were hypothetically proven that Islamic dogmas were preventing progress and prosperity, the Muslims should still stick" to their ways no matter what.[200]

The ulama regained some of its early prominence and swagger in recent decades as a result of two interrelated developments. States across the region increasingly felt the need for religious legitimacy in the face of Islamist parties' growing popularity. Even though postindependence secular regimes almost universally relied on secular and nationalist discourse to legitimize their power, their failure to deliver on promises of modernization, economic development, and an overall better life for their societies enabled Islamist activism. Islamist movements took advantage of this sociopolitical milieu and emerged as the primary forces of opposition with a piercing religious discourse. It is this recognition of political reality and the shifting political ground that pushed regimes across the region to rely on religion as a source of legitimacy. State religious agencies and other state-controlled religious institutions assumed a more prominent role and public voice as states propped them up. Al-Azhar in Egypt, Zaytouna in Tunisia, and the Diyanet in Turkey are among the most important of these ulama-populated institutions. While the tendency is to assume that the relationship between the state and state religious institutions (or the ulama) is unidirectional, it goes both ways, allowing the ulama ample opportunity to expand its influence. And the ulama certainly noticed and seized the opportunities to grow their authority. The ulama correctly identified where the competition for religious influence and authority lay; for the ulama to win over the masses and to become relevant again, they had to beat the Islamists at their own game. In Egypt, Al-Azhar gradually took command of official Islamic discourse, freely expressed conservative views on cultural and social issues, and acted with notable institutional autonomy. In Turkey, the Diyanet does not only control all the mosques and their imams but has also increasingly extended its influence over the Internet to become an actor in "monitor[ing] and censor[ing] religious content." Likewise, the Diyanet assumed an international character recently with its reach in countries in Europe and Asia.[201] In Tunisia, Zaytouna expanded its influence in the field of religious education and acted as an autonomous religious

---

[198] Bein 2011, 21.
[199] Bein 2011, 34.
[200] Bein 2011, 43–44.
[201] Lord 2018.

institution. Zaytouna's growing authority compelled the Islamist Ennahdha to reverse its previous position on "state-controlled Islam."[202]

The results of a recent public opinion survey show that the ulama have been successful in their quest for relevance. This 12-country online public opinion survey conducted across the Middle East indicates that state religious officials – who are a good proxy for the traditional ulama – have the trust and approval of large segments of respondents in all countries in the study. The results hold in the endorsement experiments in the survey as well. Reinforcing an earlier point raised here, state-affiliated religious leaders command the most influence in countries such as Saudi Arabia, Morocco, Iran, and Jordan where the state resorts to religion and religious discourse for legitimacy and national identity.[203]

CONCLUSION

In this chapter, I presented a thorough analysis of the religious institutional structures and religious authority in Catholicism and Sunni Islam. The content does not merely describe religious institutions and authority in both religions; it analyzes how religious authority is maintained and the conditions under which it changes. This discussion is instrumental in setting up subsequent analysis of the political implications of the conflict over religious authority by various religious actors in the modern period. In Catholicism, the early development and ensuing institutionalization of the church structure enabled a centralized and hierarchical institutional framework to ensure orthodoxy in religious doctrine and praxis among Catholics worldwide. This strict hierarchy affords the Church an advantage other religious actors lack: the legitimate authority to speak on behalf of the religion and the concomitant legitimacy in representing the religion and its adherents in various platforms, including the political arena. The Church, consequently, has been averse to competition in its religiopolitical authority.

By contrast, Islam has historically lacked a comparable centralized and hierarchical institutional structure. At times, states attempted to control religion within their polity by establishing religious agencies; such attempts fell short of being encompassing or long-lasting and typically did not enjoy broad legitimacy. At other times, the ulama functioned as the main religious body. Widespread recognition of the ulama's religious authority notwithstanding, it lacked hierarchy and a centralized structure, enabling fierce competition among religious actors. This competition intensified following the demise of the ulama class during the early twentieth century. By thoroughly analyzing the constraints against political action that religious institutions present, this chapter laid the foundation for examining the distinct ways that religious authority shapes religious party politics in Chapter 3.

---

[202] Donker and Netterstrøm 2017, 145–46.
[203] A detailed description of the survey and more findings are available in Yildirim 2019.

3

Anticlericalism, Religious Revival, and the Rise of Religious Political Identities

Conventional thinking against a comparison between Christian and Islamic political actors rests on the lack of comparability between their respective religions. Focusing on how political a religion Islam is and the political language Islam is imbued with, any comparison with Christianity – or with many other world religions for that matter – proves to be problematic. Bernard Lewis, for example, has been a prominent proponent of the idea that Islam is innately political, and secularism is beyond the realm of possibility for Muslim societies because the origins and holy scripture of the religion are infused with political language. Lewis claims: "In classical Arabic, as well as in other languages which derive their intellectual and political vocabulary from classical Arabic, there were no pairs of words corresponding to spiritual and temporal, lay and ecclesiastical, religious and secular."[1] Others have similarly emphasized the political discourse of the Qur'an to account for the relative lack of secularism in the Muslim world.[2] In a comparative analysis of Islam, Christianity, and Hinduism, Michael Cook focuses on religious doctrine and textual sources to explain Islam's politicization and difference from other major religions.[3] Shadi Hamid calls this "Islamic exceptionalism."[4]

Yet, these arguments attempt to draw a sense of false distinction between Islam and other religions, particularly Christianity. The contemporary fusion of religion with politics in the Muslim world is not a simple continuation of historical paradigms; instead, it is a modern reconstruction of an imagined "golden age" where religion and politics constituted an integrated Muslim society. As Ira Lapidus argues, various religious organizations, schools, and brotherhoods

[1] Lewis 1988, 3.
[2] Hamid 2004.
[3] Cook 2014.
[4] Hamid 2014.

Anticlericalism, Religious Revival, & Rise of Religious Political

historically developed independent of the state and were primarily interested in protecting and promoting Islamic symbols: "By the 11th century, Middle Eastern states and religious communities were highly separate. States were officially committed to the defense and patronage of Muslim worship, but they were not inherently Islamic institutions ... Thus, despite the common statement that Islam is a total way of life defining political as well as social and family matters, most Muslim societies did not conform to this ideal ... the state was not a direct expression of Islam but rather a secular institution whose duty it was to uphold Islam."[5] Kuru convincingly shows that only after the eleventh century did religious and political spheres in the Muslim world morph into a mutually reinforcing unified front.[6] In many ways, religion's role in the pre-modern Muslim societies of the Middle East resembled that of European Christian societies in the same period.

Similarly, arguments about Islam's distinctiveness do not hold because of the notion of religious political identity. Today, we tend to think of Catholic or Islamic political identities as timeless elements of the political landscape. Because religion embodies a crucial aspect of social identity in many societies, a religious political identity is a natural expression of this identity and sentiment. That depiction, however, fails to capture how political identities, including religious ones, are created in the first place in a historical perspective.

Pre-modern societies in both Western Europe and the Middle East were largely characterized by the dominance of religion. Societies generally agreed on the pre-eminent role of religion in undergirding the society's moral and ethical foundation. Religion stood above partisan conflicts and was rarely politicized; in a way, religion was deemed above politics. However, this changed considerably with the onset of modernization in the nineteenth century. The advent of the nation-state, modernization, and secularism transformed and diversified the political role of religion for many societies. In what follows, I examine the changing public role of religion in Western European and Middle Eastern societies with the onset of modernity.

Building on the historical analysis in Chapter 2, I analyze the origins of the Catholic and Islamist political identities. Grounded in Katznelson's theory of political identity formation, this chapter examines how the Catholic Church and Islamic actors have created respective religious political identities in response to the rise of modernity, secularism, and brewing anti-religion sentiment in Western Europe and the Middle East. In the nineteenth and early twentieth centuries, anticlerical attacks, secularization of public education, and adoption of secularism as a principle of government generated a strong reaction from the Church in Western Europe and religious leaders throughout the Middle East. In response, religious actors – both Catholic and Islamic – mobilized around

---

[5] Lapidus 1992, 5.
[6] Kuru 2019.

88 *The Politics of Religious Party Change*

the idea that no part of human existence lay outside the scope of religion. The emergence of Catholic mass movements in nineteenth-century Western Europe and Islamist movements in the twentieth-century Middle East represents the manifestation of this pushback against anticlerical and anti-religion attacks. This chapter offers a comparative account of the emergence of religious political identities in Catholic and Islamic contexts, leaving country-specific discussion of the rise of these identities to Chapters 4 and 5.

POLITICAL IDENTITY FORMATION

Political identity formation is the process through which a group begins to "recognize [them]selves as a 'we'," using common "values and principles" and often "choosing elements from past history and giving them a new order and significance."[7] Similarly, political identity formation refers to "the 'we-ness' of a group, stressing the similarities or shared attributes around which group members coalesce."[8] In contrast to the in-group perspective, the out-group approach underscores the role of outsiders in the process of political identity creation. Political identities can arise from "outsiders ascrib[ing] a common group identity to certain populations" regardless of the fact that members of these groups might not accept those characterizations.[9] Katznelson's theory of political identity formation combines the in-group and outsider perspectives. In his analysis of how class turns into a strong political identity, Katznelson shows that the process of identity formation involves workers' increasing realization of their class status and then proactive politicization of that class status. Workers began seeing the regime as "them" versus "us," eventually forming political parties to contest "them." Thus, class had become a political identity.[10]

In principle, there are various possible sources of political identity by which members of a group can be characterized such as party affiliation, ethnicity, religion, national origin, economic status, and language. The modern nation-state, with its singular force of appeal, is one of the most important sources of political identity.[11] A national political identity is formed when "the people in a new state must come to recognize their national territory as being their true homeland, and they must feel as individuals that their own personal identities are in part defined by their identification with their territorially delimited country."[12] Likewise, a shared political identity can emanate from sources such as "qualities emerging from physiological traits, psychological predispositions,

[7] Cerutti 1999, 8.
[8] Cerulo 1997, 386.
[9] Smith 2004, 302.
[10] Katznelson 1986, 34.
[11] Brubaker and Cooper 2000, 15.
[12] Mackenzie 1978, 31.

Anticlericalism, Religious Revival, & Rise of Religious Political

regional features, or the properties of structural locations," which can suggest that members of a group share in "a unified, singular social experience, a single canvas against which social actors constructed a sense of self."[13] In a study of contemporary American society, Yates and Youniss find that political identity formation – which is defined as "an outward-looking process in which youth anticipate their lives as adults and struggle to understand who they are within a social and historical framework" – is greatly shaped by the "social-historical context" individuals share.[14]

In this regard, religion also carries great potential to be a major marker of political identity. Yet, the process is far from being automatic. As Smith underscores, potential political identities turn into real ones only when they are *politicized*: "All these possible sources, however, are only political identities when political actors treat them as such."[15] Indeed, religion remained a latent political identity marker until the religious establishment and religion came under fire in the modern period, when religion gradually ceased to be the eminent common social denominator and the moral and ethical compass of the society. Modernization and the rise of the nation-state brought religion and religious establishment under closer scrutiny. Not only did individual members of society veer away from religion as their primary identity attribute, but many also called to strip religion and religious actors of their privileged status in the state and society. This process unfolded in similar ways in Western Europe and the Middle East. I discuss anti-religion and anticlerical attacks of the nineteenth and twentieth centuries next as processes instrumental to the politicization of religion and creation of religious political identities.

WAVES OF ANTICLERICAL AND ANTI-ULAMA ATTACKS

Changing public opinion and public policy toward religion in Western Europe typically took the form of anti-religion attacks and anticlericalism. Anticlericalism evolved into "a catch-all phrase" to denote most forms of anti-religion attacks in nineteenth-century Europe as part of the modernization process.[16] Anticlericalism can be defined as "an attitude of hostility to power and influence of the clergy, in social, economic, and political terms."[17] This attitude of hostility entails "emotional attacks against the clergy and is more punitive toward the religious."[18] As Remond explains, however, "anticlericalism is not merely a negative ideology; it cannot simply be reduced to the rejection of clericalism, even if its destiny is intimately linked with the fortunes

---

[13] Cerulo 1997, 387.
[14] Yates and Youniss 1998, 495.
[15] Smith 2004, 302.
[16] Sanchez 1972, 6.
[17] Barnett 1999, 16.
[18] Sanabria 2009, 10.

and the ambitions of the latter. Anticlericalism is concerned with a particular vision of the truth, of society, of human liberty."[19] Hence, separation of church and state is a predominant element of this anticlerical vision.[20]

Anticlerical figures were an eclectic group motivated by various factors. They included not only those Christians who were opposed to the Church's political influence or called for church–state separation: "[Anticlericals included] those atheists and agnostics who criticized the clergy as a way of criticizing organized religion. They included practicing Catholics who felt that clergy were abusing their power ... they included a small number of persons who were truly bent on the destruction of the church ... Ideological anticlericals are convinced that the powers of the clergy are inherently abusive, no matter to what use they are put." Similarly, antisacerdotalists who were not only opposed to the clergy but also viewed them "as symbols or representatives of an opposed institution" are also included in the larger group of anticlericals that espoused the idea of disputing the powers and the abuse of those powers by the clergy.[21] Lastly, humanists showed little restraint in their enthusiasm for anticlericalism: "With their regard for classical lore and the treasures of antiquity, they could not look upon the Middle Ages with equanimity. They tended to see the medieval period as dominated by clericalism, to which they attributed most of the defects of medieval life."[22]

Early on, anticlericalism was a myth propagated by some members of the clergy, believing "that anticlericals had hatched a diabolic plot to weaken the Church by striking at the clergy. The humanists, the scientists, and the Freemasons had formed a conspiracy against the clergy. Usually based in Paris, the anticlerical conspirators sent agents throughout the Catholic world to stir up antagonism against the clergy."[23] However, this myth soon turned into reality. A key development that precipitated anticlerical sentiment in Western Europe was "the deepening antagonism between bourgeois liberalism and the clerical and religious prerogatives of the Roman Catholic Church."[24] Germany's Kültürkampf in the 1870s perfectly illustrates the battle between secular liberal anticlericals and the Catholic Church. Protestants mobilized the anticlerical campaign, enabled by the advent of mass printing:

[It was a story of] gross spiritual betrayal and fleshly corruption of the beating heart of European Christianity. Christians were informed that the sanctity of Rome and the popes had been only a tale concocted to lull the suspicions of Christians, whilst the popes had pursued worldly and antichristian goals. Believing the actions of the papacy to represent divine will, Christians had unwittingly allowed popes and prelates

[19] Remond 1983, 121.
[20] Sanabria 2009, 10.
[21] Sanchez 1972, 6–10.
[22] Sanchez 1972, 39.
[23] Sanchez 1972, 6.
[24] Farr 1983, 249.

Anticlericalism, Religious Revival, & Rise of Religious Political   91

to rule the Church despotically. High ecclesiastics had amassed great wealth and power and, as aspiring tyrants are wont, had undermined and challenged the legitimate secular powers of kings and emperors. All had been justified by a body of Church law designed to deceive the faithful and draw Europe steadily away from its rightful Christian heritage.[25]

Deists believed that "cunning clerics" had held Europe back since the days of the Roman Empire. In order to sustain their privileged position in society, "the clergy had never allowed reason to claim its rightful role in society."[26] German anticlerical discourse described Catholicism as "a religion of popular superstition based on absolute obedience," which was "incompatible with enlightenment, reason, and progress" and undermined democratic ideals. Moreover, at a time when the nation-state became one of the most critical political ideas, Catholics failed to prioritize their loyalties, according to anticlericals in Germany: "Catholics were nationally unreliable, as their primary allegiance belonged to Rome and not to Berlin."[27] Mork further states, "The liberals looked upon that conflict between the German state and the Catholic Church as a struggle for modern culture against medieval superstition and intellectual obscurantism."[28]

Many anticlerical attacks came in the form of scientific arguments, and this was no coincidence. As anticlericals increasingly recognized the overlap between their hatred of the *ancien régime* and the unscientific (or even anti-science) stance of the Church, they increasingly couched their criticism of the Church in broad criticisms of the religion: "If man's ability was elevated there was less need for a clergy to act as intercessor between God and man. The emphasis upon naturalism and the renewed interest in studying the material world made the clergy less relevant, for they had no special qualifications enabling them to interpret natural phenomena. Individualism stressed the individual's accountability for his own actions, as opposed to the idea of corporate unity in the Middle Ages."[29] It was not just the Church's religious and interpretative authority that came under attack. Anticlericals assaulted the veracity of key pillars of Christian and Catholic dogma such as "the creation story in Genesis, the authorship of various parts of the Bible, the virgin birth, and the authority of the pope" as well as the Catholic dogma in its entirety and "the very existence of Catholicism."[30] Put differently, scientific arguments turned into "weapons" for anticlericals to attack religious doctrines, thereby debilitating the Vatican's influence over the society.[31]

---

[25] Barnett 1999, 3.
[26] Barnett 1999, 8.
[27] Altinordu 2010, 529–30.
[28] Mork 1971, 69.
[29] Sanchez 1972, 38.
[30] Kurtz 1983, 1092.
[31] Kurtz 1983, 1099.

The causes of anticlericalism in Europe were many. One of the pivotal reasons for this variety of causes was rooted in the advent of liberalism and universal suffrage, and the Church's opposition to these developments: "[Anticlericalism] was believed to be concerned with the question of questions, whether liberalism and Catholicism could be reconciled. We find its consequences running all across Europe; in the discomforts between Ireland and the British Government, in the conflict between Poland and the Russian Government, in the politics of education in Belgium, in Bismarck's Kulturkampf and above all in the French political strife after 1871."[32] Pope Pius IX became one of the most vocal critics of the extension of universal suffrage across the continent and referred to it as the "horrible plague." At its core, such criticism reflected the Church's deep sense of political vulnerability. With the advent of universal suffrage, frontal assaults on church power and influence accompanied liberal parties' surging popularity, resulting in greater politicization of religion and facilitating a religious political identity: "The old alliance of throne and altar, though still standing nominally, could no longer protect Catholics against these assaults, and therefore Catholic leaders engaged in power politics to protect their endowments or their privilege in education. Because Spain was more clerical than Belgium, the anticlerical movement was more bitter. But in both cases its full flowering was due to the coming of universal suffrage."[33]

In Germany, anticlericalism culminated in the Kültürkampf, which began shortly after the Declaration of Papal Infallibility as well as the introduction of a "democratic franchise on the widest scale of any great power in Europe." Consequently, as Anderson (1986) further underscores, the German Kültürkampf revolved around the introduction of mass politics and the future shape of state and society: "The Kulturkampf – in the sense of legislation to reduce the influence of the Catholic Church – began as a defensive reaction of local elites to the challenge of subordinate groups to their local dominance. Its onset was determined less by the Catholic religious revival, the needs of a modern state, or the parliamentary calculations of Bismarck – to name just three currently fashionable views – than it was by the anxiety of Germany's elites faced with the sudden emergence of mass politics."[34]

Just as important was the cultural dimension of anticlericalism. The origins of anti-Catholic activism in Germany lie in the state-church clash over Baden schools in the 1870s and 1880s, but it quickly evolved into a nationwide conflict on anti-Catholic legislation. Catholics perceived liberal Protestants bent on "Protestantizing" Catholics as part of a "state-decreed attempt," whereas liberals viewed the entire process as "the dismantling of backward religious institutions 'in the name of material, social and moral progress'."[35]

---

[32] Chadwick 1990, 113.
[33] Chadwick 1990, 116.
[34] Anderson 1986, 89–90.
[35] Drury 2001, 112.

Anticlericalism, Religious Revival, & Rise of Religious Political

This "struggle for civilization," as liberals conceived it, entailed a series of major policies that left Catholics unimpressed, to say the least. The bulk of the reforms concerned the Catholic clergy, their political activism, and educational roles: "It [reforms] began in 1871 with the disbandment of the Catholic Department of the Prussian Ministry for Education and Religious Affairs. The first major Kulturkampf legislation soon followed with the Pulpit Paragraph of 1871, which criminalized the political speech of the clergy in places of ecclesiastical activity, making it punishable by up to two years of prison (in 1876, the law was extended to the writing of the clergy). This was followed in the spring of 1872 by the Prussian School Supervision Law that ended the clergy's role as school inspectors."[36] Likewise, Jesuit orders were banned with the 1872 Jesuit Law and foreign Jesuits were deported from Germany, which was a result of a popular "anti-Jesuit campaign."[37] By the early 1880s, "approximately one third of the parishes in Prussia had lost their priests to government persecution."[38] While Germany was an important battleground for anticlericalism, such attacks rampaged throughout the continent: "The liberals looked upon that conflict between the German state and the Catholic church as a struggle for modern culture against medieval superstition and intellectual obscurantism; some of the Kulturkampf legislation – like that establishing civil marriage and secular control of education – was similar to the anticlerical legislation supported by liberal parties throughout Europe."[39]

Anticlericalism, which had long existed in the form of general opposition to the authority of the Church, merged with nationalism and liberalism in nineteenth-century Italy in response to the Italian unification movement, or *risorgimento*. The *risorgimento* was mostly complete by 1861 with the establishment of the Kingdom of Italy and culminated in the overthrow of the Papal States in 1870. Camillo Cavour became the first prime minister of the Kingdom of Italy in 1861 and was a proponent of "a free church in a free state," thus planting the seed for future leaders to advocate for the separation of church and state.[40] However, Pope Pius IX censured the separatist doctrine in the 1864 Syllabus of Errors and adamantly established the Church's opposition to a secular state. The overthrow of the Papal States stripped the pope of temporal authority, but the Italian government attempted to settle the "Roman question," or conflict over the pope's civil authority, in the Law of Guarantees in 1871. This law still gave the pope full spiritual autonomy in his role as a religious leader and established the Holy See's freedom, but Pius IX rejected it and claimed territorial sovereignty was the only way he could adequately rule. The pope went so far as to recommend that Italian Catholics refrain from

---

[36] Altinordu 2010, 530.
[37] Altinordu 2010, 530.
[38] Anderson 1995, 653.
[39] Mork 1971, 69.
[40] Halperin 1947, 22.

94   *The Politics of Religious Party Change*

political participation in the kingdom in his 1874 *non expedit*.[41] However, some clericals refuted the notion that Catholics should refrain from political participation, seeing them as a potential source of opposition to the anticlerical forces at work in the Italian Senate and Chamber of Deputies. The state had already made religious instruction in schools optional and passed a bill that eliminated chairs of theology in state universities, marking the beginning of many government measures aimed at reducing the power of the papacy.[42]

Hence, the 1870s through the 1890s was a period of intense ideological and political conflict between the Church and anticlericalists. While the Vatican displayed hostility toward the Italian state and mobilized its efforts to restore the Holy See's temporal power, anticlericalists continually pushed to eliminate ecclesiastical influence in state affairs, particularly in the areas of divorce, religious instruction in public schools, marriage, and charitable organizations. Many of the political factions within parliament also supported abolishing the Law of Guarantees, which they felt gave too much autonomy to the pope. After the advent of Pope Leo XIII in 1878, there was hope among those seeking a resolution between church and state that his tenure would help ease tensions between clericalists and anticlericalists. However, he quickly proved inflexible on the Roman question and thus unwilling to compromise with anticlerical politicians. The new penal code promulgated in 1889 imposed more restrictions on the clergy's political activities, and Italian Prime Minister Francesco Crispi brought all public charities under the control of the state. Crispi declared the clergy "the principal enemy of Italy" in 1883 and thus pursued anticlerical policies while in office, including abolishing ecclesiastical tithes and removing Italian schools in the Levant from Franciscan control.[43]

A series of events took place in this period in which the multitude of anticlerical factions demonstrated their discontent with papal authority. The state sponsored numerous ceremonies commemorating victims of papal violence throughout the 1880s, much to the chagrin of the Church. In 1881, an anticlerical mob attacked Pius IX's funeral procession as his remains were moved to San Lorenzo, thus provoking anger from clericals.[44] One particularly provocative instance occurred in 1889, when a statue of the philosopher Giordano Bruno was erected at the place of his martyrdom by the Church in Campo de' Fiori. Pope Leo XIII declared the statue a "war against Catholicism" and saw it as part of the broader scheme to undermine the papacy.[45] The procession and ceremony surrounding this instance helped temporarily unify anticlerical forces but did not ensure their long-term stability.[46] Similar instances ensued in

[41] Halperin 1974, 592.
[42] Halperin 1947, 23.
[43] Halperin 1947, 25–26.
[44] Lyttelton 1983, 229.
[45] Halperin 1947, 28.
[46] Lyttelton 1983, 229.

Anticlericalism, Religious Revival, & Rise of Religious Political

the following years such as the unveiling of a statue in 1895 commemorating Giuseppe Garibaldi, a well-known champion of Italian unification who defied the authority of the *curia*.[47]

Divides existed within the anticlerical camp as well. Within parliament there were regalists, who saw the Church as "the eternal and implacable enemy of everything modern" and thought it must be democratized and "subordinated to the state." There were also separatists, who favored complete separation of church and state.[48] These factions occasionally found enough common ground to pass regulations against the Catholic Church. Anticlerical views were also espoused by some radical and socialist lawmakers. The most fervently anticlerical group, however, was the freemasons – a cross-party group who drew from modern science and liberal thought to form their movement. Freemasons viewed Roman Catholicism as inherently at odds with democracy and were especially adamant about the removal of religious influence in educational institutions, which helped this issue receive continual attention from anticlerical governments.[49] Other freemason societies sought to eliminate the Catholic monopoly on charities and to influence workers' groups.[50]

The haphazard organization of anticlerical factions also led to confusion and ineffectiveness in their actions, helping to strengthen the Church's response. When Premier Zanardelli reintroduced a divorce bill in parliament in 1902, the Church was outraged and said it would produce a "nationwide *crise de conscience*." Pope Leo XIII entered the controversy, describing divorce as menace to the essence of Italian life; the government quickly faced steep opposition from the public and the clergy emerged triumphant. Some Socialist anticlericals like Leonida Bissolati also tried to prohibit religious teaching from schools, arguing that the state should use education to allow youth to develop unhindered by religious constraints. Bissolati faced steep opposition from clericals in addition to moderate liberals and conservatives, and his motion was handily defeated.[51] Overall, even though anticlerical attacks were sometimes ineffective or defeated by the Church, the general movement sowed the seeds for future separation between church and state. A détente was reached with the signing of the Lateran Treaty in 1929, which made the pope the ruler of Vatican City and resolved the "Roman question."[52]

The Belgian Revolution of 1830 had the peculiar effect of establishing "the most liberal regime in Europe" in the most Catholic country north of the Alps. French occupation during the eighteenth and turn of the nineteenth centuries strengthened popular adherence to Catholicism, and influence from Spanish,

---

[47] Halperin 1947, 30.
[48] Halperin 1947, 20.
[49] Halperin 1947, 18.
[50] Lyttelton 1983, 231.
[51] Halperin 1947, 33.
[52] Kunz 1952, 309.

96 The Politics of Religious Party Change

Austrian, and Dutch occupiers all shaped the Belgian Church to become a mix between Latin and Germanic models.[53] The Belgian fight for independence from the Dutch temporarily united the nation's Catholics and liberals in a "Union of Oppositions" but did not create lasting peace between these two factions. When the country's first constitution was created in 1831, the Church took advantage of the support it granted to religious institutions, such as subsidies to all religious groups and full religious freedom.[54] Catholics managed to maintain their hold over the education system, hospitals, and charitable institutions thanks to these constitutional guarantees, which in turn provoked the rise of the Liberal Party. The Church's organizational presence "in all fields of life" made 1830s Belgium a Catholic country with liberal institutions; fifty years later, the state was still very Catholic, with conservatives trying to remodel institutions. During the half-century in between, "liberalism was the motor force of Belgian political life, and the position of the Church in a free society the pre-eminent bone of contention between itself and political Catholicism."[55] The stage was thus set for conflict between and amongst Catholics and anticlerical liberals.

Belgian politics and society followed a unique course in the anticlerical attacks of the nineteenth century. The state was governed first in a coalition of "rationalist" Liberals and "liberal" Catholics.[56] In contrast to fellow Catholic nations Italy, France, and Spain, where the Church did not quickly adjust to changing political conditions, Belgian Catholics actively defended against the expansion of liberal measures while also taking advantage of the policies that gave the Church more freedom.[57] Since liberalism was concentrated in urban areas in Belgium, the Catholics were able to use mass mobilization in rural areas to win a solid base of popular support.[58] Growing polarization between the two factions prompted the Liberals to officially establish a political party in 1846, resulting in the first partisan cabinet in 1847.[59]

The 1850s marked a rise in anticlericalism in Belgium, especially among the "enfranchised classes" who accounted for only about 2 percent of the population at the time. The proposal and passage of a new school law in 1850 by a group of young Liberal deputies is a prime example of this anticlerical surge. This law created 60 new schools in which all instructions would be controlled by the state, including religious instruction; this, in turn, angered the national Catholic hierarchy.[60] Freemasonic societies were the "ideological and social

[53] Viaene 2001, 26.
[54] Strikwerda 1988, 335.
[55] Viaene 2001, 9–10.
[56] Kittell 1961, 420.
[57] It is possible that the Church played a greater role in Belgian political life due to its role in combatting Dutch protestant rule in 1830 (Viaene 2001, 10).
[58] This would come to benefit them especially after the establishment of universal male suffrage.
[59] Kalyvas 1998, 298.
[60] Kittell 1961, 425.

Anticlericalism, Religious Revival, & Rise of Religious Political

backbone" of the Belgian liberalism. In 1857, anticlerical riots occurred in Brussels and a monastery was sacked in Jemappes in response to legislation that would have allowed Church control over local charities. That same year, the Liberals won power in both houses of parliament and began pursuing further anticlerical policies. The militant anticlericalism of the Liberals found only moderate opposition within the ranks of parliamentary Conservatives (through the *Association Constitutionelle Conservatrice*) much to the chagrin of the Church, who desired more robust political support from the right.[61] However, ongoing agitation by Liberals and more radical factions led to the dissolution of the agreement that previously united them with Catholic conservatives.

The Liberals and anticlericals continued their opposition to Church involvement in state affairs; they deemed the Church's dominant control over various facets of Belgian civil life problematic. They were especially concerned with education, charitable institutions, marriage, and burials in cemeteries.[62] The education issue came to a head in 1879 when the Liberal government passed the Van Humbeck Law, a measure that reduced the Church's influence in schools. This legislation resulted in a "true ideological civil war" between the two sides that remained unresolved until Conservatives' rise to power in 1884.[63] Other legislation on secular education followed during this period.[64] The Vatican responded to the Van Humbeck Law by severing diplomatic relations with Belgium in 1880.

While anticlerical attackers were comprised of multiple groups, ranging from moderate Liberals to radicals and socialists, Church supporters were also divided during this time between the Church itself, moderate Conservatives, and radical Catholic activists. The Church typically acted as a mediator between moderates and radicals during the contentious 1870s, but eventually sided with the moderates before the critical election of 1884. This was a strategic move on the Belgian Church's part, influenced by the Vatican. The Church had always seen the constitution as a grudging compromise, and the Vatican became more vocal in its denunciation of liberalism during the 1860s. Pius IX was especially avid in his support for the radical ultramontanes, a group of devout bourgeois lay Catholics who tried to wrest political control of the right from the parliamentary Conservatives. This conflict was only resolved once Pope Leo XIII intervened in 1879 and stated that the Belgian constitution, while containing some distasteful principles, should still be upheld by

---

[61] Kalyvas 1998, 299.

[62] Kittell 1961, 425–26.

[63] Kalyvas 1998, 299.

[64] The "school wars" reflected an earlier debate between anticlericals and Catholics over Article 12 of the new Belgian constitution in the 1830s. Article 12 forbade state involvement in religious affairs, but anticlerical liberals declared that this would prevent the state from enforcing civil over religious marriage, thus propagating religious marriage for the vast majority of the peasantry (Viaene 2001, 29).

98 *The Politics of Religious Party Change*

Catholics.[65] Anticlericalism left a history of antagonisms in Belgian culture that continued to threaten national unity well into the twentieth century, just as the Church has remained a strong force in the makeup of Belgian society.[66]

While different anticlerical groups had varying motivations for their anti-clericalism, as discussed above, what ultimately mattered for Catholics was their perception that these attacks were anti-religion at their core. This perception arose for a number of reasons. First, the Church maintained a major influence over public life. When the faithful claimed to follow the religion, this often referred to following the Church and the clergy. Consequently, an attack on either amounted to an attack on the religion and what they represented.

Another reason why anticlerical attacks were viewed as anti-religion was the lack of separation between the Church and religion on the part of the anti-clerical groups. Opposition to the Church meant opposition to the religion by default. In some forms, anticlericalism mandated the separation of church and religion; yet, many still carried out attacks against religious forces, indicating opposition to religion as a whole rather than just its influence in public life. Lastly, anticlericalism evolved over time from its earlier anticlergy stance into a decidedly anti-Catholic dogma stance. This was especially the case among many liberals: "Since its origin, the anticlerical caricature criticizes the clergy under the angle of its morality. It also criticizes its political statements and its role, considered as oppressive in society. At the end of the nineteenth century, the caricature becomes antireligious. From now, it attacks on the dogmas. The Ancient and the New Testament are widely parodied and illustrated with caricatures. This maturing of the caricature against the religion is in fact based on centuries of rationalist or satiric criticism of the Bible."[67]

Compared to how anticlerical attacks unfolded in Western Europe, modernist attacks on religion and religious establishment took a different form in the Middle East during the nineteenth and twentieth centuries. A key reason for this difference is the institutional structure of religion in both contexts. Cognizant of how anticlerical attacks in Europe spilled over to criticizing the entire Catholic faith and religion as a whole, anti-ulama critics were generally more measured in how they framed their criticisms, directing the brunt of such criticisms toward the ulama class. Despite the fact that the ulama was not technically the equivalent of a clergy class, their centuries-long dominance in speaking for Islam as the "established scholars of Islam" made them the main target of attacks.[68] Two main avenues of anti-ulama attacks can be identified, tying back to the analysis of Islamic religious authority's transformation at the turn of the twentieth century. The ulama were criticized not only by liberals and advocates of modernist and secular reforms who desired to see religion's

[65] Kalyvas 1998, 306.
[66] Kittell 1961, 419.
[67] Doizy 2006, 63.
[68] Kingston 2001, 297.

Anticlericalism, Religious Revival, & Rise of Religious Political

role in the state minimized like in Europe but also by new breeds of religious actors – proto-Islamists, Islamists, and Salafis being chief among them – who were dissatisfied with the authoritative interpretations on doctrine doled out by the ulama. These criticisms from both sides against the ulama, and to a lesser degree against religion, resonated in a political and social context where the ulama were already losing their religious clout.

Secular reformists considered "traditional civil society ... a threat to state power," remarking that "the modernization efforts began with a very sensitive cooperation with powerful groups within the traditional civil society, such as the ulama, but was soon transformed into enmity and confrontation with these groups."[69] It soon became evident to secular activists that the ulama were too deeply entrenched as guardians of religious authority for co-optation toward modernist reforms; this realization led to more antagonistic relations between secular-minded reformists and established Islamic scholars. A fundamental criticism of the ulama was that these scholars were unable to deal with the myriad challenges that came about with managing complex social relations in modern society: "Critics [of the ulama] note that Islam knows no clergy and that the classical Islamic educations of many ulama ill prepare them to respond creatively and effectively to modern realities. Instead, they believe, the conception of the ulama, or scholars, must be broadened to include many new areas of expertise, ranging from economics to medicine."[70]

The Ottoman ulama were often compared to Europe's Christian clergy, along with the suggestion that they should similarly be marginalized, for they could similarly bring negative consequences to society. Critics usually railed against the religious establishment – that is, the ulama – "for inadvertently strengthening the antireligious camp through the ulema's inaptitude, excessive traditionalism, and self-interest, just as the clergy in Europe helped bring about the spread of secularism and atheism."[71] The Young Turks in the Ottoman Empire were a movement largely influenced by the modernization process in Europe and viewed it as a model of progress for their own society. Their efforts featured a limited role for religion, viewing the sultanate and the religious establishment as the "main obstacles" to efforts of modernization: "They attacked the ulema (Islamic Scholars) stating that there should not be any intermediary authorities between God and subjects. They pursued policies that weakened the political power of the ulema."[72] The Young Turks' publications featured more pointed criticisms of the ulama, depicting them as the country's spiritual class similar to clergy: "[The ulama] were collectively accused of abuse of their status and office similar to the transgressions of the Catholic priesthood. In other cases, their long-term impact on Muslim societies was equated with the

---

[69] Kamali 2001, 470.
[70] Esposito 1997, 10.
[71] Bein 2011, 22.
[72] Tarhan 2011, 11.

negative influences of the clergy in European history. They were thus accused of fulfilling similar obscurantist roles in instituting and enforcing corrupt religious doctrines and practices, and in deliberately impeding the advance of freedom and prosperity through scientific progress."[73]

In 1909, novelist Omer Seyfeddin called the ulama "enemies of progress" and stated, "History has shown us that it is only the priests who had mobilized against every form of freedom and liberty, and that in the end, they were defeated." A former Grand Vizier claimed that the ulama only cared for "their personal and institutional prerogatives while impeding the progress of the Muslims as a whole."[74] Others accused the ulama of being a "clerical priesthood"; some ulama even faced death threats. They were often criticized for "rigidness of interpretation and jurisprudence, their unwillingness to reform religious education, their excessive defense of their authority and prerogatives, and their general narrow-mindedness and inability to grasp the challenges of the day and respond to them effectively."[75] Similarly, Mustafa Kemal Atatürk, the founder of Turkey, stated in 1923: "Let us know this as a certain fact that there is no special class [of people] in our religion. This religion [Islam] that rejects priesthood does not accept [religious] monopoly. For example, the responsibility of enlightenment is not the exclusive purview of the ulama and our religion certainly prohibits it."[76]

The similarities in how the modern(izing) state approached the religious establishment in Western Europe and the Middle East are remarkable. Secular criticisms in the Middle East went beyond discourse and transformed the religious and political landscape of the region, in a process analogous to the one in Western Europe. The rise of secular institutions squeezed the life out of the ulama and their authority:

... despite the initial "centralizing" effects which state-building reforms had on Middle Eastern Islam, these same reforms would eventually do serious damage to the roots of its authority. Public schools sponsored by the state, utilizing a curriculum based upon technical and scientific rather than religious knowledge, were created alongside the *madrassa*; secular courts using legal codes from the West were introduced which, as their mandates expanded, lessened the jurisdiction of the once dominant religious courts, eventually confining their authority to issues of personal status; the participation of the ulama in the affairs of state was gradually replaced by that of Western trained technocrats at the highest levels; and, where religious institutions and personnel maintained their connections with the state, it was in a subordinated and relativized fashion relegated to such bureaucratic categories as the Directorate of Religious Affairs, the Department of Religious Endowments, or the Office of the Grand Mufti.[77]

---

[73] Bein 2011, 23.
[74] Seyfeddin and the Grand Vizier quoted in Bein 2011, 23–24.
[75] Bein 2011, 26.
[76] Atatürk quoted in Sarikoyuncu 2002, 76.
[77] Kingston 2001, 298.

Anticlericalism, Religious Revival, & Rise of Religious Political　　　101

Moreover, such developments make it clear that the growth of secular bureaucracy also led to a bureaucratization of Islamic religious authorities. No longer were the ulama authoritative experts lying outside of the grip of the state; instead, religious affairs became roped into departments within a larger state administered by predominantly secular technocrats. The institutional transformation of Damascus, Syria in the late nineteenth and early twentieth centuries illustrates this point further. Before the Ottoman Tanzimat reforms came into effect (1839–76), "the ulama of Damascus dominated local judicial and educational institutions in addition to administering pious endowments (sing. *waqf*), articulating religious beliefs, and conducting religious practices." Yet, in the second half of the nineteenth century when various judicial and educational institutions were not formed *nor* controlled by the ulama, this arrangement "implicitly devalued their cultural capital and shunted them off to the periphery of society."[78]

What is really striking here is that the religious institutional structure and weakening of the ulama class enabled modernist reformers to successfully act on their criticisms of the ulama and initiate secular reforms. Because the ulama lacked a solid institutional structure like the Catholic Church in Western Europe, the ulama's loss of power was not always due to damage from direct attacks. The very creation of new institutions with a more secular character was sufficient to effectively marginalize the ulama. The ulama were always the prime exponents and practitioners of civil society throughout history. Once new political and civil organizations came about that effectively opened participation in the state and society to more than simply learned Islamic authorities, the ulama's very authority inevitably waned.[79]

The anti-ulama attacks did not always arise from secularist discontent with religion. The second line of attack against the ulama came from more conservative circles. These attacks arose from avowed Islamists who felt that the ulama's brand of jurisprudence was too tepid to transform society through Islamic means. Chapter 2 thoroughly analyzed various criticisms leveled by newly bourgeoning Islamists and Salafis against the ulama and the religious establishment; I will not repeat these anti-ulama criticisms and attacks here. However, a few points are worth highlighting.

A key reason for the rise of Salafism – the fundamentalist streak of Islam – has been "witness[ing] the social marginalization of the ulama and ascrib[ing] it to the ulama's failure to teach and practice 'true' Islam" in the late Ottoman period.[80] Many early Salafis were of the mindset that the ulama must be mistaken in their teachings; if their teachings were truly authoritative, Islamic law would have never been sidelined by various secular and Western ideological

---

[78] Commins 1986, 407.
[79] Seyit 2006.
[80] Commins 1986, 408.

currents that arose during Ottoman reforms. Focusing on the most important Islamist organization of the twentieth century, Kingston notes that "[Hassan al] Banna's founding of the Muslim Brotherhood in Egypt in 1928 must also be seen in the context of debates about the inability of the established Islamic leaders and institutions to deal with the threats to Islam's moral integrity posed by foreign occupation. With the rise of the interventionist secular state in the region in the mid-twentieth century, the ulama, once thought reformable, was now looked upon as being irredeemably corrupt and often referred to as 'the stockbrokers of Islam' or 'the palace ulama'."[81]

The Young Ottomans were the first to attempt to "formulate Islamic answers from the original Islamic sources" in opposition to the ulama. They "blamed their rulers for their corruption and for not returning to authentic Islam."[82] Intellectual Ahmed Hilmi called the ulama "disingenuous guardians of Islamic law and charged that they claimed undue monopoly on the faith despite the absence of priesthood in Islam," further arguing, "They are simply incapable of analyzing and evaluating the present circumstances because they are unaware of the contemporary level of human knowledge and the power and influence of modern science. This ignorance is so profound that these wretched people assume that the maintenance and perpetuation of an opinion that was produced eight hundred or a thousand years ago by their predecessors is more beneficial and useful for Islam than recourse to ideas that could regenerate the present-day Muslim society." Ahmet Hilmi also expressed concern about how ulama's traditionalism, combined with secular modernism, would prevent society from moving toward his preferred "evolutionary progress combining modernism and religiosity."[83] In Azerbaijan, a comic magazine called *Molla Nasreddin* "routinely poked fun at traditionalist ulama whom it accused of sloth and ignorance or of actively lending a hand in the destruction of Islam and nation," having a fictional character state, "The activities of your self-proclaimed ulama are the reason for the extinction of your nation. But there's no need to grieve, brother, since your ulama aren't the only ones like this. The fact is, ulama all over the Muslim world in the last three centuries have committed similar crimes."[84]

In summary, two broad factors shaped the anti-religion and anti-ulama sentiments in the Middle East from the end of the nineteenth century to the early twentieth century. First, marginalization of the ulama did not always come about through aggressive, forced secularization (though this was certainly the case in some instances). The creation of new, secular institutions often filled a vacuum left behind by the ulama's decline and did not raise as serious

---

[81] Kingston 2001, 299.
[82] Yilmaz 2011, 250.
[83] Bein 2007, 613.
[84] Khalid 2015, 136.

Anticlericalism, Religious Revival, & Rise of Religious Political

questions about the legitimacy of such institutions. Second, pushback against the authority of the ulama arose among both secularists and conservatives such as Islamists and Salafis. The fact that religious conservatives criticized the ulama implies a different path for religious revival than was the case in Western Europe.

RELIGIOUS REVIVALISM

The historic wave of anticlerical, anti-religion attacks in Western Europe and the Middle East stirred a strong response to re-establish religion's place in public and private lives. These waves were so powerful that Heilbronner considers nineteenth-century Europe not the "Age of Revolution, the Age of Capital, nor the Age of Imperialism" but rather the "Age of Catholic Revival."[85] Likewise, the twentieth century marks the age of great Islamic revival.

Religious actors did not simply accept anticlerical, anti-religion attacks passively; instead, they put up a fight.[86] The threat, as perceived by religious actors in both contexts, did not directly concern the possibility of establishing separate spheres for religion and politics or a form of secularism. After all, as Driessen puts it, such notions of separate spheres for religion and politics had "precedent in both traditions." Religious actors' perceptions of the recent and impending changes were largely shaped by how their religious authority and power would be affected by these developments. For Catholics, it meant that the Church's authority and influence was shrinking. For Muslims, it implied that those who represented Islam – that is, the ulama – were being marginalized by secular leaders and colonial powers. Religious revival movements during this period – both Catholic and Islamic in character – mobilized against the perceived danger that "the religious nature of state and society was under threat."[87]

The specific shape that religious revival efforts took greatly depended on the structure of prevailing religious institutions. While Islamic revivalism was marked by its decentralization, Catholic revivalism was primarily characterized by its organized nature. The resulting character of religious revival movements reflected not only an effort to revive religious life and elevate religion's place in modern life but also a genuine effort to re-assert the authority of the Catholic Church in Western Europe. By contrast, in the Middle East it was the new religious actors who asserted leadership in religious revival efforts, with dramatically different ramifications for the emergence of Islamic political identity.

Two pivotal dynamics were at work in the episodes of religious revival in Europe, one proximate and one structural. At the macro level, various changes

[85] Heilbronner 2008, 236.
[86] Keddie 2003, 20.
[87] Driessen 2013, 21.

The Politics of Religious Party Change

that took place over the course of the modernization period paved the way for a renewed religious fervor in Western Europe. Factors such as "demographic changes, changing economies, urbanization, and increased literacy" created a split between the interests of the Catholic Church and society at large. The Church was unsurprisingly reluctant to accept this rapidly changing society and took to the streets to create mass religious revival, attempting to counter a perceived decline in religiosity and public morality and restore respect for traditional religious authority.[88] Importantly, however, these reactions to the challenges presented by modernity were not "simply reactionary regressions to an unchanging tradition"; instead, they represented "reactive attempts, often awkward ones, to fashion its own Catholic versions of modernity."[89]

The proximate cause of religious revival movements directly concerned the anticlerical and anti-religion attacks of the nineteenth and the early twentieth centuries. Anticlerical attacks of the nineteenth century catalyzed this renewed religious fervor in Europe. The Church believed that "the people had been 'blinded' and 'bewildered,' 'bewitched' and 'bedazzled' by modern and fashionable philosophies: materialism, rationalism, liberalism, and democracy, all propagated, church leaders claimed, by an endless number of anti-Christian and antisocial newspapers."[90] Overwhelmed by liberal anticlerical attacks, the Catholic Church began mobilizing Catholics across the continent in order to usher in an episode of religious revival.[91] The revival movement was not a spontaneous response but rather centrally planned and organized by the Church.

Religious orders such as the Jesuits, Redemptorists, and Franciscans played important roles in carrying out the Church's mobilization efforts; their work was supported by local clergies all over Western Europe.[92] The Catholic orders swept across Europe "and initiated a counterrevolutionary, antiliberal, anti-Enlightenment mass religious and cultural movement." For example, missionary groups plowed through Germany beginning in 1849 and continued their missions until 1872 when religious orders were shut down as part of Kültürkampf.[93] In order to confront anticlerical attacks, address the issues of "sharp decline in religiosity, morality, and respect for traditional authority," and restore its authority, the Church "gathered German archbishops and bishops in Wurzburg and devised a plan for the restoration of Catholic religious authority across Prussian territories." This multi-pronged plan laid out various methods to achieve this goal including missionary activism, new religious organizations, and penetration of secular organizations.[94]

[88] Heilbronner 2006, 236; Altinordu 2010, 525.
[89] Casanova 2008, 12.
[90] Gross 2004, 31.
[91] Altinordu 2010, 525.
[92] Altinordu 2010, 526.
[93] Gross 2004, 35.
[94] Altinordu 2010, 526.

Anticlericalism, Religious Revival, & Rise of Religious Political

This mass revivalism was a desperate attempt by the Church to "fashion its own Catholic versions of modernity" after having "remained for centuries adamantly anti-modern and developed a negative philosophy of history, which conceptualized modern processes as so many heretical deviations from the Catholic ideal of Medieval Christendom."[95] The Church had repeatedly opposed and resisted many historical developments, including the Protestant Reformation, the Enlightenment, 1848 democratic revolutions, the rise of the secular state, and the scientific revolution. Now, the Church "had officially condemned as 'modern errors' or heresies the discourse of human rights, liberalism, Americanism and Modernism."[96]

The religious revival movement was passionate in its condemnation of "socialism, democracy, and the Enlightenment as the work of Satan" and attempted to reform both political and popular culture. Not only was "obedience to political authority as a religious duty" encouraged but "alcohol consumption and tavern life, dancing, playing cards, gambling, reading novels, foul language, and sexual license" were discouraged.[97] A Spanish clergy member's observation is a testament to the prevailing sentiment among Catholics during this period. Sarda and Salvany argued that liberalism is a sin because it contains "all heresies and errors in itself" where "a person, an organization, a book or a government for whom the Catholic Church is not the single, exclusive and only measure in matters of faith and morals" should be deemed liberal. This "social atheism" led to the Church's loss of temporal power.[98] Local authorities generally tolerated these missionary activities because they believed they contributed positively to social order.[99] The revival movement was able to reverse the secularization trend to some degree. More importantly, however, this revivalism helped create a robust Catholic political identity.

As for the Middle East, its encounter with modernity came in a somewhat different form. The demographic, economic, and educational changes occurred at a slower pace compared to Europe. For many Middle Eastern societies, modernity came in the form of colonialism, social modernization, and centralization of the state apparatus. Yet, the effect was largely similar. Religion and religious establishment came under increasing pressure and were "manipulated and marginalized by non-Muslim colonial rulers and strong-armed secular elites."[100] Like Catholics, Muslims in the Middle East faced dual challenges as modernity set in. On one hand, they faced the deep-seated structural challenges of modernity that led to the collapse of "traditional forms

---

[95] Casanova 2008, 12.
[96] Casanova 2008, 13.
[97] Altinordu 2010, 527; Gross 2004.
[98] Sarda and Salvany quoted in Lease 2000, 44–45.
[99] Gross 2004.
[100] Driessen 2013, 21.

of social solidarity";[101] the "Islamic mind" and "its belief in God and human limitations" were the direct targets.[102] Colonialism and state modernization accompanied this long-term trend. On the other hand, religion and the religious establishment were subject to anti-religion attacks.

In response to the anti-ulama, anti-religion wave in the Middle East and elsewhere, a worldwide Islamic revival emerged, owing in large part to popular disappointment with the rise of secularism, secular nation states, and Westernized ruling elites. The elite and the newly emerging regimes were increasingly seen as authoritarian, ineffective, and lacking cultural and religious authenticity. Absent the centralized and hierarchical religious structure that Catholicism enjoyed, the response to anti-religion attacks in the Middle East took different forms. In contrast to the Catholic case where the Church took on the leading role as the pre-eminent religious authority, revival efforts in the Middle East were decentralized and mobilized without the traditional ulama. The ulama lacked the organizational capacity, religious credibility, and legitimacy to initiate any such effort. Instead, the Islamic revival in the early twentieth century was spearheaded by various reformist Islamist movements throughout the region, such as the Society of Muslim Brothers in Egypt established by Hassan Al-Banna in 1928. We can identify two main responses that constitute the backbone of the Islamic revival movements in this period.

The first of these responses was Islamic modernism. Personified by Muhammad Abduh, Islamic modernism aimed to meet the challenges presented by the rise of Europe and modernity. For these modernists, casting Islam as the "religion of reason" would revitalize Muslim society and Islam in the face of European dominance.[103] The approach of Abduh, his contemporary Afghani, and fellow Islamic modernists were characterized by three predominant features: a return to the pristine form of Islam in Islam's first century, Pan-Islamism, and "selective" adoption of Western technological and social advances.[104]

The modernist response of Abduh and others was largely met with criticism. The principal critics were Islamists – the second group aiming to instigate Islamic revival. While Islamic reformists mobilized their efforts around the structural problems faced by Middle Eastern societies, Islamists first and foremost aimed to counter colonialist expansion and the receding social significance of religion. Abduh's efforts to rebrand Islam as the religion of reason was dismissed as an "apologia for Western dominance." Islamists, instead, insisted on "repudiation" of the West and its modernity.[105] For Islamists, the issues of modernity were in large part the result of societal degradation. Various Islamist ideologues presented plans for countering this degradation.

---

[101] Sedgwick 2012, 62.
[102] Abu-Rabi 1997, 12.
[103] Euben 1997, 432.
[104] Mozaffari 2009.
[105] Euben 1997, 434.

Opposition to secularism constituted a key element of Islamist revival. While the Muslim societies of the Middle East had some limited experience with secular governance in the pre-modern period, the unfolding of secularism as a uniquely modern concept in the nineteenth- and twentieth-century Muslim Middle East elicited a strong Islamist backlash. The Islamist rejection of secularism was justified in two interrelated ways. First, secularism was perceived as a foreign, colonial idea that was incongruent with Islamic ideals. Unlike Western Europe where secularism grew out of indigenous social and political dynamics, secularism in the Muslim Middle East was viewed as an imported Western idea that would be implemented by the state as part of its modernization project.[106] This association and equation between secularism and Westernization in popular conception was such that it became virtually impossible to talk about "secularism in isolation from Christian (Western colonial) supremacy."[107] Many Muslims drew a direct connection between secularism as an ideology and Western imperialism: "The fatal association of secularism with autocratic rule and Western influence helps account for the general trend against secularism in the Muslim world; when people want to be free of Western control, they don't generally envision the path to their salvation in the secularist ideas sovereign in the West."[108] Western dominance over Muslim territories in this period served to justify these fears about perceived threats from Western political ideas like secularism.[109] This concern was more pronounced among Arab societies who experienced direct colonization by European powers.[110]

The second reason for secularism's negative perception by Islamists (and broader Muslim populations) was its close association with atheism in the region. Secularism was often – and still is to a certain degree – conflated with atheism. This perception was fueled in part by the conception of secularism as a personal matter of faith. The efforts made by secular leaders such as Turkey's Atatürk to push religion out of not only politics but also public life reinforced such perceptions.[111] Likewise, secularism symbolized "human autonomy and freedom towards the moral authority of God and of religious doctrines."[112] So while many in the region held tolerant views on the separation of religion and state, at a personal level secularism and its association with atheism and irreligiosity meant that it was "much less acceptable."[113] Secularism's association with lack of religious belief did not just exist among the conservative flank of

[106] Nasr 2003, 68.
[107] Masud 2005, 364.
[108] Keddie 2003, 25.
[109] Salama and Friedman 2012, 105.
[110] Keddie 1972, 52.
[111] Nasr 2003, 68.
[112] Hoebink 1999, 39.
[113] Rabasa et al. 2007, 125.

Muslim societies – even moderate figures such as Fazlur Rahman would suggest that "secularism destroys the sanctity and universality (transcendence) of all moral values … Secularism is necessarily atheistic."[114] Likewise, state efforts to control religion as opposed to refraining from any interaction with the religious sphere reinforced the anti-religion perception of secularism in the region, which Kuru characterizes as "assertive secularism."[115]

Like Catholic revivalist movements, Islamic revival movements were motivated largely by their distaste for (secular) modernity. Despite its deep-rooted distaste for modernity and motivation to promote greater adoption of Islamic faith and culture among Muslims, Islamic revivalism was deeply embedded in modernity and can be viewed as an "expression" of modernity: "[Islamic revival movements] are a response to and an expression of Muslim modernity, but they are also rooted in a deep historical and cultural paradigm for how Muslim peoples should cope with changing political, economic and cultural realities."[116] In this regard, such movements believed that Islam offered "the blue print for a total modern society, an ideological and political alternative to liberalism, socialism or communism."[117]

The specific issues raised by Islamists included the disintegration of traditional social solidarity structures,[118] the need for unifying Muslims against colonial powers and mobilizing toward the establishment of a "powerful Islamic empire,"[119] and dismantling the Western presence and dominance in Muslim societies to revive more traditional Muslim values of society.[120] Further, Lapidus states: "They call, at least in theory, for a return to the Shari'a, or Islamic law. They call for a stripping away of many of the traditional practices and beliefs of Muslims as a false historical accretion to the pure Islam. They call for a renewed commitment to Islam in the hearts and minds of individuals as the basis of communal solidarity, social justice, and the fair treatment of the poor. They want women to return to family roles. They want to remove corrupt regimes and create Islamic states to be the protectors and enforcers of Islamic morality in Islamized societies."[121] In other words, Muslims' lives should revolve around the indivisible trinity of "Dîn [Religion], Dunya [Way of life] and Dawla [Government]."[122] For Rashid Rida – one of Abduh's disciples and an early Islamist ideologue – the panacea to the "decadence of Islam" was the restoration of "the true Islamic state," a hitherto unknown phenomenon.[123]

---

[114] Fazlur Rahman quoted in Sonn 1987, 284.
[115] Kuru 2007.
[116] Lapidus 1997, 457.
[117] Lapidus 1997, 447.
[118] Sedgwick 2012, 62.
[119] Mozaffari 2009, 4.
[120] Haider 2002, 109.
[121] Lapidus 1997, 445.
[122] Mozaffari 2007, 23.
[123] Mozaffari 2009, 10.

Anticlericalism, Religious Revival, & Rise of Religious Political

This idea of an "Islamic state" became the bedrock of the Islamist political identity; in their calls for an Islamic state, Islamists invoked various Islamic concepts and harkened back to the early Muslim history, thereby giving the ideology a distinctively historical authenticity despite its utter modernity. Early caliphs, divine sovereignty, consultation (shura), and Qur'anic references to governance frequently appeared in Islamist discourse.[124] Islamist conceptions of the perfect Islamic society were largely conditioned by a nostalgia for the past while simultaneously rejecting the present conditions that had befallen the Muslim world. In this, many found the solution "in a return by the individual Muslim and the state to the pure sources and practices of Islam, the rejection of Western influence and values, and the creation of an Islamic state."[125] Despite the yearning for a return to the glorious Islamic past, they are firmly grounded in the contemporary political context and "an abstract concept of community and moral authority."[126] Rejecting secularism as a principle of governance, Al-Banna claimed that Islam demands an Islamic form of government "as a pillar of social order."[127]

The anti-ulama and anti-religion attacks around the turn of the twentieth century led to the construction of a novel Islamic political identity that drew "new inner and outer boundaries through modern consumer goods, dress styles, manners, educational networks, demeanor, and diets" and raised "political consciousness by framing issues through the political language of Islam."[128] This identity was flexible enough to respond to changing circumstances and reinforced itself through the socialization of new recruits to Islamist movements.

The onset of modernity and secularism ushered in an episode of reimagining and reconstructing what the public and political role of religion should be not only among the liberal, secular, and anticlerical groups but also among religious sectors. Religion is politicized and new forms of religious political identities are drawn; religious actors identified the boundaries of what it means to stand up publicly for their faith; and political consciousness is now formed on the basis of religious identity and symbols. What are these new forms of religious identity? What does the modern religious consciousness look like? What are the political ramifications of such consciousness? In Chapter 4, I examine the rise of mass religious movements as the catalysts of these new Catholic and Islamic political identities, what they lay out in terms of their social and political visions, and the society they envisioned.

---

[124] Afsaruddin 2006, 154.
[125] Wetenschappelijke Raad vor het Regeringsbeleid 2006, 64.
[126] Lapidus 1997, 448.
[127] AbuKhalil 1994, 686.
[128] Yavuz 2003, 6.

4

The Origins of Religiopolitical Identity

The politicization of religion and emergence of a religious political identity in the modern period is firmly anchored in the rise of mass religious movements – a hitherto unknown phenomenon. These religious movements became the main instruments for fulfilling the newly developed religious sociopolitical vision. Not only did they play a crucial role in raising a religious generation to confront social change, secularization, and secularization of education, but they also aimed to confront deviant ideologies and remake the political system in line with their religious visions. In this distinctly political objective lie the seeds of religious political parties, which carry the missions of religious mass movements into the political arena and fight for their goals.

Religious movements embody the ideal organizational form of modern religiopolitical activism – they can lay out a vision for societal and political transformation, teach and preach this vision, and mobilize resources and communities to achieve their vision. Tracing the rise of these movements in varying religious, social, and political contexts will help to explain a crucial part of the causal argument of this book. These movements translated the bourgeoning religious responses to modernization and secularization into tangible social, religious, and political agendas. As these movements grew more political, they became the focal point of conflicts among religious actors over power and influence. Variegated trajectories of religious mass movements ultimately shaped the future of the religious parties that they produced. Despite the various forms they assumed in different contexts, what remained constant was how these movements responded to modernization and secularization, and how they competed for greater religious and political influence. This chapter analyzes the emergence of mass religious movements in the Middle East and Western Europe.

The arrival of modernity served as a major shock to the Muslim conscience in the late nineteenth and early twentieth centuries, similar to its effect on

The Origins of Religiopolitical Identity

Christianity in the nineteenth century. Increased levels of education and secularization had weakened religion and religiosity. Likewise, the Muslim societies of the Middle East experienced widespread material underdevelopment and colonial expansion. They clearly lagged behind Western societies; many lacked the political autonomy to respond to the challenges of the modern era. Following independence, the new regimes pursued secularization policies as part of their ambitious modernization reform efforts. Religion and religious actors were marginalized despite high levels of conservatism and religiosity among the population, political and economic underdevelopment reigned, and a major political opportunity emerged for the representation of religion in the political arena. These developments collectively amounted to a perfect storm for the politicization of religion.

Like their counterparts in Western Europe, religious movements of the Middle East faced a favorable political environment. Those segments of society that identified with Islam viewed religion as under threat and considered religiopolitical activism to be the way of addressing this threat, ultimately endowing religion with its rightful place in the state and society. The rise of these hybrid Islamist movement-parties, in this regard, aimed to meet societal demand for religiopolitical activism and representation. Unlike in Western Europe, however, the religious environment was permissive for these Islamist movements. Not only does Sunni Islam have a decentralized and nonhierarchical institutional structure, but the secularization policies in the early twentieth century weakened or eliminated many of the existing religious authorities. Islamist movements emerged to fill this major void.

The cases of Islamist movements and parties in Egypt, Tunisia, and Turkey illustrate how the permissiveness of the existing religious institutional structure can affect the formation and evolution of Islamist movements. As these Islamist movements first emerged in their respective societies, they faced minimal resistance from existing religious actors. The religious landscape was not dominated by any actor in a way that resembles the Catholic Church's presence in Catholic societies. Therefore when Islamists emerged, claimed to have been tasked with reestablishing religion's rightful place in state and society, and represented Islam politically, they encountered minimal if any opposition to their claims. It was only the state that pushed back against Islamist movements, yet state pushback was political in nature rather than religious. This political and religious landscape allowed Islamists to thrive as they deemed politically advantageous. As is the case with religiopolitical mobilization elsewhere, Islamist parties traced their roots to hybrid organizational structures that served many purposes. These movements aimed to revive the religious life of society not only by focusing on religious education and dawah (missionary) activism but also expanding their activism into different sectors such as healthcare, charity, and politics. Such hybrid structures fundamentally affect the audiences that Islamists target and attract. Unlike Catholic parties, who are constrained to act strictly as political parties and appeal to the whole electorate rather than a subset, Islamist parties aim to both satisfy the movement base with conservative rhetoric and appeal to the broader electorate as a political party. As a result, Islamist parties embraced unapologetically anti-system positions under pressure from movement leadership. Provided that change in the religious landscape is unlikely to happen in a short period of time, the only feasible avenue for change in Islamist parties is in the political arena. Some Islamist parties relinquished their anti-system characters only when they recognized the necessity of change due to shifts in the political arena, as I show in Chapter 5.

The Egyptian Muslim Brotherhood's rise as the first Islamist movement – and subsequent emulation of its model elsewhere in the Middle East – owed its success to the religious and political conditions in Egypt that were mirrored in the rest of the region. Hassan al-Banna established the Brotherhood in response to the degeneration of Muslims he witnessed in Egypt and carefully positioned his movement to take advantage of sociopolitical conditions at the time. In order to appeal to both members of his Brotherhood and a larger segment of Egyptians, he claimed that the Brotherhood faithfully represented the "true" Islam while preferring to craft a comprehensive – and ambiguous by nature – discourse as to what the movement stood for. As such, the Brotherhood aimed to take advantage of the space ripe for a religiopolitical actor in both the political and religious arenas.

Tunisia's Ennahdha followed a similar path to capitalize on the vacuum in both the religious and political spheres. The intensive secularization process in society left many Tunisians desiring a religious revival in the country. Ennahdha proposed a comprehensive Islamic solution to Tunisia's societal and political problems. Having sustained its anti-system stance for decades, Ennahdha underwent a monumental process of organizational change shortly after Ben Ali's removal from power. When the political faction within Ennahdha won over the religious faction, Ennahdha decided to discontinue its hybrid party-movement structure as part of its "specialization policy."

Turkey's National Outlook Movement (NOM) has roots in the permissive political and civil environment of the 1950s and the 1960s. Marginalized by the center right parties of the time, Necmettin Erbakan collaborated with a leading Sufi order to create a robust Islamist powerhouse in Turkey. Like in Egypt and Tunisia, the poor state of social, economic, and political development and disenfranchisement of society's religious segments precipitated the formation of the NOM with the explicit goal of uprooting the existing political and economic system. The process leading to the formation of the Justice and Development Party (AKP) crystallized the conflict between the politically motivated Reformist faction and religiously motivated Traditionalist faction within the NOM.

Unlike Islamist parties where efforts in the creation of a religious political identity and mass movements were decentralized and lacked a hegemonic religious authority, the rise of Catholic mass movements and subsequently

The Origins of Religiopolitical Identity

Catholic political parties in Italy, Germany, and Belgium shows the Church's central role. Growing tension between the Catholic Church (aided by ultramontanes) and the more politically oriented liberal and social Catholics came to a head in the second half of the nineteenth century.[1] By opposing efforts to establish Catholic political parties and taking measures to undermine such efforts, the Catholic Church used its institutional control over Catholicism and forced those politically inclined Catholics to make a choice: either remain subservient to the Church and accept the Church's authority or move in an independent direction for Catholic political activism outside of the Church's authority. The Catholic Church had "vested interest" in opposing Catholic parties. The Church wanted to preserve its institutional hegemony within Catholicism by refusing to legitimize a Catholic party that "claims religion as its central mission, incorporates mass Catholic organizations, and becomes a competing agent for the representation of the faithful."[2] Likewise, the Church preferred to deal with states directly in order to maintain "the immunities, prerogatives, temporalities and spheres of jurisdiction she enjoyed" as a political actor.[3] Although this choice did not directly concern Catholic parties' ideological stance and position on the existing political system, i.e., whether they were anti-system or not, autonomy from the Church turned out to be decisive.

In Germany, anticlerical and anti-Catholic attacks and discriminatory policies toward the Catholic Church mobilized Catholics into social, religious, and political activism under the church hierarchy's leadership. Catholics organized themselves into associations (Vereine) in order to more effectively fight these attacks against the Church and the Catholics. The socioreligious activism of German Catholics gave rise to a new, modern Catholic consciousness that was political in nature. This new Catholic political identity envisioned a fundamentally different religiopolitical structure where the state had a Catholic character. However, this is also the time period where two conflicting views emerged on how to achieve the Catholic political vision. The ultramontanes advocated for a strict control of the Catholic religiopolitical activism under the Church hierarchy. By contrast, the middle-class German Catholics who shouldered the Catholic activism during this period favored a degree of independence for Catholic political activism to allow Catholics to attain their political objectives. This division served as the foundation for later emergence of the Center Party despite opposition by the Church and ultramontanes.

In Italy, the Catholic Church made sure that the burgeoning Catholic social and political activism that emerged in the face of anticlerical attacks remained within the Church's hierarchical organizational umbrella. When the Church felt that Opera dei Congressi e dei Comitati Cattolici was gradually slipping away from its control in the late nineteenth and the early twentieth centuries, the

---

[1] Vaillancourt 1980, 38.
[2] Kalyvas 1998, 300.
[3] Bonacina 1951, 4.

Opera was replaced by Pope Pius X with Catholic Action. The move aimed to stem the independent-minded Catholic political activism such as the Christian Democratic movement spearheaded by Romolo Murri. Catholic Action was organized under the direct control of the Catholic Church in a parallel structure to that of the church hierarchy.

In Belgium, the religious and political mobilization of Catholics came about in response to major anticlerical attacks. When faced with the anticlerical attacks of the Liberal government in the 1850s, particularly in education, it was the collaboration between the ultramontane elements of the Catholic mass mobilization, such as the Federation and the Church, that responded to these attacks. The Catholic mass movement in Belgium formed under three major organizations that corresponded to socioeconomic divisions that existed among Belgian Catholics at the time: the Federation of Catholic Clubs and Conservative Associations, Boerenbond, and the Belgian Democratic League. The Catholic Church adamantly opposed a separate Catholic political party and instead preferred to work with the Conservative politicians in the parliament. Divisions among Catholics at the time about their preferred political strategy shaped how the Catholic Party was formed in the late nineteenth century and led to the initial marginalization of the Democratic League within the broader Catholic mass movement.

The rest of this chapter will comparatively analyze the emergence of Islamist and Catholic political identities in Egypt, Tunisia, Turkey, Italy, Germany, and Belgium, respectively. The similarities in the formative stages of these religious political identities gave way to systematic differences across the Islamist and Catholic cases; the institutional differences in religious authority structures steered the formation of religious mass movements in diverging trajectories. I trace these divergent paths to the formation of religious mass movements and brewing conflict between the religious and political factions in each case.

THE EGYPTIAN MUSLIM BROTHERHOOD

The Egyptian Muslim Brotherhood (Ikhwan al-Muslimun) is the quintessential Islamist organization. The Brotherhood's significance emanates from the success of its founding leader, Hassan al-Banna, in overseeing the "transition [of Islam] into an ideology" at a pivotal moment in modern Islamic history.[4] This was critical to the objectification of Islam in the modern age; with the new Islamist ideological blueprint at their disposal, new religious actors could assess what was happening in society, whether it conformed to their newfound Islamic visions, and how to shape society along the lines of their ideology. The movement's ability to create an ideological framework that resonated with the sentiment of its time resulted in the Brotherhood and its philosophy

---

[4] Lia 1998, 72.

The Origins of Religiopolitical Identity

permeating much of the Muslim world. Throughout the Brotherhood's long life it has survived two revolutions, multiple regime changes, and near-constant conflict, change, and reorientation, within *and* without itself. In this sense, the Brotherhood's story is one of remarkable stability amid momentous change.

The Brotherhood's value as a critical case in my analysis derives from its unique ability to reign in the political element within its body as a religious movement, which is in sharp contrast to Catholic parties that were forced to forge a distinct political path. Despite its initial political orientation, the Brotherhood resisted forming a separate political body until the 2011 Revolution. In terms of the separation between the religious movement and the political party, the Brotherhood's trajectory reflects the balance of power between the two within the organizational structure of the movement. Even when many young Brothers gained invaluable political experience throughout the 1970s, 1980s, and 1990s on college campuses and in professional associations, the Brotherhood frustrated their passionate efforts to carry the movement's presence into the political arena. This was never about the ideological direction of the proposed political party; organizational control and maintaining the hierarchical structure superseded all other considerations. When the opportunity for legalization arose in 2011, the Brotherhood made a deliberate choice to create a political party that operated fully subservient to the movement. The Freedom and Justice Party (FJP) leadership maintained their official positions in the Brotherhood's general leadership body, regularly held coordination meetings with high-ranking Brotherhood officials, and largely outsourced mobilization and recruitment to the Brotherhood organization. This decision reflected the movement's deep-seated concern with sustaining its comprehensive approach to religiopolitical activism. The Brotherhood's claim to speak on behalf of religion necessitated a hierarchical organizational structure that upheld its venerated position.

The Origins of the Movement

Decades before Islamism emerged in other countries as an organized religiopolitical movement, Hassan al-Banna, a schoolteacher and imam, founded the Muslim Brotherhood in 1928 in response to the sociopolitical changes facing Egypt.[5] During this time, Egypt had gained partial independence from Britain, albeit with significant restrictions on its domestic and foreign policy. To the dismay of many, British colonialism, along with broader intellectual currents in the region, was gradually Westernizing and secularizing Egypt.[6] Hence, al-Banna and his followers concerned themselves with developments within and beyond the Muslim world. On one hand, the West constituted a

---

[5] Bilinski 2013, 27; Rodrigo 2014, 7.
[6] Sattar 1995, 9.

constant source of corrupting influence on the Muslim world, both materially and morally.[7] European civilization was, according to al-Banna, afflicted not only with "apostasy, doubt in God, denial of the soul" but also a variety of "materialistic traits" and sins such as "licentiousness, unseemly dedication to pleasures, versatility in self-indulgence, unconditioned freedom for the lower instincts, gratification of the lusts of the belly and the genitals, the equipment of women with every technique of seduction and incitement ... Individual selfishness ... class selfishness ... [and] usury." These ills in Western societies ultimately led to the "corruption of the spirit, the weakening of morality, and flaccidity in the war against crime."[8] The West brought their "wine, women, and sin."[9] Moreover, the West corrupted Muslim countries with "their half-naked women ... their liquors, their theaters, their dance halls, their amusements, their stories, their newspapers, their novels, their whims, their silly games, and their vices"; schools and cultural organizations established by Western countries served to "disparage their [Muslims'] religion and their fatherland, divest themselves of their traditions and beliefs."[10] For al-Banna, Western civilization was built on "scientific perfection" but faced a declining trajectory and "crumbling" foundations.[11] As such, the Christian West posed as the diabolical antagonist of the Muslim East. The leaders of Muslim societies faced a choice between the "way of Islam" and the "way of the West."[12] In important ways, this conception of the West mirrored Catholic mass movements' demonization of modern, secular Europe as a threat to Catholicism and the Catholic faithful.

On the other hand, the Brotherhood bemoaned Muslims' own failures to uphold the Islamic moral character and reform themselves. The problem, however, went beyond individual failures; it was systemic and demanded national action and governmental response. Muhammad Abduh's reformist efforts failed because they faced a secular backlash viewing religion and religious activism as "reactionary," leading to a weakened religious class that was extremely "anxious" about the rise of secularism.[13] In this context, a call for state action sets the Brotherhood and all subsequent Islamist movements apart from previous forms of Islamic reformist activism. Al-Banna wrote that each nation should bring its laws and regulations in line with "the proprieties of religion and consistent with Islamic legislation and its ordinances"; laws such as those that legalize prostitution are "a mark of shame" for nations, particularly so for Muslim societies because Islam "commands them to wage war on prostitution and to punish

---

[7] Aly and Wenner 1982, 337.
[8] Al-Banna 1978a, 26.
[9] Mitchell 1993, 223.
[10] Al-Banna 1978a, 28.
[11] Al-Banna 1978d, 106.
[12] Al-Banna 1978d, 104–05.
[13] Kandil 2015, 124.

The Origins of Religiopolitical Identity

adulterers severely."[14] Likewise, al-Banna took issue with the fact that alcohol was promoted on the "most prominent streets … and the most elegant quarters" of Egyptian cities when Islam prohibits alcohol consumption.[15] There was an "ethical duality" between Islamic and Western lifestyles, particularly evident in the legal and educational systems.[16] This sharp duality underlaid the ideological foundation of Islamist groups throughout the region in the twentieth century, including the NOM in Turkey and Ennahdha in Tunisia.

For al-Banna, these social developments were not happening in isolation; rather, what happened in the political realm carried major ramifications for social and religious spheres. The promotion of "freedom and democracy" by some political actors during this time merely served to promote "dissolution and libertinism" at the societal level: "I saw the social life of the beloved Egyptian people, oscillating between her dear and precious Islam which she had inherited, defended, lived with during fourteen centuries, and this severe Western invasion which was armed and equipped with all destructive influences of money, wealth, prestige, ostentation, power and means of propaganda."[17] Such "Western invasion" spared neither the caliphate in Istanbul nor Egyptian institutions.

These dual problems faced by Muslims – Western influence and Muslims' failure to morally reform themselves – necessitated a two-step political solution. First, the Muslim lands needed to be emancipated from all forms of foreign occupation and domination. Because foreign, that is, Western, influence and control permeated all areas of life, no reform or reconstruction could take place unless such influence ceased first. Second, an "Islamic state" – an entirely novel and modern concept – should be established to uphold Islamic principles; the "Muslim state" of the pre-modern period did not suffice.[18] Crucially for al-Banna, the creation of this Islamic state was not merely voluntary but incumbent on all Muslims: "For as long as this state [Islamic state] does not emerge, the Muslims in their totality are committing sin, and are responsible before God the Lofty, the Great, for their failure to establish it and for their slackness in creating it."[19] Yet, the idea of such an Islamic state was grounded in "generalities" and "imprecision."[20]

It is here that the Brotherhood's relevance to the solution of Egyptians' woes, and those of Muslims' more broadly, becomes apparent. Al-Banna did not want to constrain the movement to a purely religious or political organization. Instead, the Brotherhood needed to engender a "new spirit" that would

[14] Al-Banna 1978e, 89.
[15] Al-Banna 1978e, 90.
[16] Mitchell 1993, 223.
[17] Lia 1998, 28.
[18] Mitchell 1993, 235.
[19] Al-Banna 1978a, 31.
[20] Mitchell 1993, 245.

find its way to the "heart" of the nation by reviving it through the Qur'an.[21] Belief without action – much like Muslims have been doing for centuries – reinforced the separation and growing dissonance between the religious and political spheres. Muslims had to "translate their faith into sociopolitical activism" and bring their "religiosity" over to the public arena.[22] Al-Banna's comprehensive approach to religion and religiopolitical activism resembled Catholic mass movements' organizational response to the secular modernist threat against religion. Both Catholic and Islamist movements were convinced that the totality of religion was under attack; therefore, the response needed to be comprehensive in nature.

The line between the political and the religious was blurred by design. An "Islamic state" aims to inform the political through the religious and relies on the existence of a porous relationship between the two spheres; a clear division would defeat this purpose. For the Brotherhood, Islam defied compartmentalization or being constrained to certain religious rites and rituals; there could not be any distinction between religion and politics.[23] Rather, Islam stood for *shumuliya* (comprehensiveness). Because Islam encompasses and regulates all aspects of life, the political cannot be divorced from the religious – an assertion that al-Banna draws from the Qur'an and the practice of the first generation of Muslims.[24] The Fifth Congress of the Brotherhood dealt with "the Islam of the Muslim Brothers"[25] and defined *shumuliya* thusly: "We believe that the rules and teachings of Islam are comprehensive in organizing people's affairs in this life and the next, and that those who believe that these teachings only cover worship and spiritual matters are mistaken. Islam is belief and worship; homeland and citizenship; religion and state; spirituality and practice; revelation and sword."[26] This comprehensiveness, however, lacked substance and applicability. As Mitchell stated, the Brotherhood used comprehensiveness "without much specification as to what [it] meant in terms of government theory and practice."[27] Nonetheless, the certainty of this comprehensive approach comforted those who sought safety in an "uncertain world."[28]

Importantly, the Brotherhood did not restrict its domain to Egypt when it was founded. Islam's universal message tasked the Brotherhood with the responsibility to "establish sovereignty" around the world in order to institute Islamic principles for humanity's well-being[29] and restore the caliphate.[30]

---

[21] Al-Banna 1978a, 36.
[22] Kandil 2015, 51.
[23] Krämer 2010, 51.
[24] Al-Banna 1978c, 46.
[25] Mitchell 1993, 14.
[26] Kandil 2015, 86.
[27] Mitchell 1993, 40.
[28] Pargeter 2013, 21.
[29] Al-Banna 1978e, 72.
[30] Pevna 2014, 8.

The Origins of Religiopolitical Identity

Islam should shape the constitutions of each Muslim society; any law that does not conform with Islam should be "expunged."[31] Likewise, the legal system should derive from "the prescriptions of the Islamic Sacred Law, drawn from the Noble Qur'an, and in accordance with the basic sources of Islamic jurisprudence."[32] Al-Banna's religiopolitical activism fed off his deep personal connection with Rashid Rida, whose Islamic journal, *al-Manar*, al-Banna closely followed.[33] Al-Banna visited Rida frequently,[34] leading Rida to believe that al-Banna shared his vision and held great promise to combat secularism, revive the caliphate, and establish the inseparability of Islam and state.[35] As a testament to the strength of their relationship, al-Banna continued the publication of *al-Manar* in 1939 after Rida's death.[36] Al-Banna even contributed to the journal by publishing fatwas himself. But by September 1940, *al-Manar* was shut down by the Egyptian government.[37]

Creating the Brotherhood Brand

The kind of religiopolitical discourse and activism promoted by al-Banna was unprecedented in the Muslim world; it aimed to catapult the Brotherhood into the crowded space of contemporary religious actors. This was a key difference between the rise of Islamist movements and Catholic mass movements in Europe; while Catholic movements enjoyed the Church's status as the dominant religious actor, Islamists felt the need to carve a niche for themselves in a growing field of religious actors. This key difference ultimately shaped how each viewed the function of religiopolitical activism, thereby affecting the future organizational structures of Catholic and Islamist political parties. There were approximately 135 Islamic associations in Egypt in the post–World War I period.[38] As such, it meant that the Brotherhood would have to compete – and clash, if necessary – with existing religious actors. The views promoted by the Brotherhood and al-Banna on religious topics were "novel and unconventional," frequently pitting them against the well-established "religious elite" of Ismailia.[39] Al-Banna was careful in how he treaded the religious landscape of Egypt. Instead of repeating what existing religious actors had done, he aimed to create a niche for his brand of religiopolitical activism and gain legitimacy in the process. To achieve this goal, he undertook a series of steps. Al-Banna

---

[31] Al-Banna 1978e, 88–89.
[32] Al-Banna 1978e, 89.
[33] Krämer 2010, 16.
[34] Mitchell 1993, 5.
[35] Kandil 2015, 125.
[36] Lia 1998.
[37] Krämer 2010, 54.
[38] Zakariyya Bayumi quoted in Al-Anani 2016, 172.
[39] Lia 1998, 21–22.

first distinguished between religious doctrine and religious authority. In doing so, al-Banna contrasted the (Catholic) West and the Muslim world; religious authorities had a fundamentally different role in Islam compared to how clergy produced and reinforced religious doctrine in the West: "The jurisdiction of the religious authorities in Islam is circumscribed and limited, powerless to alter its statutes or to subvert its institutions, with the result that the fundamental principles of Islam, across the centuries, have kept pace with the changing eras, and have advocated progress, supported learning, and defended scholars."[40] This distinction critically underscored the limits of the power wielded by the current religious establishment. Not only that, al-Banna clearly created a wedge between Islam as a faith and the religious authorities that represented the faith – he blamed the religious establishment for the flaws associated with religion in this period, effectively absolving the faith itself. Such flaws included "selfish interests and worldly ambitions over the welfare of the country and the nation" – a line of attack that aimed to undermine the religious establishment in a period of colonialism.[41] For their part, the ulama did little to dispel the attacks from both seculars and Islamic reformists. The ulama collectively failed to rise to the occasion and ensured their ultimate irrelevance, leading to their marginalization "as a fossilized lot."[42]

Al-Banna was wary of how the clergy was treated with "an annihilatory attitude" in the West, ultimately leading to the marginalization of religion in the public sphere. He wanted to avoid the same fate for Islam; the faith had to remain central, yet those religious authorities who drifted away from Islam could be repudiated without impunity.[43] Al-Banna did not hold back in his criticism of such ulama and how they, in his perception, failed the Muslim community. For example, his first publication in Majallat al-Fath in 1928 asked of the ulama: "What catastrophe has befallen the souls of the reformers and the spirit of the leaders? What has carried away the ardour of the zealots? What calamity had made them prefer this life to the thereafter? What has made them … consider the way of struggle [sabil al-jihad] too rough and difficult?"[44] Just like Rashid Rida did,[45] al-Banna clashed with Youssef al-Digwi and berated him "for being insufficiently concerned with the secular onslaught,"[46] although al-Banna sought him out to recruit him to his cause in the first place.[47]

The path forward entailed reforming the current religious authority structure as represented by the ulama and the religious establishment toward "true"

---

[40] Al-Banna 1978d, 122.
[41] Al-Banna 1978d, 123.
[42] Kandil 2015, 123.
[43] Al-Banna 1978d, 123.
[44] Al-Banna quoted in Lia 1998, 33.
[45] Ryad 2009, 32.
[46] Kandil 2015, 127.
[47] Krämer 2010, 23.

The Origins of Religiopolitical Identity

Islam – a conception of Islam in line with the Brotherhood's view of Islam.[48] This notion of "true" Islam represents an effort by the Brotherhood (and other Islamist groups) to legitimize their approach to religion in marked contrast to the Catholic cases, who did not need such legitimization because of the Church's dominant religious authority. The General Law of the Muslim Brotherhood stated that the organization's goal was "to raise a generation of Muslims who would understand Islam *correctly* [emphasis added] and act according to its teachings."[49] This "true" Islam was best represented by the "illustrious ulama" of Islam's Golden Age who would "burst in upon kings and princes, past their gates and walls, censuring them, forbidding them, rejecting their gifts, declaring what the truth was before them, and bringing them the demands of the nation."[50] This unmistakable commitment to "true" Islam revealed itself in the way religion was contrasted with modernity, grounded in neo-traditionalist rhetoric of authenticity, and rebuffed deeper penetration of modernity in the society.[51] Despite this distaste for modernity, the Brotherhood viewed Islam as capable of providing answers to many modern social, economic, and political problems in sharp contrast to the "religious scripturalism" of the contemporary ulama.[52] Islam was transformed into an active "operative force" to solve modern problems.[53] By doing this, the Brotherhood rejected the idea of constraining religion to the private sphere. Instead, the group opted to expand the scope of religion's applicability to all areas of life. The "functionalization" of Islam by the Brotherhood mobilized religion for a variety of "social and political projects."[54]

Al-Banna justified expanding the scope of what religious authority means and entails.[55] The Brotherhood's conception of Islam demanded that each believer be equipped with religious authority "from the least to the most outstanding of them."[56] As a bourgeoning religiopolitical actor, the Brotherhood needed a niche in the religiopolitical space. Such a drastic reshaping of what religious authority meant served to justify the Brotherhood's depiction of themselves as "the voice of Islam."[57] Because of the Brotherhood's commitment to "true" Islam, al-Banna cautioned his followers against the pushback they might experience; the Brotherhood's activism could potentially alienate the

---

[48] Mitchell 1993, 232.
[49] Lia 1998, 102.
[50] Al-Banna 1978d, 123.
[51] Meijer 1995, 33.
[52] Lia 1998, 74.
[53] Cantwell Smith 1957, 156.
[54] Starrett 1998, 10.
[55] For a discussion of contemporary conflicts over religious authority in Egypt, see Karim El Taki, "Rivalry for Religious Dominance in Egypt," *Sada*, December 21, 2017. Available at: https://carnegieendowment.org/sada/75093 (accessed September 18, 2020)
[56] Al-Banna 1978d, 124.
[57] Krämer 2010, 38.

ulama and draw their antagonism.[58] Al-Banna claimed that "ignorance" about what Islam means and what it requires might undermine the Brotherhood's activism: "... you will find among the clerical classes and the religious establishment those who will regard your understanding of Islam as outlandish, and censure your campaign on that account."[59] Understandably, this redefinition of religious authority put the Brotherhood on a collision course with al-Azhar – the premier historical institution of Islamic learning in Egypt and the rest of the Sunni world – and turned them into direct competitors. Al-Banna called into question al-Azhar's claim to speak on behalf of Sunni Islam and "bitterly disputed" their weak opposition to raging currents of atheism and missionary activity.[60] The Brotherhood's disputation of al-Azhar's status as the "voice of Islam" served to reinforce the claim that the Brotherhood now stood as "champions" of Islam.[61] It was al-Banna's personal relationship with al-Azhar Shaikh Mustafa al-Maraghi that mitigated the severity of the conflict.[62]

Hassan al-Banna grew increasingly frustrated with the religious disputes undertaken by the ulama in mosques, the weak state of the religious establishment, and those who represented Islam in the late 1920s in Ismailia. He decided that his religiopolitical activism would be best served outside traditional religious spaces such as the mosque, an idea that would be emulated by many Islamist groups around the region in following years.[63] A novel idea at the time, the move sought to expand the religious field, find greater resonance with Egyptians, and gain traction among a segment of the population that typically fell outside conventional religious spaces. To this end, al-Banna visited coffee houses early on to recruit new members. As one Brotherhood member explains, "It is better to come with an empty glass. You learn faster. This is why Banna frequented coffee houses and popular neighborhoods not mosques and intellectual salons."[64] Al-Banna would visit approximately 20 coffee houses every night and deliver five-minute speeches early in his activism. According to one account, he visited nearly three quarters of more than 4,000 Egyptian villages.[65] The preference for reaching out to those outside of the traditional base of religious activism continued well into the 1970s and more recently. For example, Abdel Moneim Aboul Fotouh – a former top official in the Brotherhood – recounts that he and his associates back in the 1970s had "little [religious] heritage or political tradition to draw on. We did not know much about the logic and philosophy of the state, and made do with

---

[58] Kandil 2015, 116.
[59] Al-Banna 1978a, 34.
[60] Mitchell 1993, 5. For a recent analysis of how Egyptian President Abd al-Fattah al-Sisi's policies might be compromising al-Azhar's moral authority, see Bano (2018).
[61] Mitchell 1993, 212.
[62] Krämer 2010, 60.
[63] Lia 1998, 33.
[64] Mikkawi quoted in Kandil 2015, 10.
[65] Kandil 2015, 186.

The Origins of Religiopolitical Identity

very primitive ideas".[66] Targeting nonconventional audiences boosted the Brotherhood's claim to represent Islam.

Despite the Brotherhood's reservations about the religious establishment, the group pursued a nonconfrontational attitude toward other religious actors. If the Brotherhood was to gain popularity and assume a leadership role in the revival of the Muslim world, gaining legitimacy through commonalities – instead of confrontation – had to be the key tactic to achieve this goal. In order to avoid direct confrontation with the religious establishment, the Brotherhood chose to focus on issues that brought together Muslims from across the theological spectrum instead of harping on divisive issues. The Brotherhood's primary mobilization focused on uncontentious issues from a conservative perspective, such as upholding religious rituals, increasing religious education, and eliminating prostitution. Issues with obvious political relevance and massive popularity such as support for the Palestinian cause, anticolonial mobilization, and anti-Christian missionary action constituted the front and center of Brotherhood activism.[67] This ability to harness political activism with religious flavor and remain politically engaged appealed to a generation of predominantly younger Egyptians, who grew up in conventionally religious environments while feeling disillusioned by the apolitical and aloof disposition of the traditional religious elite.[68]

Yet, despite expressing strong commitment to the unity of the Muslim community,[69] the Brotherhood tended to view itself differently from the rest of the faithful. It saw itself as "an avant-garde elevated above them" that was tasked with the mission to bring other Muslims out of their inertia and mobilize them with their "true" conception of Islam.[70] The Brothers did not consider themselves an "ideological movement"; instead, they were simply "an island of awakened Muslims amidst an oblivious community."[71] For the Brotherhood, the movement was well positioned to lead the community because of its "proper program of action," devout members, and "trustworthy" leadership.[72]

The Brotherhood's organizational structure was key to this process of enlightenment. The Brotherhood formally registered as an organization with the Egyptian state in 1930 when members of the Brotherhood built a mosque on land donated by Muhammad Effendi Sulayman.[73] The kind of organization al-Banna conceived was different than its contemporaries. The first few years of its existence were shaped largely as a welfare organization, though

---

[66] Aboul Fotouh quoted in Kandil 2015, 10.
[67] Lia 1998, 113.
[68] Lia 1998, 74.
[69] Mitchell 1993, 216.
[70] Lia 1998, 85.
[71] Kandil 2015, 50–51.
[72] Al-Banna 1978c, 64.
[73] Lia 1998, 40.

with significant differences from its contemporaries. Prioritizing the Islamic education of "a new generation of Muslims," the Brotherhood focused on the "moral upbringing" of its members with a sense of Sufism.[74] In this sense, al-Banna saw the "nucleus" of the Brotherhood in the Hasafi Benevolent Society (al-Jam'iyya al-Khayriyya al-Hasafiyya) of the 1920s as a hybrid of a Sufi order and a modern association.[75]

Despite having its roots firmly grounded in a traditional structure of an Islamic charitable organization, the Brotherhood was innovative and adapted to the needs of a new age. In order to appeal to a younger audience, the Brotherhood mobilized youth preacher corps. Acknowledging how mass communication and increased literacy shifted the way religious authority and leadership were constructed,[76] al-Banna ensured that the Brotherhood engaged in modern techniques for disseminating its message and propaganda.[77] To this end, the Brotherhood published fatwas on various contemporary issues such as Qur'anic recitation on the radio and women's dress.[78] Focus on novel techniques of engagement reflected the Brotherhood's new ideological vision that viewed religion as capable of producing comprehensive solutions to the social, economic, and political problems of society.[79] This comprehensive outlook contrasted sharply with the traditional Islamic activism of the ulama that operated on a "division of labor" and only focused on the religious sphere. The nature of the Brotherhood's approach ran counter to Islamic history.[80] In the words of Hazem Kandil, Ikhwan was "making an unusually inauthentic bid in the name of authenticity."[81] While the explicit politicization of the movement's agenda took some time to materialize in its program, the Brotherhood was deeply steeped in political activism since its formation despite claims to the contrary.[82] Islamist groups throughout the region, including Tunisia's Ennahdha and Turkey's NOM, emulated the innovative organizational structure ushered in by the Brotherhood.

It is crucial to emphasize that the Brotherhood did not want to be simply another political party on the block or toe the line with an existing party. Al-Banna's relationship with the Young Men's Muslim Association (YMMA) illustrates this point. Al-Banna became a member of the YMMA in 1927 before he established the Muslim Brotherhood;[83] over time, however, he grew

---

[74] Lia 1998, 37.
[75] Krämer 2010, 16.
[76] For example, Brooke and Ketchley (2018) find that the Brotherhood expanded in areas with higher rates of literacy and railway connection.
[77] Mitchell 1993, 13; Lia 1998, 53.
[78] Krämer 2010, 115.
[79] Mitchell 1993, 232–33.
[80] Zubaida 2005; Hallaq 2012.
[81] Kandil 2015, 116.
[82] Munson 2001.
[83] Mitchell 1993, 7.

The Origins of Religiopolitical Identity

dissatisfied with the YMMA for two reasons. First, al-Banna became increasingly uneasy with the lack of emphasis on Islamic education in the YMMA. Without tackling the main issue that crippled Egyptians, that is, the Egyptian youth's "excessive fascination and infatuation with Western culture and habits" at the expense of the Islamic traditions and culture, al-Banna believed YMMA stood no chance of success.[84] The extent of the educational activism and activities of Christian missionaries in the Muslim Middle East during this period required that Islamic education take a central role in the reform effort, a position that paralleled the Catholic preoccupation with education policy in Western Europe. Islamic education had to go "beyond the mosque, the school and the press" and needed to be linked to "larger social and political concerns, giving it new shape and momentum."[85] Second, the YMMA's overt ties to the political establishment through Hizb al-Watani potentially undermined their seriousness of purpose and commitment to the idea of Islamic reform. For al-Banna, the commitment had to be first and foremost to the Islamic cause; politics and political connections could aid in realizing this Islamic vision but they could not supplant it.[86] At a pragmatic level, the Brotherhood also avoided overt political activism that mirrored other political groups because of the skepticism they faced from local authorities. The use of traditionally religious spaces such as mosques for political activism was frowned upon by these authorities, yet the Brotherhood boosted its legitimacy with the use of mosques.[87] When the Brotherhood called for "reinstating Islamic values and traditions" rather than plain political goals, it resonated deeply with local authorities who witnessed a gradual process of secularization undermining their social and political relevance.[88] Overall, the Brotherhood took on the character of a modern social movement with "the attributes of a mass political party."[89]

Politicizing the Islamist cause offered key advantages for the Muslim Brotherhood. Existing religious communities and societies faced significant challenges in their largely nonpolitical orientations; they were not able to attract committed members and mobilize their members with purely religious activism. Likewise, many simply lacked the resources to expand the scope of their activities or the geographic areas they served. The Brotherhood, by contrast, embraced politicization of religious discourse. For example, the organization did not merely preach against prostitution but pro-actively courted governmental action, recognizing the growing role that the state assumed in organizing social life; al-Banna wrote to the Minister of Interior asking for an

---

[84] Lia 1998, 55.
[85] Krämer 2010, 29.
[86] Heyworth-Dunne 1950, 36.
[87] Mitchell 1993, 9.
[88] Lia 1998, 132.
[89] Krämer 2010, 36.

end to legal prostitution in 1932.[90] Al-Banna redefined Islam as an inherently political religion; politics was "an integral part of Islam" and the Brotherhood youth had the freedom to engage in causes that were political in nature.[91] In the early 1930s, al-Banna argued that the "Islamic mission" was the responsibility of the government, the parliament, and the wealthy elite, in descending order. This duty of Islamic mission fell upon scholars and others only after that. As the Brotherhood grew in size and reach across Egypt, Sufist elements within the movement were marginalized in favor of more explicit politicization that took public positions on issues, such as the nationalization of the Suez Canal. Note that al-Banna's stance on Islam being a fundamentally political religion dates back to the early days of the Brotherhood's foundation; explicit politicization of the movement such as acquiring an outright anti-imperialist and liberationist tone,[92] however, followed in later years after Brotherhood statutes dropped the political noninvolvement clause.[93] In May 1938, al-Banna declared in the weekly magazine al-Nadhir "the beginning of their involvement in the external and internal political struggle."[94] This explicit politicization lacked an agenda or specific political program; instead, it was characterized by a rejection of party politics and factionalism.[95]

While critical to their success, politics was not the only popular draw for the Brotherhood. The group undertook a slew of activities that tackled social justice issues, engaged in charitable work, and provided healthcare and educational services.[96] Such social work was particularly instrumental in expanding the Brotherhood's presence into rural and poor suburban areas. The social work of the movement helped the Brotherhood in another way as well. Christian missionary activism was viewed as a particularly pernicious threat to Egyptian (Muslim) society because of the pervasiveness of poverty, which could leave many poor Egyptians vulnerable to missionaries' religious messages. As Lia explains, "Although very few Muslims actually converted, rumours of Muslim girls being kidnapped and forcibly converted to Christianity by foreigners aroused strong feelings among many Muslims in Egypt."[97] Throughout the 1920s and 1930s, Christian missionary activism spurred the growth of Islamic activism. A direct political implication of this close association between missionary activity and corresponding Islamic activism was the perception that the state was incapable of defending the faithful. By offering social services, the Brotherhood filled the vacuum created by the government and reduced

[90] Lia 1998, 67–68.
[91] Lia 1998, 58.
[92] Krämer 2010, 29.
[93] Lia 1998, 68.
[94] Mitchell 1993, 16.
[95] Krämer 2010, 52.
[96] Lia 1998, 109.
[97] Lia 1998, 112.

The Origins of Religiopolitical Identity

Egyptian society's perceived susceptibility to missionary activism, thereby building its societal base in the process. As a result of the combination of these factors, the movement grew to be the largest mass movement in the country at the time.

Early Years of the Brotherhood

Al-Banna's organization was founded in Ismailiyya, near the Suez Canal Zone. The British presence and influence permeated all corners of life here, "where all the signs of Western civilization, oppression and colonization were most clearly visible ... creat[ing] a sense of alienation in the Egyptian in his own country."[98] Al-Banna soon gained followers and branches of the Brotherhood started opening throughout Egypt. The first official Muslim Brotherhood branch opened in Ismailiyya in 1931. Al-Banna made frequent trips to each branch in Egypt, ensuring uniformity of operation across branches. In 1932, the main headquarters of the Brotherhood moved to Cairo, where the movement was gaining ground among university students. Fifteen branches were established (most being in the Nile Delta region), and annual conferences commenced. The first general congress was held in 1933 with a focus on Christian missionary activity.[99] In this congress, the General Guidance Bureau was established, consisting of 15 members and remaining the central decision-making body of the movement to this day. Unsurprisingly, al-Banna was the first General Guide of the movement.[100] A three-tiered membership structure was also established during this conference. At the lowest level, members only had to hold a membership card and pay dues. At the middle tier, they were "required to demonstrate a knowledge of the Society's principles, attend meetings regularly, and perform an oath of obedience." On top of the prior level's obligations, members at the highest level had to study the Qur'an regularly, observe all Islamic religious practices, and engage in physical exercise.[101] The membership structure changed shape over time; since the 1970s, it has maintained a five-tiered structure.[102]

Serving to further aid in the movement's cohesion, an official weekly Brotherhood newspaper (Jaridat al-Ikhwan al-Muslimin) was established in 1933, although it suffered over the years from poor funding and lack of readership.[103] The Brotherhood printed a handful of other publications between 1939 and 1941 until the Egyptian government, pressured by the British, shut all of them down. Around this time, the movement had approximately 150

---

[98] Aly and Wenner 1982, 399.
[99] Mitchell 1993, 13.
[100] Rodrigo 2014, 10.
[101] Munson 2001, 497.
[102] Al-Anani 2016, 93.
[103] Krämer 2010, 44.

official branches and 20,000 members.[104] Some estimates put membership up to 500,000 and the total number of branches between 1,000 and 1,500 by the mid-1940s.[105] This exponential increase in membership was due to a series of factors: "Its [Brotherhood's] activities and the numerous services it provided through the construction of private mosques, hospitals, modest commercial projects and the creation of educational foundations for religious teaching and the eradication of illiteracy; to its proselytism through the publication of books and magazines; and to its position on certain geopolitical issues, notably its support for the Palestinian uprising of 1936"[106] where they "raised funds, purchased weapons, and sent volunteers to fight."[107]

Al-Banna is often considered to have been a Weberian charismatic leader, but the movement was not without schism and dissent. The most serious break occurred in 1939 with the formation of a new group called Muhammad's Youth, which was inclined toward violence.[108] Despite these internal conflicts, the Brotherhood's growth pushed it to rival the Wafd for the largest mass movement in Egypt at the time. The Brotherhood planned on running in the parliamentary elections of March 1942, but the plan was shelved under pressure. The Brotherhood, including al-Banna, ran in the legislative elections of January 1945 but failed to win seats.[109] The Brothers who took part in political activism and public affairs during this period did so "in the name of Islam."[110] The Brotherhood offered guidance to the community and leaders of Egyptian society in line with their vision of a comprehensive Islamic order, or *al-Nizam al-Islami*, although this comprehensiveness came across as vague to others.[111] Addressing branch leaders in 1945, al-Banna defended the Brotherhood's ambiguity by declaring that "We are Islam."[112]

Al-Banna was briefly imprisoned by the British for his political activities in the early 1940s. Upon his release, al-Banna agreed to the establishment of a secret paramilitary wing of the Brotherhood. The wing was so secretive that even fellow Brotherhood members did not know who was or was not involved.[113] This militia based on volunteers from the movement came to be known as the Special Order (al-Tanzim al-Khass) under Saleh Ashwami's leadership.[114] It took part in the 1948 War in support of Palestinians and carried out targeted attacks against the British in the Suez Canal region. Increasing

[104] Lia 1998, 94–97.
[105] Lia 1998, 154; Krämer 2010, 69.
[106] Rodrigo 2014, 7.
[107] Sattar 1995, 10.
[108] El-Ghobashy 2005, 376.
[109] Krämer 2010, 64.
[110] Krämer 2010, 39.
[111] Mitchell 1993, 234; Krämer 2010, 50.
[112] Kandil 2015, 86.
[113] Zollner 2009, 12.
[114] Mitchell 1993, 205; Krämer 2010, 70; Pargeter 2013, 27.

The Origins of Religiopolitical Identity

unrest and uncertainty in post–World War II Egypt ultimately led the regime to declare a state of emergency, and the Muslim Brotherhood organization was dissolved on December 8, 1948. In response, the Special Order resorted to "urban violence, assassinating politicians and judges, and blowing up public buildings" although al-Banna "disowned" these acts of violence directed at Egyptians.[115] The paramilitary wing assassinated the prime minister, Muhammad Fahim al-Nuqrashi on December 28, 1948. A few weeks later, the government in turn assassinated al-Banna.[116]

Hassan Ismail al-Hudaybi succeeded al-Banna as General Guide (1949–72), but he was not the leader al-Banna was. At the time he received criticism for his failure to maintain the unity of the movement, perceived weakness, and not doing enough in the face of Nasser's despotism. More recently, however, many recognize al-Hudaybi as being of vital importance to the Brotherhood, especially in terms of its shift toward and solidification of nonviolent ideology.[117]

By the early 1950s, the Muslim Brotherhood had replaced the Wafd Party as the largest political and social actor in Egypt. In 1952, it became involved with the anti-British campaign and the activism to overthrow the Egyptian monarchy. Along with the Free Officers and other revolutionary groups, the Brotherhood undertook operations against the British in the Suez Canal Zone. Meanwhile, groups in urban centers began protesting, leading to the withdrawal of the British and eventual downfall of the monarch, King Faruq.[118] This resulted in independence for both Egypt and Sudan, the establishment of a republic in Egypt, and the installation of Gamal Abdel Nasser – leader of the Free Officers – as president of Egypt.

Due to their association with the Free Officers and help in the revolution, Nasser gave the Brotherhood preferential treatment in the post-1952 period, even after banning all of Egypt's political parties.[119] Nasser's motivation for this treatment rested on the belief that the Brotherhood could counter Marxist forces in the country. The honeymoon did not last long for either side, however; al-Hudaybi soon realized that Nasser's socialism was incompatible with the Brotherhood's ideology. The Brotherhood called on Nasser to pursue an Islamic course in government with demands such as prohibiting alcohol and gambling. The Brotherhood was especially displeased with the Suez Canal agreement between Nasser and the British; movement ideologue Sayyid Qutb even went as far as calling to seize control of the government.

After a rogue member of the Brotherhood attempted to assassinate Nasser in 1954, the organization was declared illegal and thousands of members were imprisoned, including al-Hudaybi, who received a life sentence. Nasser later

---

[115] Kandil 2015, 91.
[116] Sattar 1995, 10; Pargeter 2013, 30.
[117] Zollner 2009, 9.
[118] Sattar 1995, 17; Alexander 2011.
[119] Zohny 2019.

granted amnesty to the Brotherhood in 1964, again becoming uncomfortable with the growing influence of Marxism in the country. However, another crackdown occurred just a year later when Nasser declared that the Brotherhood was planning to assassinate him and overthrow the government. Most notably, Qutb was executed during this second crackdown.[120] Qutb's legacy outlived him significantly in large part due to the inspirational nature of his writings to Islamists around the world, especially among the more violently inclined groups in Egypt such as Gama'a al-Islamiyya and Islamic Jihad. Qutb advocated that Egyptian leaders and the bulk of Egyptian society should be considered part of *jahiliya* and therefore were legitimate targets.[121] Qutb did not believe in democracy, asserting that "popular sovereignty ... is a usurpation of God's sovereignty and a form of tyranny, for it subsumes the individual to the will of other individuals." As such, the only proper form of governance was an Islamic state under which citizens lived according to God's law, or shariah. For Qutb, legislators enacting laws for others to follow was an obstacle to the "absolute dignity" of humankind.[122] Still under the direction of al-Hudaybi, the Brotherhood had largely disavowed Qutb's anti-systemic tendencies.[123] Younger Brothers became displeased with the older Brothers they perceived as "passiv[e] in the face of government aggression." As a result, many younger members left and formed violent organizations while the remaining members turned to the nonviolence of al-Hudaybi.[124] However, the Brotherhood maintained its ideological and organizational ambiguity in this period and remained "noncommittal" to a specific agenda. When al-Hudaybi was questioned on what the Brotherhood stands for, he responded by emphasizing "the need for Islam to dominate the affairs of state and society."[125] This nonresponse committed the Brotherhood to its current structure and reinforced the idea of comprehensiveness that underlies the Brotherhood's organizational and ideological orientation.

Political Activism and Growing Tensions

Nasser's successor, Anwar Sadat, ushered in an era of tolerance for the Muslim Brotherhood. He granted amnesty to those in prison and released them in stages from 1971 through 1975, also encouraging those in exile to return home. Sadat's motivation was to counter the "Nasserist left," similar to how Nasser had used the Brotherhood to counter Marxists.[126] According

---

[120] Aly and Wenner 1982, 342; Sattar 1995, 17; Soage and Franganillo 2010, 42; Pevna 2014, 8.

[121] Pargeter 2013, 35.

[122] Esposito and Piscatori 1991, 435–36.

[123] Bilinski 2013, 27; Pevna 2014, 8.

[124] Soage and Franganillo 2010, 42. Non-violence was entrenched as the Brotherhood's political strategy during al-Tilmisani's leadership (Al-Arian 2014, 104).

[125] Kandil 2015, 86.

[126] Wickham 2015, 30.

The Origins of Religiopolitical Identity

to Pevna, "Sadat stylized himself as a 'believer president' and legitimized himself by religion"; his softening of relations with the Brotherhood was one of the ways he accomplished this.[127] The Muslim Brotherhood was also strengthened by Sadat's neoliberal economic policies, which reduced state-based welfare and allowed the Brotherhood to fill the void.[128] They were also gaining ground at universities that would subsequently be a major asset in the 1980s and 1990s as the Brotherhood made its way into the formal political space.[129] The Brotherhood largely drew from the educated and middle-class segments of society,[130] in addition to some from the lower classes due to their charity and welfare work.[131] In the words of the third general guide, Umar al-Tilmisani (1972–86), the group maintained its closed structure and prioritized loyalty to the Brotherhood as "allegiance to God."[132] Throughout the 1970s and 1980s, the Brotherhood had relatively ambiguous and ill-defined ideological leanings.

Following Sadat's assassination, Hosni Mubarak came to power and released the imprisoned Brothers, as his predecessor had done.[133] The ensuing period until 1988 brought about another softening of relations and major growth for the organization. The Brotherhood bolstered its grassroots operations, expanded its charity and welfare networks, and even took control of many professional unions. They were also allowed to contest elections, provided that they ran as independents unaffiliated with the Brotherhood. Despite lacking an official political party status, the Brotherhood could take part in alliances with other political parties.[134] In the 1984 parliamentary elections, the Brotherhood ran with the New Wafd Party and won 12 seats. In 1987, the "Islamic Alliance" between the Brotherhood, Socialist Labor Party, and Liberal Party won 32 seats on a platform calling for economic reform, greater democracy, and an implementation of shariah.[135] Thousands of antigovernment Islamists were arrested in 1989 after protesting in the streets and demanding shariah law. As a result, the Brotherhood, along with other opposition parties, boycotted the 1990 elections.[136]

The Islamist FIS' 1991 electoral victory in Algeria understandably alarmed the Mubarak regime, and this new era of repression continued. The following year, Mubarak's fears were realized when Egyptian security forces raided a Brotherhood member's business and found documents detailing a scheme

---

[127] Pevna 2014, 8.
[128] Tadros 2012, 6.
[129] Wickham 2002; Eisenhart 2010, 81.
[130] Munson 2001; Masoud 2014; Brooke 2019.
[131] Tadros 2012, 6.
[132] Quoted in Kandil 2015, 50.
[133] Pevna 2014, 8.
[134] Sattar 1995, 20.
[135] Esposito and Piscatori 1991, 429; Sattar 1995, 20.
[136] Esposito and Piscatori 1991.

called the Enablement Project. This was a plan of the Brotherhood to "infiltrate government institutions and civil society organizations gradually with a view of taking over power. [The documents] also showed that the Muslim Brothers had re-created the state by setting up sections dealing with all the domains in which they deemed it necessary to have influence: students, professionals, the security services, elections, human rights, and so on." Most of the organization claimed the documents were fabricated but some younger members declared the documents authentic, albeit nothing more than "the delusions of a handful of hardline old guards."[137]

TUNISIAN ENNAHDHA MOVEMENT

Today, Ennahdha is largely synonymous with Tunisian Islamism, with an overwhelming majority of Islamists belonging to the group. Yet, the signs of religious–secular conflict that would give rise to an Islamic revival date back to the late nineteenth century, particularly the era of European colonialism. Efforts to replace Islamic law with a Western-style constitution effectively turned Islam into "a symbol and rallying point of interest."[138] With escalating secularization in the state and society – partly due to European and French influence – and advocacy by Young Tunisians to limit Islam's public role, traditional religious authorities, that is, the ulama, gradually lost their influence. An episode of low societal trust in these authorities ensued as Tunisians doubted their ability to defy colonial control and subordination of Tunisians, and to ultimately practice Islam. Although it would take several decades for pan-Islamism to take an institutionalized form, the seeds were sown for conflict between secular and religious forces. This conflict continued well into the independence struggle of Tunisians. In this regard, the emergence of a religious political identity in Tunisia parallels similar processes in the rest of the Middle East; however, colonial experiences of the Middle Eastern and Western European cases remain notably different.

Habib Bourguiba's crusade against the religious establishment in the postindependence period distanced Tunisian conservatives from his rule and ultimately facilitated the birth of an organized Islamist movement in Tunisia. The movement that would later grow into Ennahdha began at Zaytouna Mosque in postindependence Tunis. Here, men participated in discussion groups and shared their feelings of marginalization resulting from Bourguiba's secularizing and modernizing reforms.[139] One of these men explains: "I remember we used to feel like strangers in our own country. We had been educated as Arabs and Muslims, while we could see the country being totally moulded in the

---

[137] Soage and Franganillo 2010, 47.
[138] Wolf 2017, 16.
[139] Willis 2012, 159.

The Origins of Religiopolitical Identity

French cultural identity."[140] Bourguiba's reforms, especially the French education system, were a key catalyst in the rise of the movement as they recognized this non-Tunisian education system was threatening Tunisians' culture and identity.[141] Bourguiba's assault on religion also took its toll as fundamental tenets and symbols of Islam such as the hajj, fasting, and hijab were under attack. Rachid Ghannouchi, the future leader of Ennahdha, recalled those days by the feelings of alienation they went through: "For us, the doors to any further education were closed since the university had been completely Westernized."[142] Moreover, Ghannouchi and his colleagues were convinced that Bourguiba's Westernization reforms wiped the country of its Islamic heritage. They lamented the gap between their understanding of what Islam was and what Tunisian public institutions cultivated.

In the late 1960s, this group of Rachid Ghannouchi, Abdulfattah Mourou, and Hmida Ennaifer went on a speaking tour, visiting mosques and secondary schools.[143] The "Islamic Group" (or *al-Jamaa al-Islamiyya*) preached on the urgency of "rebuild[ing] the Arab-Muslim character of Tunisian society." With their "trimmed beard[s], white jallaba, and red chechia," these "sheikhs" drew crowds that many of these mosques had not been graced with in decades.[144] Not only did they aim to raise Islamic awareness among Tunisians, but they also attacked the country's symbol for traditional Islamic learning and authority – Zaytouna. They argued that Zaytouna was "archaic" and "failed to adapt its curriculum to the demands of the contemporary world." Instead, founders of al-Jamaa al-Islamiyya aimed to re-institute Islam's "dignity and power."[145] Like its counterparts in the Middle East and Western Europe, the movement's early focus was on religious, cultural, and societal issues.

In the following years, two developments proved instrumental in further entrenching the political nature of the group. First, the Bread Riots erupted in 1978, culminating in the harsh government suppression of labor unionism and thus the leftists at large.[146] This suppression, coupled with the growing socioeconomic disparities in the country and the Islamist infiltration of student organizations, left the movement with an even broader sociopolitical vacuum to fill.[147] Second, many in the movement were inspired by the 1979 Iranian Revolution.[148] Rachid Ghannouchi himself went to some length to justify their interest in postrevolutionary Iran and their Islamic regime. In particular, he

---

[140] Quoted in Willis 2012, 160.
[141] Okumus 2014, 5.
[142] Ghannouchi quoted in Wolf 2017, 30.
[143] Willis 2012, 160.
[144] Jones 1988.
[145] Wolf 2017, 36–40.
[146] Allani 2009, 259.
[147] Willis 2012, 160; Bilinski 2013, 17.
[148] Kaminski 2014, 36.

argued that relations between Iranian Islamic groups and Sunni Islamists went back to the first half of the twentieth century.

In August 1978, the Islamic Group held a formative convention gathering all its disparate cells. They established general rules for the movement, including agreeing to hold a congress every three years and creating several offices, such as a 25-member Consultant Council, a 9-member Executive Bureau headed by the Emir, or leader of the movement, and movement officials at various regional levels.[149] Rachid Ghannouchi was the first Emir and still holds this office today. The group also changed its name to the Islamic Tendency Movement (MTI) in this meeting. Due to security concerns, this first congress and most other activities were held in secret.[150]

Movement activities continued in secret until police stumbled upon a group meeting in December 1980. The movement decided at its second congress in April 1981 to cease being a clandestine organization; in June, the movement officially applied for government recognition. Their decision was motivated by a desire to enter a coalition with other opposition parties in attempts to replace the Bourguiba regime.[151] Nonetheless, the movement's ideological orientation lacked precision and embodied the typical comprehensive nature of an Islamist movement: "The party failed to produce an official manifesto or a program. Its only official public statement emphasized the goals of Islamic revival, anti-westernization, reformulation of the Islamic thought and social justice."[152]

With the movement emerging from the shadows, the regime began to feel threatened by the ever-growing Islamist opposition. Ennahdha's request to begin directly controlling mosques felt especially concerning as it targeted the government's sovereignty over religion. The government also believed Ennahdha was an Iranian proxy bent on establishing an Islamic state, although the government lacked evidence to this effect.[153] Thus, using the Gafsa events as a pretense, the government began prosecuting numerous movement members in 1981. Charged with various crimes such as "forming an illegal organization, publishing false news, and defaming the president," 107 members were sentenced, some with up to 11 years in prison.[154] Unsurprisingly, the movement's application for official recognition was declined.[155]

In November 1987, Zine el Abedine Ben Ali deposed Bourguiba in a coup d'état, citing the president's alleged medical incapacity and advanced age.[156]

---

[149] Allani 2009, 260. Anne Wolf puts the date of this congress as July 1979 (2017, 50).
[150] Allani 2009, 260.
[151] Allani 2009, 261.
[152] Bilinski 2013, 18.
[153] Jones 1988; Esposito and Piscatori 1991, 431.
[154] Allani 2009, 261–62; Willis 2012, 164.
[155] Wright 1988, 55.
[156] Allani 2009, 257; Ayari 2015, 136.

The Origins of Religiopolitical Identity

The Islamists believed this new regime would bring them better fortunes, and it did, but only temporarily. Ben Ali released many political prisoners from the Bourguiba era, including Ghannouchi and other members of the MTI.[157] In 1989, Ben Ali's regime passed a new law prohibiting parties from referring to Islam in their names, as this could be interpreted as monopolizing "the claim to be Islamic." As such, the MTI renamed itself Harakat Ennahdha, or Renaissance Movement.[158] Ennahdha was allowed to officially establish a student union called UGTE and publish a magazine called *al-Fajr*.[159]

Ennahdha then participated in the 1989 parliamentary elections, albeit by running as independents, similar to the Brotherhood in Egypt and many other Islamist groups throughout the region. Although Ennahdha likely won roughly 30 percent of the vote, official results indicated only 12 percent support for Ennahdha candidates due to vote-rigging on the part of Ben Ali. Ennahdha performed better than all the secular opposition parties combined, and in some areas, its candidates won up to 80 percent of the votes.[160] Ben Ali subsequently announced that parties were now prohibited from mixing religion and politics, thus blocking Ennahdha's pursuit of legalization.[161] Ghannouchi left the country in self-exile, first to Algeria and then London.[162] Ennahdha then boycotted the next local elections in June 1990 in protest of the regime's new rules.[163]

Ennahdha's successful comeback and performance in 2011 following the revolution was a legacy of its support base from the movement's early days. As Ghannouchi was touring mosques and secondary schools, he built a solid base of young Islamists who took their new ideological leanings with them to university, eventually surpassing the traditionally strong leftist student groups. Islamism was also brought into the workplace, as Ghannouchi told workers that Islam is "on the side of the poor and the oppressed." As the university students graduated and joined the labor force, a swath of middle-class professionals such as doctors, engineers, and teachers remained attuned to the movement.[164] The university-to-middle-class-profession trajectory that Ennahdha relied on proved to be a steady pipeline of recruits and activists for Islamists around the Middle East. The lower classes and unemployed became a movement stronghold partly due to welfare programs established by the MTI, which provided free medical care and legal help as well as aid to the families of those detained or fired from their jobs for supporting the Islamists.[165] This constituency grew

[157] El-Khawas 2012, 2.
[158] Esposito and Piscatori 1991, 431; Ayari 2015, 136.
[159] Allani 2009, 263.
[160] El-Khawas 2012, 3.
[161] Zollner 2019, 6.
[162] Affan 2017, 5.
[163] Esposito and Piscatori 1991, 431; Ayari 2015, 136.
[164] Jones 1988.
[165] Jones 1988.

through the 1970s and 1980s due to the regime's neoliberal policies, increasing birthrate, and global economic developments.[166] By some estimates, in 1987, the MTI was supported by up to 25 percent of Tunisians.[167] The strong showing by Ennahdha in 2011 reflects the fragmentation of other opposition parties in addition to Ennahdha's superior organizational capacity.[168]

The MTI was widely believed to be one of the most moderate Islamist organizations in existence[169] and has remained as such into the present. As the movement's central intellectual architect, Ghannouchi considers himself less of a politician and more of an activist and reformer in the style of Sayyid Qutb and Hassan al-Banna, both of whom he considers influences. In its early days, the movement had a strong relationship with the Egyptian Muslim Brotherhood.[170] As such, Ghannouchi believes societal reform must be bottom-up, not top-down.[171] The movement does not believe in theocracy and does not seek to establish an Islamic state. Ghannouchi himself argues that such extreme interpretations of Islam are incompatible with Tunisian society, going so far as to even oppose the Constituent Assembly's suggestion of using shariah as a source of legislation.[172]

Ghannouchi was a high school philosophy teacher by trade; this brought him a unique understanding of how to present Islamism to the masses, an ideology that not only addressed individuals' spiritual needs but also their economic and political troubles. He understood how to make religion relevant again, and of this, he stated, "What concerns the young people of today? The position of the Mu'tazilites on the attributes of God, whether the Quran is pre-existent or created? Was Islam revealed for this kind of useless, sterile argument? I wonder how our students feel studying 'Islamic philosophy' when it offers them only a bunch of dead issues having nothing to do with the problems of today. I propose that these shrouds be returned to their graves, that these false problems be buried and that we deal with our real problems – economics, politics, sexual license."[173]

Movement publications were strongly reminiscent of the ideas of Qutb and al-Banna, speaking of jahiliyya, the time of the Prophet, and anti-Western sentiment. They maintained that Western hegemony would soon fall, bringing capitalism, socialism, and Christianity down with it. They also frequently

---

[166] Gasiorowski 1992, 90.

[167] Wright 1988, 55.

[168] Chamkhi 2015, 138–39.

[169] Wright 1988, 55.

[170] Despite this early strong influence, Ennahdha developed as a Tunisian movement in response to local socioreligious dynamics. The movement's leaders took inspiration from religious figures like Sheikh Hmed Ben Miled and Tahar Ben Achour, more so than they did from Egyptian Muslim Brotherhood leaders. See Sayida Ounissi's discussion (2016).

[171] Torelli 2012, 73.

[172] Ottaway 2013, 3; Wolf 2013, 561.

[173] Ghannouchi quoted in Jones 1988.

The Origins of Religiopolitical Identity

criticized early reformist figures such as Afghani and Abduh, believing them to take too much inspiration from the West.[174] Nonetheless, the movement's ideology was not entirely clear, with official statements focusing on revival and social justice with little emphasis on actual policy.[175] In this regard, Ennahdha bore the hallmark features of many religiopolitical movements: ideological purity and policy ambiguity. The founding document of the MTI mentioned topics such as the necessity of a marriage between politics and religion, ensuring the Islamic identity of Tunisia, pan-Islamism, and restoring the mosques "as centers of worship and popular mobilization."[176]

Despite the movement's anti-Western sentiment, they consider democracy to be compatible with Islam and in fact of utmost importance.[177] For them, democracy is not an ideology but a tool, and it is not inherently secular.[178] Ghannouchi maintained that Islam is antithetical to tyranny, that it must ensure human rights, including minority rights, and that no one group or individual can be the sole source of religious authority.[179] He argues, "religion prospers within democracy; it is within dictatorship that it fades. Look at what happens to Muslims: they escape dictatorships in the Muslim world to look for freedom in established democracies … [Islam] is both spiritual and social freedom."[180] Ghannouchi is not anti-system, instead believing in the necessity of Islamist participation in elections in order to establish a government inspired by Islam.[181] He wants a "system that features majority rule, free elections, a free press, protection of minorities, equality of all secular and religious parties, and full women's rights in everything from polling booths, dress codes, and divorce courts to the top job at the presidential palace. Islam's role is to provide the system with moral values."[182] He also consistently rejects the use of violence and openly accepts modernity, "intellectual freedom, scientific progress, and democratic ideals."[183]

Ennahdha has refined its platform since 2011. According to Cavatorta, Ennahdha considers itself "not a religious party which is preoccupied with Islam [rather] a political party which is engaged in economic and social issues but whose values come from Islam." Their slogan is "freedom, justice, and development."[184] Ghannouchi made sure to distance his party from the Muslim Brotherhood on several occasions, instead drawing an analogy to

[174] Allani 2009, 260.
[175] Bilinksi 2013, 18.
[176] Affan 2016, 3.
[177] Grewal 2020.
[178] Okumus 2014, 10.
[179] Dorraj 1998, 16.
[180] Cavatorta and Merone 2013, 869.
[181] Okumus 2014, 7.
[182] Wright 1996, 73.
[183] Bilinski 2013, 22.
[184] Cavatorta 2012, 20.

138   *The Politics of Religious Party Change*

Turkey's AKP with a focus on political moderateness, tolerance, democracy, and protection of human rights, including women's rights, and pluralism.[185] In an interview with Alfred Stepan in 2007, Ghannouchi condemned the Muslim Brotherhood platform item declaring that the Egyptian president could never be a woman or Christian, stating "Democracy means equality of all citizens. Such a platform excludes 60 percent of all the citizens and is unacceptable. [I am an] advocate of absolute equality of men and women."[186] The evolution of Ennahdha can perhaps best be described by the following statement from a speech Ghannouchi gave at the movement's 10th congress: "Ennahdha has evolved since the 70s from an ideological movement engaged in the struggle for identity, to a comprehensive protest movement against an authoritarian regime, to a national democratic party devoted to reform."[187]

THE NATIONAL OUTLOOK MOVEMENT OF TURKEY

The rise of political Islam in Turkey differs from the rise of Islamists elsewhere in the region in important ways. Public expression of religion and religiosity in Turkey was heavily suppressed by the early Republican governments; organized religious activity beyond the confines of the mosque was faced with government suppression, if not deemed outright illegal. Even then, mosque activity was limited to congregational prayers. Religion, as such, faced strict government regulation. As a result, the emergence of a large-scale movement with a religiopolitical agenda was delayed by several decades following Turkey's foundation in 1923.

Unlike other Islamist movements, the NOM emerged and grew predominantly in a formal institutional setting.[188] The movement took advantage of this opportunity and accessed the formal political structure through successive political parties that were formed shortly after its rise. These Islamist parties embodied profoundly anti-system discourses that relied on their organic relationship with the movement. It was not until its complete break with the movement that the latest party's approach to politics underwent a major transformation, leaving behind the conventionally anti-system approach.

Despite these differences, however, the early development of the Islamist movement in Turkey through the NOM relied on similar dynamics. It also yielded a religiopolitical movement that was nearly identical in discourse and objectives to its peers in the Middle East and the Catholic mass movements of Western Europe. The NOM harnessed the state's suppression of religion to build its discourse around a religiopolitical identity. Likewise, to promote its

---

[185] El-Khawas 2012, 17. See McCarthy's discussion of how the AKP served as a possible model for some Ennahdha officials (2018b, 370–71).

[186] Stepan 2012, 95.

[187] Affan 2016, 3.

[188] Sezgin 2011, 7.

The Origins of Religiopolitical Identity

goals, the movement embraced a hybrid organizational structure that catered to both political and nonpolitical dimensions of life in Turkey.

Ataturk's secularization policies in the 1920s and 1930s set the tone throughout the Middle East for modernization reforms between the 1940s and 1960s. Leaders around the region such as Reza Shah, Nasser, and Bourguiba emulated reforms that introduced secular education, undermined the power of religious institutions, embraced secular lifestyles, and established secular governance as a pillar of the state. Collectively, these reforms aimed to fashion Middle Eastern societies and states into a Western European mold. As a result, the reforms in the postindependence period turned secular-religious conflict into the principal axis of the socio-political divide in Turkey and beyond.[189] The secularism implemented by the Turkish state was particularly pernicious, undermining conservative Muslims' trust in the state and modernization reforms.[190] Unlike the Anglo-American model of secularism, the state was not neutral toward religion and public displays of religiosity; that the state was separated from religious institutions did not suffice. Instead, it proactively attempted to privatize religion and sanctioned a secular public sphere; religion unequivocally belonged to the private sphere in Turkey. This assertive secularism, or *laiklik*, drew its inspiration from the French model of secularism, *laïcité*.[191]

Ataturk's secularization reforms and heavy-handed approach to organized religious activism and traditional religious institutions catalyzed a profound reactionary current among conservatives. Occasionally leading to spontaneous protests and uprisings, the first true political opportunity for religious mass movements in Turkey materialized in the 1950s.[192] A new political party, the Democrat Party (DP), won in 1950 the first free elections since Turkey's transition to a multiparty democratic system in 1946. The DP did not embrace the strict secularism of the Kemalist era. Thanks to its unprecedented stance on religion, the party gained a significant level of support, especially among those disenfranchised by Kemalism. Under the DP, the state allowed mosques to again recite the call to prayer in Arabic instead of Turkish, mandated religion classes in schools, resumed the use of state resources for training imams, and established religious high schools known as Imam-Hatip schools.[193] After a military coup in 1960, however, the DP was banned due to its tolerant attitude toward religion and its increasing authoritarianism. A new party formed in the same mold under the name Justice Party (AP), enjoying widespread support among conservatives and budding religious groups.

The 1961 constitution, with its emphasis on freedoms of expression and association, paved the way for greater Islamic as well as leftist and Alevi

---

[189] Benedikter 2020.

[190] Gingeras 2019, 304.

[191] Kuru 2006, 2009.

[192] Landau 1974.

[193] Sarfati 2014.

activism. With civil liberties guaranteed by the constitution, Islamist activists found more freedom to organize and operate.[194] They geared their activities toward Islamic education, publication of Islamic material, and associational organization,[195] where groups such as the Turkish National Student Union, Association for Fighting Against Communism, Nationalists' Association, and Nationalist Teachers' Association emerged.[196] The relatively open political environment facilitated the growth of a lively and diverse Islamist network across Turkey. Throughout the 1960s, Islamists established religious alternatives to the state's secular business, professional, cultural, and women's associations.[197] Pluralism and a high level of competition, in turn, characterized the religiopolitical sector in this period; no single actor dominated the field. The competitive nature of the religious political environment pushed the founders of the NOM to contemporaneously establish a formal political organization to grow into one of the two major mass religious movements. In the words of Süleyman Arif Emre, the effort to establish the NOM in this context "was not like transforming an unclaimed piece of land into a farm. It was more like acquiring a plot in an already ... parceled out ... place like Taksim Square."[198]

The opportunity to experiment with social, religious, and political activism proved crucial for the development of Islamists' religiopolitical identities. Islamists first entered the political arena in the late 1940s with the permissive proportional representation electoral system that offered smaller parties a chance to exist. Parties such as the Nation Party and the Islam Democratic Party did not fare well, either because of the bans they faced or poor electoral performance. As a result, prominent Islamist personalities found political refuge in various parties of the center-right. These personalities included Hasan Aksay, Hacı Tevfik Paksu, Osman Yüksel Serdengeçti in the Justice Party, Süleyman Arif Emre in the New Turkey Party, and Fehmi Cumalioğlu and Abdurrahman Şeref Laç in the Nation Party.[199]

The Rise of the National Outlook Movement

It is in this context that Turkey's first Islamist movement, the NOM or Milli Gorus Hareketi, emerged as the result of years of disenfranchisement and marginalization of religious Turks by the Kemalist establishment and leadership of the Justice Party (AP). Although somewhat linked to the writings of Qutb and al-Banna and the regionwide Islamic awakening that such thought catalyzed,

---

[194] Karasipahi 2009, 95; Sezgin 2011, 8.
[195] Alam 2009, 364.
[196] Sezgin 2011, 71.
[197] Yilmaz 2012, 364.
[198] Sezgin 2011, 127–28.
[199] Sezgin 2011, 73.

The Origins of Religiopolitical Identity

the NOM had more specific domestic roots.[200] In the 1960s, a Naksibendi Sufi leader, Mehmed Zahid Kotku, became influential among a small number of male university students. He sought to attract "new recruits from urban and educated segments of society and aimed to turn the Order from 'a mosque-based community into a semi-political movement' by encouraging his followers 'to capture the higher summits of social and political institutions in the country and establish control over the society'."[201] These students were interested in science and technology and believed that these were the keys to Western power. Kotku pushed his followers to acquaint themselves with the economic, cultural, and political issues of their time.[202] NOM was formed in the late 1960s "as an umbrella organization" for Islamist politicians and the Naksibendi Order.[203]

Historically, all National Outlook parties used nearly identical ideological frameworks, with contextual variation on the deeply anti-system posture of the NOM. The movement had both socioeconomic and cultural dimensions, building its rhetoric on a sharp religio-cultural divide overlaid with calls for socioeconomic equality. Culturally, the movement subscribed to a binary worldview between the West and the East, that is, the Muslim world. This view was akin to the Brotherhood and Ennahdha's conceptualization of the secular West and their own society's position vis-à-vis the West. Turkish society's political, economic, and social problems resulted directly from the Western model of modernization; this was "a historic mistake" that had to be corrected. The panacea for the ills of society rested on erecting a "national order" where "national" stood for the Ottoman–Islamic culture.[204] In this regard, Islam and Muslimness defined the nation and the movement was the true representative of this identity. The NOM was a radical "religious critique of laicism" and declared that Westernization led to "moral decay" and alienated Turkish Muslims from their traditional Muslim values and culture.[205] As such, the movement espoused "an antiglobalization and anti-Western attitude."[206] The movement first and foremost sought to abolish Westernization in order to return the country back to its cultural roots in its Islamic identity. The movement's mission was to arouse the "Islamic truth" in society[207] because they believed that moral development constituted the foundation for "material development."[208] Muslims

---

[200] For a brief overview of the National Outlook Movement's early contacts with Egyptian Muslim Brotherhood, see https://yetkinreport.com/2020/06/10/turkiyede-reislamizasyon-musluman-kardesler-ve-cia/.
[201] Kirdis 2016, 7.
[202] Mardin 2005, 157–58.
[203] Kirdis 2016, 7.
[204] Yildiz 2007, 73; Rabasa and Larrabee 2018, 40.
[205] Kirdis 2016, 7; Neslihan 2016, 32.
[206] Kuru 2005, 268.
[207] Kirdis 2016, 7.
[208] Atacan 2005, 188.

were suppressed for practicing their faith, lacked basic religious rights such as having their weekly holiday off, and suffered from insufficient public funding for religious education. By contrast, Christians and Jews had their holidays off, and ballet schools "raised prostitutes"; education, according to the movement, had become a tool of moral and material desolation. Utilizing anti-Semitic language, movement officials claimed students across Turkey "were taught sociology and philosophy texts authored 'by Durkheim, a Jew' and psychology books 'written by a Jewish rabbi'."[209] As Muslims, therefore, citizens bore a religious obligation to combat the moral degeneration of society. This singular focus on religion aimed to boost the value of religion as a political resource, in turn sanctioning the movement's activism and gaining greater popular ground. While this focus on moral degeneration appears to be a broad criticism of the West by Turkish – and, more generally Middle Eastern – Islamists, fundamentally it aimed to tackle the secular and modern influence of the West. As such, there exists an important similarity in how Catholic mass movements framed their own identity. Islamist and Catholic movements were unified in their opposition to Western secular modernity; both viewed this new secular approach to the state and society as detrimental to their faiths and their faithful.

The focus on moral development led movement leaders and activists to boast about their personal religiosity as a sign of their commitment to this Islamic identity. Embracing stricter religious observance also helped distinguish them from other actors in a competitive religiopolitical field. Erbakan was pitched as a "model Muslim" who had the gravitas to "represent" not only the movement but also "the nation"; movement activists were framed as "an enlightened cadre" who righteously embodied Quranic values.[210] In their travels across the country for grassroots mobilization, movement leaders would make their first stop the most prominent mosque in each city as an act of religious symbolism.[211] This process of "differentiation" was a deliberate exercise to legitimize the movement's presence in the religiopolitical arena: "Not only a Muslim needed to be redefined as a politically conscious and active subject but also in an environment where religiousness was equated with religious stringency the NSM activists were forced to refashion themselves according to ever more-stringent interpretations of religion to be 'more Muslim' than other Muslims worthy to represent the nation."[212] In this regard, the NOM's actions mirrored the Brotherhood's own efforts to legitimize its own cadres' religiosity and religious credentials. In the same vein, there was plenty of religious dog-whistling. Politicians, big business owners, and other prominent members of the society were accused of being freemasons, a potent

---

[209] Sezgin 2011, 178.
[210] Sezgin 2011, 193.
[211] Sezgin 2011, 134.
[212] Sezgin 2011, 197.

The Origins of Religiopolitical Identity

insinuation in conservative circles to this day, suggesting that these individuals were not real Muslims. At its core, the movement framed its activism as a conflict between *hak* and *batıl*, or between godly and heathen. It was clear who the believers should side with.

In a key difference from Islamist groups elsewhere in the Middle East, the historical roots of the re-imagined ideal Islamic state for Turkish Islamists did not correspond to the typical conception of the Golden Age, that is, the first few generations of Muslims starting with Prophet Muhammad. Instead, the NOM harkened back to the Ottoman Empire as its historical and cultural model.[213] The movement's ideology as conceived by Erbakan rested on the idea of "just order" (*adil düzen*), although this specific phrase would become the Welfare Party motto only in the 1980s. The just order is nationalist, but not in the same way as the Kemalist establishment, which movement leaders deemed divisive. Ottomanism is a proto-Turkish identity; Ottomanism and modern Turkish identity are held together not by ethnicity or class, but by Islam.[214] This form of nationalism, therefore, does not exclude Kurds who constitute 15 to 20 percent of Turkey's population. For some, it seemed that the movement had found a solution to the Kurdish problem, as well as the problem of the disengaged and disenfranchised Muslim periphery.[215]

Compared to other Islamists, economic inequality occupied a larger share of the NOM's political framework. The movement found greater success in incorporating the language of inequality from the political left in its economic discourse. A deep and growing economic disparity existed between "white Turks" – the economically privileged, secular, urban, educated, and modernized sectors of society that are close to the state power – and "black Turks" – the economically disenfranchised, conservative, and undereducated segments of society who identified with an Islamic identity.[216] The NOM identified with those in the periphery, that is, the black Turks, and aimed to be the voice of those excluded populations. Just as importantly, the movement was a response to the marginalization of a young generation of conservatives within the center-right parties of Turkey. Even though the economic and political openings of the 1950s and 1960s created limited opportunities for peripheral constituencies, their demands for greater economic prosperity were largely ignored by those who claimed to politically represent them in the Justice Party and others.

Economically, the just order was pitched as a compromise between two evils: communism and capitalism. Although the movement opposed capitalism, it favored the free market. They promoted the industrialization of

---

[213] Yavuz 2000, 34.

[214] Yildiz 2003, 188; Mardin 2005, 157–58; Hintz 2018, 84.

[215] Yavuz 1997, 74. See Türkmen (2021) for a recent analysis of the religion's role in the conflict between Turks and Kurds in Turkey.

[216] Yavuz 2000, 22.

Anatolia – the abode of the periphery – and small enterprises as the movement sought to alleviate social injustice and inequality. This goal was especially relevant to conservative Turks, even leading to calls for a state investment program in the Kurdish areas of Southeastern Turkey.[217] In interviews with movement members, Yavuz found that for them the just order meant "justice, a secure social and economic environment, an end to nepotism and corruption, cooperation between the state and society, protection of the unity of the state, and an end to undue Western influence over Turkey."[218] Although they hailed from diverse backgrounds, the base of the movement was united in their defiance of the Kemalist policies and system, and in their demand to replace them with an Islamic identity.[219]

Despite Milli Görüş's similarities with Arab Islamism, a notable difference lies in how Sufism played a central role in the creation of the movement. Kotku's main gripe with the Islamism of Qutb's followers was that they conceived of the state as an "absolute enemy," while he believed in slowly infiltrating the government and bureaucracy in order to overtake the state.[220] Nonetheless, in both forms of Islamism, the state is seen as the key to engineering a top-down transformation of society.[221] While work on Islamizing society at the grassroots level continued, the centrality of the state in the Islamization process became increasingly evident; "capturing the state" would not only allow for changes at the policy and governmental level but also further facilitate Islamization at the societal level by undertaking social reforms.[222] Like the Egyptian Muslim Brotherhood, the NOM viewed itself as "vanguards" of society "with a mission to awaken an Islamic 'truth' in the people."[223] This conviction, again, represents an innate belief among Islamists that because their society is Muslim, all citizens are therefore potential supporters of their ideology. Islamist ideology is once again equated with Islam itself: "Their mission was not to represent the society but to convince people to come to their ranks. In this, NOM leaders believed their vanguards had 'potential' support in the society, because almost everyone in Turkey was a potential NOM supporter as practicing Muslims."[224] In a striking similarity with the Egyptian Muslim Brotherhood, the NOM, specifically the MNP, claimed it represented "the embodiment of the Muslim nation" and as such was not merely a political party; the movement was essential to the revival of the nation.[225]

---

[217] Atacan 2005, 188; White 2014, 17; Neslihan 2016, 43.
[218] Yavuz 2003, 222.
[219] Gulalp 2001.
[220] Mardin 2005, 158.
[221] Yilmaz 2011, 256.
[222] Bulac 2010, 106.
[223] Kirdis 2019, 76.
[224] Kirdis 2019, 77.
[225] Sezgin 2011, 174.

The Origins of Religiopolitical Identity

One strategy the movement employed to rise above the political fray was denying the partisan and political nature of the movement, like the Brotherhood. The NOM aimed to dissociate itself from the pejorative connotations of party politics. To this end, the movement did not expressly accept its intention to form a political party until the end of 1969, eschewed the use of such language in their published material, and referred to themselves as a movement (including the movement parties).[226] Reducing the broad reach of the movement, that is, the entirety of Muslim nation of Turkey, to one singular political identity would undermine its grandiose claims about what the movement stands for and what it aims to achieve. In this sense, the NOM and other Islamist groups' avoidance of an explicit partisan association parallels the Catholic Church's insistence on nonpartisan Catholic mass movements in Western Europe.

A mechanical engineer and Kotku's disciple, Necmettin Erbakan ran to lead the Union of Chambers and Commodity Exchanges of Turkey (Turkiye Odalar ve Borsalar Birligi, TOBB) in 1968. Having lost once to the ruling Justice Party (AP) leader Suleyman Demirel's favored candidate, Sırrı Enver Batur, Erbakan ran a second time on May 25, 1969, and won despite opposition from the Demirel government. The government did not recognize Erbakan's election on procedural grounds. After resisting against the government, Erbakan was finally ousted from that position by the ruling Justice Party in August 1969 through police force. In a surprising move, Erbakan applied to be an AP parliamentary candidate shortly after his ouster from the TOBB; he was denied a second time.[227] The conflict with AP leadership and the fight over TOBB put the nail in the coffin for Islamists' hopes of working toward their ideological goals through the AP. Frustrated with the Justice Party and center-right governments' failure to meet their demands, a group of Islamist politicians – including Erbakan – left the party before the 1969 parliamentary elections. In what was known as the Independents Movement, Erbakan and other Islamist politicians ran in the elections as independents. These politicians collectively concluded that the political context called for a separate Islamist path.

This group of politicians was already meeting with a diverse group of individuals from various religious communities, public servants, and business owners dating back to 1967. They aimed to form a religiopolitical movement that could fill the void of Islamic leadership in society and politics. The group included names like Tevfik Paksu, Ahmet İhsan Genç, Husamettin Akmumcu from the Nur Movement, Osman Yuksel Serdengecti, and Süleyman Arif Emre.[228] Ali Fuat Başgil and Osman Turan briefly led the group before they settled on Necmettin Erbakan as its leader, due to his formidable eloquence and political skills.[229] The movement served as the

---

[226] Sezgin 2011, 184.
[227] Caha and Baykal 2017, 791.
[228] Caha and Baykal 2017, 793.
[229] Sezgin 2011, 90.

materialization of this social, religious, and political activism that aimed to transform Turkish society and the state. The latest developments and fallout with the Justice Party served to expedite these efforts toward forming an Islamist political party as part of the NOM (Milli Gorus Hareketi). A competitive religious field also compelled the founders to harness the advantages of an institutionalized party to carry out the agenda of the NOM. Despite Erbakan's savvy political leadership, the group was lacking in one critical aspect – grassroots mobilization. In a crowded field of religiopolitical actors, it was virtually impossible to build a movement without the support of a well-established religious organization. Erbakan and his colleagues did not have much of a popular following, which is where Mehmed Zahid Kotku enters the fray. Erbakan and some of his friends, including Suleyman Arif Emre and Hasan Aksay, visited Kotku, explained their vision, and sought his blessing and support.

This invitation aligned well with Kotku's vision. Since he assumed the leadership of the Iskenderpasa lodge of the Naksibendi Order in the 1950s, Kotku had hoped to transform the small religious community into "a semipolitical movement"; in this regard, Kotku played a seminal role in "creating a model for the majority of contemporary Turkish Muslim socio-political movements."[230] On this vision, Kotku stated: "Following Sultan Abdulhamid II's removal, those West-imitating Masons have captured power in the country [Turkey]. They are a minority. They cannot represent our nation; it is an unavoidable historical responsibility for you to work to transfer power back to the true representatives of our nation. Join this endeavor and take leadership if your friends ask you to do so. Get to work. It is already too late."[231] Kotku urged other Naksibendi leaders to lend their support to this effort, including Ali Efendi from Suluova and Mustafa Bağışlayıcı from Samsun.[232] As a Sufi group, however, overt political activism did not sit well with the dignity of the group; a collaboration with others more willing to take on direct political activism appealed to Kotku. A successful religiopolitical movement would infuse new life into the Sufi order with a reservoir of potential recruits for the order to tap into.[233]

The Early Years: Party–Movement Relationship

The Kotku–Erbakan partnership was grounded in a natural division of labor that benefited both leaders in their common objective – ending the moral decline of Turkish society. Kotku offered spiritual leadership for the movement and mobilized the Order's base in aid of the movement. The alliance gave

[230] Kumbaracibasi 2009, 158.
[231] Kotku quoted in Emre 1990, 185.
[232] Sezgin 2011, 118.
[233] Sezgin 2011, 113.

The Origins of Religiopolitical Identity

Kotku an opportunity to expand his small community[234] while bringing state capture to the realm of possibility via the prospective Islamist political party: "In this, like the Moroccan MUR [Movement for Unity and Reform], which feared political marginalisation if it chose not to participate in party politics, the NOM saw party politics as a way to escape the ongoing marginalisation of Islamic leaders and orders within centre-right parties."[235] Although Kotku did not have much love for partisan politics as a Sufi leader, the Naksibendi yearning to regain its historical significance in the political arena dating back to the early nineteenth century ultimately prevailed.[236]

Erbakan spearheaded the political arm as part of the broader movement. The partnership allowed Erbakan to bring together individual Islamist politicians who lacked the supportive power of an organized movement. Iskenderpasa Lodge, therefore, provided the requisite infrastructure for the NOM and subsequently the political party in their formative phases. Party organization would enable these Islamist politicians "to voice their demands louder" and "unify" them, according to Erbakan.[237] Likewise, it would provide them with an opportunity to separate themselves from other conservative political parties through a clear platform. Indeed, Mahmud Esad Cosan, who followed Kotku to assume Iskenderpasa Lodge's leadership, testified to the role of the Lodge in the NOM's formation when he stated that the NOM "started as an action" of the Naksibendi Sufi Order; they supported the movement "from head to toe" with its grassroots mobilization by providing them "people for their central administration, presidencies, vice-presidencies, [and] youth branches."[238]

Compared to other Islamist movements, the NOM featured a more harmonious relationship between its religious and political arms. This relationship was facilitated by the NOM's ability to formalize its political arm early on in view of the country's permissive political environment. Depending on the context and occasion, the movement could invoke its religious or political identity. This allowed the movement to reap the benefits of malleable organizational identity. On one hand, formalization of the political wing allowed access to primarily state financial resources to facilitate the movement's activism. On the other hand, the informal nature of religious activism offered opportunities to build support and raise loyal cadres in society.

By January 1970, the movement had gathered considerable steam; Necmettin Erbakan founded the first Islamist political party in Turkey based on the NOM's ideology and principles and with Kotku's support on January 26, 1970. The party's name was, as proposed by Esref Edip, the National Order Party (MNP).[239] Various conservative groups including some Sufi orders

---

[234] Caha and Baykal 2017, 793.
[235] Kirdis 2019, 79.
[236] Caha and Baykal 2017, 798–99.
[237] Kirdis 2019, 77.
[238] Cosan quoted in Kirdis 2019, 76.
[239] Caha and Baykal 2017, 793.

148 *The Politics of Religious Party Change*

and Nurcu groups lent support to the party in its formation; likewise, dailies such as *Sabah* and *Bugün* pitched the MNP as the voice of the disenfranchised pious Muslim majority. The makeup of the party's founding members – where engineers and small business owners dominated the list – boosted the party's claim to represent the voiceless.[240] The party's founding declaration reflected Kotku's vision and the NOM's blueprint for Turkey's Islamic revival; it frequently harkened back to the glorious history of the Turks and decried the "spiritual invasion" of communist and cosmopolitan movements. The party founders preached about how the Turkish nation was "chosen to enjoin the right and forbid the wrong."[241] This view aligned with Erbakan's conviction that the NOM and its religiopolitical activism would "bring awareness from the top" and steer the society in the right direction as an act of "compassion."[242]

Yet, the party was short-lived. A military coup occurred on March 12, 1971; by May 20, the MNP was banned by the Constitutional Court, charged with wanting "to alter the secular principles of the state and institute an Islamic order."[243] Party leader Erbakan left the country for Switzerland until his return in 1972. Undeterred by this major setback to its religiopolitical activism, the National Outlook Movement sought the right time to step onto the political scene again. One development that worked to the movement's advantage was the growing concern among some generals about the Justice Party and its leader Suleyman Demirel's dominance over Turkey's political system. The generals sought to mobilize those close to Erbakan to form a new party to compete with Demirel; because party officials of the banned MNP did not face individual charges, there were no legal obstacles to pursuing this avenue.[244] Süleyman Arif Emre took on the task of forming the new party while Mehmet Zahid Kotku remained central to mobilizing the movement's resources for the new party.[245] Emre belonged to the Iskenderpasa Lodge and the NOM and was a member of the MNP before it was banned. The National Salvation Party (MSP) came into existence on October 11, 1972, just in time for the next parliamentary election. Erbakan, in the meantime, officially became a member of the party in May 1973 and assumed party leadership following the October 1973 elections. The current Prime Minister Recep Tayyip Erdogan got his political start as a youth organizer for this party.[246]

Ideologically, the MSP walked in its predecessor's footprints. The party harped on an anti-Western, anti-secular, and pro-religion populist tone that underscored socioeconomic inequality faced by masses and small business

---

[240] Yavuz 2003, 209.
[241] *Milli Nizam Partisi Kuruluş Beyannamesi*, 1970. Available at: https://acikerisim.tbmm.gov.tr/xmlui/handle/11543/798 (accessed July 30, 2020)
[242] Kirdis 2019, 77.
[243] Yavuz 1997, 66.
[244] Caha and Baykal 2017, 803.
[245] Yavuz 2003, 209.
[246] Mardin 2005, 159.

The Origins of Religiopolitical Identity

owners.[247] The fusion of Turkish nationalism with Islam yielded the motto "A Great Turkey Once Again" (Yeniden Büyük Türkiye), where a return to Islam and a "Muslim way of life" undergirded Turkey's triumphant return to leadership of the Muslim world. The idea of a Muslim Common Market and a Muslim defense alliance reflected this fixation with the pursuit of anti-Western objectives.[248]

The MSP won 12 percent of the vote in 1973, corresponding to 11 percent of the parliamentary seats and making it the third largest party; a coalition government could not be formed without it.[249] The party first entered into government with the Republican People's Party (CHP), the party of Ataturk; later, the MSP joined a coalition government under Prime Minister Süleyman Demirel and his Justice Party, along with two other nationalist parties, known as the Nationalist Front.[250] These coalition governments enabled the NOM to pursue a more prominent role for religion in public education.[251] Although longer lived and more successful than its predecessor, the MSP fell victim to another coup in 1980. In contrast to the previous coup, which only banned the MNP, this coup banned all political parties for three years, nonetheless specifically accusing the MSP of being anti-secular.[252]

The Welfare Party

Not to be deterred, after the three-year ban expired, the NOM returned to full force yet again, this time under the name Welfare Party (RP). Under Turkish law (Constitution, Article 69), "members of a party who are found to be responsible for the closure of a party due to their speeches and activities are banned from politics for five years and cannot be founding members, members, administrators or inspectors of another political party during this time." Likewise, the same individuals cannot stand for election for a parliamentary seat.[253] When the generals decided to gradually open up the electoral system, the movement decided to form the Welfare Party (RP).[254] Although the movement faced some challenges to put together the party's founding cadre, in part due to opposition to some names by the military, Ali Türkmen and Ahmet Tekdal officially established the party on July 19, 1983. Erbakan's political ban remained in effect until a 1987 referendum allowed politicians who were banned by the military to return to active politics. Upon his return, Erbakan

---

[247] Yavuz 2003, 212; Karasipahi 2009, 95.
[248] Rabasa and Larrabee 2018, 41.
[249] Yilmaz 2012, 365.
[250] Atacan 2005, 187.
[251] Gümüscü and Sert 2009, 953.
[252] Kuru 2005, 269; Yilmaz 2012, 365.
[253] Atacan 2005, 196.
[254] Akinci 1999, 78.

assumed the party's leadership.[255] Simultaneously, following Kotku's death in 1980, Erbakan gradually centralized power within the NOM and pushed out the Iskenderpasa Lodge, now led by Esad Cosan, throughout the 1980s.

The party's initial years were marked by sluggish performance due to strict military oversight. Also, the RP did not achieve electoral success until the early 1990s partly because Turgut Ozal's ANAP dominated the conservative electoral space during this period.[256] Following the intense period of political polarization and violence between the Left and the Nationalist Right in the late 1970s, the military decided to utilize religion as a potential antidote to future ideological polarization. In addition to this development, associational life thrived significantly. Between 1980 and 1995, there were 39,369 newly formed associations, whereas between 1926 and 1980, only 24,272 new associations had been established. Crucially, many of the associations were Islamic in orientation.[257] These associations gradually helped build the societal base for the Welfare Party.

One of the distinguishing traits of the RP was that they organized voter registration drives and transported voters to the polls on election day, something no Turkish party had done before but is commonplace among European social democratic parties. The party was particularly well organized in reaching out to the Muslim periphery and the Kurds.[258] Party members regularly attended weddings and funerals in their neighborhoods and extended financial or other help to those in need.[259] While this sort of political mobilization was foreign to Turkish political parties, it was standard among Islamist religiopolitical movements in the rest of the Middle East. These newly mobilized sectors of society had previously not engaged in politics, tapping into a resource that had largely been ignored up to this point (specifically the Muslim periphery and the Kurdish population).[260] A socioeconomic shift in favor of the periphery coincided with the rise of the RP, creating a political vacuum that eventually led to the electoral success of the AKP.[261] Supporters of Milli Gorus came to include "entrepreneurs, civil activists, students, theologians, pious intellectuals, and women's groups" many of whom were "upwardly mobile [and] urbanizing."[262]

The RP's ideological stance did not change significantly from its MSP days; the party's ideological pillars remained firmly anchored in Islam, opposition to secularist Kemalist ideology, economic justice, and anti-Westernism.[263] For the

[255] Yavuz 2003, 218.
[256] Atacan 2005, 187; Kuru 2005, 269.
[257] Alam 2009, 364.
[258] Yavuz 1997, 66.
[259] Yavuz 1997, 77.
[260] Yavuz 1997, 66; Yavuz 2003, 217.
[261] Insel 2003, 298; Ahmadov 2008, 18.
[262] Neslihan 2016, 33.
[263] Gulalp 2001, 440; Kuru 2005, 270; Alam 2009, 368; Rabasa and Larrabee 2018, 42.

The Origins of Religiopolitical Identity

conservative and marginalized masses, the party offered a radical, anti-system critique combined with a shot at socioeconomic mobility. The growing public perception of corruption among secular parties fueled interest in the RP's anti-system discourse among urban working-class voters. The party's official motto, *Adil Düzen* (Just Order), resonated with the disillusioned suburbanites. Erbakan's core Islamist vision was incorporated into the RP platform: "A stable, well-ordered society will emerge if Turkey achieves four objects: a Milli Görüş philosophy that is not in conflict with its own past; a just order; an economically and militarily powerful country to lead the union of Muslim countries; and a new world order where Muslims have an important voice."[264]

The RP was opposed to EU and EEC membership, arguing that it was a "Christian club" and that Turkey should instead associate itself with Muslim countries. Erbakan mocked those who supported European integration, calling them "naïve imitators of the West."[265] The party believed "international institutions and norms [to be] extensions of the Western hegemony" and generally avoided international outreach and cooperation. This was despite the fact that promoting the norms of democracy and human rights in Turkey could have saved the RP from repeated repression by the state.[266] Erbakan promised to "restore the hurt national pride" that had supposedly been harmed by the secular elite; repeated rejections by the EU constituted a national embarrassment, in his opinion. Instead, the party's foreign policy was "directed to other Muslim nations" instead of Europe.[267] The party actually advocated for the establishment of an "Islamic monetary union, Islamic common market, [and an] Islamic NATO", desiring to create Islamic parallels to Western institutions.[268] With Erbakan as Prime Minister, the party established "an economic cooperation pact with [the] eight biggest Muslim nations under the name D-8."[269]

Erbakan's rhetoric proved controversial at times both inside and outside of the party. In voicing his opposition to the EU, his and the movement's anti-Zionist, and occasionally anti-Semitic, tendencies surfaced.[270] He stated that if Turkey joined the EU, Israel would join immediately after, and Turkey and Israel would become the same state.[271] While some of Erbakan's controversial statements can be classified as populist attempts to normalize the RP, others

---

[264] Yavuz 2003, 221.
[265] Yilmaz 2005, 401.
[266] Kuru 2005, 269.
[267] Yilmaz 2012, 369; Neslihan 2016, 55.
[268] Atacan 2005, 188.
[269] Yilmaz 2011, 256.
[270] Erbakan, Kotku, and other leaders of the National Outlook Movement and the parties associated with it used anti-Semitic, anti-Israel, and anti-Masonic tirades to mobilize and recruit supporters since the formation of the movement. See Çaha and Baykal (2017, 799).
[271] Atacan 2005, 188.

reveal the primal instincts of conventional Islamism: "Other parties have voters whereas RP has believers"; "elections are the counting of Muslims in Turkey"; and those who do not vote for RP belong to the "religion of potato"; "the Prophet Adam was a Welfarist. Likewise, all past prophets were partisans of RP, so was the Sultan Mehmet II"; if "Ataturk had been alive, he would have been a Welfarist."[272] Erbakan's controversial approach to politics was a key reason why the NOM failed to ever garner a mass following.[273]

The RP's breakout electoral performance came in the 1994 local elections, where the party won 19 percent of the vote. Most importantly, the party won the mayoral contests in Turkey's two largest cities – Ankara and Istanbul, the latter of which belonged to Erdogan – which shook the secular establishment to its core. The party's fortune continued in the 1995 parliamentary elections where the RP won 21.4 percent of the vote. At its previous national contest in 1987, the party won only 7.2 percent of the vote, failing to surpass the country's 10 percent electoral threshold to win seats in the parliament. After the 1995 election, the RP entered into a coalition government with the True Path Party (DYP), and Erbakan became the first Islamist prime minister in Turkish history.[274] Erbakan's time as the prime minister was fleeting, however, as he was forced to resign after only 11 months due to the "postmodern" coup on February 28, 1997. In deciding to undertake this coup, the National Security Council and the military "declared that ... Islamic fundamentalism in Turkey has become as dangerous as Kurdish separatism and should be fought by all available means."[275] In 1998, the movement again found itself in front of the Constitutional Court as the RP was banned for violating secularism, in the same manner as its predecessors.

Its political institutionalization notwithstanding, the Turkish Islamists stuck to their hybrid movement-party organizational structure. The movement was crucial for recruitment, grassroots mobilization, and religious legitimization of the political party. Hence, the similarities prevail despite the notable differences between the NOM in Turkey, on one hand, and the Egyptian Brotherhood and the Tunisian Ennahdha, on the other hand. It is the religious movement that constitutes the bedrock of Islamist activism in all three cases. Political activism constitutes only one component of the multifaceted Islamism in this period.

CENTER PARTY IN GERMANY

The origins of the German Catholic mass movement can be traced to three distinct developments in the nineteenth century: anticlerical attacks, de-Christianization, and the Social Question. The process generally recognized

[272] Yildiz 2003, 191 & 193; Yilmaz 2011, 258.
[273] Mardin 2005, 158.
[274] Atacan 2005, 187–88; Kuru 2005, 269; Yavuz 1997, 63.
[275] Atacan 2005, 193.

The Origins of Religiopolitical Identity 153

as de-Christianization is dated back to either the mid-eighteenth century or the early nineteenth century. Increasing public approval of anticlerical views, lower rates of church attendance, and the broader movement of social life away from the Church characterized this process. Likewise, the growth of radical leftist political ideas paralleled the process of de-Christianization.[276] The Lutheran Church operated as "a pillar" of the state and held the Catholic Church and its claims in contempt.[277] Anticlericalism therefore did not exist because the German state of the time sought to be especially secular, but rather due to the primacy held by the Lutheran Church and the expected anti-Catholic sentiments arising from leaders of the Lutheran faith.

Long before the Kültürkampf, the Prussian state drew widespread resentment among Catholics for pursuing discriminatory policies toward the Catholic Church. The Cologne Troubles of 1837 (also known as the Cologne Incident or Kölner Wirren) is instructive in this regard, illustrating the evolution of the difficult relationship between the Catholic Church and the Prussian state. As part of an effort to expand state authority over social issues vis-à-vis the Catholic Church, the Prussian state began officially recognizing marriages between Catholics and Protestants in 1825. Unsurprisingly, the state's new policy of performing mixed marriages irked the Catholic hierarchy.[278] Around the same time, the state decided to take complete control of higher education via Humboldtian reforms. While the state's primary goal in monopolizing university education seemed to have been facilitating the provision of "competent state servants through neo-humanistic training," the inclusion of theological training in this educational reform disturbed Catholics. Eventually the church hierarchy challenged these policies, leading to the Cologne Troubles. When the state's stance on mixed marriages conflicted with that of the Catholic Church, Catholics expressed their discontent via "violent street disturbances and peaceful public demonstrations."[279] Cologne Archbishop Droste-Vischering was arrested in 1837 because of his objections to the state's accommodation of mixed marriages and his refusal to accept the authority of Bonn University's Catholic Theological Faculty to teach Catholic theology.[280]

This episode ushered in the discernably ultramontane Catholic revival. Ultramontanism refers to the movement among Catholics in the nineteenth century that called for a stronger form of papal authority and relied on increased religious consciousness and identity in Germany as well as Italy and Belgium.[281] It promoted strict commitment to papal orthodoxy by excluding those perspectives that did not fully conform. The movement began under Pope Gregory

---

[276] Sperber 1982, 306.
[277] Epstein 1959, 27.
[278] Evans 1999, 60.
[279] Sperber 1986, 47.
[280] Atkin and Tallett 2003, 98.
[281] Atkin and Tallett 2003, 106

XVI (1831–46) but attained perfection under Pope Pius IX (1846–78), who introduced a series of teachings that ultimately defined what papal orthodoxy stood for; such teachings were anti-Liberal in orientation and culminated in the dogma of papal infallibility of Vatican I, furthering divisions among Catholics in Germany.[282] For Catholics, the Cologne Troubles helped mobilize and unify German Catholics toward greater social and political activism and fostered the ultramontane perspective among Catholics. Father Johannes Becker's efforts to spur "anti-Prussian sentiment" among lower class Catholics embodied the overall sentiment of Catholics at this time. Those who did not share the ultramontane perspective were castigated as Hermesians.[283]

In the decade following the Cologne Troubles, religion attained greater significance in the lives of German Catholics. The first half of the nineteenth century was marked by the crumbling of the social and cultural structure that shaped religious life in Germany much like elsewhere in Europe; it was unclear what the new social structure would be at this time. By mid-nineteenth century, religion re-assumed its central role in the "practices and institutions" of German Catholics. As Sperber argues, this was not merely "an organizational phenomenon"; the plethora of Catholic organizations popping up during this time was only part of the bigger picture. As important was the fact that "popular [Catholic] consciousness" among Catholics dramatically increased, ultimately allowing the Catholic Church to regain influence lost before 1850.[284] There was a change in the way religious identity was conceptualized among Catholics, however. Before the 1830s, the Catholic Church displayed some openness to modernization and could be characterized as "enlightened" by some measures. The events of the 1837 Cologne Troubles changed the Church's overall attitude to modernity. The Church no longer embraced the civil society activism of the thriving Catholic middle classes; instead, the defining features of the new Catholic identity revolved around papal orthodoxy and the apparent tension between Catholicism and modern society. Pius IX asked bishops in Germany and elsewhere to defy state controls. In one instance, Hermann von Vicari – Archbishop of Freiburg – made clerical appointments without governmental approval and refused to hold masses following the death of Grand Duke Leopold. He also called on the government to put an end to state certification of Catholic clergy, supervision of schools by the state, and state interference with church finances and administration.[285]

Jonathan Sperber's thorough analysis of the wills left by German Catholics between 1800 and 1870 offers some empirical support for this shift in Catholics' religious self-identification in Germany. Catholics in the Rhineland

[282] Yonke 1990, 23; Ross 1998, 36.
[283] Yonke 1990, 34.
[284] Sperber 1982, 318.
[285] Evans 1999, 97.

The Origins of Religiopolitical Identity

and Westphalia display a remarkable shift in how they justified their bequests. In the decades before 1850, it was fairly common for wills to have secular justifications; however, in the years following 1850, if German Catholics justified their will, they did so using religious justifications: "Between the invocation of the most Holy Trinity and clauses regulating the distribution of property, the expression of exclusively secular ideals faded away."[286] While it is possible to interpret this observation and construe the dynamics of this change in different ways, the fact that religion assumed a more central role in the lives of German Catholics should be a starting point for any discussion.

Rise of the Catholic Mass Movement

This new Catholic consciousness predated the tumultuous anticlericalism of the 1860s and 1870s and the challenging political climate therein for Catholics. It was the thriving Catholic consciousness and increase in "Catholic religious sentiment" against the early wave of anticlerical attacks that prepared Catholics for their strong reaction to anti-Catholic developments in the 1860s and 1870s; they stood by the Catholic Church with "an astonishing tenacity."[287] This growing importance of religion in the lives of Catholics correlated with the growth of Catholic mass movements, associations, and organizations across Germany following Archbishop Droste-Vischering's arrest in 1837. Understanding the emergence of Catholic associations is essential to understanding the evolution of Catholicism in Germany. These new associations typically fell under one of the following four issue areas: educational, charitable, social, or political. While each association had its own specific focus, several overarching goals unified these organizations, creating a collective identity and the semblance of a united Catholic front.[288] In their efforts to defend Catholicism from attacks, these Catholic organizations aimed "to undertake works of mercy and charity; to teach the common folk so as to protect them from the intellectual and cultural pitfalls of a secularized society; to provide a Christian form of socialization; to organize the faithful politically against the intrusions of the state into religious matters."[289] Prior to this period, Sperber observes, "there were essentially no sociopolitical organizations in German Catholicism ... The predominant form of association remained religious brotherhood whose sociopolitical workings were limited to the possible existence of a mutual benefit fund."[290]

In this regard, these voluntary associations (Vereine) were an entirely new phenomenon among Catholics in Germany and expanded remarkably during

[286] Sperber 1982, 310.
[287] Sperber 1982, 316.
[288] Atkin and Tallett 2003, 126.
[289] Yonke 1990, 68.
[290] Sperber 1980, 84.

this period.[291] Hundreds of new Catholic organizations such as reading circles, casinos, popular missions, sodalities, miners' associations, and new pilgrimages were formed. These organizations did not merely enable Catholics to socialize or meet their religious needs – they functioned as forums for Catholics to engage in political and social debate, social activism, and Catholic cultural identity-building. Many Catholics, especially the middle classes, enriched themselves with "civic pride and self-consciousness"; these associations most critically helped Catholics across Germany to mobilize "against the intellectual as well as political threats to the Church."[292] The extent of the Prussian and Protestant threats to Catholics' cultural and religious identity facilitated the process of creating guardians of the faith from Catholic laity via these associations. While these associations were previously decentralized, the subsequent rise of Volksverein solidified their organizational cohesion and unity. The rise of associational life among German Catholics was mirrored among Catholics in Italy and Belgium; likewise, Islamist organizations in the twenty-first century pursued organizational structures that operated in social, political, charitable, and religious areas.

Brewing Intra-Catholic Conflict

The Catholic associations and broader Catholic mass movement also served as the medium through which the two modern views of Catholicism conflicted: ultramontanism vs. liberalism. For the Church hierarchy, various Catholic associations (Vereine) were far from independent organizations; they served the Church and operated as "an extension of the Church" such that church records laid out "internal machinations as well as the Christian goals and intentions behind them."[293] As such, these associations pushed the agenda of the ultramontanes and their conservatism in various ways, including higher levels of religious participation and morality. This conservatism with ultramontanism at its core, however, turned into a source of friction among Catholics. Catholics who hailed from middle-class and educated backgrounds took great issue with this fundamentalist movement that prioritized papal authority at all costs.[294]

But the conflict was not merely an ideational one about where society was headed or how Catholics should orient themselves in a modern world. The new Catholic associations were largely under the control of the middle-class laity, who "reveal[ed] a heightened middle-class and cultural consciousness that would eventually express itself politically."[295] The struggle for power

---

[291] Atkin and Tallett 2003, 146.
[292] Yonke 1990, 6–7.
[293] Yonke 1990, 12.
[294] Evans 1999, 102.
[295] Yonke 1990, 81.

The Origins of Religiopolitical Identity

and influence defined the ensuing conflict between these liberal middle-class Catholics and the conservatives as the ultramontane tendency among German Catholics gained greater traction. Ultramontanism became the expression of a new orthodoxy that worked against the liberalism and secularism of the modern age. Moreover, ultramontanes were deeply anti-intellectual, militating further against the middle-class Catholics.

This friction inevitably raised serious questions about the Catholic Church and the direction of social, religious, and political activism among Catholics in Germany. Where did the educated lay Catholics fit in the future design of the Catholic Church? Would their modernist and liberal conceptions of political and social reform be compatible with the fundamentally anti-liberal orientation of the Catholic Church and the ultramontane movement within Catholicism? Despite this fundamental conflict between the two, middle-class German Catholics did not sever ties with the Church and continued to uphold the Church hierarchy.

As a result of the conflict between ultramontane and middle-class factions of Catholicism, conflicting views on the state, society, and political activism emerged. At its core, these conflicting views bred confusion among Catholics. For liberal Catholics, modern society presented serious challenges that needed to be met head-on. Catholic theologians like Johann Baptist von Hirscher and Anton Günther called for a renewal of the Catholic Church's position in modern society, underscoring the necessity of incorporating the changing social circumstances associated with modernity. In a bold reform effort, they called for integrating the educated laity into the church hierarchy.[296]

By contrast, the Catholic Church mobilized the faithful around the apostolic vision that prioritized the centralized authority of the Church and its vision above all else. In order to facilitate this ultramontane effort, Piusverein (Pius Association) was established in 1848 as an umbrella organization for Catholic associations across the country.[297] During the spring and summer of 1848, a circle of priests and laymen in Mainz worked with conservative Catholic journals to promote the founding of a new association – an umbrella organization originally named the Pius Association for Religious Freedom. By August, hundreds of cells of this new Pius Association had formed, and Father Adam Franz Lennig issued the call for a general assembly to convene in Mainz.[298] The Pius Association operated under the auspices of the archbishop and claimed to represent Catholic interests as the "political voice of Catholicism" in Germany. In reality, however, the association was far from unifying all Catholics and most certainly failed to represent all political interests of Catholics in Germany.[299] The political orientation of the Pius Associations posed problems for the state,

---

[296] Yonke 1990, 89.
[297] Evans 1999, 68; Gross 2004, 34.
[298] Atkin and Tallett 2003, 126.
[299] Yonke 1990, 113.

which ultimately stripped these associations of their ability to engage in political debates.

German Catholics came together in October 1848 to unify the Pius Association's goals. Ultramontane Catholics dominated the meeting, which is subsequently described as the "second Pentecost" by the convention report: "It was the first great assembly of Catholic Germans – yes, the whole of Catholic Germany was assembled here in spirit and substance. Until now we were scattered, isolated; each surrounded in his circle of opposition, misunderstood, persecuted, restrained – but now we were here one and peerless; and free and joyous, as never in living memory, we conferred on our own matters – a spiritual parliament of the Catholic folk. Was it then a miracle, when the enthusiasm ultimately unleashed itself and poured out in full force – and the locked-up thought soared high and brilliantly?"[300] However, Wilhelm Emanuel Ketteler – later Bishop of Mainz and a leader in the German Church hierarchy – led a splinter group from the nascent Pius Associations to form the *Katholischer Verein Deutschlands* (KVD) and focus on the "moral regeneration of the German people."[301] The KVD aimed to address issues such as freedom of the church, freedom of education, intellectual and moral education, self-regulation for Catholic institutions, and alleviation of social incongruities. Ketteler's orations inspired the creation of charitable organizations under KVD auspices and laid the foundation for Catholic charitable and social engagement throughout Central Europe, referred to as social Catholicism. Meanwhile, the Pius Associations "distributed leaflets, held rallies, and gave sermons denouncing the left and calling on the voters to support moderate or conservative candidates."[302] The organizations proved ephemeral; most of them had disappeared by the early 1850s because of a lack of interest, and the few that remained chose to focus on religious or charitable matters. Eventually, the KVD turned into an organization that represented all Catholic voluntary associations. Middle-class Catholics commanded a disproportionate influence within the KVD during this time, shaping the Church's response to socioeconomic issues, that is, the Social Question. Such activism in the KVD was supplemented by the middle-class Catholics' extensive network of "semi-exclusive clubs" where their Catholic political consciousness flourished in the 1850s and 1860s.[303]

The extent of the chasm between the Catholic Church and ultramontane Catholics on one hand and middle-class liberal Catholics on the other was most evident in the political arena. Middle-class Catholics' influence over the Catholic Church on political issues remained largely muted as the Church maintained close control over political activism. For example, the Catholic newspaper *Volkshalle*'s editorial policy confined the meaning of Catholicism

---

[300] Quoted in Yonke 1990, 95.
[301] Yonke, 2005.
[302] Sperber 1984, 50.
[303] Yonke 1990, 184.

The Origins of Religiopolitical Identity

and its political interests to a strictly ultramontane conception. Such stringent control turned away many liberal middle-class Catholics. Remarkably, many of these Catholics did not take issue with the interests of the Church; rather, they willingly advocated for Church interests and Catholic concerns. The crux of the disagreement lay in the way ultramontanism came to define Catholicism. This schism between the ultramontane Catholics and the more politically oriented middle-class Catholics in Germany exhibited strong parallels in the way Islamists experienced intragroup divisions between the religious and political factions in Egypt, Tunisia, and Turkey.

The emergence of the "Catholic politician" around 1848 attests to the evolution of political activism on the part of politically inclined liberal Catholics during this period. The strong interest in politics and political activism exhibited by middle-class Catholics did not materialize as a Catholic party until the 1870s – a delay observed in Catholic and Islamist parties elsewhere. Yet, middle-class laymen intent on entering the political arena to promote Catholic interests took action and came together in the Frankfurt Assembly. As members of the Catholic Club, these Catholic politicians found homes in different political convictions, brought together by their motivation to promote Catholic interests.[304] They were characterized by two key attributes that aimed to harness religion's political draw in their political ambitions to its fullest extent. On one hand, they expressed subservience to the church hierarchy – a strategy that intended to secure the Church's support or, at the very least, to avoid the Church's disapproval in their political endeavors. On the other hand, these Catholic politicians tended to overplay their political sway and asserted that they spoke "for all Catholics"[305] – a claim certainly not condoned by the Church. Yet, these two seemingly conflicting strategies helped them obtain the support of many Catholics in elections when Catholics sought "good" Catholic candidates in state and national legislative elections; Catholic support for such candidates came predominantly from the associations dominated by middle-class Catholics.

The Social Question increasingly captured middle-class Catholics' social activism as they viewed it not only as an urgent issue but also as an outlet for their political consciousness. At its core, the Social Question referred to the "worker question."[306] At the 1848 convention of the KVD, the Social Question was defined as "the growing division between rich and poor, between possessors and non-possessors."[307] While socioeconomic in nature, the Social Question deeply reflected the ongoing political conflicts in German society and offered an opportunity for Catholics to play a larger political role. In what would later become the theoretical origins of Catholic Socialism, Wilhelm

[304] Evans 1990, 69.
[305] Yonke 1990, 131.
[306] Misner 1992, 581.
[307] Yonke 1990, 137.

Ketteler – theologian and bishop of Mainz – drew attention to the insufficiency of traditional charity organizations of the Catholic Church in addressing the Social Question;[308] a fundamental transformation toward "Christian poverty and love of neighbor" was imperative to address this problem created by modernity and, in particular, by the industrialization process. The Social Question was also viewed from a cultural perspective. As the Kültürkampf drew closer, many middle-class Catholics perceived the Social Question as a "cultural struggle" and a consequence of the "perceived cultural crisis of secularization."[309]

The expanded role and influence of middle-class Catholics in German Catholicism's efforts to tackle the Social Question was remarkable. In addition to being the main ideological force in engaging with the Social Question, middle-class Catholics became the chief patrons of this process. Their financial contributions facilitated both the expansion of the institutional infrastructure to deal with the Social Question and the clergy's growth in numbers.[310] While socioeconomic inequality featured as an important aspect of Islamist parties in Egypt, Tunisia, and Turkey, its connection to the process of modernization and industrialization was more tedious for Islamists. This was unlike their Catholic counterparts, who took issue with the inequalities brought about by industrialization more seriously. The difference between Islamist parties in the Middle East and Catholic parties in Western Europe reflected the difference in the underlying processes of modernization and industrialization in these regions.

Such disproportionate influence over what the Social Question encompasses and how to address it elevated middle-class Catholics' position within German Catholicism but fell short of shaping the political activism of the Church. In fact, the Catholic Church tightened its grip over Catholics in Germany. The long tenure of Pope Pius IX (1846–78) entrenched the dominance of ultramontanism among the clergy and the rank and file.[311] This was not simply a matter of persuasion – it reflected the Church hierarchy's direct confrontation with the heterodoxy and revolt that plagued many middle-class German Catholics. For liberal middle-class Catholics, the core issue at stake was not defending the Church's interests in the political arena; all Catholics concurred that the Church and Catholics were under attack and these attacks threatened their key interests. Rather, the liberal Catholics concerned themselves with the best way to address this existential threat, keeping in view the deeply transformative effects of modernity. Liberal Catholics in particular wanted to ensure that science, education, and rationalism became pillars of the Catholic response to these challenges. However, Pope Pius IX's approach did not seek

[308] Evans 1999, 70.
[309] Yonke 1990, 184–85.
[310] Yonke 1990, 149.
[311] Gross 2004, 51.

The Origins of Religiopolitical Identity

a compromise; by contrast, it looked for ways to consolidate the ultramontane power, openly defying liberal Catholics in Germany and deepening the tension between the two.

Like elsewhere in Western Europe, by empowering ultramontanism in Germany, Pope Pius IX sought to weaken and undermine German theology and liberal Catholicism. In this struggle, the Catholic Church commanded a vast array of resources to shape the direction of the Church and sentiment of the laity. It utilized the institutional advantages offered by Catholic seminaries and the episcopal hierarchy. Clergymen were brought in line with the ultramontane conception of Catholicism. The pope communicated the Syllabus of Errors and dogmatized the doctrine of papal infallibility. Moreover, the pope resorted to a range of symbolic instruments to reinforce the Church's centrality: "His [Pope Pius IX] vigorous promotion of Marian religious feasts, canonization of new saints, and distribution of papal indulgences appealed to Catholics seeking spiritual solace in a difficult age."[312]

The Church was disturbed by the political activism of lay Catholics through the 1860s as it increasingly took on a more autonomous form.[313] In an effort to maintain the Church hierarchy's monopoly on Catholic involvement in the political arena, the Church did not allow priests "to stand for office, nor to preach" on politics in any form.[314] It was the Church's concern with losing political and religious power that pushed the Church to limit outright political activism – a process absent in the Islamist context. When openly political organizations emerged toward the end of the decade despite church policy, the Church put vigorous effort into controlling how these associations unfolded. For example, the Swabian Vereine was established in 1871–72 and contained statutes "identically or nearly identically worded, suggesting, besides a concerted effort by Catholic activists, the existence of church coordination."[315]

Liberal Catholics pushed back against the ultramontane pressure in 1869, shortly before Vatican Council I. In an open statement known as the Koblenzer Laienadresse (Koblenz Laity Address) directed to the Bishop of Trier, approximately 50 middle-class lay Catholics criticized the convocation of Vatican Council I and the intention to lay out new doctrines. The address read: "Nowhere at present time do we see an emergent heretical point of confession touching upon schism, as had invoked earlier councils to the formulation of church teaching. The unbelief that rings about us is supported by philosophical opinions, whose falsehood was brought to light by great Christian truths long ago. And a union with our Christian brothers separated in faith would not be facilitated if one increased the sum of the articles of faith with a few new

---

[312] Yonke 1990, 207–08.
[313] Sperber 1980, 270.
[314] Sperber 1980, 248.
[315] Kalyvas 1996, 206.

formulations."[316] The address is significant in that it displays the inherent tensions between different strands of European Catholicism, particularly in how different Catholics conceptualized progress. Liberal Catholics implicitly recognized the Church's authority over Catholics, yet remained concerned about how the creation of new doctrines would likely lead to further factionalism rather than facilitating reconciliation.

The Koblenz Laity Address clearly communicated liberal Catholics' discontent with the Church hierarchy and papal authority. The signatories demanded freedom for the Church from state authority and an active strategy to meet the challenges created by "the social maladies of the age," which correspond to the ultramontane perspective. Crucially, the signatories of the Address sought to ensure a fundamentally religious vision for the state, affirming their Catholicity:

...they fear those times would return when the state authority intervenes with worldly means of coercion for the dogma and laws of one particular religious confession; ...We do not deny that the life of the state also has a *religious foundation* [emphasis added], insofar as the order of the state and its authoritative power rests upon the recognition of a personal God and of the moral planted by Him in the soul. However, we are also fully convinced that the sphere of the state, like the church, moves in complete independence within its inherent realm. It is confined by those spiritual perceptions and moral laws that are obtained through the natural strengths of humanity.[317]

Where the Address differed from the Church was calling for reconciliation with Protestants, embracing modern education and science (Wissenschaft), and making the laity a more integral part of decision-making within the Church. It declared, "It already contradicts the interests of the Church as the first cultural power not to be represented at the great educational institutions of our nation ... Suffice a glance at the relationship between the clergy and the educated laity in most Latin countries to frighten us away from the consequences of a one-sided education and cultivation of future ministers."[318] The signatories of the Koblenz Address were convinced of the need to fundamentally restructure the relationship between the laity and the clergy and alter the hierarchical vision of the Church. In other words, the Koblenz Laity Address sought to "de-mystify the clergy by placing them in the center of the community, instead of above it."[319] These requests fundamentally challenged the hierarchical authority of the Church and further demonstrated the depth of the friction between the two sides.

[316] Yonke 1990, 210.
[317] Yonke 1990, 212.
[318] Yonke 1990, 212.
[319] Yonke 1990, 212.

The Origins of Religiopolitical Identity

Initially, other similar statements were made by middle-class German Catholics such as the Bonn Statement addressed to the archbishop. It was after papal infallibility was dogmatized in 1870 that the outcry from liberal German Catholics turned into protests. The doctrine of papal infallibility served as "a millstone around the necks of liberal Catholics"; it was the "articulate and vociferous" ultramontane block who engineered such a radical pronouncement and sought to bring liberal Catholics back into the fold.[320] The Königswinter Protest statement read: "Considering that the assembly held in the Vatican deliberates without total freedom and important resolutions were formulated without the requisite agreement, the undersigned Catholics publicly state that they do not recognize the decree concerning the absolute authority of the pope and personal infallibility as the decision of an ecumenical council, furthermore rejecting the same as an innovation standing in contradiction to the traditional faith of the Church."[321] The Church responded fiercely to demands it accurately perceived as a challenge to its hierarchical authority. Those who signed the statements faced bans from the Church and were asked to recant in front of the clergy. Catholic theologians who took part in protests, however, faced greater rebuke. They were asked to withdraw their support; failure to do so would lead to their excommunication. Many were eventually excommunicated when they did not recant. While those who were excommunicated moved on with a new church they established (the Old Catholic Church),[322] those who were critical of the hierarchy but remained within Catholicism – upon renouncing their criticism of the church hierarchy in the face of pressures from the clergy – posed a major challenge to the Church.[323] The doctrine of papal infallibility and the Church's strong reaction to critics of this new doctrine would characterize the ultramontane camp's victory and early course of political Catholicism.

However, calls for a Catholic political party grew louder and gained greater traction among German Catholics at the end of the 1860s and very early 1870s. Jacob Lindau – a Catholic leader from Baden – demanded the establishment of a Catholic party in the Catholic Congress of 1869. Likewise, Cologne's Archbishop Melchers called on the Catholic hierarchy to guide the faithful on fateful political issues of the time in the annual meeting of Katholikvereine. On his part, Archbishop Melchers lifted the proscription on clergy's political participation and urged Catholics to elect "devout Catholics" in 1870 in view of the upcoming elections in Prussia.[324]

The emergence of the Catholic mass movement crystallized a growing division within German Catholicism upon the onset of modernity. While

---

[320] Atkin and Tallett 2003, 141.
[321] Yonke 1990, 220.
[322] Evans 1999, 98.
[323] Ross 1998, 37.
[324] Kalyvas 1996, 209.

164 The Politics of Religious Party Change

German Catholicism was united in pushing back against the marginalization of the Catholic Church and protecting the interests of Catholic Germans in an ever-secularizing modern environment, the religious and political factions of Catholicism called for different approaches. The religious faction – comprised primarily of the church hierarchy with its ultramontane orientation – envisioned a unified Catholic religiopolitical movement subservient to the Church hierarchy and legitimized by its religious authority. As a result, the Church maintained control of the activism of Catholic mass organizations. The political faction of German Catholics gradually emerged as a competing force in this period, empowered by the enthusiasm and organizational skills of middle-class Catholics. They occasionally confronted the religious faction on how to best meet the challenges of a secularizing state. Occasional episodes of politicization of the Catholic identity reflected small-scale anticlerical efforts in this period. Ultimately, it was the Kültürkampf that dramatically changed the political and religious landscape for German Catholics. The creation of a mass Catholic socioreligious movement in this earlier episode was followed by greater calls for the politicization of the Catholic identity.

POPULAR PARTY IN ITALY

The origins of the Catholic mass movement in Italy were highly decentralized, tightening its organizational structure and central control over time similar to Catholic mass movements in Germany and Belgium. In its formative years, it was structured around Opera dei Congressi e dei Comitati Cattolici, subsequently morphing into Catholic Action.[325] The Opera was formed at the Italian Catholic Congress in Venice in 1874 as "a loose federation of parochial societies of committed laymen"; the Opera's leaders were supported – sometimes directly appointed – by the Holy See or the church hierarchy.[326] The theme of the Opera's first congress was "the necessity of Christian education," and it unmistakably rebuked the anticlerical attacks by the Italian state, particularly laws that aimed to limit the influence of the Church and religion in schools. The declaration issued at the end of the congress underscored the need for Catholics to mobilize "in concerted and unified action" in order to maximize the Church's power and influence.[327]

The ideological roots of the Opera date back to the Society of Italian Catholic Youth (Societa della Gioventu Cattolica Italiana), which was founded in 1867 by Mario Fani and Giovanni Acquaderni. The creation of this movement marked the first ever effort by Italian Catholic laymen to form an organization at the national level in "defense of the Church."[328]

[325] Agocs 1975, 32.
[326] Poggi 1967, 16.
[327] Vaillancourt 1980, 39.
[328] Poggi 1967, 15.

The Origins of Religiopolitical Identity

The Society convened the first Italian Catholic Congress in Venice in 1874, leading to the creation of the Opera. In resemblance of the Jesuit lay sodalities of the sixteenth century, the Society was made up of "aristocrats and wealthy members of the bourgeoisie" with an eye toward social change in response to the growing anticlerical character of the post-Risorgimento Italian government.[329] Pope Pius IX (1846–78) immediately granted his approval of the organization as he viewed it as an instrument to defend the Church against modernity and secularism. Pius IX's trust in the Society rested in part on the conviction that the organization posed a limited threat of independence in view of its elite origins.

In 1875, a permanent national liaison committee began giving shape to the Opera. The standing committee behind the Opera was led by a president appointed by the pope, speaking to the close relationship between this Italian Catholic movement and the Church akin to the unified structure of Islamist parties. With clerical supervision, the organization established local parish committees that constituted the real power of the Opera. Such national organization and geographical division into diocesan and parochial committees emulated the Church's ecclesiastical structure, unlike the decentralized nature of the German Catholic mass movement. The specific goals of the Opera included "the defense of the pope's rights, the fight for freedom in teaching and against compulsory public education, and the support of guild-like solutions in social relations."[330] In addition to upholding the Church's goals and authority, the Opera helped empower laypersons through the formation of separate associations that served specific Catholic demographic groups. The Opera toed the Vatican's line in world affairs, particularly on issues such as education and political noninvolvement. The Opera faithfully followed Don Giacomo Margotti's 1861 mandate, "Ne eletti, ne elettori," and Pius IX's 1874 Non Expedit.[331] Opera congresses aimed at "doctrinal influence, not the winning of parliamentary seats"; for example, Pope Leo XIII (1878–1903) demanded the 1881 congress delegates to "regroup Italian Catholics in a common and unified action for the defense of the rights of the Holy See, and the religious and social interests of Italian Catholics, in conformity with the desires of the pope and under the direction of the episcopate and the clergy."[332] Catholics were concerned about the growth of anti-Catholic sentiment in Italy as the Italian Prime Minister Antonio Starrabba di Rudini took actions against the Opera in 1898 and some Catholic dailies such as *L'Osservatore Cattolico*.[333]

As Opera members felt the need to organize more cohesively to protest against the secular government, the term "Catholic Action" was popularized

---

[329] Vaillancourt 1980, 39.

[330] Banti 2000, 54.

[331] Cunsolo 1993, 23.

[332] Vaillancourt 1980, 40.

[333] Cunsolo 1993, 27.

to refer to a new network of Catholic groups and associations "connected by the Opera's parish and diocesan committees."[334] Hence, over time a growing number of organizations fell under the broad umbrella of the Opera, including associations that catered toward the youth, women, and workers. By the end of the nineteenth century, 17 regional committees, 188 diocesan committees, 3,982 parochial committees, 688 workers' organizations, 708 youth organizations, 17 university student groups, 24 dailies, and 155 periodicals were part of the Opera.[335]

In 1904, however, the Opera was abolished by Pope Pius X (1903–14).[336] Why would the pope abolish an organization that already maintained strong ties with the Church and the Catholic faithful? Pius X had two reasons for abolishing the Opera, the first being ideological in nature. He felt that the organization was too susceptible to the "modernistic heresy" and feared the influence of left-leaning Catholic leaders within the group – a reference to the politically oriented members of the Catholic mass movement in Italy, or the political faction. Second, Pius X viewed Christian democratic and political sentiments within the Opera to be a "challenge to hierarchical control over lay organizations."[337] At its core, this concerned the Church's religious authority and how the Opera was deemed close to charting an independent course. Similar concerns existed against middle-class German Catholics and Belgian Catholic activists. The Vatican adamantly opposed the idea of lay Catholic organizations such as the Opera taking on a more political and independent direction. Indeed, the narrative of the Opera was characterized by the constant clash over control of the movement between the Church and the old leaders of Opera, on one hand, and lay Catholic activists such as the young Christian Democrats, on the other.[338] Romolo Murri and fellow Christian Democrats threatened the Church's authority: "The Vatican had escaped the danger of an Italian Catholic party, which under Murri would have cut loose from any hierarchical control and might have dragged the church into dangerous adventures. Murri's party would have been Catholic without being papal, and its leader would have been a political primate imperiling the unity of command within the church."[339] The attitude of the pope and the Church toward the organization was defined by "formal approval, but distrustful and discouraging detachment."[340] Pope Pius X ultimately decided that the Opera dei Congressi organization interfered with the Church's hierarchical control over the Catholic social movement in Italy, and thusly abolished it in order to push his own, more papal-influenced course for Catholic Action in Italy.

[334] Poggi 1967, 16.
[335] Kalyvas 1996, 217; Banti 2000, 54.
[336] Poggi 1967, 18; Agocs 1975, 32.
[337] Agocs 1974, 18.
[338] Agocs 1975, 32; Dawes 2011, 493.
[339] Webster 1960, 15.
[340] Belardinelli quoted in Kalyvas 1996, 180.

The Origins of Religiopolitical Identity

The Rise of Catholic Action

It is somewhat difficult to pin an exact date for the founding of Catholic Action (Azione Cattolica Italiana, Italian Catholic Action), in great part because Catholic Action referred to "the whole phenomenon of organized lay undertakings" on behalf of the Church in addition to the specific organizational structure that followed the Opera.[341] Different lay organizations founded at different points were all considered part of the larger Catholic Action movement in the first decade of the twentieth century. Once the Opera was dissolved, however, Pope Pius X directly intervened in the initial steps to create Catholic Action by "establishing hierarchical control" over its organization and activities; such control was established through the appointment of lay leaders for the administration of the Catholic Action movement.[342] A 1904 papal circular explicitly stated that "Azione Cattolica would be in the future under the direct control of the bishops. Diocesan congresses would be held only under episcopal control, and national congresses could not be held without the authorization of the pope. The pope would also have the exclusive right of appointing the head of Azione Cattolica."[343] By 1915, Pope Benedict XV (1914–22) formed a "central office" for these different organizations which led to greater consolidation of Catholic Action, transforming it from a loose movement to an organized effort to bind like-minded Catholic groups together. The leadership cadres of these associations would be subservient to the clergy in the Church hierarchy through direct episcopal supervision.

Indeed, some young Catholic activists who would later form the backbone of Christian Democracy in Italy viewed Catholic Action and its subsidiary associations such as the Unione Popolare as popular instruments "to confirm the pope's decisions."[344] Unquestioning loyalty and unswerving orthodoxy were the sine qua nons of belonging to Catholic Action; those who did not conform were systematically pushed out or marginalized in order to sterilize the movement. Young Christian Democratic activists like Filippo Meda and Don Luigi Sturzo, in response, decided to leave the new organization.

Like other Catholic mass movements, Catholic Action aimed to promote the interests of Catholicism. Yet, two factors complicated this process. First, the movement was a conglomerate of various organizations that served different functions. Hence, going beyond the fray of individual organizations and finding the commonalities across specific organizations was key. Second, and more importantly, the relationship of the movement to the Catholic Church greatly shaped what the movement did and did not do. Two issues here were of great concern to the Church: leadership and ideological direction of the movement.

---

[341] Misner 2004, 654.
[342] Misner 2004, 655.
[343] Quoted in Kalyvas 1996, 181.
[344] Agocs 1973, 76.

The Church wanted to maintain reign over Catholic Action. The fresh memory of the Opera's ventures into independent activism worried the Church hierarchy; the prospect of losing their control and authority over the Catholic faithful loomed large for the Church. In this regard, the movement sought to appeal primarily to lay persons on the cultural and religious issues of the time, rarely delving into political ones. Pope Pius X laid out the broad charge of the movement thusly in the papal encyclical *Il Fermo Proposito*: "The field of Catholic Action is extremely vast. In itself it does not exclude anything, in any manner, direct or indirect, which pertains to the divine mission of the Church. Accordingly one can plainly see how necessary it is for everyone to cooperate in such an important work, not only for the sanctification of his own soul, but also for the extension and increase of the Kingdom of God in individuals, families, and society."[345] What is so remarkable about this statement is that by painting the scope of Catholic Action – a modern, mass religious movement – in such broad strokes, the pope's statement draws an unmistakable analogy to Islamist movements in the twentieth century. Both Catholic and Islamist movements were all-encompassing in their nature and left nothing beyond the realm of religion's reach. Their missions are sacred and the movements serve as God's instruments to touch their societies.

Pope Pius X clearly viewed Catholic Action as more than simply a movement of people, but as a movement that is on a divinely ordained mission to engage the Catholic populace of Italy in the Church's holy mission of spreading the gospel. Pius X thusly gave the movement ecclesiastical sanction. The encyclical further elaborated on the mission of the movement: "Our Predecessor, Leo XIII, of blessed memory, has pointed out, especially in that memorable encyclical 'Rerum Novarum' and in later documents, the object to which Catholic Action should be particularly devoted, namely, 'the practical solution of the social question according to Christian principles.' Following these wise rules, We Ourselves in Our *motu proprio* of December 18, 1903, concerning Popular Christian Action – which in itself embraces the whole Catholic social movement – We Ourselves have laid down fundamental principles which should serve as a practical rule of action as well as a bond of harmony and charity."[346] The encompassing nature of Catholic Action, as envisioned by the Church, applies to both its scope and organization. Pope Pius X desired for the movement to bring about "the participation by the laity in the hierarchical apostolate of the Church."[347] The crucial word here is "hierarchical" as it clearly signals that the Church had little sympathy for independent activism in the name of religion.

Catholic Action as a religious movement did not merely emerge as the more centralized metamorphosis of the Opera; it also evinced greater cohesion and

---

[345] *Il Fermo Proposito*, 1905, paragraph 3.
[346] *Il Fermo Proposito* 1905, paragraph 13.
[347] Poggi 1967, 23.

The Origins of Religiopolitical Identity

cast a wider net in terms of its organizational reach. Catholic Action inherited the organizations associated with the Opera and established control over a wider and newer conglomerate of Catholic organizations, many of which arose after the Opera was abolished. Among the organizations that came to be known as Catholic Action were the Society of Italian Catholic Youth (the original organization within the movement), Unione Donne (later became the Italian Catholic Young Women), Electoral Union, Popular Union, and Economic-Social Union. The latter three were the significant so-called "unions" within Catholic Action. Such organization was intended by the Church to ensure that Catholic Action would be "regulated and united" in its efforts which were "varied and multiple in form while directed toward the same social good."[348] In this organizational structure, laypeople effectively formed into their own distinct organizations within the broad umbrella of the Catholic Action movement. For instance, the Italian Catholic Young Women organization (previously the Unione Donne or "Women Movement") was a branch of Italian Catholic Action that "organized unmarried women under thirty" and was spearheaded by laypeople.[349] While laity did not necessarily lack a voice in their organizations, the movement was, by and large, subject to clerical dominance.

To align the movement with the Church hierarchy, leaders of Catholic Action were laymen appointed by the Vatican or other important clerics. It was therefore imperative that the hierarchy between Catholic Action leaders and the clergy was clearly established to ensure the Church's control over the movement: "The constitutional provisions ensuring this are: (1) Above ACI's [the Catholic Action's] organizational structure, not merely at the summit of it, there exists a supreme governing body made up exclusively of members of the hierarchy. (2) The key leadership positions within the organization are held by laymen appointed by the hierarchy; these officials are responsible to those who have appointed them."[350] Clergy within the Church hierarchy ultimately reigned supreme, governing the entire movement and making their own choices about who the most qualified lay leaders were.

As such, it would be fair to suggest that although it was a lay movement, Catholic Action was "directly controlled by the [Church] hierarchy."[351] Like its predecessor the Opera, Catholic Action's organizational structure mirrored the Church's governance where "regional and diocesan committees were constituted at the intermediate level."[352] The Catholic Action movement, in this sense, notably never separated from the Church. This precedent was set from the mid-nineteenth century on as the Italian Social Catholicism movement (which gave birth to the movements that coalesced into Catholic Action) was

---

[348] *Il Fermo Proposito* 1905, paragraph 13.
[349] Poggi 1967, 20.
[350] Poggi 1967, 68.
[351] Lyon 1967, 83.
[352] Poggi 1967, 16.

heavily organized through church structures. For example, Pope Benedict XV pushed for the Unione Popolare to expand its grasp through founding diocesan committees, thus structuring its efforts around ecclesiastically defined geographical regions.

Besides exerting power over the leadership of Catholic Action, the Church viewed the movement as being directly under ecclesiastical authority and did not mince words to make Catholic Action's subservience to the Church hierarchy publicly known. Pius X reminded the faithful that just as Catholic Action's work in support of the ministry came under the authority of the bishops and the Church, its social work that aimed to establish "true Christian civilization" could not be imagined "independent of the counsel and direction of ecclesiastical authority" because Catholic Action "must conform to the principles of Christian faith and morality." Much like in the Islamist movements, the Catholic movement in Italy – as well as in Germany and Belgium – tended to boost its religious authority in order to ensure organizational cohesion and legitimize their religiopolitical visions.

While some degree of freedom in the affairs of Catholic Action was warranted, Pius X was clear on the limits of such freedom: "Since Catholics, on the other hand, are to raise always the banner of Christ, by that very fact they also raise the banner of the Church. Thus it is no more than right that they receive it from the hands of the Church, that the Church guard its immaculate honor, and that Catholics submit as docile, loving children to this maternal vigilance."[353] Here, the Pope explicitly delineates that Catholic Action must subordinate itself to ecclesiastical authority because the holy responsibility undertaken by the movement must be carried through with the guidance of the Catholic Church, which represents the presence of Christ on Earth. The following extensive quotation is instructive in contextualizing the control that the Church wielded over Catholic Action:

As far as Italy is concerned, the main critical points in ACI's [the Catholic Action] history regularly correspond to decisions taken by the Holy See. The formation of the Opera dei Congressi was both the first and the last major policy decision spontaneously made inside the Italian Catholic movement. While it can be said of the German Volksverein that its social policy derived from two great inspirations, Leo XIII's social encyclical and Wilhelm II's social policy, the corresponding movement in Italy was inspired only by the encyclical ... At the beginning of the twentieth century, an autonomous development in the Italian Catholic movement that had much in common with a contemporaneous development in the German Zentrum was abruptly ended by Pius X's beheading of the Opera dei Congressi. All previous and successive historical turning points of ACI witnessed, with monotonous regularity, comparable interference by the Holy See.[354]

---

[353] *Il Fermo Proposito* 1905, paragraph 22.
[354] Poggi 1967, 166.

The Origins of Religiopolitical Identity

Catholic Action was more directly tied to the ecclesiastical organizational structure than other Catholic mass movements in Europe, such as the Volksverein in Germany. This reflected the value that the Church attributed to Catholic Action. For Pope Pius X, the greatest assets of Catholic Action were its organizational and propaganda capabilities, and those strengths had to be mobilized. The Church wanted to fight "dangerous" ideologies of the time by relying on Catholic Action's organization "to counter the successes of the Socialists" and its propaganda machinery "to convince the Catholic masses that in the face of the 'socialist menace,' they had to close ranks behind the leaders of the Church."[355]

Just as with the German Volksverein, the Italian Catholic Action movement developed in a social setting where socialist doctrine was gaining popularity. Lyon's historical background on how liberalism similarly proved a source of conflict for the Church, likely pushing the Church in Italy to create an outlet to express their views which would not be tied up in political matters, is illustrative. She states: "In general the church was wary of the nineteenth century's constitutional governments, which for the most part were founded on anticlerical liberalism and the beliefs condemned by Pius IX's 1864 Syllabus. So Catholic parties were slow to emerge in France and Italy, where there was open hostility between church and state."[356] The Unione Elettorale Cattolica (Catholic Electoral Union) functioned as "the organizational instrument" for Pius X's political goals. As the socialists grew in strength, Pius X aimed to steer the Catholic vote toward trustworthy "moderate" candidates from the bourgeois parties without allowing a Catholic political party to form.[357] Thus, the Electoral Union certainly did not operate as a political party nor did it cooperate with the Italian state on behalf of the Church. Rather, the Union functioned as an instrument of the Church to influence voter sentiment after the Pope allowed Catholic citizens to participate in state elections. Fighting against socialism constituted its primary objective in this process; the Union did not act out of enthusiasm and zeal for religiously influenced political action. La Piana echoes this idea; Pope Pius X "granted to the Catholics permission to take part in the electoral campaign, not, however, with a platform and candidates of their own, but only to help with their votes men of the various reactionary parties in order to defeat the Socialist candidates for Parliament."[358] The war between Roman Catholicism and socialism raged on in the political arena.[359] For example, when socialism supplanted liberal government as the most significant threat to Catholicism, "Catholic Action conservatives and allied bishops put pressure on the Vatican to relax its policy of noncooperation with the

---

[355] Agocs 1975, 36.
[356] Lyon 1967, 71.
[357] Poggi 1967, 18.
[358] La Piana 1920, 168.
[359] Badè 1911, 156.

172 The Politics of Religious Party Change

liberals. Thus, by the end of the century, the movement that had been intended to fight liberalism became – first in local politics, then national elections – a moderate, pro clerical support for liberalism against more radical forces."[360]

Catholic Political Activism

Developments in the political arena were not the only concern for the Church leadership. Ideological issues and political activism inside the Catholic world deeply troubled the Church, especially left-leaning Catholic leaders such as Romolo Murri, Guido Miglioli, and Luigi Sturzo. This "democratic" wing of Catholic activists aimed to "destroy" the liberal order in favor of a democratic and Catholic one.[361] The most notable of these leaders was Romolo Murri, a young priest and the leading figure of the Christian Democratic current that contained the seeds of the future Catholic party in Italy. Despite some early traction with Pope Leo XIII, Murri ultimately ended up unable to gain favor with the Vatican. Leo XIII encouraged Murri to rely on the Opera in order to boost the legitimacy of his group, yet any traction Murri might have had was undermined soon after Pius X was elected Pope.[362] This falling out was rooted in the ideological orientation of this movement and the perceived threat to the Church's authority: "The left wing, led by the ardent young priest Romolo Murri, might well have gained the upper hand. But the death of Leo XIII and the peculiar convictions of his successor, Pius X (1903–14), arrested this development. Pius X saw the 'Christian democratic' movement led by Murri both as a challenge to hierarchical control over lay organizations and as a sociopolitical expression of the modernistic heresy he was determined to drive out."[363] The pope barred Christian Democrats from taking any independent political initiatives. Christian Democrats had to "go to the bishops and to the Pope for the approval of every project, every book, pamphlet, or article which comes from them. They cannot open their mouths to utter a word of their social, political or religious programme, until the Italian Episcopate grants them permission."[364] Worried by the Christian Democratic trends that he viewed as heretical, Pius X decided to repress the national standing committee of the Opera dei Congressi and transfer control of the Opera's many regional units to local priests themselves.[365]

Faced with Pius X's censure of his efforts to organize a Catholic political party, Murri decided to relinquish appeal to Catholicism or Christianity in his group's name to alleviate the Church's concerns and evade its reproach.

[360] Vaillancourt 1980, 41.
[361] Cunsolo 1993, 25.
[362] Vaillancourt 1980, 43.
[363] Poggi 1967, 18.
[364] A Catholic Priest 1907, 40.
[365] Poggi 1967, 18.

The Origins of Religiopolitical Identity

Murri's group adopted National Democratic League (Lega Democratica Nazionale) as its name in 1905[366] and announced itself as a secular[367] and nonconfessional[368] organization that drew inspiration from Catholic ideas. The League claimed autonomy from ecclesiastical hierarchy in view of the nonreligious nature of the activities they engaged in, while simultaneously declaring its ultimate objective as the implementation of "the principles of Christianity, the realization of Roman Catholic ideals, the Catholicization of society."[369] This duality in the origins of the Italian Catholic party as a religious party portended the institutional duality of Islamist parties across the Middle East later in the twentieth century. Murri and his fellow Christian Democrats reasoned that in order to take the "Christian message" to Italians, Catholics needed to directly engage in the national political life.[370] However, the pope argued that actions in the political and social spheres held "moral consequences, therefore they had to be subject to ecclesiastical oversight.[371] The Church considered the League a "rival" to the Church and Church-sanctioned organizations like the Popular Union.[372] Fully convinced of his infallibility and the "divine character of his authority," the pope did not accept any restrictions or intermediaries in his relationship with the Catholic faithful.[373] Unimpressed with the changes undertaken by Murri, Pius X publicly condemned the League in July 1906 for being a "heretical organization"[374] and prohibited priests to join the League via the encyclical *Pieni l'animo*; subsequently, the pope "suspended Murri *a divinis*" in 1907, and excommunicated him in 1909 once he was elected to the parliament from the left.[375] Importantly, Murri's condemnation by the Church was for political rather than doctrinal deviation.[376]

Pius X feared that the philosophy of Christian Democracy too closely approached liberalism. This fear, coupled with his desire to have all Catholic groups fall under the Church hierarchy, seems to have contributed to the overall spirit of discord between the pope and those who identified as Christian Democrats. Pius X viewed it as his mission to check "the movement in European Catholicism toward liberalism in both religious and nonreligious spheres" and undertook "a reign of intellectual terror."[377] His 1907 encyclical *Pascendi Dominici Gregis* stated, "Note here, Venerable Brethren, the

[366] Badger 1937, 46.
[367] Dawes 2011, 494.
[368] Kalyvas 1996, 175.
[369] Agocs 1973, 84.
[370] Dawes 2011, 493.
[371] Agocs 1973, 84.
[372] Agocs 1973, 79.
[373] La Piana 1920, 167.
[374] La Piana 1920, 167.
[375] Badger 1937, 46; Almond 1948, 743; Vaillancourt 1980, 43.
[376] Dawes 2011, 494.
[377] Vaillancourt 1980, 41.

174 *The Politics of Religious Party Change*

appearance already of that most pernicious doctrine which would make of the laity a factor of progress in the church."[378] In particular, Pius X attributed the shift toward "progressive ideas" in Italian Catholicism to "foreign influence," specifically that of German middle-class Catholics.[379]

The relationship of the Catholic Action movement to the idea of Catholic political activism or parties is somewhat complex, especially viewed in the context of the Catholic Church's complicated relationship with political participation in general. The many organizations that loosely formed the Opera first and the Catholic Action movement subsequently in the late nineteenth and early twentieth centuries were united by their advocacy for abstention from voting in national elections.[380] Considering the bold measure by Pius X to intervene in the already smoothly functioning affairs of the Catholic social movement in Italy during this period, it may seem surprising that the pope and other church leaders expressed a sharp hesitancy to involve the Church in the larger political sphere in Italy, especially after bringing the movement under the Church hierarchy. Catholic leaders in Italy eventually developed more open views toward political involvement when the threat of socialist parties grew, yet political advocacy in the Church was initially tepid.

Ironically, the Church's wariness toward political participation diminished the possibility for tangible social change in line with the Catholic vision – created in the aftermath of the anticlerical attacks – that could have resulted from the propaganda and organizing efforts of Catholic Action's different arms. While Catholic Action stood for "the independence and liberty of the Holy See," as its leader Giuseppe Dalla Torre announced in a 1913 speech,[381] the goals set for it by the Church were self-defeating. Catholic Action lacked a consistent direction, program, or platform through which it could corral its propaganda and organizational efforts toward the Church's political objectives.[382] At the core of the Church's distance from Christian political activism lay the risk of losing hierarchical control over "any political group that claimed Catholic inspiration," despite a sizeable group among the clergy favoring religious political activism in some fashion. Murri and his fellow Christian Democrats rooted themselves in "the principle of autonomous responsibility of Catholics in the political and social field," worked toward "independent Catholic organizations," and ultimately aimed to create a Catholic party. Such a view fundamentally contradicted the Church's and ultramontanes' views on how Catholic mass organizations should function as "a papal auxiliary" to combat secular liberalism.[383] Ultramontanes were more interested in attacking

---

[378] *Pascendi Dominici Gregis*, September 8, 1907.
[379] Vaillancourt 1980, 42.
[380] Poggi 1967, 17.
[381] Cunsolo 1993, 34.
[382] Agocs 1975, 46.
[383] Kalyvas 1996, 218.

The Origins of Religiopolitical Identity

"liberalizing and modernizing" Catholics as a reflection of their belief in "strict adherence to all papal directives and traditional Church teachings" than they were against non-Catholics.[384] Yet, the Church's disinclination toward Catholic political participation was self-defeating:

> But Pius X's refusal to allow Catholic participation in politics, in a world in which even the Catholic laity desired freedom from the hierarchy on matters of temporal politics, was in practice nearly equivalent to the prohibition of all explicitly Catholic political participation ... Thus, in a world where Catholic lay groups were interested in political organization only if allowed some autonomy from hierarchical control, Pius X's refusal to sanction such groups simply meant that there would be no organized, political participation explicitly oriented toward furthering Catholic goals.[385]

Importantly, while the philosophy of Christian Democracy or Catholic political activism did not always sit well with Catholic leaders in the Vatican, this does not mean that Catholics who embraced Christian Democratic ideology did not express loyalty to the Church hierarchy. For example, Don Luigi Sturzo, one of the leading figures in Christian Democracy and a founder of PPI in Italy, opposed the papal Non Expedit policy early on and "succeeded in giving Christian democracy a degree of cohesive unity and adequate form." Yet Sturzo theorized about how potential conflicts between the Church and political leadership could be resolved in a way that would uphold principles of Catholicism and not sacrifice democratic principles. In fact, Sturzo presented "some provocative ideas which would attach a stronger responsibility to the Papacy for guidance in temporal affairs."[386] Sturzo was unyielding in his Catholic theology.[387] He did not favor sacrificing papal authority; he envisioned a mechanism that would allow the Church to maintain its political and religious power. Likewise, even though Murri was excommunicated, he continued professing his loyalty to the Catholic Church.[388]

This is a crucial contention for the argument developed in this book. Christian political activists were fundamentally no different from Islamist political activists when they first emerged in how they approached the role of religion in the political sphere. There was no doubt about Catholic political activists' loyalty to the Church or that they envisioned a significant role for the Church in realizing the Church's vision for the state and society. Little, if any, difference existed in the visions laid out for the state and society by the Church and Catholic political activists. Sturzo consistently stressed the preeminence of the papacy in his Catholic political vision, yet the Church remained wary of the proponents of Catholic political activism. The conflict between the two

---

[384] Seidler 1986, 866.
[385] Burns 1990, 1135.
[386] Moos 1945, 292.
[387] Moos 1945, 270.
[388] McNeill 1919, 509.

176 The Politics of Religious Party Change

reflected a deep mistrust on the part of the Church. For the Church, Catholic political activists threatened to share in the authority of the Church through one of two mechanisms. First, they could function like a liaison between the Church and the state to mediate disagreements in policy. Such a position would enable Catholic political activists to exert an outsized influence, thereby undermining the Church's monopoly on religious authority. Second, under the semblance of acting on behalf of the Church and with such authority, Catholic political activists could pursue their own political agendas without even consulting the Church hierarchy. Both prospects concerned the Vatican because of their implications for the Church's absolute authority over Catholics and its ability to be the sole speaker for the religion. Ultimately, this was the red line for the Church.[389]

The Vatican's robust hierarchical control over Italian Catholics led to the comparatively slower emergence of a Catholic political party in Italy. The Non Expedit policy established by the Vatican in 1868 enjoined that Italian Catholics abstain from the electoral process as both voters and candidates. The policy stayed in place for more than three decades until the papal encyclical *Il fermo proposito* partially permitted Catholics to vote in constituencies approved by the local bishop. This relaxation in policy came due to the growing popularity of socialism in this period, arguably the greatest source of danger to the Church. Young Catholic activists such as Murri and Sturzo viewed the policy of political inaction as "senseless."[390] In 1913, Catholics were encouraged to vote for "moderate" candidates of the "bourgeois parties" as part of the Patto Gentiloni.[391] Embarrassingly for the Church, many radicals and Masons were among the approximately 300 deputies who pledged to defend the Church's interests as part of the pact for Catholic votes. Non Expedit ultimately ended in 1918; the Vatican, however, made it absolutely clear that those Catholic candidates elected to office "could not be considered spokesmen for Catholic interests, and they did not form a unified party."[392]

---

[389] Papal objection to Catholic political activism showed variation over time, especially during Benedict XV's papacy. His experience and interactions with the Popular Union of Catholic Action were instrumental in shifting his views from his predecessors: "As archbishop of the diocese of Bologna he [Benedict XV] had been in contact with the Popular Union of Count Giuseppe Dalla Torre and Marquesa Patrizzi; as pope he supported this association of lay Catholics and made it a key element in his reorganization of Catholic Action. He fostered a differentiation between the sociopolitical and the moral-religious spheres because he wanted Catholics to be autonomously involved in politics without confusing political action with religious obligations ... He seems to have wanted above all the development of a lay apostolate in religious, social, and moral spheres rather than an authoritarian curbing of Catholic conservatism. However, his policy of giving more autonomy to lay Catholics in the political and economic arenas favored the growth of progressive and independent organizations which themselves inhibited the conservatives' power" (Vaillancourt 1980, 44).

[390] Agocs 1973, 75.

[391] Poggi 1967, 18.

[392] Whyte 1981, 53.

The Origins of Religiopolitical Identity 177

The Church was opposed to organized Catholic political action and banned those Catholics elected to the parliament from forming even a "Catholic parliamentary faction." For example, the decision of prominent Catholic Filippo Meda to participate in Prime Minister Paolo Boselli's cabinet drew a strong statement from the Vatican that suggested that "he represented only himself and his friends, not the Catholics."[393] The Church, in other words, preferred the lines to not be blurred; by creating a separation between itself – the legitimate Catholic authority to represent Catholics – and Catholic activists who needed the Church's explicit blessing to assume any such role, the Catholic Church reinforced its supremacy.

CATHOLIC PARTY OF BELGIUM

The Belgian Revolution of 1830 had the peculiar effect of establishing "the most liberal regime in Europe" in the most Catholic country north of the Alps.[394] When the first Belgian constitution was created in 1831, Belgian Catholics supported it despite an explicit denunciation of liberalism in papal encyclical *Mirari vos*. The reason for Catholics' support for the constitution lay in the state's "material support" to the Church and granting autonomy over the Church's internal affairs.[395] Over the years, the Catholic Church took advantage of the freedom the constitution granted to religious institutions, including subsidies to all religious groups and complete religious freedom. Utilizing the constitutional guarantee on religious freedom, Belgian Catholics expanded their dominance in charity work, education, and healthcare.[396] The Church had organizations in many fields of life, making 1830s Belgium a Catholic country with liberal institutions; 50 years later, the state was still very Catholic, with conservatives trying to remodel institutions along more conservative lines. During the half-century in between, liberalism operated as the "motor force" of political life in Belgium; the Church's status in this free society constituted the "pre-eminent bone of contention" between the Church and politically oriented Catholics.[397] The stage was thus set for the commencement of conflict between Catholics and anticlerical liberals.

Anticlericalism in Belgium

The history of anticlericalism in Belgium is a political history that involves numerous factions either within or closely intertwined with the government. Belgian politics and society followed a unique course of development

[393] Kalyvas 1996, 180.
[394] Viaene 2001, 9.
[395] Kalyvas 1996, 168.
[396] Strikwerda 1988, 335.
[397] Viaene 2001, 9–10.

throughout the nineteenth century. The state was first governed by a "Unionist" alliance – a coalition of "rationalist Liberals and liberal Catholics."[398] In contrast with fellow Catholic nations Italy, France, and Spain, where the Church did not quickly adjust to changing political conditions, Belgian Catholics actively defended against the expansion of liberal measures while also taking advantage of the policies that gave the Church freedom.[399] This early response is one reason why the response to anticlericalism differed from other countries in Western Europe to some degree. Since liberalism was concentrated in urban areas in Belgium, Catholics managed to use mass mobilization in rural areas to win a solid base of popular support.[400] Growing partisanship between the two factions prompted the Liberals to officially establish a party in 1846, resulting in the first partisan cabinet in 1847.[401] In response, Conservatives organized to establish a Conservative party with a nonreligious program independent of the Catholic Church.

The 1850s witnessed the rise of a potent anticlericalism, leading Belgian Catholics "to equate liberalism with godless Freemasonry" following the line pushed by Pius IX and ultramontanes.[402] This anticlericalism was particularly pronounced among the enfranchised elite who accounted for only about two percent of the population, as demonstrated by the proposal and passage of a new school law in 1850 by a group of young Liberal deputies. Known as the Rogier Law, this law created 60 new schools – primarily focused on secondary schools – in which all instruction would be controlled by the state, including religious instruction. The bill also supported and subsidized municipal schools, including Episcopal schools. Most critically, the law explicitly stated that public education had to be neutral and free from church control; the clergy could be part of the educational system only insofar as teaching religion was concerned.[403] The law infuriated the national Catholic hierarchy.[404]

Anticlerical sentiment culminated in the momentous year of 1857. Freemasonic societies had become the "ideological and social backbone" of the Liberal movement in Belgium. Beginning with the second Rogier government, Belgian Liberals adopted anticlerical measures to limit the Church's control over education and social welfare, as well as efforts to exert state control over regular clergy and the creation of new parishes.[405] Anticlerical riots occurred in Brussels and a monastery was sacked in Jemappes in response to

---

[398] Kittell 1961, 420.

[399] It is possible the Church played a greater role in Belgian political life due to its role in combatting Dutch Protestant rule in 1830 (Viaene 2001).

[400] This would come to benefit them, especially after the establishment of universal male suffrage.

[401] Kalyvas 1998, 298.

[402] Evans 1999, 136.

[403] Witte, Craeybeckx, and Meynen 2009, 83.

[404] Kittell 1961, 425.

[405] Domenico and Hanley 2006.

The Origins of Religiopolitical Identity

the monastic law legislation that would have allowed the Church control over local charities. The same year, the Liberals won power in both houses of parliament and began pursuing anticlerical policies. Liberals' anticlerical attacks intensified in the following years and throughout the 1860s, framing religion as an "obstacle to progress" and declaring Catholicism "an aberration to be destroyed at any price." Cardinal Sterckx requested the laity's help in fending off anticlerical attacks and defending the Church; the political response was largely left to the Conservative politicians.[406] The militant anticlericalism of the Liberals found only moderate opposition within the ranks of parliamentary Conservatives – who deemed themselves the *Association Constitutionelle Conservatrice* in 1858 – much to the chagrin of the Church which desired more robust political support from the right.[407] The absence of a stronger response by the Conservatives can be attributed to the fact that religion did not constitute a major point of friction between the Liberals and the Conservatives as the two main political factions. As the anticlericalism in Belgium picked up pace and intensity, however, the ongoing agitation by Liberals and more radical factions dissolved the unionist agreement that had previously united them with Catholic Conservatives.

The Liberals and anticlericals continued their opposition to church involvement in state affairs, deeming the Church's dominant control over various facets of Belgian civil life to be problematic. They were especially concerned with education, charitable institutions, marriage, and burials in cemeteries.[408] The education issue came to a head when the Liberal government of Frère-Orban passed the 1879 Education Act, or the Van Humbeeck Law. The government aimed to reduce the Church's influence in public schools and undermine the "free schools," which the Catholic Church maintained.[409] The law mandated the state to take on primary education, eliminate church oversight in schools, and minimize instruction of religion. This legislation resulted in a "true ideological civil war," remaining unresolved until Conservatives' rise to power in 1884.[410] Other legislation on secular education followed, starting the so-called School Wars.[411] The Vatican responded to the Van Humbeeck Law by severing diplomatic relations with Belgium in 1880.

While the anticlerical attacks involved multiple groups ranging from moderate Liberals to radicals and socialists, supporters of the Catholic Church fielded

---

[406] Kalyvas 1996, 187.

[407] Kalyvas 1998, 299.

[408] Kittell 1961, 425–26.

[409] Lord 1923, 34.

[410] Kalyvas 1998, 299.

[411] The "School Wars" reflected an earlier debate between anticlericals and Catholics over Article 12 of the new Belgian constitution in the 1830s. Article 12 forbade state involvement in religious affairs, but anticlerical liberals declared that this would prevent the state from enforcing civil over religious marriage, thus propagating religious marriage for the vast majority of the peasantry (Viaene 2001, 29).

a more united front in their response. Nonetheless, divisions certainly existed among Catholics between the Church, moderate Conservatives, and radical Catholic activists (ultramontanes) during this time.[412] Despite their relatively small population among Belgian Catholics, ultramontanes exerted an outsized influence on the evolution of Catholic political activism and in shaping the Catholic response to anticlerical attacks. Confrèrie de St. Michel functioned as the organizational structure that held ultramontanes together. For Belgian ultramontanes, religion and the Church had to have a dominant role in state and society. Grounded in their perception of how society was moving away from Catholicism, ultramontanes argued that the Church had a right to step in to the political sphere in order to guide "its sinful flock" to the truth and redemption, elevating the Church to a position above the state.[413] The Belgian ultramontanes dreamed of a "crusade" against socialism and liberalism and "admired" *zouaves* who fought with arms in support of the pope in Italy in the 1860s.[414] Islamist visions for a united Muslim world under the caliphate in the twentieth century mirror the ultramontane ideas among Catholics in Belgium and elsewhere in Europe.

To confront what they perceived as raging secularism and anticlerical attacks, Catholics mobilized under the Church's – particularly ultramontane clergy and laymen's – leadership to take back their nation: "Faith was manifested without restraint, and liberal ideas were aggressively attacked; it was stressed time and again that the Church had to be the centre of public life. The Vatican orchestrated the whole operation."[415] Ultramontanes were instrumental in pushing the Vatican to adopt more conservative dogmas and were, in turn, reinforced by those very same dogmas. Belgian ultramontanes became particularly influential and vocal around 1870s, mobilizing Catholics to fill the streets of major Belgian cities in the battle against anticlerical policies.

Ultramontanes aimed to establish a "Catholic state" that would be under direct papal control, inviting a striking analogy to Islamist visions of an "Islamic state." Such control by the pope would ensure respect for what ultramontanes deemed "the fundamental principles of Catholicism, i.e., the Church leading and controlling all sectors of life and society."[416] The fact that the liberal Belgian state and the Belgian constitution failed to uphold these fundamental principles galvanized ultramontanes into proposing an alternative to the current system. The logical extension of ultramontane thinking, as endorsed by its radical faction, was the formation of a Catholic state under the pope's leadership with a significant role for the clergy in the process. What Belgium needed was not change in individual policies but the entire political system

---

[412] Kalyvas 1998, 299.
[413] Witte, Craeybeckx, and Meynen 2009, 85.
[414] Strikwerda 1997, 218.
[415] Witte, Craeybeckx, and Meynen 2009, 86.
[416] Witte, Craeybeckx, and Meynen 2009, 88.

The Origins of Religiopolitical Identity

at large. This new Catholic state would be "led by the bishops and a militant Church, with an ancient-régime monarch as an ally." The more moderate faction of the ultramontanes, including the leaders of the future Federation of Catholic Clubs and Conservative Associations, aimed to establish "Catholic supremacy" by working within the parameters of the existing system. Charles Perin – a professor at Leuven University – became the ideologue of ultramontanism in Belgium with his emphasis on the "incompatibility of liberalism and Catholicism, the restoration of the Catholic state and the principle of paternalist corporatism."[417] Perin's vision had found support among a small yet powerful audience, including Pope Pius IX, Théodore-Joseph Gravez (Bishop of Namur), and Théodore Alexis Joseph de Montpellier (Bishop of Liège). Such a vision for a Catholic state closely mirrors the idea of an Islamic state among Islamists. Critically, both religiopolitical visions combine elements of an idealized original religious polity that did not exist erstwhile and a yearning for what they deem the good old days of their faithful.

The Rise of the Catholic Mass Movement

The rise of the Catholic mass movement in Belgium during this period parallels the growing prominence of ultramontanism among Belgian Catholics. Like the German Catholic mass movement, the Belgian Catholic movement was largely characterized by its decentralized structure. The movement's origins lay in Catholic associations groomed by the Church called Catholic circles, modeled after secular *cercles littéraires* that were popular in Belgium at the time. These bourgeois secular groups presented a novel form of "sociability" that offered "a whole range of more specialized cultural and scientific societies" as umbrella organizations.[418] The Catholic circles were thus viewed as an innovative way for Catholics to band together with one another and strengthen the social fabric of Catholicism in Belgium. The rising tide of anticlericalism necessitated the Catholic Church to respond with its own form of social mobilization: "Between the 1840s and 1860s ... as relations between Catholics and liberals became ever more strained, the Church began to found or encourage a new range of associations outside the parishes in order to counter the growing organizational power of anticlericalism."[419] However, as the intensity of anticlerical mobilization and policies increased over time, Belgian Catholics felt that more zealous Catholic social mobilization was the answer to stemming the tide of anticlerical liberal and socialist ideologies; better organization and the idea "that the Church had to be the centre of public life" motivated Belgian Catholics.[420]

---

[417] Witte, Craeybeckx, and Meynen 2009, 88–89.
[418] Ertman 2000, 163.
[419] Ertman 2000, 164.
[420] Witte, Craeybeckx, and Meynen 2009, 86.

The Malines Congresses were a turning point in how Belgian lay Catholics thought about and organized themselves in defense of the Catholic Church and its interests. The first Malines Congress took place in 1863 in the city of Malines (Mechelen). The congress, followed by subsequent ones in Malines in 1864 and 1867, helped create what was probably one of the first Catholic political organizations in continental Europe, inspiring other similar Catholic political and social organizations in the rest of Europe.[421] The Malines Congresses were an important landmark in the development of church–state relations. They became a harbinger of the shift from the traditional alliance of the throne and the altar toward a more modern way of doing politics, containing "the seeds of the future Catholic political identity."[422]

The Malines Congress was convoked by Cardinal Engelbert Sterckx, the archbishop of Malines, to unify Catholics against anticlerical measures adopted by Belgian liberals in control of the government. The congress brought together both the ultramontane and the Liberal Catholics. They discussed the question of whether and how "to reconcile the just autonomy and secularity of the political sphere – especially if organized democratically – and the freedom of the conscience of citizens and their right to be immune from State oppression in religious matters, with the Church's responsibility to be the voice of truth that includes moral criteria for judging the exercise of political power and the ordering of human society."[423] Prominent Liberal Catholic Charles Montalembert gave two critical speeches during the 1863 congress, in which he urged separation of the church and the state, Christianization of democracy, and religious freedom.[424] Montalembert drew sharp criticism for his ideas particularly from ultramontane Catholics for failing to sufficiently defend the Catholic doctrine.[425] While Montalembert avoided direct public censure by the Church, his ideas were strongly rebuked by the papal encyclicals *Quanta cura* and the *Syllabus of errors* issued in 1864. The Malines Congresses were also significant for incubating several Catholic associations. In 1864 and 1868, the Federation of Constitutional Conservative Associations (*Fédération des Associations Constitutionnelles Conservatrices*) and the Federation of Catholic Clubs (*Fédération des Cercles Catholiques*) were founded, respectively. Both organizations brought together various lay Catholic associations throughout Belgium, the latter being subject to church oversight.[426] These organizations provided a platform for Catholic politicians and other lay persons with an interest in socio-political developments, facilitating the formation of a Catholic political identity. Crucially, neither organization operated as a political party;

---

[421] Domenico and Hanley 2006.
[422] Kalyvas 1996, 188.
[423] Rhonheimer 2013.
[424] Atkin and Tallett 2003, 134–35.
[425] Altholz 1962.
[426] Kalyvas 1996, 188.

The Origins of Religiopolitical Identity

in the absence of a common political platform or program, they simply lacked unity among the individual associations that made up the federations.

By the time the Van Humbeeck School Law of 1879 was in effect, the Catholics observed that Liberal political designs would severely undercut the power of the Church and realized the need to "isolate" themselves and become more cohesive. This process of social strengthening was not possible without Catholics utilizing their resources and taking on more political power: "... it was a liberal education law (Van Humbeeck's School Act of 1879) that provided the impetus for a religious community, in this case the Catholics, to begin to organize and isolate their subcultural milieu. Also, as we have seen, some of the raw materials for the construction of the future Catholic pillar were already in place well before the late 1870s in the form of a growing network of Catholic social work, instructional, and leisure-time bodies and their electoral associations had arisen during the 1850s."[427] Hence, this latest wave of anticlerical attacks and the Van Humbeeck Law ultimately crystallized the necessity of political action for Belgian Catholics to defend their interests. The increasing intensity of anticlericalism resulted in religion's emergence as a cleavage in Belgian politics.[428]

As an umbrella Catholic organization, the Federation of Catholic Circles (Clubs) incorporated direct political activism when it became more crucial for Catholics to hold not just social but political sway in Belgian society. From early on the Federation was a movement with political undertones, supporting those men who would represent Catholics politically in the country. While the Federation was "an association of non-political Catholic groups, it formed the structural backbone of the future Catholic party."[429] At its core, the Federation of Catholic Circles was "Church-sponsored,"[430] and thus could be judged as more closely related to the Catholic Church than the Catholic lawmakers who were wary of Catholic sociopolitical movements.

Belgian Catholics upped the ante once the 1879 Van Humbeeck Law was passed. In order to "fight a total war," the Church mobilized all Catholics in the country; Archbishop Victor Augustin Isidore Dechamps led the effort and asked dioceses across Belgium "to create committees composed of clerics and laymen to take over the running of a new network of primary confessional schools."[431] In a decisive move signaling the politicization of the Catholic movement, the Federation of Catholic Clubs (*Fédération des Cercles Catholiques*) and the Federation of Constitutional Conservative Associations (*Fédération des Associations Constitutionnelles Conservatrices*) merged to create the

---

[427] Ertman 2000, 171.
[428] Kalyvas 1996, 169.
[429] Witte, Craeybeckx, and Meynen 2009.
[430] Ertman 2000, 164.
[431] Kalyvas 1996, 189.

Federation of Catholic Clubs and Conservative Associations (*Fédération des Cercles Catholiques et des Associations Conservatrices*) in 1879.

The Catholic mass movement of Belgium was marked by its variegated character, particularly along socioeconomic lines. The early formation of the Federation of Catholic Circles resembled its secular "sister" Literary Circle organizations because it appealed to more socially established and economically prosperous, middle-class Catholics across Belgium.[432] The variegated nature of Belgian Catholicism's social movement structure embraced a social policy geared toward the working classes several years before the Vatican took steps in this direction with the encyclical *Rerum Novarum*.[433] Toward the end of the nineteenth century, however, the Belgian Catholic mass movement was supplemented by two major mass movements that appealed to different segments of the Catholic population in Belgium: the Boerenbond and the Belgian Democratic League.

The Boerenbond, or the Farmers' League, was founded in 1890 in Leuven by Joris Helleputte. It arose out of largely the same circumstances as the Belgian Democratic League. The Boerenbond sought to keep would-be socialist farmers within the Catholic fold, yet it also worked against established Catholic voices in Belgium by mobilizing Catholics lower on the economic scale. The US Bureau of Labor Statistics noted that the Boerenbond was "one of the most influential organizations in Belgium."[434] Boerenbond had almost half a million members in the 1920s.[435] Boerenbond's goal was to organize the rural peasants of Belgium to provide them with "moral rather than economic support."[436] Instead of being an advocacy or charitable organization meant to help Belgian farmers ascend the social ladder, the Boerenbond functioned as a large support association designed to uplift the spiritual well-being of these farmers; maintaining faith took priority over advancement of social status.

The Boerenbond primarily consisted of Flemish farmers due to the significance of farming in the Flanders region,[437] making the organization both religiously and ethnically homogenous. One could say that while the organization existed to stem the tide of socialism, it also valued being thorough and careful in attracting members and being a doctrinally pure organization. Maintaining Catholic values in the organization, in other words, was equally important as fighting against non-Catholic norms outside of the organization: "Anyone interested in farming may join a [Boerenbond] guild, but one of the strict requirements is 'that prospective members fulfill their church obligations'."[438]

---

[432] Parsons 1910, 506.
[433] Day 1932, 308.
[434] BLS 1929, 559.
[435] Day 1932, 310.
[436] De Stoop 1931, 325.
[437] Strikwerda 1997, 219.
[438] BLS 1929, 559.

The Origins of Religiopolitical Identity

The Boerenbond, as such, posed a key "challenge" to the upper class Catholic Conservatives and political activists by mobilizing lower class Catholics in a particular sector.[439]

Clerical involvement enabled the establishment of the Boerenbond as several priests were among the founders of the organization.[440] Beyond the fact that priests were founding figures, the organization's structure mimicked that of the Church and its direction was "largely in the hands of the priests of the church ... the parish priest is the spiritual director of each of the guilds and in his position as chaplain he has great influence over the members and can intensify the work for the general uplift of the peasant. It must be said parenthetically that this system has worked very well both from the standpoint of the religious worker and from that of the agricultural expert."[441] This cleric-led organization of the Boerenbond echoes the close relationship between the movement and the Church that we observe in the Italian Catholic Action movement. Although the Boerenbond and Catholic Action had comparable levels of clerical involvement, the Boerenbond had a relatively more independent organizational structure than Catholic Action, which was more closely tied to the Catholic hierarchy. The Boerenbond consisted of various organizational components such as the Supreme Council, Administrative Board, Annual Meeting, General Secretary's Office, local farmers' associations, and young farmers' associations. Still, the extent of clerical involvement in the organization was remarkable: "The central organization is directed by a committee composed of seven members, three of whom are priests and four are laymen. This committee is 'appointed by and under the guidance of a council composed of 40 prominent citizens from the arrondissements or districts. Approximately half of this council are priests'."[442] The overlap with the organizational structure of the Church and the extensive presence of clergy in leadership positions suggest that the Boerenbond aimed to cater to its base while submitting to clerical control.

The Belgian Democratic League was formally established around the same time as the Boerenbond in March 1891, although the origins of Christian Democracy – the ideological movement that gave rise to the League – date back to the 1870s. The League's membership grew considerably over time; it reached 16,000 members in 1901, and by 1913, the figure rose to 102,000 members.[443] According to the 1891 Manifesto of the Belgian Democratic League, the group aimed to "improve the social situation of the workers, to bring peace to the world of labor, to induce respect for the rights of all, both employers and employees" as defined by Pope Leo XIII's Encyclical *Rerum*

---

[439] Strikwerda 1997, 222.

[440] De Stoop 1931, 325; Strikwerda 1997, 220.

[441] BLS 1929, 559.

[442] BLS 1929, 141.

[443] Day 1932, 309. Strikwerda (1997, 220) puts the membership number at 10,000 in 1891 and almost 100,000 by 1898.

novarum "On The Condition of the Workers" (1891).[444] Among the leading founders of the League were Arthur Verhaegen, Joris Helleputte, and Abbé Pottier. These men mobilized throughout the 1880s workers clubs and local unions in cities across Belgium that rivaled socialist ones. The League declared its loyalty to the Catholic Church, yet called for economic equality and social justice, charting a slightly different course of sociopolitical activism.[445]

Because socialism was quickly gaining ground in the late nineteenth-century Belgium, the Belgian Democratic League was tasked with reaching out to working-class Catholics and mobilizing a more cohesive network of Belgian Catholics. Even before the formal establishment of the League, Christian democrats were trying "to gather the workingmen into societies" affiliated with broader Catholic mass movement.[446] Arthur Verhaegen, one of the Belgian Democratic League leaders at the time, emphasized the movement's goal as "win[ning] over the masses" in reference to the increasing popularity of socialism among Belgians in this period.[447] The founders of the Belgian Democratic League were not simply satisfied with religious freedom wherein they could practice their faith; they instead believed it imperative to change the fabric of society, reaching out to various strata of society to ensure that workers and others would not be tempted by imminent socialist propaganda. For example, Abbé Pottier – a Christian democratic leader from Liege – stated, "No God, no master, promiscuity of women, promiscuity of property – voilà in four phrases, the Socialist doctrine. At the international Socialist congress in Ghent in 1887, the public sessions were one long blasphemy against God as well as one immense curse against society."[448] Socialism now supplemented liberal anticlericalism and "ungodliness": "From a religious point of view, however, the appearance of new socialist subculture merely added to the forces of the ungodly, and hence quickened the resolve of Catholics and Calvinists to complete the construction of their own self-contained life-worlds."[449] Thus, the necessity of mobilizing a large segment of Belgium's Catholic society resulted partially out of a real concern that lower classes could be reached by socialists and partially out of the broader worldview of the zealous Christian Democratic movement, of which the Belgian Democratic League "took charge" upon its formation.[450]

Christian Democracy as an ideology envisions compatibility between democracy and Catholicism, seeking to "apply new techniques to social and economic problems within the framework of constitutional, law-limited

---

[444] "Manifesto of the Belgian Democratic League" in Moody and Joseph 1953.

[445] Linden 1920, 327.

[446] Vauthier 1894, 718.

[447] Strikwerda 1997, 222.

[448] Strikwerda 1997, 218.

[449] Ertman 2000, 167.

[450] Day 1932, 309.

The Origins of Religiopolitical Identity

government."[451] Within these parameters, the group did not act like a "church party"; instead, Christian Democrats sought to advocate for workers by helping them to become "responsible partner[s] in the economic process of which [they are] part."[452] On the pragmatic side, Christian Democrats were also concerned about the ground that socialists would gain with the universal suffrage campaign underway. Although uncertainty surrounded the extent of the suffrage's expansion, it was only a matter of time that the expansion would take place. The expansion of suffrage also meant that working class voters would make up a significant proportion of the electorate. Therefore, the Catholic Party faced a choice. The party could choose to remain oblivious to this tremendous shift in the electoral arena, allowing socialists to make major electoral gains at the expense of the Catholic Party. Alternatively, the party could embrace the expansion of electorate and actively recruit and mobilize the working class to broaden the party base. The Belgian Democratic League and the Christian Democrats would fill this gap for the Catholic Party, as Christian democracy held vast potential to reach a wider audience than the Catholic Party's current base. Ultimately, this task of reaching out to different social circles to proclaim Catholicism as greater than Socialism turned out to be the crux of the League's mission.

Strikwerda writes that "with some justice, in fact, Christian Democrats could see themselves as the true defenders of the Church. The elitist and quietist conservatives had hoped a liberal state controlled by a Catholic party would merely allow the faithful to be true Christians. Christian Democrats were building a Christian society and battling the worst enemies of Christianity, the Socialists."[453] It was not immediately evident in any way that these politically oriented Belgian Catholics pursued objectives fundamentally different, that is, more moderate and democratic, from those of the ultramontanes. For example, one of the movement's preeminent founders was Joris Helleputte, a Leuven University professor and an ultramontane. As an ideological school in Catholicism, ultramontanes prioritized undisputed loyalty to the pope as part of the Church's holy war against socialism and liberalism. They pushed for a fully Catholic Belgian society, which accounts for their vision to win back the working class for the Church.

Despite a streak of ultramontane sentiment in the foundation of the Belgian Democratic League, the Church's involvement in the organizational structure of the movement was less pronounced compared to the Boerenbond. Nonetheless, the formal Catholic hierarchy was a crucial ally to the Belgian Democratic League because they believed the movement was necessary to avoid socialism, and to a lesser degree because they hoped the Belgian Democratic League might

---

[451] Bouscaren 1949, 60.
[452] Bouscaren 1949, 61.
[453] Strikwerda 1997, 218.

188   *The Politics of Religious Party Change*

help to "Catholicize" Belgium in line with the ultramontane vision. Such support by the Church stood in opposition to the upper class Catholic Conservative politicians' and the Federation's skepticism of the Belgian Democratic League because of their focus on workers and lower class Catholics more broadly. Aware of the conflict between two, church leaders typically opted for more tacit forms of approval of the Belgian Democratic League rather than enthusiastic promotion: "The clergy and hierarchy were willing to support Christian democracy to stop socialism, so long as it retained some distinctly Christian aspects. It was not to become an ally of socialism, which they saw as the sworn enemy of the Church's institutional position. Only the clergy and hierarchy kept Catholic conservatives from vigorously repressing Christian democracy."[454] The release of Pope Leo XII's *Rerum Novarum* encyclical a month after the League's formal establishment – which recognized workers' rights to create unions to protect their interests – can be viewed as a nod to the Belgian Democratic League. However, the Vatican was careful to underscore the need for a formal connection between the Church and the Catholic workers' associations.[455] The objective here was to maintain the unity of the Catholics and discourage them from independent action. A case in point here is what happened to Father Adolf Daens when he defied the Church. A priest in the city of Aalst, Daens embraced socialist ideas, mobilized lower class Catholics who were discontent with the (upper class) Catholic political leaders, and established the Christian People's Party (Christelijke Volkspartij) with Christian Democratic ideals. Once he was elected to the Belgian parliament in 1892, he did not shy away from openly lending his support to socialists on social policy and expanding suffrage. Daens faced a coordinated opposition campaign by the church hierarchy and the Conservative politicians of the Catholic Party.[456] The Vatican "officially" censured Daens in 1905 thanks to Charles Woeste's efforts,[457] while the Bishop of Ghent issued an interdict against him.[458]

These three associations – the Federation of Catholic Clubs and Conservative Associations, Boerenbond, and the Belgian Democratic League – collectively provided the societal foundation upon which the Catholic Party rose and thrived. In this tripartite, informal division of labor, the Federation appealed to the middle class Catholics, Boerenbond to the peasants, and the Democratic League to the industrial working class: "The idea of association has been worked out in great detail ... All classes are provided for ... For the peasants of the country districts has been instituted the 'boerenbond,' a savings-bank, a syndicate for the material expansion and self-protection, and a

---

[454] Strikwerda 1997, 222.
[455] Strikwerda 1997, 220–21; Witte, Craeybeckx, and Meynen 2009, 111.
[456] Linden 1920, 327; Witte, Craeybeckx, and Meynen 2009, 112.
[457] Evans 1999, 169–70; Witte, Craeybeckx, and Meynen 2009, 113.
[458] Linden 1920, 327.

The Origins of Religiopolitical Identity

means of religious propaganda all in one. For the industrial workmen, social and political in its aim, the 'Ligue Democratique' run by such democrats as Levie, Verhaegen, and Helleputte, and for the middle class the 'Federation of Catholic Circles,' a chain of societies spread over the whole country, and presided over by M. Ch. Woeste. The scheme is perfect, well-planned, almost invulnerable."[459] This organization at the grassroots level ultimately helped to strengthen the Catholic Party and entrench it in Belgian political landscape. These associations helped the party defy Socialism and Liberalism. The fact that the Catholic Party felt threatened by Socialism and Liberalism mirrors the fears of Catholic movements and parties in Italy and Germany.

The Catholic Church in Belgium opposed the formation of a Catholic political party for many years. The Church's objection lied in its desire to avoid "an obstacle to their leadership" as the church leadership "feared that religious influence might pass to the hands of laymen."[460] Clearly, the emergence of a Catholic party and a politicized Catholic mass movement indicated, for the Church, that it had to compromise in its uncontested leadership of the faithful and possibly losing its political clout as the voice of Belgian Catholics. Indeed, these concerns pushed the Church to take action against the Catholic congresses that are organized by the Catholic laity in the 1860s and the Union Catholique in 1871 in order to regain control of the Catholic fight against anticlericalism.[461]

[459] Parsons 1910, 506.
[460] Kalyvas 1996, 176.
[461] Kalyvas 1996, 174 & 177.

5

Intraparty Conflict

The rise of religious political parties in the modern era exhibits great variation across different religiopolitical contexts. The source of variation concerns the strategies that religious movements adopt as they seek to enter the political field. The difference is particularly sharp between Islamist and Catholic parties. In this chapter, I explain how the distinctive institutional environments and their corollary ramifications on religious authority drive religious movements to adopt different strategies in shaping their political activism and creating religious parties. Religious competition and conflict lie at the core of the analysis in this chapter. Islamist movements, unperturbed by a hierarchical religious authority, found the liberty to pursue hybrid organizational structures. This carte blanche to assume religious authority enabled Islamist movements to operate both as a religious movement that serves in religious, social, and educational areas and as a religious party in the political arena. The Church hierarchy, by contrast, forced Catholic mass movement leaders to choose between expulsion and avoiding political activism in the name of Catholicism. Catholic political activists largely responded to this challenge by formally parting ways with mass movements and creating their own Catholic parties without the blessing of the Church, ultimately deprived of the ability to rely on religious authority in their political ventures. In addition to chronicling the conflict over religious authority and the distinct trajectories of Islamist and Catholic parties, this chapter focuses on the implications of divergent organizational trajectories on the electorate. If organizational structures truly matter and religious authority plays a decisive role in how religious parties craft their discourse, then we should observe that Islamist and Catholic parties target different audiences in their political discourses. Indeed, while Catholic parties attempted to forge broad-based electoral coalitions and were not constrained by the demands of a particular religious movement, Islamist parties had to tread carefully in order to simultaneously not alienate their core support base in Islamist movements and appeal to the general electorate.

Intraparty Conflict

The Egyptian Brotherhood opted to maintain its unitary organizational structure and undertake its political activism under the umbrella of the movement. Over the years, a small group of politically motivated Brotherhood leaders pushed for a separate Brotherhood political party in Egypt; fearing independent activism and rivalry, Brotherhood leaders rejected the idea. Absent a major shift in the political arena, the Brotherhood retained its anti-system stance even after the 2011 Revolution. When the Freedom and Justice Party was established following the overthrow of Hosni Mubarak, the party did not enjoy autonomy from the movement; rather it operated as a subservient arm of the main movement. The conflict between the political and religious factions within Ennahdha played out differently. Despite some early inclination to form a separate political party, the political faction within the movement failed to prevail. When the political faction finally won over the religious faction after Ben Ali's removal from power in 2011, Ennahdha decided to discontinue its hybrid party-movement structure as part of its "specialization policy." The Ennahdha party congress formally abandoned its religious activism and religious movement and constrained itself to being only a political party. Unsurprisingly, the party's embrace of the Muslim democratic ideology simultaneously came at the expense of political Islam. Party officials justified the decision on the grounds of a major political and electoral shift in the aftermath of the 2011 Revolution. The process leading to the formation of the Justice and Development Party (AKP) crystallized the conflict between the politically motivated Reformist faction and the religiously motivated Traditionalist faction within the National Outlook Movement. The Reformists recognized a fundamental shift in the political arena that necessitated a change in how the movement approached politics. In particular, the Reformists cited the shift in the electorate's position on the religion–politics relationship. According to Reformists, the path to influencing policy was through winning electoral power and required them leaving behind the National Outlook Movement. The AKP's formation in the early 2000s represents the culmination of the Reformist approach to politics and abandonment of its religious activism.

One of the most important challenges that Catholic parties faced at their inception was choosing a name for themselves. On one hand, these parties wanted to identify themselves with Catholicism, as their founders' religious identity helped inspire their religiopolitical activism. An explicit association with the Catholic faith would signal their commitment to the religion. On the other hand, these parties were hesitant to carry a close association with the faith, and thereby with the Catholic Church; such association with the Church could compromise their independence as a political actor and undermine their electoral reach and recruitment. In view of this dilemma, several Catholic parties (including the Italian and German parties) chose nondenominational titles for themselves.

Catholic parties aimed to appeal to an electorate broader than that of their religious identity. At a time when socioeconomic inequality disadvantaged the industrial working classes and the agricultural sector, the social question and expansion of suffrage created a broad electoral opening for Catholic parties. While the Church resisted calls for reform to address this social question for a long time,[1] Catholic parties were able to reach segments of the electorate that were previously unavailable. Catholic parties, however, not only faced opposition from the Church to their activism addressing the social question; they also had to compete against the socialist movement to win over these constituencies. Indeed, Christian Democracy and Social Democracy were contemporaries in direct competition with each other.[2] Success in the political arena for Catholic parties often implied conflict with the Church. Common to the Church's opposition to Catholic parties' formation and addressing the social question was how both developments threatened the Church's interests and its institutional privileges.

In Germany, middle-class Catholics increasingly clashed with the Church over its response to modernity and the state's church policy. Continuously sidelined by the clergy and its ultramontane flank, middle-class German Catholics aired their frustrations in a more public fashion. Throughout the 1850s and 1860s, middle-class Catholics' attempts to form a Catholic party failed, in great part due to ecclesiastical opposition. It was only when the Kültürkampf incapacitated the Catholic Church in the 1870s that middle-class Catholics' mission of forming a Catholic party bore fruit. Desperately in need of its laymen and unable to oppose their sociopolitical activism, the Church mounted minimal resistance to the Center Party in its formative phase. Nonetheless, once the Church moved on from the shock of the Kültürkampf, it began dealing directly with the German state; the Church demanded that the Center Party follow the Church's preferred policies and bring the Kültürkampf to an official end. The Center Party's refusal to concede to the Church on important policy matters underscores the extent to which the Center Party values its independence from the Church as a Catholic political party.

In Italy, the primary axis of conflict was between the Church and Christian Democrats. The emergence of the Catholic mass movement with the Opera and Catholic Action occurred under the Church's strict organizational control. Although Christian Democratic figures like Sturzo and Murri took on leadership roles within these organizations, their attempts to steer these groups in a more political direction with Christian Democratic ideals were rebuffed by church hierarchy. When Sturzo and Murri assured the Church of their intent to uphold Catholic interests and not speak on behalf of the faithful, the pope did not accept the PPI's formation as legitimate and discouraged Catholics and the clergy from supporting the party. The Vatican's geographical proximity and concomitant control over the Catholic movement in Italy deprived the PPI of

[1] Hennesey 1988, 398.
[2] Whyte 1981, 71.

Intraparty Conflict

the ability to co-opt Catholic Action. The PPI, as a result, continued its path as a nonclerical and pro-system party. Despite PPI leaders' personal commitment to the Catholic faith, their party remained completely independent of the Church's influence.

Lastly in Belgium, the rise of political Catholicism and the Catholic Party followed a different path than in Italy and Germany. The liberal nature of the Belgian constitution and the Church's access to the political system through well-established Conservative Catholic politicians delayed the rise of political Catholicism in Belgium. The Christian Democratic activists who later formed the Belgian Democratic League were marginalized by ultramontanes. The expansion of suffrage in the 1890s allowed Belgian Christian Democrats to rise to prominence within the party; the League's expansive reach among the working classes boosted its political salience for the party. The Christian Democrats gradually took over the Catholic Party and ousted the ultramontane Federation.

THE MUSLIM BROTHERHOOD IN EGYPT

Internal differences and conflict between the political and religious wings of the Brotherhood over the 1980s and 1990s eventually split the organization.[3] Following many years of discussion and resistance from the older generation, the General Guide finally sanctioned a group of middle-generation leaders to draft a political party proposal in late 1995. The work on a draft party program reflected an informal agreement that would pave the way for the establishment of a political party with a separate organizational entity.

The Brotherhood's success between the 1970s and the 1990s, first on college campuses and later in professional associations such as engineers, dentists, doctors, journalists, and pharmacists associations nationwide, nurtured a generation of politically oriented Brotherhood leaders who envisioned a shift in the Brotherhood's organizational structure to carry out its mission.[4] Other Islamist groups mirrored the Brotherhood's experience in professional associations throughout the region, which differed from the path Catholic parties took toward formally establishing a political party. This politically oriented group of Brothers included figures like Issam Al-Aryan, Abdul Munim Aboul Fotouh, Aboul Ela Mady, Salah Abdel Karim, and Issam Sultan.

This group recognized the shifting political ground and the growing importance of grassroots Islamic activism to political success in Egypt. In order to win power and take steps to realize the goals set by Al-Banna, the Brotherhood needed a dedicated political organization. While they remained committed to the fundamental goal of the Brotherhood, this group's pedigree in campus and professional association politics – the main and most free arenas of political

---

[3] Pargeter 2013, 17.
[4] Wickham 2002, 115; Zollner 2019, 6.

activism during Sadat and Mubarak years – convinced them of the necessity of a separate political organization to achieve this goal.

Once the draft proposal was completed, the Guidance Bureau dominated by the Brotherhood's religiously oriented old guard suspended the initiative indefinitely in order not to "provoke the regime appearing too aggressive."[5] The old generation leaders' preference for the current organizational structure was in part informed by Al-Banna's aversion to formal political parties.[6] The Brotherhood's Deputy General Guide, Ma'moun Hudeibi, unequivocally threatened those who did not backtrack on the new party initiative with expulsion.[7] The persistent effort toward a political party was seen as an attempt to create a separate, parallel structure to the movement that could potentially challenge the Brotherhood's authority.[8] While many abandoned the effort, Mady and Sultan forged ahead to legalize the Wasat Party; the party's repeated attempts at becoming officially licensed were rejected until after the 2011 revolution.[9]

While this attempt to form a legal Muslim Brotherhood party did not bother the Brotherhood in the grand scheme of things, the debate surrounding the Wasat Party's formation underscores the division and the balance of power between the religious and political wings of the Brotherhood. Even though the division does not strictly concern age, it still falls along generational lines. The older generation tends to embrace the comprehensive organizational structure and remains suspicious of a separate political party and activism. Decades of state suppression hardened their convictions about the utility and wisdom of comprehensive organizational structure for political activism. By contrast, the younger and middle generations were socialized into Islamist activism in an environment of political competition. For them, the path to realizing the political vision of the Brotherhood passed through direct political activism in a functionally separate political entity from the Brotherhood while upholding the Brotherhood's Islamist ideology; this model resembled how political activists from other ideological orientations operated on college campuses and professional associations. Decades of organizational ambiguity and lack of separation between the political and the religious in the Brotherhood reinforced ideological ambiguity and comprehensiveness (*shumuliya*). The Brotherhood's need to address "several different constituencies simultaneously" underlaid its persistent fuzziness and internal conflict.[10] The lack of specificity and the ubiquity of ambiguity in what the Brotherhood stood for, in turn, facilitated the religious wing's dominance over the political wing. Over the course of

---

[5] Kandil 2015, 147.
[6] Moussalli 1993.
[7] Stacher 2002.
[8] This was certainly not the first initiative to form a political party; similar efforts were taken before. See Pevna (2014, 16).
[9] Rodrigo 2014.
[10] Pargeter 2013, 16.

Intraparty Conflict

many decades in secrecy and underground activism, the Brotherhood's survival took precedence over other concerns. Religious activism constituted the very core of the movement, subduing direct political activism. It is the prospect of charting of an independent course of action, in this case by the Wasat Party, that rendered it a threat for the Brotherhood. So, while the demand for a separate Brotherhood political party represented a mere tactical move by the younger, political generation, the old guard felt it threatened the existence of the Brotherhood as a religious activist organization. Note that this is the very concern that the Catholic Church carried about the formation of Catholic political parties in Western Europe. The prospect of escaping the Church's authority pushed the Church to fiercely oppose the formation of Catholic parties in Western Europe, just as the Brotherhood and other Islamists opposed the formation of a separate formal Islamist political entity outside the movement's organizational structure.

The years following the Wasat Party fallout were a time of mixed fortunes for the organization. The Brothers returned to elections in 2000, gaining only 17 seats. In 2005, they increased their seat share to 88 (one-fifth of the total number seats), despite widespread electoral fraud and the fact that the Brotherhood ran only in 35 percent of the districts to avoid repression. But this somewhat unintentional show of strength again disturbed Mubarak. By 2007, almost 1,000 Brotherhood members had been detained in the worst crackdown since the Nasser era.[11]

Despite repeated crackdowns, near-constant illegality, and flirtations with formalizing the movement's political operation, the Muslim Brotherhood remained remarkably unified and well organized, surviving to witness and benefit from the 2011 Egyptian Revolution.[12] After Mubarak was deposed, the Brotherhood finally created its first political party, the Freedom and Justice Party. An estimated 80 percent of party members were also members of the movement.[13] In the first postrevolutionary parliamentary election, the FJP won 37.5 percent of the vote and 47 percent of the seats. Another Islamist party, al-Nour Party, which is Salafist and unaffiliated with the Brotherhood, received 28 percent of the vote and 25 percent of the seats. Despite gaining legal standing, the Wasat Party failed to find electoral success. The Brotherhood's good fortune continued as the FJP presidential candidate, Mohamed Morsi, was elected to office in June 2012. The FJP platform and Morsi's actions displeased many, however, and the first truly democratically elected leader of Egypt was removed in a coup only a year later and sentenced to life in prison in 2015. Abdel-Fatah al-Sisi, an army general and leader of the coup that replaced Morsi, and the Brotherhood once again found itself face-to-face with harsh state repression.

---

[11] Eisenhart 2010, 65–66; Bilinski 2013, 30.

[12] Shehata 2018.

[13] Pevna 2014, 16.

In 2005, the Brotherhood created its first official platform based on the organization's long-time motto, "Islam is the solution." The platform showed a clear commitment to democracy and pluralism, but it was not without controversy. For example, despite asserting a belief in gender equality and religious freedom, the platform declared that the presidency could only be held by a Muslim man. A subsequent platform in 2007 advocated for a body of clerics to advise parliament on whether legislation conformed to shariah, similar to the Iranian system. Unsurprisingly, seculars and Copts were uncomfortable with such a suggestion. The official Freedom and Justice Party platform was quite similar to that of the Brotherhood, although it abandoned the idea of a shura council and made no mention of banning alcohol or requiring women to wear the hijab.[14] They also no longer openly called for an Islamic state, instead desiring a "civil state with Islamic reference." Salafists, on the other hand, took up the call for an Islamic state.[15]

The 2011 Revolution and the Nonevolution of the Brotherhood

The 2011 revolution introduced a unique opportunity for the Muslim Brotherhood to operate as a legal political party for the first time in its long history. According to the inclusion–moderation theory, the Brotherhood's foray into the legal political space and inclusion in the system should have offered significant incentives for the movement to change its fundamental approach to how the religion–politics relationship should be structured and what the role of religion in the political arena should be. The movement should have dropped its anti-system stance. As Bermeo shows, not all social movements abandon their anti-system discourse during periods of (democratic) transition.[16]

However, if my argument holds, there should not have been any fundamental changes in how the Brotherhood conducted itself in the new political environment for two reasons. First, there had not been any changes to the underlying structure of religious institutions and authority in Egypt during this transitional period. Second, the level of religious competition increased significantly in the postrevolutionary political space. The limits placed on religious actors' political participation during Mubarak's presidency no longer constrained the infusion of religious and political discourses. Hence, a series of religiously oriented parties emerged to compete for power and influence. Many of these parties had fairly conservative ideological outlooks and competed for the same conservative electorate as the Muslim Brotherhood. The result was an increasingly conservative Brotherhood that aimed to win over this constituency with its recalibrated posture. When the Brotherhood formally established the Freedom and Justice Party (FJP) to conduct its political activities, the party

[14] Bilinski 2013, 29.
[15] Bilinski 2013, 31.
[16] Bermeo 1997.

Intraparty Conflict

lacked autonomy and operated fully subservient to the parent organization.[17] As a result, the party's ideological stance reflected the Brotherhood's self-image as a vanguard organization that speaks for and represents religion. The FJP existed only insofar as to act on the Brotherhood's goal of Egypt's Islamization and needed to be "centrally directed."[18]

The creation of the FJP came about in the wake of a decidedly conservative takeover in the upper echelons of the Brotherhood by its "iron man" Mahmoud Ezzat and "kingmaker" Khairat al-Shater.[19] Throughout the 2000s, Ezzat and Shater used their organizational and financial clout over the Brotherhood to strengthen the movement's conservative power center, which was loyal to them before anyone else.[20] At its core, this strategy was about gaining power within the organization. By controlling membership in the Guidance Bureau, Ezzat and Shater indirectly ruled over the Brotherhood. This was in part because the bylaws of the Brotherhood remained beyond the reach of the membership, giving the Guidance Bureau "absolute power" and the "right to rule."[21]

The succession in leadership of the Brotherhood from Mohammed Akef to Mohammed Badie in late 2009 and early 2010 solidified the conservative hold on the Brotherhood as engineered by Ezzat and Shater. Akef's tenure as the Supreme Guide (2004–10) was marked by an effort to achieve greater balance between the hardliners and the more politically oriented reformists. In a process mired in ambiguity, the Shura Council first elected a new and predominantly conservative Guidance Bureau. Subsequently, on January 26, 2010, the Brotherhood announced that Badie was elected "by consensus by members of the consultative council" as the new leader of the Brotherhood.[22] The conservative victory utterly marginalized the burgeoning political/reformist wing of the Brotherhood. This was not necessarily about the political direction of the Brotherhood and a potential Brotherhood political party; rather, the conflict reflected a battle over control of the Brotherhood. As the Mubarak regime collapsed in less than a year, the reformists who envisioned a different path for the political orientation of the group broke off to chart their own political course in a more open political environment. Likewise, the Brotherhood, who avoided formally establishing a separate political party for years, formed the FJP shortly after the 2011 Revolution despite some internal opposition that the Brotherhood should continue as a movement.[23]

The reformist faction within the Brotherhood was not too happy about how the movement proceeded with forming the new party. In particular,

---

[17] Personal interviews with Hussein Rabee (2017) and Sameh El-Essawy (2017).
[18] Zollner 2019, 6.
[19] al-Anani 2016, 151–52.
[20] al-Anani 2016, 152.
[21] Kandil 2015, 68.
[22] al-Anani 2016, 154.
[23] Pargeter 2013, 226.

criticisms centered around two issues. Abdel Moneim Aboul Fotouh most vocally took issue with the Brotherhood's decision to establish a political party, arguing that the movement should operate only as a religious movement.[24] A larger group that did not take issue with the movement's decision to establish a political party criticized Brotherhood leader Badi's unilateral decision on party formation, sidestepping the broader movement leadership and its base. It was the absence of "autonomy" that was the most damaging for the new party.[25] Eventually, several leading figures from the politically oriented reformists were pushed out of the Brotherhood, including Abdel Moneim Aboul Fotouh, Islam Lotfi, Ibrahim Za'frani, and Muhammad al-Qassas.[26]

The Brotherhood viewed the FJP as its subdued organizational arm operating in the political arena on a tight leash. This lack of separation between the party and the movement was not by chance, but by design. As such, the FJP was entrusted to proven Brotherhood leaders who would prioritize and uphold the movement's interests and preferences over those of the politically oriented Brotherhood leaders. Mohamed Morsi was named the leader of the new Freedom and Justice Party by the Brotherhood on April 30, 2011. Essam el-Erian became the vice chair, while Saad el-Katatny served as the secretary general of the party. As far as the Brotherhood was concerned, these appointments would serve the movement well and ensure that the hierarchy between the movement and the party would be maintained in favor of the former. All three leaders were members of the Brotherhood's Guidance Bureau and had proved themselves as faithful members of the movement in their tenure as parliamentarians throughout the 2000s, including the leadership of the Brotherhood's parliamentary bloc. The draw of these names, therefore, was first and foremost grounded in their loyalty to the movement. On May 18, 2011, the Brotherhood formally submitted its application to establish the FJP with around 9,000 founding members, more than 70 percent of them being active members of the Brotherhood. Crucially, the list consisted predominantly of the conservative faction rather than the more politically oriented reformists. It achieved legal status on June 6, 2011.[27]

Discipline in political participation was the name of the game for the Brotherhood. Those members and leaders who did not follow the directives of the movement faced the ire of the Brotherhood. Indeed, time and again, the Brotherhood imposed strict discipline over vocal dissent within its ranks, that is, those members and leaders who called for a distinct political operation to grow out of the Brotherhood. The movement's Deputy

[24] Hussein Rabee, personal interview, 2017.
[25] Wickham 2015, 175.
[26] Zollner 2019, 9.
[27] al-Anani 2011; Wickham 2015, 175.

Intraparty Conflict

Supreme Guide Khairat al-Shater was clear during this period on where the Brotherhood stood regarding internal dissent. Al-Shater said that individuals who did not agree with the movement's decisions could "either comply or leave the organization."[28] In the Spring of 2011, a youth conference attacked the Brotherhood leadership for its political strategy in the post-revolutionary period; the membership of around 4,000 youth Brothers was frozen in the period immediately preceding Fotouh's presidential announcement.[29] To make matters worse, when Abdel Moneim Aboul Fotouh – a former member of the Brotherhood's Guidance Bureau – announced his intention to run for president a couple of months after the youth conference in May 2011, the movement briskly responded by removing Aboul Fotouh from the Brotherhood a month later.[30] These actions came on the heels of the Brotherhood's statement that the movement would seek neither the presidency nor the parliamentary majority in the post-Mubarak period.[31] When asked why a separate political party was established in addition to the Brotherhood's main religious organization if the goal was not to win power, the Brotherhood's deputy leader at the time Rashad al-Bayoumi responded by resorting to the movement's standard line on this issue: "Political work is an integral part of Islamic work, for Islam is a comprehensive religion and politics is part of general Islamic work."[32]

Aware of the potential criticisms that FJP leadership's continued ties to the movement might raise, the Brotherhood preemptively removed the three FJP leaders from their membership in the Guidance Bureau as a sign of their political independence. Brotherhood spokesperson Walid Shalabi insisted that the party and the movement were separate from each other in leadership and finances, although both shared the "same Islamic ideals" and would assist the other when needed.[33] Yet, Morsi, el-Erian, and al-Katatny continued as members of the Shura Council – the general leadership body of the movement – attesting to their deep connection and commitment to the movement. Overall, the FJP maintained an ideologically and politically "subordinate" relationship to the Brotherhood. The Brotherhood's control over the FJP was so evident that when the FJP won the 2011–12 parliamentary elections, the US Ambassador in Cairo did not visit FJP leaders to congratulate them on the victory; instead, Ambassador Anne Patterson visited Brotherhood Supreme Guide Badie on

---

[28] Traeger 2016, 73.
[29] Traeger 2016, 128.
[30] Pargeter 2013, 231.
[31] Farag 2012, 220.
[32] "A Talk with Muslim Brotherhood's Rashad al-Bayoumi," *Asharq Al-Awsat*, February 27, 2011. Available at: https://eng-archive.aawsat.com/theaawsat/features/a-talk-with-muslim-brotherhoods-rashad-al-bayoumi (accessed September 14, 2020)
[33] "Freedom and Justice Party," *Jadaliyya*, November 22, 2011. Available at: www.jadaliyya .com/Details/24642 (accessed September 14, 2020). Wickham also notes the financial, logistical, and mobilizational dependency of the FJP on the Brotherhood (2015, 314).

January 18, 2012.[34] More telling of what this visit meant for the relationship between the FJP and the Brotherhood was the fact that neither Morsi nor FJP officials took issue with the visit.[35] The absence of critical voices from within the party attests to the party's subservience to the party.

Ideologically, the FJP seemed to confirm its subservient status to the parent Brotherhood organization. Islam constituted the main pillar of the party platform, aiming to "enhance Islamic morals, values, and concepts in individuals' lives and society."[36] Brotherhood Deputy Supreme Guide Khairat al-Shater argued that the FJP's electoral victories provided the party with the mandate for "an explicitly Islamic government": "The people are insistent … All institutions should revise their cultures, their training programs and the way they build their individuals in the light of this real popular choice."[37]

While the FJP was physically separated from the Brotherhood through using different office spaces, the party began undertaking virtually identical functions to the Brotherhood such as "medical clinics, educational programs, vocational trainings, and food-distribution efforts," essentially blurring the lines between the party and the movement. Moreover, the FJP relied on key Brotherhood leaders to mobilize the party base as events featuring Brotherhood leaders drew thousands.[38]

In terms of decision-making on issues that fell within the purview of the FJP as a political party, the Brotherhood did not recognize a separation as such and frequently appropriated tasks that the FJP was expected to carry out,[39] including running for positions within the party.[40] For example, in preparation for the parliamentary elections of 2011–12, the Brotherhood leadership asked regional and local offices to select candidates to run in FJP lists. Interested Brotherhood members were required to obtain endorsement of their local Brotherhood leaders up in the hierarchy for consideration by the Brotherhood leadership for candidacy. The names that went through the hierarchy with endorsements were then passed on to the FJP leadership.[41] While it may be easy

---

[34] John Hudson, "Knives Come Out for U.S. Ambassador to Egypt Anne Patterson," *Foreign Policy*, July 3, 2013. Available at: https://foreignpolicy.com/2013/07/03/knives-come-out-for-u-s-ambassador-to-egypt-anne-patterson (accessed September 14, 2020)

[35] Personal interviews with Wael Haddara (2017), Ibrahim Mounir (2017), Mohamed Soudan (2017), and Gamal Heshmat (2017).

[36] al-Anani 2011.

[37] David D. Kirkpatrick, "Keeper of Islamic Flame Rises as Egypt's New Decisive Voice," *The New York Times*, March 12, 2012. Available at: www.nytimes.com/2012/03/12/world/middleeast/muslim-brotherhood-leader-rises-as-egypts-decisive-voice.html (accessed September 14, 2020)

[38] Traeger 2016, 80.

[39] Brown 2011.

[40] Zollner 2019, 13.

[41] Traeger 2016, 101. For example, Abdul Mawgoud Dardery's nomination by the local party office was rejected by the movement multiple times before it was finally approved and passed on to the party leadership. Dardery subsequently won the election to become a member of the Egyptian parliament (Abdul Mawgoud Dardery, personal interview, 2017).

Intraparty Conflict

to dismiss this as a one-off incident or attribute it to the newness of the FJP as a political party, it is important to note that an overwhelming majority of the nominated names were well-established members of the movement who were unquestionably committed to the Brotherhood. The Brotherhood similarly solicited nominations for prospective minister appointments following the parliamentary elections and these names were passed onto the FJP. However, the party leadership had some room to navigate suggestions.[42] Once in the parliament, the committee chair appointments by the FJP reflected a similar pattern; of the 12 committee chair appointments, 11 were members of the Brotherhood while the lone exception was a former member of the Egyptian military to lead the sensitive Defense and National Security Committee.[43] In Traeger's words: "So while the Brotherhood didn't know what its leaders would actually do in power, it knew that its leaders needed to be in power. And the Brotherhood was very prepared for advising Morsi on his governmental appointments: By the time that Morsi won the presidential election, the organization had already selected potential ministers and deputy ministers for every cabinet post, and it later drafted a list of gubernatorial candidates for Morsi to appoint in certain governorates."[44]

The Brotherhood's supervision of the FJP went beyond appointments, however. The movement made sure that party decisions were made together with the movement,[45] and a formal structure was created to facilitate the hierarchy between the two organizations. FJP's top leadership (Morsi, el-Erian, and al-Katatny) held weekly "coordination" meetings with four top Brotherhood leaders: Brotherhood secretary general Mahmoud Hussein, spokesperson Mahmoud Ghozlan, and Deputy Supreme Guides Khairat al-Shater and Mahmoud Ezzat.[46] These coordination meetings ensured that the party remained under the direct control of the "new" conservative leaders of the movement, al-Shater and Ezzat.[47] Moreover, when calls for Morsi to drop out of the second round of the 2012 presidential elections intensified, it was not Morsi's own campaign or the FJP but the top Brotherhood leadership, including a statement by the Supreme Guide Mohammed Badie that referenced the Guidance Bureau's decision to that effect, that announced Morsi's intention to stay in the race.[48]

Similarly, the Brotherhood took FJP's grassroots mobilization into its own hands, further blurring the lines between the two organizations. The

---

[42] Personal interviews with Ibrahim Mounir (2017), Gamal Heshmat (2017), Hussen Rabee (2017), Wael Hadddara (2017), and Sameh El-Essawy (2017); Traeger 2016, 120.

[43] Traeger 2016, 113.

[44] Traeger 2016, 155.

[45] Wickham 2015, 314.

[46] Traeger 2016, 111. Brotherhood and FJP officials such as Ibrahim Mounir, Gamal Heshmat, Mohamed Soudan, and Wael Haddara confirmed in personal interviews that these meetings took place.

[47] al-Anani 2016, 149.

[48] Traeger 2016, 140–41.

Brotherhood's Guidance Bureau asked Brotherhood members to become members of the FJP,[49] to campaign for the FJP,[50] "to distribute campaign literature, knock on doors, hang banners, and organize political rallies all over the country."[51] In the early days in office, the Brotherhood's Shura Council mobilized members to help President Morsi and the FJP to achieve the 100-day plan goals. Early party publicity material included the logos of both the FJP and the Brotherhood as well as the "Islam is the Solution" text on Brotherhood material attached to FJP posters.[52] Such utter lack of separation between the FJP and the Brotherhood was a key failure during this period, according to a leading Brotherhood and FJP figure Amr Darrag.[53]

The Brotherhood also aimed to control the political behavior of its base.[54] The movement unequivocally declared its support for the newly established FJP;[55] Supreme Guide Badie released a statement on March 15, 2011 that laid out the main parameters of the Brotherhood members' political activism: "Members of the [Brotherhood] cannot establish, participate, or join any other parties."[56] The main advantage afforded to the FJP by the Brotherhood was the movement's ability to maintain control over its base within this hierarchical structure and ensure high turnout in support of the FJP when turnout rates remained historically dismal for the broader Egyptian electorate. For most of the movement base, this was a noncontroversial statement. The FJP leadership felt confident about the support they would receive from the Brotherhood and its ability to whip up votes on the eve of the 2011 constitutional referendum. As an expression of this confidence in the Brotherhood's ability to mobilize, FJP Vice President Essam el-Erian stated, "When we say that we accept the constitutional changes, and we vote 'yes', then this is a clear message to the entire Brotherhood front, which is to vote 'yes'."[57] A small youth faction, nonetheless, revolted against this direct order and criticized the Brotherhood leadership by demanding clear separation between the party and the movement.[58]

This point is crucial to the nature of the relationship between the FJP and the Brotherhood organization because it directly speaks to the Brotherhood's claim to Islamic authority and represents Islam. The Brotherhood unequivocally equates Islam with itself and vice versa. A Brotherhood member recently recounted, "We come to believe that Islam is the Brotherhood (al-Islam howa

---

[49] Zollner 2019, 12.

[50] Personal interviews with Gamal Heshmat (2017) and Mohamed Soudan (2017).

[51] Traeger 2016, 106.

[52] Traeger 2016, 165, 80, & 106.

[53] Hamid 2017.

[54] Personal interviews with Abdul Mawgoud Dardery (2017), Gamal Heshmat (2017), Hussein Rabee (2017), and Mohamed Soudan (2017).

[55] Brown 2011.

[56] Pargeter 2013, 227; Traeger 2016, 68.

[57] Traeger 2016, 67.

[58] Pargeter 2013, 237.

Intraparty Conflict 203

al-Ikhwan)."[59] This expression is no gaffe; it truly represents the sentiment across the Brotherhood's organizational structure. In fact, the wording is intentional and mirrors what some senior Brotherhood officials openly expressed in the past. For example, Amany Aboul Fadl Farag, a leading woman Brotherhood leader from Cairo, declared "Islam is Muslim Brotherhood and Muslim Brotherhood is Islam."[60] Farag was not alone in her assertion. AbdelHamed Al-Ghazali – the former member of the Brotherhood Shura Council, the former head of the Brotherhood's political bureau, and advisor to the former General Guide Mohammed Akef – repeated the same phrase verbatim and stated in a personal interview, "Islam is Muslim Brotherhood and Muslim Brotherhood is Islam."[61] The suggestion is clear; there is no difference between what Islam lays out for Muslims and what the Brotherhood preaches: "Islamic point of view and Muslim Brotherhood point of view … are identical."[62] The logical conclusion of this equivalence of the movement with Islam is the sanctification of the Brotherhood. Representation of the sacred, in this regard, leads to a "sacred" Brotherhood, in the absence of which "there can be no return to Islamic rule."[63] Hence, turning one's back to the Brotherhood implies rejecting one's faith rather than merely a political ideology, "abandoning God not Hassan al-Banna."[64] While Sunni Islam lacks the kind of hierarchical religious authority structure that Catholicism enjoys, this claim by the Brotherhood to represent Islam paralleled the Catholic Church's effort to establish religious and political control over the faithful. No independent political action would be tolerated so as not to threaten the religious and political power of the Church, or in this case the Brotherhood.

Some Brotherhood and FJP officials like Abdul Mawgoud Dardery and Gamal Heshmat hinted at the beginnings of an independent trajectory for the party despite its brief existence; some initial discussions were held within FJP about separating the party and the movement. For example, Heshmat states: "The party [FJP] had its finger on the pulse more, it was attuned to the real problems of the masses. In addition, it was better positioned to know when to form coalitions with other parties, what individuals would make good ministers, etcetera. By contrast, the jama'a [the Brotherhood] was more focused on social services and was not as directly involved in broader political life. But party decisions were made jointly by the FJP leadership and the jama'a. In fact, the jama'a dominated political decisions that should have been left to the party leadership."[65] Some senior Brotherhood officials, however, did not take issue with the nature of the relationship between the movement and the party. For

[59] Kandil 2015, 48.
[60] Amany Aboul Fadl Farag, personal interview, 2008.
[61] AbdelHamed Al-Ghazali, personal interview, 2008.
[62] AbdelHamed Al-Ghazali, personal interview, 2008.
[63] Kandil 2015, 48.
[64] Memoir of Sameh Fayez quote in Kandil 2015, 50.
[65] Heshmat quoted in Wickham 2015, 314.

example, Mohamed Soudan – member of the Brotherhood's arbitration committee and former foreign affairs committee secretary with FJP – argued that the relationship was cooperative in nature and "there is no conflict between the two [FJP and the Brotherhood] because they have the same agenda, they have the same policy."[66] Likewise, despite the movement's support for the party and widespread coordination between the two entities, Brotherhood's Deputy Supreme Guide and Acting General Guide Ibrahim Mounir claimed that the party was "totally independent" from the movement.[67]

The Muslim Brotherhood's rise and later growth epitomizes how unfettered access to religion and religious authority in the absence of a centralized religious institution shapes religiopolitical activism. In sharp contrast to Catholic parties that felt the need to separate themselves from existing religious institutional structures in order to emerge as political parties, the Brotherhood established itself with a firm grasp of a religious mantle. As others have shown, the Brotherhood has always been a multifaceted organization capable of speaking to different constituencies and winning their support. Nonetheless, the movement never faced significant religious or political pressure to change its hybrid organizational structure. Secure in the movement's mobilizational and recruitment potential, the Brotherhood instead suppressed internal calls for disentangling its religious and political activism. Even when the Brotherhood formally established a political party after Mubarak's removal from power, the party operated as a subsidiary of the Brotherhood in every imaginable way rather than showing signs of independence; as Zollner observes, "the boundaries between social movement and party were in fact fictional."[68] As such, its fundamentally anti-system orientation and self-image as the true representative of Islam in Egypt did not waver.

ENNAHDHA MOVEMENT IN TUNISIA

The nature of the relationship between Islamist parties and the religious movements from which they hail constitutes one of the most crucial institutional settings that Islamist parties operate within. I analyze the recent specialization policy of Tunisia's Ennahdha Movement, which separated its movement and dawah (movement)-related activities from its political arm in Spring 2016. The nature of the relationship between the party and the movement fundamentally alters the political landscape and meaning of electoral politics for Islamist parties, with major ramifications for the party's ideological rigidity. Religious parties prefer the party-movement hybrid organizational structure because it allows religiopolitical movements to operate as encompassing organizations

---

[66] Mohamed Soudan, personal interview, 2017.
[67] Ibrahim Mounir, personal interview, 2017.
[68] Zollner 2019, 13.

Intraparty Conflict

that align with the broad-based religious transformation they envision in the state and society. Likewise, it allows them to harness the power of religion more fully in the political arena. Ennahdha provides an intriguing contrast to how the Egyptian Brotherhood decided to handle its movement-party dynamic in 2011. Likewise, Ennahdha's careful examination of European Catholic parties while adopting its specialization policy and the party's reasoning to do so help illustrate the underlying effect of religious authority structures on religious party organization and ideology.

The case of the Ennahdha Movement in Tunisia and its departure from the party-movement hybrid structure is important for several reasons. Ennahdha currently serves as the posterchild for Islamist moderation and democratization. Its organizational restructuring offers useful insights into the party's ideological transformation. Ennahdha is also the most recent example of organizational overhaul by an Islamist party. Therefore, party leaders are well suited to recollect details of the process, decision-making, and rationale for the specialization policy. Lastly, Ennahdha leadership approached this question of organizational change with great care and deliberation, underscoring the significance of the party's move. In this regard, the justifications and discussions among different party leaders on this issue are quite valuable in illustrating the hybrid structures of conventional Islamist parties.

Specialization Policy

Ennahdha's recent adoption of *Takhassus*, or specialization, policy marks a critical turning point in its evolution as an Islamist party.[69] The specialization policy was adopted in 2016 and aims to directly tackle the organizational predicament that Islamist parties typically find themselves in: What does the group aim to achieve? Who is their audience? What kinds of policies can be adopted? To complement the specialization policy, Ennahdha renounced political Islam as the party's ideology in favor of Muslim democracy. Both policies required Ennahdha to rethink its relationship with religion and the country's religious sphere.[70]

The specialization policy was adopted at the 10th party congress (2016) with an overwhelming majority vote. It recognizes politics and religion as separate spheres of activity, that is, "functional specialization," which is a sharp departure from Islamist parties' conventional position on the two as interwoven areas of activity much like the Egyptian Brotherhood.[71] While the new policy may appear to suggest two distinct organizational arms to oversee the political and religious activism of Ennahdha, that is not the case. The policy

---

[69] Rached Ghannouchi, "The Ennahda Party and the Future of Tunisia," *Foreign Affairs*, September/October 2016.

[70] Merone, Sigillo, and De Facci 2018; Meddeb 2019.

[71] McCarthy 2018a, 1.

essentially constrains Ennahdha to the political sphere only and mandates it to operate purely as a political party. As a result, Ennahdha abandoned its religious activism entirely; individual party members were left to pursue their religious enrichment and activism on their own. What motivated Ennahdha to change its organizational structure? Ennahdha went through a lengthy period of internal review and soul-searching to determine what course of organizational change the party wanted to pursue. The process leading to the adoption of the specialization policy is particularly crucial in understanding the dynamic between the religious and political elements of religious parties and how the claim to religious authority plays out.

The answer to why Ennahdha embraced this policy of specialization and decided to pursue such a fundamental change in its organizational structure rests on various factors. The movement's former hybrid structure shaped the different ways that Ennahdha leaders imagined the party's nature and function in the process leading up to the specialization policy. Where an Ennahdha official stands on the division between the religious and political factions of Ennahdha colored their perception of the political context, how they justified the specialization policy, and what they expected of it. In a way, this is a group torn by divided – and, at times, conflicting – allegiances.[72] Such division between the political and religious factions has parallels in other Islamist parties and Catholic parties. On one hand, a group of Ennahdha officials – who can be characterized as the religious faction who make up the core of Ennahdha's religious movement – view Ennahdha as a comprehensive Islamist movement because Islam speaks to all aspects of life. For this faction, Ennahdha has a responsibility in all aspects of life to effectuate the Islamic vision. On the other hand, Ennahdha leaders who comprise the political faction consider Ennahdha to be a primarily political organization – a political actor that aims to find (Islamic) political solutions to the social, religious, and economic problems of Tunisians. This more politically oriented group attributes Ennahdha's past decision to pursue a comprehensive organization to the political conditions of the time. As such, a change in political conditions opens up the possibility for renouncing the movement side and focusing on political activism. The division between the two factions existed in the pre-2010 period, it is not a function of the specialization policy.[73]

While the differences between these two visions appear sharp in the abstract, most Ennahdha officials fall somewhere on a continuum of this religious–political division. Individual positions are typically not mutually exclusive; Ennahdha members subscribe to both visions to differing degrees, with the important difference being how these two visions are prioritized. Both factions believe in the necessity of defending the "Islamic identity" of the Tunisian

---

[72] McCarthy 2018a, 3.
[73] McCarthy 2018a, 116 & 54.

Intraparty Conflict

society in the face of threats coming from the regime – first from Bourguiba, subsequently from Ben Ali – and fighting against dictatorship.[74] Importantly, the difference between the two groups is less about the ultimate goal – a version of the "Islamic project" on which both factions agree on – and more about the means to get there.

The idea of specialization, or organizational reform, has been part of Ennahdha's internal discussions since the 1980s.[75] The nature of these discussions in that early period, however, differs markedly from the debates in the postrevolutionary period. In the 1980s, the debates were much less thorough.[76] Following a period of hiatus from the issue, organizational reform discussions restarted in the first half of the 2000s when Ennahdha leaders began leaving prison. The discussions emerged as to what the movement stood and advocated for, yet, in turn, led to further "confusion" about Ennahdha's identity within and outside of the movement.[77] The difficulty of "combining" the religious and political activities became increasingly evident to party officials.[78] The political faction within Ennahdha viewed the separation of the political arm and the establishment of a legal political party as "a matter of principle" and was "ready to abandon" the religious movement entirely in the early 1980s.[79]

Following the revolution in 2011, the organizational change became "a necessity," according to Lotfi Zitoun.[80] The postrevolutionary period presented an entirely different set of circumstances compared to the restrictive environment of the prerevolution period. Ennahdha reemerged as a legal political party, a new and open political system was established, and a shot at governance was a real possibility – truly, a watershed moment. What did this drastic change in political context mean to Ennahdha leaders? How did they respond to it? The answer to these questions depends on where different Ennahdha leaders fell regarding the division between the religious and political factions, and what they conceived as the movement's primary task. The political and religious factions of Ennahdha had different answers, subsequently leading to important differences in how they approached the question of organizational reform and the specialization policy.

Ennahdha undertook extensive research into its strategy for organizational restructuring. Rachid Ghannouchi and Abdelfattah Morou initially spearheaded the specialization efforts but the movement subsequently took

---

[74] Yousef Nouri, personal interview, 2017.
[75] Personal interviews with Fathi Ayedi (2017), Lotfi Zitoun (2017), Mohamed Ben Salem (2017), Toumi Hamrouni (2017), and Mohammad Chiha (2017). See Cavatorta and Merone's (2015) analysis of the internal debates within Ennahdha prior to the 2010 revolution.
[76] Lotfi Zitoun, personal interview, 2017.
[77] Lotfi Zitoun, personal interview, 2017.
[78] Mohammad Chiha, personal interview, 2017.
[79] Mohamed Ben Salem, personal interview, 2017.
[80] Lotfi Zitoun, personal interview, 2017.

ownership of the issue, engaging in comprehensive discussions.[81] The initial discussions on the idea of specialization were undertaken in the period leading up to the ninth party congress (2012) under Abdellatif Makki's leadership via multiple committees (2011–12), one of which included Ghannouchi himself, although Makki's leadership was cut short once he became the Minister of Health in the Jebali government. After inconclusive deliberations, party leadership at the Shura Council level decided that further discussion and a thorough study of the issue were needed; a decision was postponed until the 10th party congress for the entire party congress to discuss and vote on it.[82] The leadership asked for a broad study that would consider the experiences of religious parties in other countries. Several committees were established to examine this issue and report back to the party leadership, the most important of which was the Committee of Content. This committee would look into a broad set of questions surrounding specialization and organizational reform, including but not limited to religion–state relationship, the party's position on religion, and democratic governance.[83] The crucial question before the leadership was the following: how did other religious parties create political parties with inspiration from religion while avoiding the "dichotomy" or "contradiction" between religious and political spheres that religious parties typically struggle with?[84]

During these deliberations, Ennahda cast a wide net and examined in detail different kinds of religious party models and their organizational structures in order to craft its own direction. The committee dedicated the bulk of its attention to Moroccan, Egyptian, Turkish, and German parties,[85] although Jordanian[86] and Sudanese[87] parties were also discussed to some degree. As part of this process, the committee studied "establishing laws" of 14 contemporary political parties, organized seminars with the German Hanns Seidel Foundation, visited the 2014 European People's Party (EPP) congress in Dublin, and invited for workshops representatives of political parties Ennahda examined.[88]

Three main models crystallized during Ennahda's research into the many forms of religious parties around the world regarding the direction that the organizational change could take. The first model entailed decoupling political

---

[81] Lotfi Zitoun, personal interview, 2017.

[82] Rory McCarthy, "Ennahda's Next Move," *Sada*, November 4, 2014. Available at: https://carnegieendowment.org/sada/?fa=57120 (accessed September 24, 2020)

[83] Personal interviews with Ahmed Mechergui (2017), Yousef Nouri (2017), Abdellatif Mekki (2017), and Fathi Ayedi (2017).

[84] Lotfi Zitoun, personal interview, 2017.

[85] Personal interviews with Rafik Abdesalam (2018), Mohamed Akrout (2017), Nawfal Al-Jamali (2017), Ossama Al Saghir (2017), Fathi Ayedi (2017), Dalila Babba (2017), Mohamed Ben Salam (2017), Hbib Idriss (2017), Abdelhamid Jlassi (2018), Mehrziya Laabidi (2017), and Ahmed Mechergui (2017).

[86] Abdelhamid Jlassi, personal interview, 2018.

[87] Toumi Hamrouni, personal interview, 2017.

[88] Personal interviews with Ossama Al Saghir (2017), Fathi Ayedi (2017), and Toumi Hamrouni (2017).

Intraparty Conflict 209

and nonpolitical activism under separate and independent organizational structures. The Moroccan Justice and Development Party's relationship with the Movement for Unity and Reform epitomizes this dynamic, a model most prominently favored by Habib Ellouze. In fact, Ellouze viewed separation and continued organizational existence of the religious movement as the most viable path forward and proposed it both before and after the revolution.[89] The second model is what Fathi Ayedi termed the "re-diffusion" model. In this model, different spheres of activity have their autonomy in, for example, politics, dawah, or charity; all activity is "overseen" by the Ennahdha movement as a singular organization. The goal here would be to "spread the energy" of the organization to different areas of activity.[90] This model mirrors the traditional hybrid organizational structure of Islamist movements; the Egyptian Muslim Brotherhood represents the best example. The third model favored political activism over the rest and required channeling the movement's energy into the political arena, effectively morphing into a political party. In this model, Ennahdha would cease to operate in nonpolitical fields of activity; the religious activism of the movement would end. It mirrors the AKP's and CDU's organizational structures in Turkey and Germany, respectively.

The grassroots members of Ennahdha were not entirely sold on the idea of specialization. There emerged some discord between the leadership and the grassroots of the party; the initial lukewarm attitude, or even resistance, among grassroots members gave way to greater reception as the intraparty discussion continued.[91] In the 10th party congress (2016), Ennahdha moved to adopt the third model with approximately 80 percent of the congress participants' support; Ennahdha renounced its nonpolitical functions and all related activities in its entirety. As such, Ennahdha committed to being purely a political party. The decision was not surprising as Ennahdha leader Ghannouchi was an ardent proponent of the idea.

The adoption of the specialization policy revealed a great deal about the factions within Ennahdha; how these factions approached the policy of specialization and what it means for the future of the party offers a wealth of information about the competition between the political and religious factions of Ennahdha. In particular, the factions collided on three issues: (1) comprehensiveness of Ennahdha's religiopolitical activism, (2) necessity of organizational reform, and (3) what the specialization policy means for the future of the party. In what follows, I discuss each line of argument by examining what Ennahdha officials said about the specialization policy in my interviews. At times, the lines are not always clear with overlapping arguments by officials, underscoring the fact that it is less about binary choices; for most officials, the issue presented itself as a matter of prioritization.

---

[89] Habib Ellouze, personal interview, 2017.
[90] Fathi Ayedi, personal interview, 2017.
[91] Rafik Abdesalam, personal interview, 2018.

Comprehensive Approach to Religiopolitical Activism

Ennahdha leaders' perspectives on why Ennahdha operated within a hybrid organizational structure prior to the 2011 revolution sheds light on how and why the specialization policy was justified, or tolerated, subsequently. Despite a deep divide between more politically oriented and more religiously oriented Ennahdha leaders, both factions agreed on Ennahdha's goals, broadly construed. For Ennahdha leaders, the movement faced a "question of religion" and a "question of identity"; the religion and religious identity of Tunisians was under threat. As such, the main goal of the movement was to challenge the regime in its official policy toward religion. Lotfi Zitoun states, "*Ennahdha* first was founded in the 1970s, it was a response to another question; it was the question of religion. After the independence in Tunisia, there have been massive aggression against the religion itself as a foundation of the society and it was a question of the identity. There was a big debate between [the questions of], are we a Muslim society or are we a Western society?"[92]

Ennahdha aimed to "revive" Islamic values and principles, reestablish the "Islamic way of life," and reenergize Tunisian society with the "Islamic spirit" following the colonial period. Ennahdha's operation as an Islamic movement would serve this end.[93] As a comprehensive Islamic movement, Ennahdha engaged in three principal activities, according to Abdellatif Mekki. First, the movement taught Islamic doctrine to Tunisians to educate them about Islam and its teachings. Second, Ennahdha guided "the conduct" of Tunisians through both the doctrines taught in the first stage and "camps or outside activities." Lastly, Ennahdha engaged the state to address the issue of Tunisia's Islamic identity. The movement "invited the state to increase its respect for Islamic provisions" in the country's legal infrastructure.[94]

For the religious faction, the movement's "comprehensive" orientation was less a response to the current political conditions on the ground and more a reflection of Islam's comprehensiveness.[95] This comprehensiveness meant that Ennahdha would be "active in all fields, the cultural life, the political, the economic, the social, the educational, everything involved in life." Such inclusiveness in regard to spheres of activity mirrored Islam's inclusiveness in "all areas of life" and the way it functions as "the curriculum of the life of the Muslim." This was not a phenomenon unique to Ennahdha – it reflected the mainstream Islamist perspective such as the Brotherhood in Egypt. Sadok Chourou states, "this understanding of Islam is the understanding that is specific to Islamic movements, especially [those] which were initiated in the beginning of the 20th

---

[92] Lotfi Zitoun, personal interview, 2017.
[93] Hicham Larayedh, personal interview, 2017.
[94] Abdellatif Mekki, personal interview, 2017.
[95] Zollner 2019, 9.

Intraparty Conflict

century and which includes the Islamic movement in Egypt, the movement of the Muslim Brotherhood, the Islamic movement in Pakistan."[96]

In contrast to the religious faction, the political faction attributed Ennahdha's organizational structure in the period before the revolution to the unique political circumstances of the time. The official policy of not allowing religious political parties – or most forms of legal political activism, for that matter – during the Bourguiba and Ben Ali regimes constitutes the main impetus for Ennahdha to embrace activism in a broader array of areas.[97] The party's explicit prohibition from engaging in direct political activity, in this regard, led to the expanded scope of its activities: "When we were prohibited from political activity, it was imposed upon us that everything had to be done; educational, cultural, social, all of it had to be done under the name of the party."[98] An authoritarian setting charged Ennahdha with the "responsibility" of engaging in dawah activities because Islam needed to be "protected"; the civil society lacked the means to protect Islam because of the oppressive regime in place. Imed Khmiri claimed the movement did not have "a choice" on the comprehensive organizational form it took; the comprehensiveness reflected a "historical necessity" because of "the climate of authoritarianism and the climate of political oppression" in Tunisia during this period.[99] Mehrziya Laabidi summarized the rationale succinctly as follows: "At the time, we needed to face this totalitarianism of dictatorship; we have a total answer, we have to work in mosques with people in their civil society. Indeed, this is the [critical] aspect of the comprehensive movement ... we kept the same people doing all these activities and, of course, we added to this activism of human rights, when majority of our people were imprisoned."[100] At a time when the secular–Islamic conflict ravaged Tunisian society, Ennahdha viewed itself as the chief representative of the "identity actors," that is, Islamic side, and served as "an umbrella" for their activism.[101] A "comprehensive opposition" was needed.[102]

The Need for Organizational Reform
Why did Ennahdha engage in organizational reform and move away from the conventional hybrid structure Islamist groups prefer? As importantly, how did Ennahdha leaders justify the specialization policy? The answers to both questions relate closely to what Ennahdha leaders envision Ennahdha's role to be in Tunisian society over time. The religious faction emphasized external factors in how Ennahdha was forced by actors inside and outside of Tunisia to change its organizational structure – and ultimately what the movement represents. By

---

[96] Sadok Chourou, personal interview, 2017.
[97] Abdellatif Mekki, personal interview, 2017.
[98] Toumi Hamrouni, personal interview, 2017.
[99] Imed Khmiri, personal interview, 2017.
[100] Mehrziya Laabidi, personal interview, 2017.
[101] Lotfi Zitoun, personal interview, 2017.
[102] Pacha Bouasida, personal interview, 2017.

contrast, the political faction focused on the changing social and political conditions in Tunisia following the revolution, and how Ennahdha is well positioned to take advantage of the new context as a matter of choice. The ultimate decision was surely a combination of both considerations.

The more politically oriented Ennahdha leadership's preferred framing for the organizational restructuring underscores Islam's role in postrevolutionary Tunisia. Before the enshrining of the new constitution (2014), Ennahdha considered itself the defender of Tunisia's Islamic identity. Pre-revolution Tunisia was characterized by the suppression of religion and religious identity. Following the French model of religion–state relations (laïcité), Tunisian state marginalized religious identity in public sphere, seeing it detrimental to the country's modernization process. In an environment where Islam and the society's Islamic identity were under attack, Ennahdha aimed to be their desperately needed defender. Between its origins in the 1960s and the adoption of the new constitution in 2014, Ennahdha clearly stood for Islam and Islam's public role.

For Ennahdha, Tunisia's Arab–Islamic heritage and its "Arab-Muslim character" cried out for a strong restoration effort.[103] The sentiment of alienation for devout Muslims reigned supreme. In the words of Ghannouchi, "I remember we used to feel like strangers in our own country. We had been educated as Muslims and Arabs, while we could see that the country had been totally moulded in the French cultural identity."[104] Since the 1970s, education and morality constituted essential pillars of Ennahdha's vision; the French origins of Tunisia's educational system were in the group's crosshairs.[105] The 2014 Constitution recognized Islam as the official religion of the country, as Article 1 states, "Tunisia is a free, independent, sovereign state; its religion is Islam, its language Arabic, and its system is republican." To that end, many official and nonofficial policies that placed restrictions on public display of religiosity were either removed or relaxed. Once the 2014 Constitution ensured a prominent place for Islam in Tunisia's future, Ennahdha's view that Islam was under threat had to be revised, according to Ennahdha officials. Ahmed Mechergui states, "The topics that [*Ennahdha*] worked on during the time of the dictatorship ... have ended. People used to defend their freedoms like the freedom of attire, they defended the right to be religious and [fought] the decree 108 that prohibited the headscarf. Thanks to the revolution, these have been settled, they are no longer demanded."[106] This formal recognition of Islam's role in the state was a key achievement for Ennahdha officials.[107] Many Ennahdha leaders consider the predominant issue they fought for in the pre-revolutionary

---

[103] Jones 1988.
[104] Ghannouchi quoted in Cavatorta 2012, 13.
[105] Okumus 2014, 5.
[106] Ahmed Mechergui personal interview, 2017.
[107] Imed Khmiri, personal interview, 2017.

Intraparty Conflict

era, that is, the question of Islamic identity, resolved in the postrevolutionary period. For example, Abdesalam stated, "I think the problem of identity is already resolved in our constitution. We mention in the constitution that we are an Arab Muslim country."[108] Yousef Nouri expressed his trust in the Tunisian society to protect Islam; he claimed that because Islam is included in the new constitution to define Tunisia's identity, "the Tunisian people will protect it ... so we are not as afraid as we were before. We are no longer afraid for our identity, our Islamic identity, and Arab identity."[109]

According to Ennahdha officials, continued focus on the problem of Islamic identity in this new era can have two undesired effects. Rehashing Islamic identity issues can alienate large segments of the Tunisian society – it risks driving a large group of Tunisians away from Islam and being perceived as a "sect," which might hinder Ennahdha's ability to govern.[110] An Ennahdha MP put it thusly: "If you aim as a political party to exercise power, to be in charge of the country, you cannot afford the fact that you are aiming a few people. You have to touch maximum number of people in Tunisia."[111] The reference to Islam in the constitution outsources the protection of the Islamic identity to the broader population, where "the state is responsible for this, and the Constitution defines this matter ... We [Ennahdha] do not talk on behalf of religion nor do we claim that we represent it."[112] Such a stance contrasts sharply with Ennahdha's position prior to the revolution. Religion's value as a political asset in Tunisia also diminished in recent years.[113] According to a series of International Republican Institute public opinion surveys conducted in Tunisia, the share of Tunisians who support a close relationship between religion and governance steadily decreased between 2014 and 2019. This shift in Tunisians' view has been a factor in pushing Ennahdha to come to terms with changing popular opinion on the role of religion in public life (Figure 5.1). The real struggle for Ennahdha was conveying its new approach to religion and religion's public role in ways that would align with changing public opinion on this issue *and* sustain its electoral popularity.

Likewise, Tunisians demand economic well-being and "social justice" more than dawah activism;[114] prioritizing dawah does not sit well with Tunisians because they take offense at the suggestion of being the objects of dawah as an overwhelmingly Muslim society.[115] Islam is "bigger than all the movements and

---

[108] Rafik Abdesalam, personal interview, 2018.
[109] Yousef Nouri, personal interview, 2017.
[110] Lotfi Zitoun, personal interview, 2017.
[111] Nawfal Al-Jamali, personal interview, 2017.
[112] Ahmed Mechergui, personal interview, 2017.
[113] Yerkes 2018.
[114] Dalila Babba, personal interview, 2017. Also, see Abduljaber (2018) for an empirical analysis on the significance of socioeconomic issues for the Tunisian public.
[115] Lotfi Zitoun, personal interview, 2017.

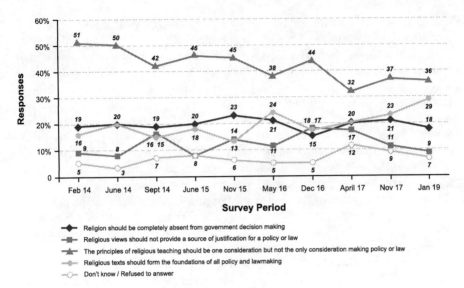

FIGURE 5.1 Religion–governance relationship in Tunisia
Source: Various International Republican Institute public opinion surveys in Tunisia.

parties" and, as such, should function as a "unifying" factor rather than a divisive one: "After the Revolution, we know that Islam should not be an issue of division among Tunisians. It should be an issue that brings them together .... the [Ennahdha] movement wanted to make sure that Islam stays as a reference for all Tunisians."[116] This reasoning naturally leads to the conclusion that Ennahdha no longer needed to "oversee" the defense of Islam in Tunisia.[117]

The postrevolutionary social and political context affords Tunisians and Tunisian civil society the liberties to uphold Tunisia's Islamic identity.[118] Therefore, Ennahdha does not need to "bear the burden" of standing up for Islam because such a task can be "fulfilled by organizations, civil society, [and] religious institutions."[119] As Hicham Larayedh stated, "So we found that now we are in a free country with democracy, with liberties, we do not need to protect Islam from anybody anymore; the society itself will be protecting Islam as it has been doing for 20 years when Ennahdha was not here."[120] Rachid Ghannouchi explains the reasoning more clearly as follows: "Tunisian society is a Muslim society. This society will produce or create its means of defending itself, to serve Islam. Once freedom is there, once the society is free, this Muslim society will create the institutions, the civil societies, to serve and protect its

[116] Najib Krifi, personal interview, 2017.
[117] Yousef Nouri, personal interview, 2017.
[118] Abdelhamid Jlassi, personal interview, 2018.
[119] Ahmed Mechergui, personal interview, 2017.
[120] Hicham Larayedh, personal interview, 2017.

Intraparty Conflict

identity. We are not the guardians of Islam, nor of society. We have left the freedom to society to produce its own tools of protecting Islam ... The role of the party is to protect the popular initiative to serve Islam, and to encourage them, not to dominate them, or to transform them as part of the party ... We believe that the society has the real capacity to protect its identity, and to create enough institutions to protect itself."[121] In this remarkable statement, Ghannouchi does not only explain why Ennahdha should move out of the religious sphere but also explains the rationale for why Ennahdha undertook religious activism in the first place. Islam needed protection; when duty called, Ennahdha served as its vanguard. Such reasoning resonates with how Islamists typically justify their claims to speak on behalf of Islam in the public arena. The civil society activism by devout Tunisian Muslims now, however, is sufficient to fend off potential threats to Tunisia's Islamic character. Because of this opportunity that did not exist prior to the revolution, Islam does not need political actors for its defense in the political arena. Instead, the focus needs to be primarily on civic reforms.[122]

The specialization policy was a response to constitutional limits on the extent of formal association between civil society organizations and political parties.[123] These are the constraints that Ennahdha signed onto in the first place: "It [specialization policy] is a response to the law and the constitution that we wrote. We had the majority in the National Constituent Assembly and the constitution that we wrote ... prohibits political parties from engaging in the activity of religious preaching or an equivalent activity."[124] The close association between civil society organizations and political parties in Tunisia was not unique to Ennahdha in pre-revolutionary period; other parties had similar control over civil society associations.[125] Separating civil society activism from political parties also aims to empower the civil society and provide them with "autonomy."[126] Decades of oppression under authoritarian rule necessitated "rebuild[ing] civil society and strengthening civil society and this would not happen until the dominance of parties [over civil society organizations] is reduced."[127] The new space available for civil society organizations in the postrevolutionary period also helps Islamic social activism à la Ennahdha by "liberat[ing] the capabilities and the energies within the movement."[128] So, incidentally, the specialization policy would simultaneously meet a legal requirement and boost the civil society, according to Ennahdha officials.

---

[121] Rachid Ghannouchi, personal interview, 2018.
[122] McCarthy 2018b, 130–32.
[123] Abdellatif Mekki, personal interview, 2017; Abdelhamid Jlassi, personal interview, 2018.
[124] Mohamed Ben Salem, personal interview, 2017.
[125] Abdelhamid Jlassi, personal interview, 2018.
[126] Najib Krifi, personal interview, 2017.
[127] Fathi Ayedi, personal interview, 2017.
[128] Imed Khmiri, personal interview, 2017.

As a party that aspires to govern and compete for power, the perception that Ennahdha favors a sectarian approach to politics poses a major challenge.[129] Openness to "all Tunisians" now underlies the party's approach as the party looks to "broaden" its electoral base.[130] This shift, according to some Ennahdha leaders, epitomizes Ennahdha's "transition from a protest movement to a movement that participates in governance."[131] The issue of "managing the state"[132] and the pragmatic necessity of providing "solutions" to Tunisians' demands in the postrevolutionary period required a new approach to politics.[133]

Several Ennahdha leaders used the term "strategic choice" to explain Ennahdha's pursuit of the specialization policy.[134] The party viewed the country's democratic future as inextricably tied to Ennahdha's own political future. By undertaking the specialization policy as a strategic choice, Ennahdha demonstrates its commitment to "the process of democratization in the country," which they signaled as being more important than the party's own fate.[135] In fact, there was major electoral concern within the political faction of Ennahdha about how the religious faction might undermine the (political) gains of the postrevolutionary period. Specifically, calls for shariah's inclusion in the new constitution undercut Ennahdha's participation in the political process following Ben Ali's removal from power. Such calls intensified during the drafting of the new constitution, not just from Salafis or Hizb al-Tahrir but from voices within Ennahdha.[136] These demands from within the movement led to furor. Likewise, when female genital mutilation came to occupy public discussions in Tunisia, some Ennahdha leaders aligned with "Gulf preachers" of Salafi background on this issue. Tunisians could not distinguish between Ennahdha and the more conservative Islamists from which Ennahdha certainly wanted to keep its distance: "So, we had to clear this confusion ... Islam became a factor of conflict in the country and we had to liberate it from this political conflict. It is a factor of unity and it is the reference of all the [Tunisian] people; during the constitutional drafting process, there were very long discussions about the place of Islam in society and politics; all parties agreed that Islam is the main reference of our identity as a people."[137] The political faction of Ennahdha wanted to avoid the use of shariah language in the constitution because they hoped to avoid making Islam a source of controversy and "a

---

[129] Sadok Chourou, personal interview, 2017.
[130] Fathi Ayedi, personal interview, 2017.
[131] Rabeh Mahdoui, personal interview, 2017.
[132] Toumi Hamrouni, personal interview, 2017.
[133] Ahmed Mechergui, personal interview, 2017.
[134] Personal interviews with Rafik Abdesalam (2018), Imed Khmiri (2017), and Sadok Chourou (2017).
[135] Rafik Abdesalam, personal interview, 2018.
[136] Zouaghi and Cavatorta 2018.
[137] Lotfi Zitoun, personal interview, 2017.

Intraparty Conflict

point of difference."[138] When Habib Ellouze along with 10 sheikhs confronted Mehrziya Laabidi – the Vice President of the Constituent Assembly at the time – to support the inclusion of shariah in the constitution, he was referred to the Shura Council of the party to make his case.[139] Sadok Chourou likewise expressed his discontentment with the lack of reference to shariah in the new constitution by saying on the day of its ratification that "today is its [constitution] birth and today is its funeral."[140]

By contrast, the religious faction highlighted the threats faced by the party and the strategic considerations for Ennahdha's decision to engage in organizational transformation. Acutely aware of the postrevolutionary political context in which they operated, Ennahdha's long term survival constituted the key strategic goal for the party despite the importance of electoral success and desire to shape the new constitution. None of these policy objectives would matter without ensuring the party's survival. Although the postrevolutionary environment welcomed the party's participation in the political process following years of exclusion, many in Tunisia harbored great skepticism about Ennahdha's true political intentions. The rising tide of terror acts undertaken by Islamist militants in the postrevolutionary period exacerbated these concerns. Not only did many ordinary secular Tunisians doubt Ennahdha's political objectives, but many remnants of the old regime were bent on minimizing the party's growth or, at the very least, containing its political and policy influence. The "pressure" from other political parties in Tunisia came in the form of accusations of "duality in discourse"; Ennahdha could not distinguish between "what is civil and what is associated with shariah."[141] The unified structure of religiopolitical activism exposed Ennahdha as an easy target, thereby intensifying political conflict. The "envy" from other parties due to "Ennahdha's unique relationship with mosque-goers" also fed this perception, according to Akrout.[142]

The high level of polarization after the assassinations of prominent secular politicians Chokri Belaid and Mohamed Brahmi in 2013 forced Ennahdha toward greater caution.[143] In a precarious episode such as this one, seculars wasted no time attacking Ennahdha in order to "damage the image" of the party, according to some Ennahdha officials; they accused Ennahdha of not being a normal political party but rather "a party with an Islamist dye" where political activism and civil society activism are not separated.[144] Regardless of their political orientations, "all" political parties called on Ennahdha "to

---

[138] Najib Krifi, personal interview, 2017.
[139] Mehrziya Laabidi, personal interview, 2017.
[140] Dalila Babba, personal interview, 2017.
[141] Dalila Babba, personal interview, 2017.
[142] Mohamed Akrout, personal interview, 2018.
[143] Rafik Abdesalam, personal interview, 2018.
[144] Mohamed Akrout, personal interview, 2017.

separate between the political activity and the religious preaching, religious activity in its entirety."[145] According to Habib Ellouze, Ennahdha was faced with "political awkwardness" in this context. On one hand, postrevolutionary developments called for Ennahdha's "participation in and reconciliation with the state" about which Ennahdha was "enthusiastic"; on the other hand, Ennahdha's Islamist ideology and hybrid organizational structure cast doubts about the feasibility of such a reconciliation.[146] The pressure from "leftist and secularist" parties ultimately pushed the party into adopting the policy of specialization.[147] Ennahdha had to take steps to assure other political actors that the party was committed to delivering on its ideological transformation, and the change in the hybrid movement-party structure constituted a critical step in this process. "The rhythm and the speed" of the adoption of the specialization policy was dictated by the political context in Tunisia as other political parties demanded Ennahdha to move in this direction.[148] Therefore, the party's decision to accept the specialization policy was simultaneously motivated by a desire to frustrate "those who want to taint the *dawah* with politics and those who want to taint politics with *dawah*."[149]

These developments in Tunisia and Ennahdha's growing political presence came about in a broader regional and global context. The political environment in Tunisia and around the world necessitated Ennahdha revisit its current stance on religiopolitical activism because "the West does not believe in this relation."[150] Some Western and Gulf countries were concerned with the possibility that Ennahdha might "control" and "Islamize" the state.[151] During this period, Islamists in the rest of the region gained larger political roles, upset the status quo, and alarmed many seculars. The Egyptian Muslim Brotherhood's ascension to power, alignment with Salafists in the constitution drafting process, and competition with Salafists for the conservative vote carried major implications for the trajectory Ennahdha might follow in Tunisia.[152] Neither Ennahdha officials nor secular Tunisian actors desired a scenario like Egypt where an unchecked Islamist wave led to a reversal in the revolutionary course that culminated in the 2013 coup. Not only did the Sisi-led coup ushered in a period of violent crackdown on Islamist opposition, but it also erased virtually all gains of the 2011 revolution. Such a prospect presented the worst possible scenario for Ennahdha leaders.[153] After decades of exclusion from the Tunisian political system, the party was willing to take on a limited governing

[145] Sadok Chourou, personal interview, 2017.
[146] Habib Ellouze, personal interview, 2017.
[147] Sadok Chourou, personal interview, 2017.
[148] Hassan Meddeb, personal interview, 2017.
[149] Mohamed Akrout, personal interview, 2018.
[150] Mohamed Akrout, personal interview, 2018.
[151] Sadok Chourou, personal interview, 2017.
[152] Marks 2015.
[153] Ounissi 2016.

role (despite the party's electoral popularity) in return for continued legal existence. Ghannouchi himself stated that "There was sort of a temptation in 2013, to imitate or follow the Egyptian experience but we succeeded in stopping this temptation. We withdrew from the government to avoid this scenario. We accepted withdrawing from the government without losing the election or a coup."[154] Many in Ennahdha were motivated by the goal of "protecting Tunisia from what is happening in Libya and Syria."[155]

Specialization Policy and Ennahdha's Future

Again, while both factions fundamentally agree on Ennahdha's ultimate goals, the friction over the party's organizational structure deeply relates to the nature and soul of the party. The new organizational structure embraced by Ennahdha carries with it the possibility of bringing changes unforeseen by the architects of this policy and taking on a life of its own. Some Ennahdha leaders consider this shift in the party's organizational structure via the specialization policy to be the "abandonment" of Ennahdha's Islamic identity or "shed[ding] its clothes as if it means that it [Ennahdha] no longer cares about … divine principles of religion.[156] Likewise, part of Ennahdha's electoral base – whom Sadok Chourou refers to as "the silent base of the party" that constitutes "the historical base for the Islamic movement" – views the policy of specialization as being "not in the interest of the entire Islamic project."[157] For the religious faction, the optics of the specialization policy are not favorable; it appears as if "the treasure is the political project" at the expense of the rest of the movement's activism.[158] Habib Ellouze summarizes the fear of Ennahdha's religious faction succinctly as follows: "The Movement of Ennahda has a lot of positives and a lot of advantages but I do not deny that this single objective of politicization [specialization policy] has a dangerous effect on the intellectual and educational sides because our original project was a project of civilization, a project of culture, [of] religious guidance."[159]

The political faction of Ennahdha, however, defiantly rejected suggestions that the party was leaving Islam behind. To diffuse such criticisms, Abdelhamid Jlassi qualified the specialization policy and what it aims to accomplish by disentangling two dimensions of religion–politics relationship: "This specialization has two sides. There is the side that is administrative, organizational, where it is necessary to liberate fields of [religious] activity from direct association with the political. There is the other side – the philosophical

---

[154] Rachid Ghannouchi, personal interview, 2018.

[155] Ossama Al Saghir, personal interview, 2017.

[156] Dalila Babba, personal interview, 2017. Such concern was voiced in personal interviews with Abdelhamid Jlassi (2018), Hbib Idriss (2017), Mehrziya Laabidi (2017), Andellatif Mekki (2017), and Mohammad Chiha (2017).

[157] Sadok Chourou, personal interview, 2017.

[158] Habib Ellouze, personal interview, 2017.

[159] Habib Ellouze, personal interview, 2017.

side – that establishes the relationship between [Islamic] principles and politics; Ennahdha has not abandoned this [second side]."[160] Likewise, Abdesalam argued that the separation is not "between morality and politics" but simply institutional and organizational;[161] the Islamic reference was to remain constant.[162] The critical question, then, is what is the Islamic reference and what makes Ennahdha an Islamic party, as Ennahdha officials claim?

According to Ghannouchi, the Islamic reference of Ennahdha refers to a link with Islam, and Ennahdha's program represents a kind of ijtihad (interpretation): "We define our party as a democratic nationalist party ... Islam is a reference, based off the *ijtihad*. We consider our programs as sort of *ijtihad*. We could not go ahead in contradiction with Islam, but we have an open *ijtihad*, an open vision of Islam. We are linked with Islam."[163] Al-Jamali describes Islamic reference in more specific terms: "In terms of values and civilization, the family, justice, strong link with values of Islam, we are trying to defend our identity as an Islamic people, Muslim people, and Arab people."[164] For other Ennahdha officials, the Islamic reference deals with "identity" and it represents "the identity of the [Tunisian] people,"[165] and therefore, the party will "always" protect this identity.[166]

Indeed, some Ennahdha officials broadened the scope of what was "Islamic" to grant greater legitimacy to the current path of the party. Mechergui envisions a close parallel between what the party aims to achieve and "the goals" of religion: "They [Ennahdha] are achieving justice, achieving freedom, achieving good, achieving peace, achieving brotherhood, and love; these are the purposes of religion. So when I work in the field of politics, I am working with the values of religion, with the direction of religion and here I meet with Christians and with non-Christians and even with those who do not believe."[167] Similarly, Hamrouni claimed that Ennahdha views "all activity, even political activity, is religious activity, with a broad meaning."[168] A local Ennahdha official from Sfax explained, "Islam is the [group of] values and purposes ... But, at the same time, we consider that Islam protects the value of development, the value of freedom."[169]

What if Ennahdha did not engage in specialization? According to Ahmed Mechergui, the party would have been hit with reality because politics

---

[160] Abdelhamid Jlassi, personal interview, 2018.
[161] Rafik Abdesalam, personal interview, 2018.
[162] Personal interviews with Hbib Idriss (2017), Mohammad Chiha (2017), and Najib Krifi (2017).
[163] Rachid Ghannouchi, personal interview, 2018.
[164] Nawfal Al-Jamali, personal interview, 2017.
[165] Dalila Babba, personal interview, 2017.
[166] Najib Krifi, personal interview, 2017.
[167] Ahmed Mechergui, personal interview, 2017.
[168] Toumi Hamrouni, personal interview, 2017.
[169] Rabeh Mahdoui, personal interview, 2017.

Intraparty Conflict

"demand" specialization; remaining "prisoners" to idealistic visions that do not correspond to the contemporary social and political circumstances would have cost Ennahdha votes because voters want to see betterment in development, employment, and environmental protection. The change was therefore "inevitable."[170] Some expected electoral considerations to play a role in Ennahdha's calculations into the effect of the specialization policy. For example, Idriss thought that while "a portion" of Ennahdha's base might be lost in the transition, an overwhelming majority will not find a better option among the alternatives.[171] Akrout suggested that "the loyalty" of the "sons of the movement" to the Islamist goals will lead them to continue supporting the party and voting for it. Moreover, he claimed that those who had reservations against Ennahdha would "abandon this reservation because they have begun to see that this movement now represents them. The movement is coming closer to representing all stratifications of the Tunisian society."[172]

Not everyone shares this optimism. While most leaders from the religious faction of Ennahdha were cautious in expressing their expectations from the specialization policy, Habib Ellouze did not pull any punches and seriously criticized the potential benefits of the policy. Ellouze predicted that poor election results will inevitably lead to "revisiting" the current policy. The loss of "human resources" in the movement because of this policy would be the key cause of the party's future poor performance.[173] Conservative supporters of the party might feel let down and ultimately alienated due to "Ennahdha's avoidance of moral and religious debates."[174] The lack of a strong religious movement behind the party diminishes Ennahdha's ability to serve the Islamic cause; this is why Ellouze proposed the founding of a separate religious movement around 2009, much like in the model of the Moroccan Movement of Unity and Reform behind the Justice and Development Party.[175]

The political and religious evolution of Ennahdha shares important similarities with many other Islamist groups in the Middle East, yet diverges in notable ways from Catholic parties of Europe. Ennahdha emerged as a response to perceived marginalization of religion in the Tunisian society and state. For decades, it functioned as a movement-party hybrid, standing as the defender of Islam and its faithful as Islam was under attack. The 2010 revolution and regional developments led to a major change in Ennahdha's political calculations about the utility of religion and where the party stood as its stalwart defender. The inclusion of language about Islam in the constitution relieved pressure on the party to defend it, according to party officials. A similarly

---

[170] Ahmed Mechergui, personal interview, 2017.
[171] Hbib Idriss, personal interview, 2017.
[172] Mohamed Akrout, personal interview, 2017.
[173] For example, see Ben Salem's analysis on the effects of the specialization policy on recruitment (2018).
[174] Habib Ellouze, personal interview, 2018.
[175] Habib Ellouze, personal interview, 2017.

important development was the fate of the Brotherhood in Egypt at around the same time. Ennahdha's political faction won over the religious faction's opposition to fundamentally transform the party at the organizational and ideological levels. It is crucial to note that the party saw an intimate connection between organizational and ideological change as it undertook both changes at the same time, although the organizational change failed to grab the attention of most observers.

While the long-term effects of Ennahdha's specialization policy and the concomitant organizational restructuring are not yet fully evident, the process leading up to it is instructive in illustrating the conflicts over issues, concerns, and visions for Ennahdha. On one hand, the religious faction views Ennahdha as a conventional Islamist movement that is comprehensive in its focus and organizational structure. The critical motivation for considering potential organizational change rested in the external threats faced by Ennahdha. For this faction, the organizational change required safeguarding the religious movement under a separate organization. In the absence of such an organization to oversee the dawah activities, there exists the real risk of compromising the Islamic identity and vision of Ennahdha. On the other hand, the political faction's primary commitment is to the political vision of Ennahdha; the only reason for Ennahdha to incorporate nonpolitical activism in its body was the pressure exerted by the Bourguiba and Ben Ali regimes to begin with. The inability to engage in open and free political activism forced Ennahdha to broaden its scope in order to serve as the defender of Tunisia's Islamic identity. The freedom afforded by the 2011 revolution paved the way for Ennahdha to mobilize its resources exclusively for its political vision. This was a unique political opportunity for Ennahdha to take advantage of – Ennahdha could legitimately be part of the political system and engage in political compromise to promote its own political agenda.

THE JUSTICE AND DEVELOPMENT PARTY IN TURKEY

The case of the National Outlook Movement and the AKP offers an intriguing variation on the trajectory of Islamist parties. Once the relationship with the parent movement was severed, the evolution of the AKP in the post-2001 period revealed two pivotal insights. The party no longer positioned itself as the defender or representative of Islam; instead, the party aligned itself with the common Muslim values of Turkish society and promoted these values in policymaking. However, this new relationship with religion does not imply the disappearance of religious discourse from the party's political repertoire. Shifting political and electoral contexts can and do lead to variation in the extent that the party draws from religion. When the party relies on religious discourse, such discourse typically serves to boost the party's electoral prospects.

Intraparty Conflict

Despite its relatively quick political resurrection after each setback over the years, successive banning cases against its political parties nonetheless caused problems within the National Outlook Movement. According to the law, each new party not only had to create a new name but also had to reconvene under different leadership. This created rifts within the movement.[176] After the 1998 banning, the movement yet again formed a new political party, the Virtue Party (FP), with Ismail Alptekin as the party's caretaker leader at its formation as preferred by the National Outlook Movement, followed by Recai Kutan.[177] RP's parliamentary members switched to the FP *en masse*. Unlike past instances, this time around some members of the movement grew dissatisfied and uncomfortable with how the party was being run. Even though Erbakan was banned from active politics for five years, he remained firmly in control of the movement and in a position of influence over the party. Recai Kutan and, to some degree, Oğuzhan Asiltürk served as the link between the party and Erbakan. In particular, the choice of Kutan as party leader reflected Erbakan's trust in him as "a non-charismatic but moderate person able to get along well with the military as well as the younger and more radical elements within the party."[178]

As a result of the February 28 process, the FP adjusted its political discourse in significant ways, softening its stances and rhetoric. Concern about another secular pushback turned the party into an "apolitical" one, in a peculiar turn of events. The party largely stopped speaking of the just order and advocated a free-market economy more strongly than before. The FP also called for greater democracy, rule of law, and human rights in Turkey. However, most notable were the party's shifts in foreign policy and secularism. Regarding the former, the FP began supporting European Union membership and, for the most part, disavowed anti-Westernism. Instead of believing the EU to be nothing more than a "Christian club," the party recognized it as an institution that advances democratic values. Regarding secularism, the FP took a more neutral stance on religion, believing that religion should not be imposed onto the populace. While they opposed the headscarf ban, they couched their reasoning in the language of freedom and human rights rather than a moralistic, religious one.[179] Yet, this shift in the party's rhetoric did not convince many; it was widely perceived as "nothing more than a show that masked the party's true motives."[180]

The FP had a poor showing in the 1999 parliamentary election; as a result, the cracks within the National Outlook Movement grew irreversibly. Dissenting members blamed party leadership and out-of-touch policies for the

---

[176] Atacan 2005, 196.
[177] Şen 1995.
[178] Gulalp 1999, 41.
[179] Atacan 2005, 188.
[180] Mecham 2004, 346.

electoral failure, specifically because the party "let religious issues dominate its political agenda, it underplayed the importance of consensus-seeking and dialogue-building with other sectors of the society, and it did not address itself to a broader public."[181] This was, for the first time in the movement's history, a frontal assault by some of its members on the movement's approach to politics. The "Traditionalists" (Gelenekçiler) defended the historical trajectory of the National Outlook Movement around Erbakan and his closest associates. They did not view a fundamental need to change course; the comprehensive movement-party hybrid structure served them well and represented the best path forward. The "Reformists" (Yenilikçiler), by contrast, recognized some fundamental problems with their approach to religiopolitical activism.[182] They recognized how the traditional comprehensive approach to religiopolitical activism failed the movement. In this regard, the differences between the two sides were not merely cosmetic, relating only to minor policy differences; nor was it about the ultimate goal of religiopolitical activism, as both sides concurred on the vision of a more Islamic Turkey. The essential difference related to the question of *how* to achieve this goal. At the 2000 party congress (May 14), the reformists mounted a challenge to take over the party leadership; this was the first instance of competition inside the National Outlook Movement and a formal challenge to Erbakan's authority within the movement. Erbakan and the traditionalists opposed this challenge by the reformists, threatening them with banishment from the movement and the party. Abdullah Gül became the reformist candidate for party leadership against Kutan. Gül received 521 votes to Kutan's 633 votes, losing the election for party leadership by a small margin. The reformists initially intended to wait until the next party congress to make a stir;[183] before the party congress arrived, however, the FP predictably found itself banned in 2001 for anti-secular activities.[184] Thus, after the banning of the Virtue Party, the AKP was formed alongside the Felicity Party (SP), the latter retaining the character of Milli Gorus (National Outlook). The AKP, by contrast, disavowed Milli Gorus and political Islam.

A quadrumvirate composed of Abdullah Gül, Abdullatif Sener, Bulent Arinc, and Tayyip Erdogan broke away from the National Outlook Movement, spearheading reformist efforts to eventually found the Justice and Development Party (AKP). This was a definitive break with the National Outlook Movement; Erdogan's statement, "We removed the mantle of National Outlook on February 28,"[185] marked the end of an era. Two explanations that account for this shift stand out: change in the political preferences of the conservative Muslim electorate and the secular-military establishment's historical repression

---

[181] Cizre and Cinar 2003, 326.
[182] Mason 2000, 57; Kuru 2005, 270; Rabasa and Larrabee 2018, 45.
[183] Atacan 2005, 193.
[184] Aydin and Cakir 2007, 114.
[185] "Erdoğan: Milli Görüş Gömleğini 28 Şubat'ta Çıkardık," *Akşam*, August 14, 2003.

Intraparty Conflict 225

of the Islamist movement in Turkey. In important ways, Ennahdha's internal deliberations to engage in an organizational transformation in 2016 mirror the reformists' rationale in the National Outlook Movement. On one hand, the religious constituency looked to move beyond the conservatism of conventional Islamist discourse. This constituency thrived under the new economic regime of the post-1980 period and became the chief beneficiary of the liberalization process, thereby leading to a deep-rooted transformation of their political preferences.[186] The confrontational and anti-system ideology of the Erbakan-led National Outlook Movement and the Welfare Party that sought to represent this constituency turned out to be self-defeating; this is best illustrated by the military's 1997 economic boycott that sanctioned "green capital" businesses owned by conservative Muslim business owners.[187] Continuing down the path of Erbakan-esque Islamist ideology entailed alienating a significant electoral base and increasing political marginalization.

On the other hand, it became increasingly clear that the secular-military establishment was unwilling to allow Islamists a governmental role even via legitimate electoral processes. For secularists, Islamism represented everything the founders considered detrimental to the principles of the Turkish Republic. Many concerns about Islamists were voiced publicly, and even relatively minor Islamist policy shifts or discourse were considered existential threats, eventually leading to the removal of the Islamist Welfare Party from power following the February 28, 1997 National Security Council meeting.[188] Like Islamists in other secular contexts, their commitment to democracy and pluralism was constantly in question. The secular-military elite dominated the political system and dictated the parameters of Islamist engagement. Any serious aspirations for power had to take these parameters into consideration.

These two explanations coalesce around reformists' fundamental motivation for opposing the traditionalists: the anti-system nature of the Islamist National Outlook Movement undermined their ability to win power and affect policy. Winning elections and power necessitated leaving behind the National Outlook and its anti-system discourse. Once the reformists publicly broke away from the National Outlook Movement, they revised their religious discourse and subjected themselves to outside scrutiny. They sought counsel from "all sectors" of society in assembling a political ideology to help them attain power. Many who were involved in the AKP's formation in the early 2000s expressed the idea that the "ideological" orientation of the Islamist movement in Turkey emasculated the party and hindered any real possibility of winning elections, creating a virtual electoral ceiling. For example, a founding AKP member and later Minister of Foreign Affairs Yaşar Yakış underscored the gap between the ideology of Erbakan's Welfare Party and the "realities" of the

[186] Gülalp 2001; Bugra 2002.
[187] Lombardi 1997; Bacik and Aras 2002.
[188] Ozel 2003.

Turkish state and society: "Erbakan and later Mr. Recai Kutan were trying to pursue policies that were perhaps in line with their religious convictions but detached from Turkey's realities. The reformist movement's point of departure is this observation ... and, this has been the policy stance of AK Party."[189] Reha Denemeç, another founding AKP member and an advisor to Erdogan in the party's formative years, recognized why such ideological stances posed a distinct challenge: "When you are an ideological party, you lose the opportunity to embrace the society and fail to prevent coalition governments that are detrimental to politics and the economy. You are unable to surpass 20% [of electoral support]."[190]

Other officials from the party echoed these ideas regarding the country's "realities" and problems created by being an anti-system Islamist party.[191] "Turkey's realities" and being an "ideological" party were key phrases used to account for the Welfare Party's inability to resonate with the electorate; an ideological party that clings to fundamental tenets of Islamism was a nonstarter. Thus, the goal was not to exclusively identify with a small and highly ideological minority of the electorate through a religious movement that claimed to represent them in the political arena. Instead, the goal was to bring the party under the ideological canopy of the massive conservative-right electorate. Public opinion polls undertaken by the AKP founders partly informed this conclusion, including one poll with 42,000 subjects who asked a variety of questions about policy priorities and satisfaction with existing political parties.[192] Just as Islamism no longer resonated with the conservative constituency, addressing the secular military establishment's deep-seated concerns necessitated a fundamental reorientation in the party's religious outlook. Reconceptualizing the role of religion in politics and secularism were two essential components of a new ideological platform.

The AKP's ideological outlook in the post-2001 period reflected these considerations. While it appealed to the Islamic constituency with its conservative approach to social issues, the overall ideological orientation of the party was a testament to the care involved in crafting the party ideology. The AKP reformists tempered their Islamist tinge and rebranded their ideological orientation as conservative, Muslim, post-Islamist, and democratic.[193] The shift from a conventional Islamist position of representing Islam in the political arena to defending the conservative and Muslim values of the society marked the party's organizational transformation.[194] The European Union membership

---

[189] Yasar Yakis, personal interview, 2008.
[190] Reha Denemec, personal interview, 2008.
[191] Personal interviews with Feyzullah Kiyiklik (2008), Halide Incekara (2008), and Aziz Babuscu (2008).
[192] Yasar Yakis, personal interview, 2008.
[193] Tepe 2005; Ozbudun 2006; Yavuz 2009; Yildirim 2016.
[194] Akdogan 2004; Dagi 2005.

Intraparty Conflict

constituted a cornerstone of the AKP's platform during this time.[195] This contrasts sharply with the anti-EU stance of Islamists in the pre-2001 period, when the EU was characterized as a "Christian club."[196] The AKP's track record on democracy and human rights between 2002 and 2010 demonstrated a commitment to pluralism, as illustrated by successive EU progress reports.[197] Crucially, the party's position on secularism reflected its carefully weaved religious discourse and desire to appease the secular military state elite. Islamists in Turkey were historically unequivocally opposed to secularism. In the post-2001 period, though, the reformists displayed a marked shift in how they reframed their stance on this issue. While adhering to the notion of secularism as a principle of government, AKP officials qualified their embrace of secularism. They were opposed to its historical application in Turkey reminiscent of the French notion of *laïcité*, yet were open to an Anglo-American model in which the state remains neutral vis-à-vis religion and its public role.[198] Leaving behind the anti-system posture of the National Outlook presented the AKP two advantages that were inaccessible under the National Outlook umbrella. Electorally, the party eclipsed the biggest achievement of all National Outlook parties by a large margin; the AKP obtained 34 percent of the vote in its first election and never looked back. Such electoral success, in turn, meant that the party could win power and govern single-handedly. At the policy level, that the party was no longer anti-system paved the way for greater collaboration with political actors with different ideologies, particularly liberal democrats in Turkey.[199]

The AKP and Religious Discourse

The dramatic change that reformists brought to Islamist politics in Turkey, that is, leaving the religious movement behind, does not suggest that religion and religious discourse disappeared from the AKP's public platform. Shifts in the political context led to variations in how the AKP emphasized or de-emphasized its religious identity.[200] The AKP's ideological outlook remained consistent between 2001 and 2010; the political context in Turkey changed dramatically after 2010, however, leading the AKP to reevaluate its religious discourse. There were two distinct changes that facilitated the return of a more pronounced religious political discourse. First, between 2008 and 2011, the AKP government weakened the secular establishment despite challenges in bridling the military's undue influence over politics

---

[195] Kosebalaban 2005.
[196] Gunes-Ayata 2003; Onis 2006.
[197] Yildirim 2013.
[198] Kuru 2009.
[199] Arango 2013.
[200] Gontijo and Barbosa 2020; Matera 2020.

since 1923.[201] A series of court cases, collectively known as the Ergenekon Case, aimed to subdue the military and some secular figures by rounding up top-brass generals, prominent secular journalists, academics, and politicians.[202] Major reshuffling in the military allowed Erdogan to pick less political generals for top posts, eventually leading to what has been termed "the fall of military tutelage."[203] Likewise, the 2010 constitutional referendum introduced greater civilian oversight over the military. These developments collectively altered the dynamics of Turkish politics by shifting the boundaries of Islam's political utility; the military–secular opposition was no longer a constraint. Similarly, the 2010 constitutional reform changed the structure of the Constitutional Court and the number of sitting judges. This enabled the AKP to appoint several new judges and thereby cancel the possibility of being shut down due to religious discourse.

Second, the graft scandal of 2013 was a critical milestone for the shift in religious political discourse. The allegations against Erdogan and other party officials, including four ministers, charged them with the greatest corruption scheme in the Republic's history.[204] For the first time in more than a decade, the AKP felt intense electoral heat. Between March 2014 and November 2015, Turkey held four elections: local elections on March 30, 2014; presidential elections on August 10, 2014; parliamentary elections on June 7, 2015; and parliamentary elections on November 1, 2015. The real possibility of losing power and its potential legal and criminal ramifications pushed the party to employ political polarization along ethnic and religious lines as its strategy to remain in power. This revision of the party's religious discourse was facilitated, in turn, by the knowledge that there would be no backlash from the secular establishment if the party revamped its religious discourse. To reiterate, while the subordination of the secular military establishment enabled the AKP to have the *capacity* to use greater religious rhetoric, such discourse was not employed until the emergence of a serious threat to the status quo. Only when the AKP sensed a threat to losing its parliamentary majority and some AKP local governments, in fact, lost elections did the party veer toward greater use of religious discourse.[205]

In this new political context, the AKP's strategy has been to intensify social polarization, forge its popular base around a (Turkish) nationalist and (Sunni) religious discourse, reinforce their victimhood,[206] and ultimately prevent breakaways from its electoral coalition. Significantly, the AKP's electoral urgency was not about mobilizing new voters from secular-liberal

---

[201] Cizre 2008.
[202] Kaya 2009; Unver 2009; Tas 2014; Ugur 2019, 135–39.
[203] Kuru 2012.
[204] Gurbuz 2014; Salt 2015.
[205] In this same period, the AKP shifted from tutelary to delegative democracy. See Tas (2015) for a thorough discussion.
[206] Guiler 2020.

Intraparty Conflict

constituencies; instead, the party primarily aimed to sustain its support base and then draw from the base of the Turkish nationalist MHP (Nationalist Action Party) and, when possible, from the Sunni-conservative voters of the HDP (Peoples' Democratic Party). The party increasingly set the record straight on their religious credentials while questioning the faith of others. Erdogan frequently challenged opposition leaders by name, repeating "I have grown up with the Qur'an and I live with the Qur'an ... it is well-known what the [lowly] status of the Qur'an is in your sight [Republican People's Party (CHP) leader Kilicdaroglu]."[207] Declaring God to be on their side, AKP leaders criticized the pro-Kurdish HDP by saying, "They have terror organizations behind them. Allah is on our side, people on our side,"[208] and challenged Gezi Park protestors by stating "Nobody can stop the rise of Turkey, but Allah."[209]

The AKP frequently projected a unified Sunni–Muslim conception of citizenship to the entire population during this period, the roots of which date back to the rise of Islam and continue throughout the Ottoman Empire. In the lead-up to the critical June 2015 elections, Erdogan pleaded with conservative voters by relating contemporary political developments in Turkey to Islam's origin: "Don't even think that the struggle that began 1,400 years ago between the truth [Islam] and fallacy [other beliefs] is over. Don't even think that those who set an eye on these lands 1,000 years ago have given up their ambitions. Don't even think that those who turned up at the Dardanelles, and then across Anatolia 100 years ago, coming with the most powerful armies, weapons and technology of the time, have repented. No, they never did so. This long-standing struggle is going on and will go on."[210]

Furthermore, Qur'an recitations by AKP leaders also became standard in this period. In early 2016, when speaking to a group of village and neighborhood chiefs (*muhtars*), Erdogan stated, "What does the commandment say? Allah is sufficient for us, and he is the best disposer of affairs. Without this faith of ours, we could have never confronted the Byzantine army ... Without this faith of ours, we could have never established the most powerful state in history and

---

[207] "In Turkey, Erdogan's Election Rhetoric Draws Ire," *Voice of America* 2015; *Voice of America*, May 18, 2015. Available at: www.voanews.com/content/in-turkey-erdogan-election-rhetoric-draws-ire/2775833.html; "Cumhurbaskani Erdogan: Kuran'la Buyudum Kuran'la Yasiyorum," *Hurriyet* 2015. Hurriyet, Mayis 5, 2015. Available at: www.hurriyet.com.tr/cumhurbaskani-erdogan-kuran-la-buyudum-kuran-la-yasiyorum-28918354

[208] "Erdogan: Onlarin Arkasinda Teror Orgutleri, Bizim Arkamizda Allah Var," *T24* 2015. T24, August 13, 2015. Available at: http://t24.com.tr/haber/erdogan-onlarin-arkasinda-teror-orgutleri-bizim-arkamizda-allah-var%2c306189

[209] "Turkiye'nin Yukselisini Allah'tan Baska Hicbir Guc Engelleyemez," *AA* 2013. AA, June 7, 2013. Available at: http://aa.com.tr/tr/politika/turkiyenin-yukselisini-allahtan-baska-hicbir-guc-engelleyemez/239995

[210] Gursel 2015. "Erdogan Grows More Radical," *Al Monitor*, March 24, 2015. Available at: www.al-monitor.com/pulse/originals/2015/03/turkey-erdogan-grows-more-radical.html#ixzz43wwIUBPc

kept it alive for 600 years."[211] This religious discourse eerily resembles the pre-2001 religious rhetoric of Erdogan and National Outlook Islamists. Consider, for example, how Erdogan began the first meeting of Istanbul's Metropolitan Municipal Government in 1994 following his election as mayor with the recitation of the Qur'an's opening chapter.[212] In such historical symbolism, the AKP's neo-Ottomanism extended to self-conferred authority over oppressed Muslim communities worldwide.[213] The belief that "Turkey must serve as the custodian and protector" for these oppressed communities has been applied to Syria, Jerusalem, and Rabaa Square in Cairo.

By appealing to the religiously observant Kurds, the AKP strategically moved to counter a potent electoral threat from the pro-Kurdish HDP.[214] The HDP was poised to surpass the 10 percent electoral threshold for securing parliamentary representation, thereby threatening the AKP's parliamentary majority and Erdogan's constitutional reform aspirations to gain more power. In the run-up to the June 7, 2015 parliamentary elections, Erdogan unveiled the country's first "official" Kurdish translation of the Qur'an in the middle of a campaign rally: "Look, the Religious Affairs Directorate, which they want to shut down, has printed the Qur'an in Kurdish for you." The statement served as a direct attack on the HDP, as Erdogan accused the party of having "nothing to do with religion."[215]

This sharp turn in the AKP's religious discourse in the post-2011 period underscores the malleable nature of religious discourse in response to changing conditions of the state elite and the electorate. When faced with increasing electoral pressure in the wake of political scandals, the AKP resorted to a greater use of religious discourse. This was facilitated by the fact that the secular-military state elite that once controlled the political discourse was now subservient to the AKP's political dominance.

As a political party free of ties to a religious movement, the AKP began assembling a network of religious organizations subservient to the party. In an unprecedented move among Islamist parties, the AKP flipped the script and firmly established the primacy of the "political" in religiopolitical activism before the "religious," as was the case in conventional Islamist movements with hybrid movement-party structures. The party's position as the uninterrupted governing party since 2002 endowed it with valuable resources to buy

---

[211] "Erdogan: Teror Orgutu Mensubu Gibi Hareket Edenler Konusunda Meclis'in ve Yargi-nin Harekete Gecmesi Sarttir!" *T24*, January 6, 2016. Available at: http://t24.com.tr/haber/cumhurbaskani-erdogan-muhtarlar-toplantisinda-konusuyor%2c323139

[212] Heper 2013.

[213] Ataç 2019.

[214] Kolçak 2020. For an argument about the historical continuity of Turkish position on the Kurdish issue, see Mohammed and Alrebh (2020).

[215] "In Turkey, Erdogan's Election Rhetoric Draws Ire," *Voice of America* 2015. *Voice of America*, May 18, 2015. Available at: www.voanews.com/content/in-turkey-erdogan-election-rhetoric-draws-ire/2775833.html

Intraparty Conflict

the loyalty and deference of many Islamic groups and associations across the country. The AKP embarked on this strategy of building a firewall of religious organizations through two distinct but interrelated policies.[216]

First, starting in the early 2010s, the party cultivated a group of religious associations that were under Erdogan and his family's direct control, such as TURGEV (Turkey Youth and Education Service Foundation) and TUGVA (Turkey Youth Foundation). Erdogan's family and his inner circle usually take positions in the boards of these associations and shape the organizations' policies from within. Originally established as ISEGEV (Istanbul Foundation for Youth and Education Services) by Erdogan, TURGEV became a juggernaut in Turkish civil society during the custodianship of Erdogan's son (Bilal Erdogan) and daughter (Esra Albayrak). The foundation operates primarily in the educational sector serving girls and young women. The foundation likewise operates nurseries and K-12 schools. Virtually identical to TURGEV, TUGVA – where Bilal Erdogan is a board member – has served in the educational sector since 2012, operates nationwide, and focuses primarily on male youth. Both organizations have nearly identical religious identities and prioritize religious values in their education of the youth. Collectively, these two organizations serve tens of thousands young Turkish citizens. As Cevik explains, these organizations differ from typical religious organizations by "their lack of a central religious leader and religious teachings"; they do not embrace religious texts to define "an ideological core" for themselves.[217] Unlike traditional Islamist movements, therefore, religious indoctrination and inculcating a religious identity remain epiphenomenal for these organizations. Instead, the organizations revolve around loyalty to Erdogan and the AKP's power. The focus on loyalty to Erdogan and the AKP, dressed in a loose religious rhetoric, helps build a reservoir of core party supporters in the political arena for the long haul. The work of these organizations is facilitated by access to immense financial resources, courtesy of their proximity to the center of power in Turkey. Several other organizations – some of which are founded by Erdogan and his family – fall in this same category, including YETEV (New Turkey Education Foundation), Ilim Yayma Vakfi, Ensar Vakfi, Insan ve Irfan Vakfi, and KADEM (Women and Democracy Association).

Second, like other conservative parties did prior to the rise of the AKP, the party forged clientelistic relationships with Islamic communities in civil society. At its core, these relationships are largely transactional. The AKP uses its governmental power to offer these communities access to land, financial support, positions in the state bureaucracy, and the ability to shape religious education.[218] For example, religious communities such as the Gulen Movement, Ismailaga Community, and Menzil Naksibendi Order have benefited from generous

---

[216] Cevik 2019.
[217] Cevik 2019, 7.
[218] Cevik 2019, 4–5.

support of the AKP government at different times since 2002. In return, the party demanded political and electoral support from these religious communities. Such generosity by the AKP – using state resources – was conditioned on unconventional levels of support. The party viewed it insufficient for these communities to simply vote for the party; instead, religious communities were frequently asked to publicly express their support for the AKP government in order to shape public opinion at critical junctures. The party's complete control of the government puts the AKP in a uniquely advantageous position. Religious communities who choose not to cooperate with the party can and do face consequences for their dissent. Groups such as the Gulen Movement, Marifet Vakfi, and Furkan Vakfi have experienced dire consequences to varying degrees. The Gulen Movement faced utter obliteration by the AKP for directly challenging and politically undermining the party and Erdogan,[219] whereas Furkan Vakfi faced a ban due to its leader's persistent criticisms of the AKP government and its leader faced approximately two years of jail time.

The AKP similarly utilized the Directorate of Religious Affairs (Diyanet), Turkey's state religious agency, to supplement its policy of building and subduing religious organizations in support of the party. The growing budget and visible public presence of the Diyanet offers the AKP the opportunity to both mobilize the Diyanet's nationwide network in reshaping the religious discourse in Turkey and aid the legion of religious communities and associations the party has created or is courting.[220] The ultimate objective remains generating and sustaining electoral and political support for the party that is grounded loosely on a symbolic Islamic identity. Freedom from the shackles of a movement and a hybrid party-movement structure grants the AKP the ability to freely pursue political power and mobilize religious communities in its support.

The rise of Islamist activism in Turkey followed the relative opening of the political and civic spheres in the aftermath of transition to a multiparty political system. Decades of suppression of religion and public religiosity in the name of secularism created a significant Islamist response, as in the rest of the Middle East. The National Outlook Movement and the political parties associated with it crystallized this Islamist reaction to the secular regime. While the Turkish political system remained semi-open through the rest of the twentieth century with intermittent military takeovers, its semi-open nature did little to promote a change in the anti-system character of the National Outlook Movement. Critically, the National Outlook Movement faced minimal resistance to its absorption of religious authority; the informal nature of the religious movement allowed the movement to infuse the political party with its religious activism. It was only in the late 1990s and early 2000s that the intra-movement conflict led to a rupture between the two factions and an eventual complete separation of the political faction from the religious faction.

---

[219] Tas 2018; Kardas and Balci 2019.
[220] Lord 2018; Yilmaz 2021.

Intraparty Conflict

This separation resulted in the formation of the ideologically pro-system AKP, a shift Ennahdha would experience more than a decade later in Tunisia. According to party officials who took part in the formative stages of the party, the shift in voter preferences and the inability to win power and influence policy as an anti-system party underlaid the overhaul of the National Outlook Movement's Islamist ideology and organizational structure.

THE RISE OF THE CENTER PARTY

The origins of the Center (Centrum/Zentrum) Party can be traced back to the Katolische Fraktion, which came into existence in 1851 and was renamed Zentrumfraktion in 1858. Zentrumfraktion was a parliamentary bloc in the Prussian Landtag, formed by Catholic parliamentarians banding together "to defend their interests" against what they perceived to be unfair government treatment.[221] Their main goals were obtaining equality for Catholics and Protestants and addressing Catholics' educational woes arising from the state's anticlerical policies. This early Catholic political faction dissolved in 1866, only to be resurrected with greater fervency across Germany when it became clear that Otto von Bismarck intended to enact legal restrictions upon German Catholics.[222] Despite its initial goal of representing Catholics nationwide, the faction failed to gain much traction due to the prevalence of regionalism or religion among its members. Likewise, the faction lacked robust organizational mobilization at the grassroots level.[223] Several other, mostly regional, efforts at establishing Catholic parties also emerged at this time. In Prussia, the official establishment of the party can be dated back to October 1870.[224] Ross underscores the conflict between Catholicism and the German state as the main factor behind the politicization of Catholicism, thereby leading to the reemergence of the Center Party as follows: "This Kültürkampf, a grandiloquent term meaning the 'struggle for civilization,' represented a clash between Bismarck and liberalism on the one hand and political Catholicism and the Roman Church on the other. Seeking to safeguard their interests in the drastically new circumstances of a confessional imbalance within the recently created German Empire, the Roman Catholic minority, both within truncated Germany and Prussia, coalesced into an organized political movement and reestablished the Centrum Party."[225] Bismarck's condemnation of the Catholic Church's power, dating back to the 1850s, presaged how he viewed the conflict taking shape in the long term when he suggested that "the invading spirit that dominates the Catholic camp will force us, in the long run, to fight a battle."[226]

---

[221] Ross 1976, 1.
[222] Whyte 1981, 36.
[223] Kalyvas 1996, 204.
[224] Evans 1999, 108.
[225] Ross 1976, 15.
[226] Kalyvas 1996, 204.

The national rise of the Center Party on the eve of the Kültürkampf highlights the precarious and uncertain nature of this political endeavor. While some had overwhelming confidence in German Catholics' ability to organize into a viable political party and viewed the party's rise as "a palpable testimonial to the political maturity which German Catholicism had achieved in the brief period of growth from 1848 to 1870,"[227] it must be noted that the circumstances that spurred the rise of the Center Party were much bleaker than they believed. The party encountered significant adversity for many years after its founding, especially during the anti-Catholic Kültürkampf facilitated by Bismarck. This episode demonstrates how the processes of nation-building, state-building, and nationalism were intricately related to the emergence of political Catholicism in different contexts, leading to distinct trajectories in different countries and varying responses to anticlericalism by the Church. In Germany, territorial unification combined with the liberal and nationalist sentiment of Protestants to create an inhospitable political environment for the country's religious, regional, and linguistic minorities: "The Protestantverein, which numbered many influential Liberals among its ranks, explicitly aimed at completing the territorial unification of Germany with its cultural unification under a national church. In such an atmosphere, many Catholics felt their traditional interests to be threatened. All of their platforms, for example, alluded to the need to defend the religious orders, and understandably so."[228]

The rise of a Catholic party was not met with enthusiasm by all German Catholics, however, underlining the divisions that existed within the community. Throughout the 1850s, the Catholic Church spearheaded efforts to prevent the rise of a Catholic political movement; bishops publicly came out against lay Catholic political activism and the formation of a Catholic political party.[229] In the 1860s, Heinrich Hofstätter, the Archbishop of Passau, expressed serious concern about losing control of lay Catholic political engagement and fought against any form of lay Catholic political activism that "threatened to escape the guiding hand and leadership of the hierarchy."[230] He undermined the potential influence of such lay activism by isolating the Church and the clergy from it. Moreover, the Archbishop impelled local Catholic youth associations "to abandon" the use of "Catholic" in the organization's title and "ordered clergymen under his jurisdiction to cease participation in its activities."[231] Others such as the church leadership in Wurttemberg were opposed to the formation of a Catholic political party because they did not consider partisan political activism to be in the interest of the Church, as it would ultimately undermine the Church's authority and its ability to extract policy

---

[227] Alexander 1953, 455.
[228] Anderson 1981, 134–35.
[229] Whyte 1981, 31.
[230] Southern 1977, 199.
[231] Kalyvas 1996, 179.

Intraparty Conflict   235

compromises, a sentiment that was mirrored in other contexts such as Italy and Belgium.[232] When clergy were involved in such political activism, they fell victim to the Church's retaliation. For example, when a priest named Dominic Grobl mobilized and enlisted approximately 1,000 members to the Catholic Volksvereine of Beilngries in Franconia between its foundation in December 1871 and July 1872, the church hierarchy not only denounced Grobl's activism but also compelled him, through his bishop, to publicly announce "that he was quitting the organization and ceasing his activity."[233]

The Mainz Association, formally known as the Association of German Catholics, was founded by Baron Felix von Loë in 1872 and quickly became the largest and most influential official political organization in Germany during its existence.[234] The Association began with the goal of "defending the freedom and rights of the Catholic Church and bringing Christian principles to bear on all aspects of public life."[235] In the context of the ongoing Kültürkampf in Germany, the increasingly anticlerical policy of Bismarck and, in particular, the passage of the anti-Jesuit law in the Reichstag provided the impetus for the organization's formation. The organization built on the Pius Association's work by winning over local Catholic leaders to mobilize Catholic voters. The Mainz Association was meant to be a national organization, unifying German Catholics. Even though the executive committee of the Mainz Association included major Bavarian Catholic families, ordinary Bavarian Catholics did not trust the Prussians and thus many did not join. Despite its national claims, an overwhelming majority of the Mainz Association was made up of Catholics from the Rhineland and Westphalia, with a heavy concentration in the Düsseldorf and Arnsberg Districts.

The Mainz Association held massive public rallies throughout the Rhineland–Westphalia area, where its president von Loë spoke to crowds about defending Catholicism. In smaller towns and the countryside, local authorities estimated that upwards of 80 percent of adult males in the area were present for these meetings, with significant (but not as overwhelming) numbers also attending in larger urban centers.[236] The Mainz Association events built on previous apolitical missionary events and expressly politicized them, imploring faithful Catholics to defend their religion in the face of Bismarck's increasingly anti-Catholic policies.[237] The Mainz Association

---

[232] The Catholic Church's aversion to politicizing Catholic interests is also a strategy employed by the Church in some contemporary cases such as Ireland, Canada, and Poland where the Church used its influence to draft legislation, vet government officials, and veto policies. By contrast, in the United States where the Church allied itself with a political party, the extent of the influence that the Church wields is more limited (Grzymala-Busse 2015).

[233] Kalyvas 1996, 179.

[234] Cowell-Meyers 2002.

[235] Sperber 1984, 211.

[236] Sperber 1984, 212.

[237] Ross 1998, 129.

relied on mobilizing local leaders to conduct the organization's work. Leading figures in local Catholic political clubs and provincial electoral committees of the local Center Party were common local leaders, whereas the central office in Mainz acted as a political clearing house. The leaders of the association's central office were Catholic notables and clergy, not politicians. Therefore, Center Party officials harbored a certain level of skepticism about the Mainz Association, regardless of the work it did in spreading the party's organizational apparatus throughout Germany. The Mainz Association promoted the formation of Catholic political clubs in the localities it visited if an existing political network did not already exist.[238]

Within a few months of its formation, the state banned officials from joining the Mainz Association, raided local leaders, and closed meetings. In 1876, the Prussian Supreme Court ruled the association was in violation and dissolved it.[239] However, the Mainz Association had reestablished a "network of political clubs and politically active clergy and notables" reminiscent of the Pius Associations, as well as encouraging the formation of a local press that printed Catholic weeklies in addition to the larger Catholic dailies.[240] Despite its short-lived existence, the Mainz Association proved instrumental in fostering and supporting Catholic political organizations and infrastructure in Germany.

The Soest Program constituted the core of the later, nationwide foundation of the Center Party. The program refers to a political platform that arose in response to increasing attacks on the Catholic Church and aimed to defend "the freedom of the church."[241] A group of prominent Catholics from the Rhineland and Westphalia, including Burghard Freiherr von Schorlemer-Alst and Wildrich von Ketteler – brother of Bishop Wilhelm Emmanuel von Ketteler – met in Münster in June of 1870 and agreed upon a program drawn up mostly by Herman von Mallinckrodt.[242] The program addressed a number of attacks on Catholics and the freedom of the Church. Later in the month, the *Kölnische Volkszeitung* published an edited version for popular appeal by Peter Reichensperger as the first public notice that Catholics intended to enter the political arena.[243] On October 28, 1870, the official Soest Program was established, seeking to provide the common platform for Catholic politicians on the eve of elections. The Soest Program's objective was "to defend the rights of the Church, and primarily of confessional schools, against the modern state'; the program supported federalism and "sought class harmony on the basis of Catholic social teaching."[244] The

[238] Sperber 1984, 214.
[239] Sperber 1984, 221; Ross 1998, 115 & 131.
[240] Sperber 1984, 214.
[241] Kalyvas 1996, 210.
[242] Windell 1954, 278.
[243] Windell 1954, 282.
[244] Weichlein 2011, 289.

Intraparty Conflict

majority of the points raised in the program mirrored the Münster program, the Reichensperger proposals, and the Essen platform.

The Soest Program provided Catholic organizations with an agenda for grassroots mobilization in the 1870 Prussian elections, which the program successfully carried out. Forty-eight Catholics were elected on the Soest Program, and approximately 50 ultimately established the new Catholic faction – other elected Catholics joined the Free Conservatives, the Conservative party, the National Liberals, or remained independent. While this new faction was proposed to center around defending the Catholic Church, its institutions, and its freedom, there was considerable disagreement among Catholic parliamentarians on the confessional nature of the prospective party. Some parliamentarians wanted to establish the Center Party as a purely confessional party, while others insisted that the designation "Catholic" not be used at all to dampen the flames of religious controversy. Ultimately, a compromise that minimized the confessional aspects of the party was established as the official faction. It was decided that the party's name would be Zentrum Party and avoid emphasizing its Catholic origins in an effort to appeal to the Protestant vote, although the party became the subject of criticism and controversy from its constituents. The choice for the party name in some ways mirrors the Italian PPI's decision to avoid direct reference to Catholicism or Christianity in its name. The conflict over the direction of the party parallels disagreements within Islamist parties between the political and religious factions.

The official establishment of the party took place immediately after the nationwide March 1871 elections.[245] The party was founded on three principal goals: civil and religious freedoms for all, defense of the federal nature of the German state, and intraparty freedom of opinion.[246] Despite early enthusiasm, the party encountered the same problems as its earlier incarnations: poor grassroots organization, weak association with the Catholic electorate, and regionalism. The onset of the Kültürkampf, ironically, became the savior of the party.

Beginning in 1872, the German state issued a wave of laws and policies targeting the Catholic Church's historical privileges vis-à-vis the state in Germany. This process, known as the Kültürkampf, aimed to curb the Church's influence and bring it under state control. Many of these reforms were undertaken at the state level rather than national level, leading to variation across different German states as to how far these reforms were taken. These new policies limited politicization of the pulpit, secularized education, controlled clerical appointments, banned Jesuits and religious orders, brought clerical training under state control, and made civil marriage obligatory. Crucially, Catholic clergy who opposed the measures were "jailed, banished, or deprived of their stipends" and Germany cut its diplomatic relations with the Vatican.[247]

---

[245] Kalyvas 1996, 211.
[246] Windell 1954, 289.
[247] Whyte 1981, 49.

238   *The Politics of Religious Party Change*

Exasperated by the increasing pressure of the German government, Pope Pius IX declared in the encyclical *Quod Nunquam* in 1875: "A wild and unexpected storm now reigns in your land [Prussia], where the Church of God once enjoyed peace and tranquility. Other new laws have been added to those laws against the rights of the Church which were proposed recently and which struck down and removed from their positions many clerics and laymen. These new laws thoroughly overturn the divine establishment of the Church and totally destroy the holy rights of the bishops."[248] The Kültürkampf debilitated church organization to the extent that the Church was unable to staff its institutions. For example, in 1876, all Prussian bishops were either imprisoned or driven to exile; in 1880, nearly one quarter of all parishes did not have pastors (1,100 out of 4,600).[249] In a pivotal moment for the evolution of Catholic political activism in Germany, the laity stepped in to fill the void, ultimately gaining greater influence within the Church. They took on pastoral duties in parishes, oversaw church properties, and served in parish councils.[250] While in principle the Catholic Church opposed lay political activism in the name of Catholicism, the Kültürkampf debilitated the Church to such a degree that it felt compelled to rely on the activism of a political party for its survival.

This turn of events empowered middle-class German Catholics against the Church and presented them with a remarkable opportunity. The middle-class German Catholics who were convinced of the necessity of political activism – but previously denied by the church hierarchy – could now act on their vision and face limited resistance from the church hierarchy. The Catholic Church was crippled and in no position to scrutinize the faithful's actions, especially in the political arena. Such lax institutional control over the faithful had implications that went beyond the Church. The relative absence of the church hierarchy meant that, unlike Catholic parties elsewhere in Europe, the Center Party gained greater latitude for political independence. Similarly, the party could mobilize the Catholic mass movement in support of its political agenda without strong ecclesiastical resistance. Lastly, the dynamics of the Church–Catholic party relations were defined less by competition and animosity, and more by the Church's greater dependence on the party to attain its political objectives. Even though the party's relationship with the Catholic Church was fraught with friction and conflict – and, remained far from the friendly and cooperative relationship we might expect from an otherwise two coreligionist entities – the church hierarchy did not aim to terminate the Center Party.

In one such fractious episode, the conflict between the party and the Church came to a head when controversial questions of church–state relations were being considered toward the end of the Kültürkampf. As an astute politician,

[248] *Quod Nunquam* ("On the Church in Prussia"), February 5, 1875.
[249] Ross 1976, 16. Atkin and Tallett put the number of parishes without priests at 1,400, nearly one-third of all parishes (2003, 146).
[250] Yonke 1990, 234.

Intraparty Conflict

the Center Party leader Ludwig Windthorst wanted to negotiate and cooperate with Chancellor Bismarck in order to "reach a compromise with Bismarck on some parts of the Kültürkampf legislation"; Pope Leo XIII (1878–1903) opposed a compromise and instead urged Windthorst to hold out and strategically push the government longer to endow German Catholics with greater rights. However, during the negotiations for a final peace agreement between the Vatican and the German government in 1886, the Center Party leader "insisted that the Papal Curia should not surrender to Bismarck's insistence that the state retain its power to approve or veto pastoral as well as episcopal appointments, while Leo XIII ruled against him."[251]

A crucial division within the Center Party deeply influenced the party's relationship with the Catholic Church. This division revolved around regional differences and the extent to which factions of the party saw themselves as "secular" or Catholic and clerical: "... territorial relationships were important in determining the strength of the various competing factions within the German Roman Catholic community. Like the Centrum itself, the party's affiliated or quasi-affiliated organizations depended on a provincial base."[252] In view of the internal divisions within the Center Party, it is obvious that the relationship between the party and the Catholic Church was complicated and ambiguous, resting on the shifting ways in which factions within the Center Party viewed themselves across different regions of Germany. The party's factional nature underscores its relative lack of political and ideological unity across Germany and cannot be overstated. While the Center Party in Bavaria "remained in clerical hands" and in Silesia and the Trier-Saar the confessional faction of the party was dominant among limited lay Catholic politicians, the Center Party's "more influential and powerful ... secular-political wing" found a welcoming audience in the Rhineland and Westphalia.[253] Clerical involvement in the local organization of the Center Party reflected this factional variation of the party. For example, in Sieg and Geldern in 1898, priests comprised two-thirds and one half of electoral committees, respectively. In Bavaria, the party secured the support of the bishops, creating a sort of "chaplainocracy" and facilitating the mobilization of the Catholic masses.[254]

The division between the secular and confessional factions of the party was more than a mere abstraction; not only did these separate factions exist, but this fractionalization also caused actual leadership conflicts within the Center Party. In particular, the "Centrum conflict" reflected the notion that the leaders of the party's confessional, religiously identifying faction were less attuned to and invested in the substantive development of the organization as a viable political party. Catholics in Berlin were particularly culpable in this regard: "Given their

---

[251] Zeender 1984, 429.
[252] Ross 1976, 120–21.
[253] Ross 1976, 122–23.
[254] Whyte 1981, 60.

240   *The Politics of Religious Party Change*

antipathy to the Centrum's secularization through the existence of a separate party structure, it was not surprising that the 'Berliners' took refuge in the outdated church-related form of the organization and failed to gain control over this new apparatus. By relying on the acquisition of episcopal support and the backing of the church, they doomed their cause to failure. That support was of limited value in the political quarrels dividing the Centrum because the Church's influence waned in the face of the party's secularization and the laicization of its leadership."[255] What is truly remarkable about this instance is that some factions of the Center Party received assistance from a network of German bishops and viewed themselves as intricately tied to the Church. Such a close-knit relationship with the Church, however, obscured their judgment. Certain conservative members of the party became so invested in cooperating with church leaders that they overlooked accomplishing more substantial efforts at political mobilization of Germany's Catholic population, which was ironically better accomplished by the factions of the party who considered themselves secular.

The Center Party's relations with other Catholic groups and organizations in Germany, including the Volksverein, evinced the party's efforts at grassroots mobilization as a new political party. In 1872, the Catholic Church led an effort to form the Association of German Catholics to rival the Center Party; Windhorst thwarted this effort in order to "preserve the Zentrum's monopoly on political Catholicism and the tactical freedom it guaranteed."[256] The Church put up another attempt to create an alternative organization, the Leoverein, with an explicitly confessional orientation in the late 1880s.[257] Center Party leader Windhorst undermined the Leoverein by simultaneously creating the Volksverein to support the party. The extraordinary growth of the Volksverein at the expense of the Leoverein frustrated the church hierarchy in Germany, who rightly saw the Center Party's actions as a challenge to "the Catholic episcopal authority in Germany."[258] Indeed, calls for Church to rein in the Volksverein abounded during this period; for example, one unrelenting supporter of the ecclesiastical authority claimed that "the time had come to ascertain the Volksverein's position within the ecclesiastical framework and the authority to which it must subordinate itself. Lest the Volksverein be misused, [he] concluded, it must be closely supervised by the episcopate."[259] The Catholic Church's formal position notwithstanding, members of the Volksverein showed enthusiasm for the Center Party: "The Volksverein was in fact an auxiliary, an agitation and propaganda department of the Zentrum (the Center Party). With words and deeds it prepared the ground for the electoral success of the party among the Catholic masses."[260] Relations between

[255] Ross 1976, 124.
[256] Anderson 1981, 180.
[257] Kalyvas 1996, 185.
[258] Ross 1976, 59.
[259] Quoted in Ross 1976, 59.
[260] Agocs 1975, 44.

Intraparty Conflict

the movement and the Center Party were thus more than cordial, with the Volksverein essentially cooperating with the party to widen its support base among the German population. The party also drew strongly from the Catholic labor movement. The support from working-class Catholics paralleled support for the party from small and middle-sized businesses.[261]

Chancellor Bismarck could be considered the principal opponent of the Center Party in its formative years. The Center Party's perseverance throughout the Kültürkampf weakened what was the party's main rival, the National Liberals. While the anti-Church character of National Liberalism proved instrumental during the Kültürkampf, National Liberals gradually lost ground and legitimacy relative to the Center Party, thereby minimizing Bismarck's need for them. Bismarck proposed reconciliation with the Center Party and an end to his anti-Catholic pursuits as a "tactical concession" as the party grew in strength.[262] In this regard, Bismarck's view on the relationship between the Center Party and the Catholic Church is instructive:

> [Bismarck] was convinced and succeeded in convincing others in Prussia's ruling circles that the Catholic population as represented by the Center Party and its allies posed a real danger to the security of the state. That danger did not lie in its spiritual dependence on an international authority, the Pope in Rome—indeed, Bismarck frequently expressed more friendliness toward Pius IX and Leo XIII than toward any Centrist politician and, as is well known, preferred to deal directly with the Vatican in dismantling Kültürkampf legislation. The danger lay rather in ... [the fact] that Catholic clergy and its representatives were much more active than the liberals in encouraging political activity among the peasants and lower classes ...[263]

Thus, even in the mind of this German head of state who sought to diminish the influence of Catholicism within his territories, the Center Party was not tantamount to Catholicism; instead, the two were clearly distinct and presented themselves as posing distinct challenges to Bismarck's rule.

Because the Center Party arose in response to perceived religious inequality and anti-Catholic legislation in Germany, religion figured prominently in the party's platform. On the basis of the Soest program, the party demanded "parity for the recognized religions" and strived to implement "legal guarantees" to protect Catholic and church interests.[264] "Parity" in this context refers to "equal representation" of Catholics in education, bureaucracy, and other citizenship rights,[265] highlighting the arenas in which Catholics felt their involvement was lacking. Ludwig Windthorst, a key leader of the Center Party, stated the following in a speech to German politicians on May 14, 1872: "Gentlemen, I am quite aware of the fact that your notion of Liberty is totally

---

[261] Knapp 1976, 11.
[262] Alexander 1953, 459–60.
[263] Evans 1999, 112.
[264] Ross 1976, 15.
[265] Evans 1984, 101.

different from that held in North America. Your understanding of Liberty consists of according the State all sorts of rights, then making every effort to take hold of the State power and finally crushing by this very State power those who hold different views."[266] Similarly, Peter Reichensperger, another party leader in the Prussian Diet, stated the following to an audience of Prussian Liberals seen as anti-Catholic: "The principle of National Liberalism is this: Privileges for myself and my friends, none for the others. It is not a fight and a war I see here; all I see is the unilateral suppression of the interests of the Church which is helplessly exposed to a State that is possessed of all means of utmost violence."[267] Notably, religious equality and freedom from state repression characterized the party's principal stance on this issue; the vision of a Catholic state, a religiously inspired system, or other anti-system features did not make their way into the pillars of the Center Party's identity.

The Center Party encountered numerous challenges in advancing their platform against German political leaders who seemingly espoused principles of freedom while ignoring the repression of Catholic voices within their society. Matters were not helped by the fact that Chancellor Bismarck himself consistently expressed that achieving social equality between Protestant and Catholic communities was not feasible: "By their whole character the equality of both Churches in the Prussian State is impossible. They are totally incommensurate entities. Should one wish complete equality, one would have to accord to the head of the Catholic Church the identical rights given to the supreme head of the Evangelical Church."[268] Statements such as this offered the Center Party valuable opportunities in reaching out to the Catholic electorate, emphasizing how German leaders such as Bismarck failed to protect the "interests of the Church." The party complemented its stance on Catholic rights with an encompassing position serving all communities of Germany: "The moral and material welfare of all levels of society is to be promoted as much as possible; the party shall strive for the constitutional establishment of guarantees towards the civic and religious freedom of all citizens of the German Reich, and particularly, for the protection of religious communities."[269]

The Center Party was ideologically flexible and open to compromise. The party espoused a limited number of fixed ideological positions and adapted to alliances with the Right or the Left, be it with Bismarck or the opposition; the party's own priorities determined the extent of its flexibility. Since the outset, the party was determined to avoid the "narrow clericalism" of its predecessor in the Prussian lower house in the 1850s; party leaders Peter Reichensperger and Hermann von Mallinckrodt thought that such narrow

---

[266] Alexander 1953, 457.
[267] Alexander 1953, 457.
[268] Moody 1953, 456.
[269] 1871 Center Party Caucus Program. Available at: http://ghdi.ghi-dc.org/sub_document.cfm?document_id=683

Intraparty Conflict

orientation "emasculated" the party.[270] The occasional ambiguity of who exactly the Center was meant to serve constituted a central feature of the party's political platform: "The party's name of Zentrum, or Center, reflects the difficulty of choosing any more descriptive title. In 1871, the parliamentary delegation in the new Reichstag considered a number of names. They concluded that any use of the word 'Catholic' would tend to alienate potential Protestant supporters whom some conservatives wanted to attract, in order to strengthen the clerical program with backing from representatives of the Evangelical Church, and to include within the party fold federalists who might not be Catholic, such as the Hanoverian Guelphs, the Danes, and those Protestant voters who had previously supported the particularist goals of the Bavarian Patriots' Party."[271] This statement is instructive in that since the very inception of the Center Party in Germany, steps were taken to ensure that the party would not explicitly alienate supporters who happened not to be Catholics. This position aligns well with the party's desire to not be beholden to a particular confessional constituency as parliamentary Catholics; instead, by casting a wider net and aiming to appeal to a broader electorate, they wanted to be Catholic parliamentarians. Indeed, several Catholic deputies refused to become members of the party whereas some Protestants such as Ludwig von Gerlach joined the party.[272] Similar concerns about the ability to cast a wide electoral net played a major role in the AKP's break from the National Outlook Movement in the early 2000s, as I discussed previously in this chapter.

Although the Center Party had an undeniable Catholic character and Catholic allegiances, significant factions of the party defined themselves as secular, and the party was able to reach out and appeal to a relatively wide segment of German society over the years. According to Atkin and Tallett, 45 percent of German Catholics – corresponding to 56 percent of total votes cast – voted for the Center Party in 1874.[273] While the party's voter base drew predominantly from Germany's Catholic population, one advantage the Center Party enjoyed that other parties did not is the lack of reliance on a certain socioeconomic, regional, or ideological segment of the broader population. The relatively wide-reaching nature of the Center Party supporters was also the reason for the party's broad appeal and lack of specificity in policy proposals:

The electorate of the Center Party had its roots in the entire social structure of German Catholicism. At no time, not at its founding, nor during the Kültürkampf, nor in the period 1882–1918, nor during its most glorious era in the Weimar Republic, did the

---

[270] Blackbourn 1975, 823.
[271] Evans 1984, 102.
[272] Blackbourn 1975, 824.
[273] Atkin and Tallett 2003, 146.

Center Party represent special political or social interests. The historical evolution of modern German Catholicism in its particular shape has had the result that Political Catholicism, as crystallized in the forms of the Center Party, took a totally different course from that of all German political parties. All the others either had their origin in the specific conditions of the German past, as for instance the liberal and conservative parties, or in the defense of special social interests of distinctive strata, as the movement of the German Social Democrats for the interests of the workers.[274]

The primary audience for the Center Party varied across different regions of Germany. The priority to achieve religious freedom and religious "parity" with Protestants was in fact not a great concern for Bavarian supporters of the Center Party. For example, the Bavarian branch of the party formed as late as 1887 from the disintegrating Patriot Party. The party was dominated by "conservative-clerical and agricultural interests"; a prominent local Center politician, George Heim, "was known as the 'peasant king' – a title emblematic of the social character of Bavarian political Catholicism."[275] In addition to certain branches of the Center Party gaining favor with agricultural groups, the party enjoyed support by some industrial unions and allocated representation to these unions in its national- and state-level parliamentary delegations.[276] Some societal groups such as aristocratic landowners were dissatisfied with the party's policies on the military budget and agrarian tariffs, and "staged temporary walkouts from the Center's parliamentary delegation."[277] The party increasingly picked up an economic orientation that focused on social policy and reforms, in great part a response to the growing significance of social associations founded by Catholics such as the Volksverein.[278]

Liberals showed little hesitation in accusing the Center Party of treason, underscoring the party's alleged subservience to the Vatican: "Through hatred of the Catholics, the Liberals especially have not ceased their accusations against the Centre and its supporters of want of patriotism, of treachery towards their native land, and of showing allegiance to the pope to the detriment of Germany."[279] However, the matter of the Center Party's allegiance to the Vatican was more complicated than what the liberals depicted. Catholic priests played an important role in the political party's early years; in certain parts of Germany such as Bavaria and Baden, priests assumed leadership positions and were key to the party's mobilization.[280] Likewise, religious causes motivated party activism; the uncertainty of the Catholic Church's status in Germany offered plenty of motivation for Center Party officials to gear party

[274] Alexander 1953, 463.
[275] Ross 1976, 121.
[276] Evans 1984, 112.
[277] Evans 1984, 113.
[278] Blackbourn 1975, 824.
[279] Sacher 1914, 21.
[280] Anderson 1988, 367.

Intraparty Conflict

policy in favor of Catholic demands. Yet, such "clericalism" in the Center Party did not morph into ecclesiastical prescription of party policy. The party deputies fiercely defended their political independence from Church interference. As Anderson states, "No Center deputy, Roeren no more than Bachem, wanted any bishop or pope to tell him how to vote in the Reichstag."[281]

The party's position on its relations with the Church became clearer in the process leading up to the peace laws. With the ascension of Pope Leo XIII, the Vatican engaged in direct discussions with Bismarck for ending the Kültürkampf. In Bismarck's view, such negotiations with the Vatican could help contain the Center Party's growing popularity in the German political landscape. During negotiations with Bismarck for a rapprochement in 1887, Pope Leo XIII asked the Center Party to vote in favor of the septennate – a seven-year army appropriations bill. In return, Bismarck promised to change the anti-Catholic May Laws to mark the end of the Kültürkampf.

However, the party was reluctant to support the passage of the peace laws in order to bring the Kültürkampf to a close. The Center Party and the Vatican held different views on what would be the appropriate strategy to approach negotiations on these issues. Some within the party, just as the Vatican preferred, wanted to pursue a strategy in which Catholics take what they could get and end the Kültürkampf. By contrast, party leader Windthorst and other prominent party deputies opted for a strategy that ensured restoration of the status quo ante, completely dismantling the Kültürkampf. This intraparty conflict over strategy was not resolved quickly. The prolonged debate within the party revolved around whether the party should continue its opposition to septennate, or whether a second peace law should be proposed to obtain the party leadership's preferred position on ending the Kültürkampf. When the pope insisted on supporting peace laws, the party refused to toe the line, suggesting that it would rather dissolve the party than follow the Church's directive. The party's attitude toward Church pressure mirrored its response to similar pressures ahead of the 1880 septennate. Reichstag chairman Georg Freiherr von Franckenstein made it abundantly clear in 1880 that "the party was political, and independent of clerical influence," reaffirming its nonclerical character. In 1887, the party refused to change its position and upheld its "autonomy in all political matters."[282] As a result, Leo XIII "backed down."[283] Once new elections ensured a majority for Bismarck to proceed with the peace laws without the Center Party's support, Bismarck moved on without the Center Party. Bismarck introduced the vote on peace laws with the vote on the septennate of 1887. Ultimately, "a modified version" of the bill was passed in the parliament that was for three years and "gave the German

---

[281] Anderson 1988, 368.
[282] Blackbourn 1975, 823.
[283] Whyte 1981, 61.

246   *The Politics of Religious Party Change*

chancellor virtual control of the army's size and budget until 1890."[284] The
Center Party abstained in the Reichstag vote. In 1893, the Vatican yet again
attempted to instruct the party on how to vote for another military bill in the
German parliament. Cardinal Georg von Kopp and Center Party leader Franz
von Ballestrem were invited to Rome for discussions. When the pope's preference and implicit demand for the bill's passage was conveyed, party leaders
such as Ernst Lieber were "incensed" at the Vatican's intervention: "From this
date the party steered an increasingly political course which owed nothing to
clerical prompting. German Catholics who enjoyed the ear of the Curia were
far removed from power in the party, whose leaders in turn had little or no
contact with Rome: Windthorst never went there, Lieber only once."[285] While
the conflict over specific policy direction between the Catholic Church and the
Center Party was critical to shaping the Catholic Church's future in Germany,
this episode's significance derives from the Center Party's insistence on autonomy from the Church. The Church held serious concerns about how the party
might display "a disconcerting independence."[286] With its outright rejection
of the Church's intervention, the Center Party leadership adamantly defended
its independence from the Church. Islamist parties differed from the Center
Party in this case, and more broadly Catholic parties in Western Europe, in the
absence of insistence on political independence.

The Center Party was formed in reaction to the anti-Catholic and anticlerical sentiment and government policy in Germany. Coupled with the reality
of German unification, this anti-Catholic and anti-Church onslaught led the
party to embrace a strong Catholic identity. The Kültürkampf turned out to be
the biggest boost to the party's electoral prospects; the party achieved its most
notable electoral success around the Kültürkampf. Despite being predominantly a party of Catholics, the Center Party was not clerical; the party fiercely
defended its political independence from Church influence. It was this freedom
from hierarchical control that allowed the Center Party to adjust and reorient
its political platform to better respond to shifts in the political landscape, and
to survive and succeed as a political party. As a result, the party increasingly
emphasized social policies in its platform, supplementing its Catholic identity
when the latter no longer sufficed to carry the party base. As Blackbourn notes,
"At the Reichstag elections of 1912, nearly one-half of Catholics who went to
the polls voted for a party other than the Centre; while for those who remained
loyal it was not simple piety but an intricate web of interests and aspirations
which bound them to the party. In this respect, as in its parliamentary practice
in Berlin and the state legislatures, the Centre was – as its principal leaders
intended – a political party."[287]

[284] Thomas 1980, 22.
[285] Blackbourn 1975, 823.
[286] Whyte 1981, 61.
[287] Blackbourn 1980, 232

Intraparty Conflict

THE FORMATION OF PPI AND THE CATHOLIC CHURCH'S RESPONSE IN ITALY

The introduction of universal suffrage in 1912 by Prime Minister Giovanni Giolitti lent popular credibility to lay Catholic political activism in Italy, undermining the Church's work to frame political participation as an effort by the state to subjugate Catholics.[288] Direct political involvement through a Catholic political party, as Christian Democrats called for, presented dual dangers for the Vatican and Pope Pius X. On one hand, it would possibly require collaboration with socialist parties in the parliament or in the government. Such a prospect was unacceptable. On the other hand, Christian Democrats who would spearhead a Catholic party were hostages to the "Heresy of Heresies": modernity.[289] Despite Pius X's reluctance to entangle the Catholic Action movement with politics beyond simply pointing voters toward nonsocialist leaders, others in the movement were more inclined to enter the political sphere following the change in the Non Expedit policy. Don Luigi Sturzo, a Sicilian priest and former head of the Popular Union – one of the three main Catholic Action unions – founded the Partito Popolare Italiano (PPI) in 1919. As a Catholic political party, the PPI aimed to tread carefully, alienating neither the electorate nor the Church. The Church's staunch opposition, however, forced Catholic political activists to distinguish themselves from the church hierarchy and temper their religious claims. While upholding its independence from the Church, the party explicitly invoked Christian principles: "[PPI] didn't want to speak for the Church or for all Catholics or only for Catholics. [The party] wanted room for initiatives or political choices that would not commit the hierarchy or the papacy, that is, that would not require their backing or be liable to their veto."[290] Poggi writes that the PPI presented itself "formally as secular (i.e., nonreligious) and independent of ecclesiastical authorities,"[291] thereby separating itself from the Catholic Action movement that was aligned with Pope Pius XI's (1922–39) belief that the movement should operate "at the level of civil society, rather than of the state."[292]

The party's emergence overlaps with the sharp rise of social Catholicism in Italy, a fact that helped with the party's early electoral success. A well-developed Catholic social infrastructure was already in place by the time Sturzo believed it necessary to mobilize an actual political party: "... at the beginning of 1919, barely two months after the armistice there were in Italy in the hands of social Catholics more than four thousand co-operatives, some one thousand workers' mutual aid societies, about three hundred popular banks, many

---

[288] Ascoli 1935, 444.
[289] Ascoli 1935, 445.
[290] Misner 2004, 653.
[291] Poggi 1967, 20.
[292] Poggi 1967, 21.

professional unions (which had been confederated together in September, 1918) reaching within a short time a membership of almost eight hundred thousand (and in 1920 a million, two hundred thousand). Moreover, many of the students of the secondary schools and universities had been educated for a long time in the Catholic Youth Clubs."[293] Likewise, the existence of a Catholic press aided the rise of the party during this period. Modern dailies such as the *Italia* were instrumental in disseminating the party's political messaging.[294]

The party thus almost immediately garnered a wide support base, taking advantage of the momentum that the social Catholicism movement had produced in Italian society. While there were indeed numerous tensions between the Italian state and the Vatican, the PPI did not form under nearly the same stringent political conditions as the German Center Party. While the Center Party made it an urgent priority to respond to the anti-Catholic *Kültürkampf*, we do not find a similarly severe and ongoing anticlerical policy in Italy when the PPI came about. The papal *Non Expedit,* which treated the Italian state with skepticism and caution and forbade Catholics to vote, had lost power by this time.

The PPI was a party of diverse goals that aimed at achieving social justice and Christian spirit. The party embraced a platform to combat liberalism and aggressive capitalism, and institute a more Christian and humane system that would ultimately offer justice to workers. More specific elements of the PPI's platform included agrarian reform and achieving legal status for labor unions. The former policy initiative involved improving relations between landowners, tenants, and peasants, while the latter centered on giving labor unions more of a voice in the party. In its short period of existence, the party staunchly advocated in its platform for various reforms in the political arena and governance: "Proportional representation, freedom of teaching, decentralization of administration, tax reform, the right to work, the improvement of the conditions of the industrial and agricultural worker, as well as freedom for the unions, were among the most important points [in PPI platform]."[295]

In a PPI manifesto from January 1919, Sturzo expressed his own views on how the ideal state should operate: "For a centralizing state, seeking to restrict all organizing powers and all civic and individual activities we would substitute, on constitutional grounds, a state ... respectful of the natural centers and organisms – the family, occupational groups, townships, communes – giving way before the rights of human personality and encouraging its initiatives."[296] One reason why Sturzo valued state decentralization as part of his party's platform is that he hoped it would lead to the formation of stronger social networks around the country. The party ultimately laid claim to a variety of interests and

[293] Sturzo 1944, 244.
[294] De Robilant 1930, 467.
[295] Di Maio 2004, 114.
[296] Moos 1945, 278.

Intraparty Conflict

goals; yet, one can see that the general platform aimed to strengthen Italian communities through advocacy for economic justice and religious freedom for Catholics, rejecting forms of government that would threaten to revoke individual or communal autonomy in Italian society.

As with other Catholic movements and parties of the late nineteenth and early twentieth centuries, the Italian Popular Party saw itself as an opponent of socialism. Many members of the party concurred that it was the essential function of the PPI "to defeat socialism."[297] Sturzo himself indicated that "the clergy has feared, first liberalism, then socialism, and finally bolshevism"; for Sturzo, this fear was grounded in the fact that "many revolutionary leaders such as Marx and Lenin took the denial of Christianity as their point of departure. If the clergy associated itself with non-liberal regimes, it did so because the historical system changes with difficulty and because 'of lack of experience in a regime of liberty'."[298] While there were members of the PPI whose ideological views shifted toward socialist thought, outright socialism proved too controversial, iconoclastic, and ungodly to be accepted by the party.

The organizational structure of the PPI diverged from that of the Popular Union wing of Catholic Action; the PPI did not bear an organizational connection to the larger body of the Roman Catholic Church. The PPI was not Catholic in the sense that non-Catholics could enter its ranks so long as they upheld the party program. The Holy See was not involved in the party; the PPI was purely a political party, distinct from all other Catholic organizations in Italy at the time, and autonomous. The Vatican, for its part, remained distant from the platform and actions of the party, denying any responsibility for it. Baravelli writes that "the recently created Italian Popular Party relished setting aside moderate clericalism,"[299] underscoring that the intention of the party was to remain outside of the direct control and dictates of the church hierarchy. Just as the Vatican State Secretary Cardinal Gasparri referenced the "formation of a 'Party of Catholics'," Sturzo was determined "not to speak in the name of the Vatican and not to name the party either 'Christian' or 'Catholic'."[300] Such a choice by the PPI paralleled the German Center Party and their efforts to devise a name that would not appear to lay claim to speaking for Catholicism. PPI leader Sturzo wished to remain separate from the Vatican because, for him, the party's objective was to uphold Catholic principles while avoiding transformation into a clerical party. In Sturzo's view, this strategy gave them the best chance to influence policy.[301] In other words, the PPI sought to win political power and influence policy that was predicated upon electoral success rather than clerical obedience. The choice to keep the PPI out of the realm of

[297] Foot 1997, 430.
[298] Moos 1945, 282.
[299] Baravelli 2015.
[300] Di Maio 2004, 112.
[301] Di Maio 2004, 112.

clericalism reflected the party's political calculations as opposed to a fundamental difference in policy orientation between the PPI and the Church. Rather than being an anti-system party that aimed to fundamentally oppose the very foundation of the Italian political system, the PPI aimed to operate within the existing political system and affect policy.

Regarding relations between the PPI and Catholic Action, the Vatican sought to isolate Catholic Action from the PPI. Pope Benedict XV pursued a policy to distinguish and distance Catholic Action from the PPI.[302] Sturzo, for his part, ensured to find ways to take advantage of the relative autonomy of his party without a merger with the Catholic Action movement. Pope Pius XI, likewise, remained highly skeptical of the PPI during his tenure (1922–39): "In Pius XI's eyes, the inadequacies of the Popular Party were exacerbated by three factors: his suspicions regarding Benedict XV's plan for a Catholic party, his distaste for some aspects of the party's line on social and economic matters, and his attraction to a strong-man strategy for defeating 'bolshevism'."[303] Pius XI, in this regard, defined Catholic Action's essential characteristic as "the participation and the collaboration of the laity with the Apostolic Hierarchy ... [It is] outside and above all party politics."[304] This calibrated effort by the Church to maintain control of the Catholic movement against the PPI reflected the nature of religious competition in Italy at the time and the movement's critical role in this competition.

While *de jure* separation between the Church and the party was firmly established, the Church still aimed to wield *de facto* influence over the party. The fact that the Vatican is geographically contained within Italy afforded the Church the ability to exert disproportionate influence that did not exist in other contexts. As a result, the PPI faced greater pressure from the Church compared to other Catholic parties in Europe despite its independence and secular character.[305] There was a degree of ideological inconsistency within the PPI considering the fact that some of Sturzo's followers were "devoted first to their Church and secondly to the State."[306] Sturzo and many others within the party, however, were different; they went to rhetorical lengths to emphasize that their devotion to political organization remained separate from their devotion to the Church. In response to accusations that he consulted the Vatican and the Pope in political matters, Sturzo stated: "If a priest, founder and leader of a political party, is an exception in the Church, it is necessary to look at him in the whole of his life; it seems to me that I have given constant evidence that I have always safeguarded the political independence of my party as well as the ecclesiastical discipline that binds me."[307]

---

[302] Poggi 1967, 19–20.
[303] Poggi 1967, 22.
[304] Gellott 1988, 576.
[305] Di Maio 2004, 111.
[306] Moos 1945, 280.
[307] Moos 1945, 280.

Intraparty Conflict

The PPI leadership proved its independence as a political party by taking controversial positions in its pursuit of political objectives. To this end, a decisive internal conflict centered around the position of leftist voices within the party and the party's approach to forging ideological bridges with socialists. Giuseppe Speranzini and Romano Cocchi were part of a faction within the PPI known as the "estremisti" (a cognate to "extremists" in English) who opposed "the prioritization of anti-socialism within the party, [yet nonetheless] remained within the PPI, despite its interclass character, until they were forcibly expelled."[308] Speranzini's ideology and political actions, for example, closely aligned with the aspirations of socialists who aimed to organize and empower workers. Speranzini was an editor of Conquista Popolare, an estremisti newspaper, as well as a peasant organizer: "During 1919–20 he [Speranzini] returned time and again to the idea of workers' unity – arguing for trade-union alliances outside of the political parties, a sort of Catholic revolutionary syndicalism. Proletarian links were to be formed from below. Speranzini believed that alliances of this type would 'naturally' develop as Catholic unions shifted leftwards under political and economic pressure, and therefore closer to the socialist organizations."[309] In a speech at Naples, Speranzini demonstrated his belief that it was imperative for the Catholic party to form some ideological connection with socialists: "We have to ... present more courageous reforms, that otherwise will be exploited by the socialists and so we will have built a bridge towards the more intelligent elements of the socialist party."[310] Don Luigi Sturzo disapproved of the outspoken leftist voices arising inside the party, as he viewed them as a challenge to the party leadership's authority. Guido Miglioli led this group of dissident leftist Catholic voices within the party. Ultimately, the party expelled Speranzini and Cocchi in early 1921. Sturzo's decision to force Speranzini and Cocchi out of the PPI aimed to isolate Miglioli and the leftist flank within the party. In turn, many within the party took a stronger stance against socialism.[311] This harsh fate that befell the "extremist" left voices in the PPI not only reveals that the party had a relatively centralized structure of authority to allow for such actions; it also suggests that this party, which boasted of social diversity in having members from many different social classes, could not always boast about ideological harmony. While views within the party spanned the political spectrum, the real consequences of holding and propagating such views at times threatened the identity of this Catholic party, leading certain figures in the party to be deemed dangerous to the party's cohesion.

The stance of the Catholic Church toward the formation of the PPI ranged from "irrelevant" in the most favorable scenario to "openly hostile" in the

---

[308] Foot 1997, 419.
[309] Foot 1997, 419.
[310] Foot 1997, 419.
[311] Foot 1997, 430.

least favorable. As Molony states, the party "was not only expendable to the Vatican, but more positively it had to be dismantled."[312] The dire threat to the Church rested in the PPI's emergence as a new religious actor that could potentially compete with the Church and claim to represent Catholics in the political arena. As Guiseppe Dalla Torre – one of the leading figures in Catholic Action until 1920 and subsequently the editor of Osservatore Romano – observed, Catholic Action, and by extension the Church, "never will admit that a Catholic party can arise in its place."[313] Moreover, the Church aimed to marginalize the PPI by refusing to acknowledge its existence or ties to Catholicism. Attacks by Osservatore Romano, the official daily of the Vatican, and bishops partially defined relations between the party and the Church.[314]

Despite great distaste for the party, outright hostility or repression were not viable options for the Church due to the high cost associated with such a policy. The Vatican gave in to the PPI's formation because "it could not prevent it."[315] The PPI, like other Catholic parties, gained strong popularity early on; direct confrontation would therefore undermine the Church's position with the laity. Moreover, as Kalyvas suggests, the PPI potentially offered certain policy advantages from which the Church could benefit, such as acting as "a political guarantee against future anticlerical attacks" and the rising tide of socialism.[316]

One way the Church aimed to counteract the rise of the PPI involved allowing a greater role for the Catholic laity inside the Church. The Vatican was not happy about the rise of the PPI; more importantly, the PPI's draw over lay Catholics underlay the pope's discontent. Ever growing numbers made their way to the PPI away from church organizations. Pope Benedict XV felt compelled to respond to this shift by reiterating the Church's paramount position for Catholics and emphasizing that "we do not want anyone to forget that the Popular Union is the principal agent of Catholic Action."[317] Through the papal encyclical *Ubi Arcano Dei Consilio*, Pope Pius XI encouraged Catholics to "unite" with the clergy "in the works of the apostolate," promote moral values of the Church, and ultimately work toward "world peace" and "true human equality" through church leadership.[318] Critically, this role for the laity entailed a pointed stance against partisan politics and underscored potential harms of politics in attaining the noble goals of the Church.

The party was not long-lived due to the ascension of fascism in the country; the Vatican took this opportunity for a decisive action against the PPI.

[312] Molony 1977, 13.
[313] Quoted in Molony 1977, 52.
[314] Kalyvas 1996, 186.
[315] Molony 1977, 6.
[316] Kalyvas 1996, 181.
[317] Molony 1977, 82.
[318] *Ubi Arcano Dei Consilio*, 1922.

Intraparty Conflict 253

The state also had an interest in disbanding the PPI; the Italian state and the Vatican therefore entered a mutually beneficial arrangement. To this end, Pius XI demanded that PPI leader Sturzo step down from his parliamentary position and take steps to dissolve the party. Once Sturzo complied with the pope's request, the Vatican mobilized the church hierarchy and the Catholic faithful to dissociate from the PPI, leading to the party's eventual end in 1926. In return, the state offered the Vatican a series of privileges they sought via the Lateran Pacts (1929), ultimately resolving the "Roman Question." In particular, the Italian state recognized the Vatican's sovereignty as a state. The Vatican received funds from the Italian state, maintained its social organizations, and enjoyed the right to teach religion in schools.[319]

The geographical proximity of the Vatican to Italy shows how the centralized religious institutional structure significantly influenced the rise of political Catholicism and the PPI as a confessional political party. The Vatican's desire to control emerging social and political activism among Catholics throughout Europe was most effective in Italy compared to Germany and Belgium because the ecclesiastical authority managed to take organizational control of Catholic social activism and associational life at its inception. The Church kept Catholic organizations such as the Opera and Catholic Action under close supervision and integrated them into the church hierarchy. Christian Democratic activists saw the future of Catholic activism as defending the interests of the Church and the Catholic faithful in the political arena. When Christian Democratic leaders like Murri and Sturzo indicated their interest in steering these Catholic organizations and the broader Catholic mass movement in a more political direction via a Catholic political party, the Church was fiercely opposed. Church leaders recognized how such politicization of its authority over Catholics and the emergence of a confessional party fundamentally challenged its power. Instead of blessing the rise of political Catholicism, the Vatican actively undermined it by directly appealing to Catholics and urging clergymen and Catholic associations to avoid supporting Christian Democrats and the PPI. The Catholic Church's hostility toward Catholic political activism was most direct in Italy.

THE RISE OF THE CATHOLIC PARTY IN BELGIUM

The formation of a Catholic political party in Belgium took on a more nebulous form in its early stages. Similarly, the Catholic Party's creation in Belgium pursued a different path than its counterparts in Germany and Italy and more starkly reflected the competition for power between the Catholic Church and ultramontanes, Christian Democrats, and Conservative Catholics – an appellation that refers to the established Catholic leaders. The role of social classes and class conflict partially fueled the intensity of the competition and conflict between these different Catholic actors. Concerned about the intensified anticlerical attacks,

---

[319] Vaillancourt 1980, 186–88.

the Catholic Church sanctioned an increasingly politicized Catholic mass mobilization to defend the Church and its interests. The outright politicization of the Catholic mass movement, in this regard, can be traced back to the creation of the Federation of Catholic Clubs and Conservative Associations in 1879 with the merger of the Federation of Catholic Clubs and the Federation of Constitutional Conservative Associations. Crucially, the Federation was led by Charles Woeste, a dedicated faithful of the Catholic Church and its interests.

It was the Catholic victory in the 1884 parliamentary elections that set the formation of the Catholic Party of Belgium on an irreversible course. The Church, along with ultramontanes, allied with Conservative Catholic politicians and mounted a major electoral campaign to win power in the upcoming elections, which turned out to be "a veritable Waterloo for the Liberals" who lost power to the Catholics.[320] The results of the election established religion as a primary political cleavage in the years that followed. The Conservatives who historically constituted the political Right in Belgium were "recast" as the Catholic Party.[321] When the decidedly Catholic electoral mobilization leading up to the 1884 elections resulted in a major victory, Catholic politicians acted swiftly to translate their electoral gains into political ones in the form of a Catholic party and pro-Catholic policies.

The early years of the Belgian Catholic Party was notably under the control of the Conservative Catholic politicians and the Federation while the Church played a mediator role between the two. The "paternalistic" Federation assumed a significant role in the Catholic Party following the 1884 elections under "arch-conservative" Woeste's leadership.[322] There were disagreements, however, among Belgian Catholics at the time of the party's founding in 1884 as to what exactly the political strategy of the party should be. The Conservatives wanted to maintain their political autonomy and hoped to remain unfazed by the Federation and the Federation-associated Catholic politicians who were largely ultramontane. The Conservatives in particular did not want accountability for their actions in the political arena to fall in the hands of an unelected body such as the church hierarchy. So long as the Church had sufficient space for its socioreligious activism, the Conservatives fundamentally accepted the basic parameters of the parliamentary system. Such position of Conservative Catholic politicians was at odds with the ultramontane Catholic politicians of the Federation, who were deeply anti-system.[323] Moreover, Conservatives repressed the power of organized Catholics such as the Federation when they felt that these Catholics were becoming too politically engaged. Despite their differences, Conservatives declared, "What divides us is not a question of doctrine but one of action (conduit)."[324]

---

[320] Lord 1923, 35.
[321] Kalyvas 1996, 191.
[322] Witte, Craeybeckx, and Meynen 2009, 154.
[323] Witte, Craeybeckx, and Meynen 2009, 87.
[324] Kalyvas 1998, 305.

Intraparty Conflict

The Church typically acted as a mediator between the Conservatives and the ultramontane wing during the contentious period of the 1870s but prior to the 1884 elections displayed a preference for the Conservative wing. This was a strategic move on the Church's part. The Church had always seen the constitution as a grudging compromise, and the Vatican became more vocal in its denunciation of liberalism during the 1860s. Pius IX was especially avid in his support for the radical ultramontanes, a group of devout bourgeois lay Catholics who tried to wrest political control of the Right from the parliamentary Conservatives.[325] This conflict was only resolved once Pope Leo XIII intervened in 1879 and stated that the Belgian constitution, while containing some distasteful principles, should still be upheld by Catholics. Having dampened the flames of the ultramontanes and the Federation, this proclamation helped the moderate Conservatives march to victory in 1884 and maintain power for three decades, all the while maintaining the liberal institutions laid out in the Constitution of 1831. Radical anticlericals were also less influential during this time and into the turn of the century but continued to have an influence on Belgian socialist ideology. They lost even more political clout after the creation of universal male suffrage in 1894, at which point the Conservatives gained more support from the mass of Catholic commoners who could now vote.[326] Anticlericalism has left a history of antagonisms in Belgian culture that continued to threaten national unity well into the twentieth century, just as the Church has remained a strong force in the makeup of Belgian society.[327]

Over the course of the next several years, the Federation gradually expanded its influence over the Catholic Party. Under Conservative Jules Malou's leadership, Federation leaders Charles Woeste and Victor Jacobs assumed cabinet positions. Although their ministerial tenure in the short-lived Malou government did not last long, they left a lasting legacy in consolidating the party organization and in Belgium's education policy. As part of the party's organizational formation, the Federation "officially" became part of the Catholic Party.[328] While the Church did not lead the initiative to create the Catholic Party, it nonetheless supported it in view of the Federation's role in this process with its commitment to ultramontanism. Indeed, the Church's directive to various Catholic organizations such as the *Union nationale pour le redressement des griefs* to leave the political arena and to priests to leave social activism reinforced the Federation's position within the party.[329] Another Conservative Catholic politician, Auguste Beernaert, replaced Malou as the prime minister. Despite his ouster from the cabinet, Woeste remained as the most central figure within the Catholic Party for years to come.[330] During his brief tenure as a

[325] Kalyvas 1998, 300–01.
[326] Strikwerda 1988, 336.
[327] Kittell 1961, 419.
[328] Kalyvas 1996, 192.
[329] Kalyvas 1996, 184.
[330] Lord 1923, 36.

minister, Woeste remained faithful to his ultramontane roots and undertook a series of reforms in educational policy that partially brought back the Catholic Church's influence in education. In particular, the law of 1884 reduced minimum educational requirements for schools and recognized schools besides public schools in the educational system. In practice, this change meant that private schools such as the church schools could be officially recognized by the state and receive state subsidies as long as they met state regulations. Gradually, the state subsidies for private schools approached the level of public schools.[331] With another legislation in 1895, Catholic schools, that is, "free" schools, began receiving subsidies from the state on a regular basis; this was part of the Catholic government's plan to decentralize education in the hopes of granting the Church greater influence in social policy. The party justified its drive for decentralization with the idea that "Education is not a public service; it is the function of the father, not of the State."[332] Likewise, religious instruction became compulsory in schools, although exemption was a possibility if requested. Overall, however, this push for decentralization was brief. Developments within and without the party led to greater centralization and eventually toward more democratic reforms.[333]

Unlike other contexts in Western Europe, the Church's position on the formation of the Belgian Catholic political party did not amount to outright opposition. This was in part fueled by the role that Conservative politicians played in the formation of the Catholic Party. The Church preferred to work with Conservative politicians who were more open to working with the Church on its preferred policies. The rise of Christian Democrats and the Belgian Democratic League to prominence in Belgium and within the party created a fundamental conflict in terms of the direction and the confessional nature of the Catholic Party, increasing the tension between the Church and the party. The Christian Democrats pushed for greater independence from the Church, posing a dilemma for the Conservatives and the Federation leaders within the party. On one hand, the Belgian Democratic League offered clear advantages in an era of mass politics; they could reach out to a critical segment of the electorate to sustain the party's parliamentary majority. The party leadership knew that the Christian Democrats of the League offered a viable way to mobilize support for Catholic leaders at a time when many suspected that suffrage would soon be extended to broader segments of the Belgian society. While they were wary of the "radicalism" that the Christian democrats presented, the League's "experience in creating associations of lower-class individuals and their more politically aggressive stance," party leaders reasoned, was necessary for the party's electoral success.[334] On the other hand, the League posed a serious threat to the party leadership; the

---

[331] Linden 1920, 325.
[332] Linden 1920, 329.
[333] Linden 1920, 326.
[334] Strikwerda 1997, 219.

Intraparty Conflict

increasing popularity of the Catholic labor movement undermined the current party leadership's hold on the party. The Boerenbond's efforts to mobilize the peasants similarly did not please the traditional, old, and upper class Catholic Conservative leadership of the party. The fact that Joris Helleputte served as a founder in both the League and the Boerenbond illustrates the competing groups in the formative years of the Catholic Party.

The process leading to the expansion of suffrage in Belgium constitutes a pivotal turning point in the Catholic Party's makeup. The Catholic Party did not fully support calls for the expansion of suffrage, as the issue was highly politicized and there was division within the party. The party leadership's middle and upper class character partly contributed to the hesitancy about suffrage reform as opposed to the Belgian Democratic League's enthusiastic support for it, recruiting and mobilizing the working-class Catholics. The Federation, however, displayed "reluctance" to mobilize the working class in order to expand the constituency of the party.[335] Hierarchical control within the party rendered deviation from the parameters set out by the leadership nearly impossible. Therefore, when the progressive wing of Christian Democrats expressed their disappointment with the party's lack of support for expanding suffrage, Catholic leaders pushed for a change in the Belgian Democratic League, seeing Verhaegen in as the new leader of the group.

Christian Democratic Belgian Democratic League's ascent within the Catholic Party gradually transformed the party's identity, as the League gained prominence at the expense of the Federation. The League's rise and its eventual status as an indispensable component of the party's electoral success came due to the suffrage's expansion. The League's deep network, a result of its recruitment and mobilization over the years, proved crucial for the Catholic Party to appeal to a wider set of interests in the era of mass politics than what the party's Conservative leadership could offer. The League reached out to higher church authorities in order to facilitate their organizational goals: "In 1901, [the League's president Arthur] Verhaegen and the leading Bruxellois Christian Democratic leaders, acting through the [Belgian Democratic League], convinced the archbishopric of Mechelen to create a Secretariat of Social Works for the arrondissement of Brussels to help priests create clubs, insurance societies, and unions."[336]

Belgian suffrage was one of the most restrictive in Europe at the time.[337] The Catholic Party's proposal to expand suffrage prioritized expanding the electorate in the rural areas, or "country districts," which were predominantly Catholic; the proposal would significantly "disadvantage" cities, which tended to support the Liberal Party.[338] However, this proposal did not find enough

[335] Strikwerda 1997, 220.
[336] Strikwerda 1997, 342.
[337] Lord 1923, 39.
[338] Vauthier 1894, 711.

support in the parliament. When faced with tremendous popular pressure in the streets by the working class, the Belgian Parliament accepted a compromise solution to the longstanding issue of the expansion of suffrage in April of 1893. The constitutional change established the "plural vote" as the new basis of suffrage with almost 80 percent support in the parliament. With this change, every male citizen at least 25 years of age became eligible to cast at least one vote. Those who were older (over 35 years of age), wealthy, educated, or served as the head of their household had one or two additional votes, depending on the combination of these factors. The constitutional change increased the number of voters from 135,000 to 1,300,000; the number of additional votes was 800,000, bringing the total number of votes to 2,100,000.[339] This expansion in suffrage helped the Christian Democrats rise to prominence within the Catholic Party. While the League demanded greater parliamentary representation from the Catholic Party in the 1890s, the League was deprived from this opportunity in part because the Church hierarchy and party officials did not view the League as an important and independent actor outside of the Federation of Catholic Clubs and Conservative Associations. This recognition would not materialize until after 1905.[340]

It was the expansion of suffrage and the Catholic Party leadership's realization – in the face of the party's gradually declining parliamentary majority – that Catholic workers had to be part of the party's core base to sustain their majority; if working-class Catholics broke away from the Catholic party (presumably to the socialists), it proved impossible for them to hold on to the government. This realization put the Belgian Democratic League and the Christian Democrats in a favorable position for a much larger role in the party and affect policy. More specifically, the League's rise came at the expense of the Federation.[341] While the Christian Democrats embraced diversity and envisioned a role for themselves in the Catholic Party, the Federation and its leader Woeste opposed these efforts. Woeste viewed the League as "a necessary evil" that had to be kept in check. When, for example, the League expressed their interest in organizing Catholic congresses to bring Catholic activists from across the political spectrum, Woeste vehemently opposed the idea and claimed that "it wouldn't be possible to restrain anyone from speaking." Therefore, Woeste sabotaged the convening of such a congress in the model of the Malines Congresses multiple times.[342]

The conflictual dynamic between the League and the Federation continued when the League changed leadership to Arthur Verhaegen. Strikwerda writes that "by 1903, Verhaegen had succeeded in getting the bishops, a few important upper-class party leaders, and even the papacy to side with the

[339] Vauthier 1894, 722.
[340] Witte, Craeybeckx, and Meynen 2009, 113.
[341] Defossez 1972.
[342] Defossez 1972, 301.

Intraparty Conflict

[Belgian Democratic League] against ... conservative opponents."[343] While the League courted the Church and sought its approval, the movement acted independently from the church hierarchy. Its cooperation with the Church aimed to convince the clergy of the legitimacy of their goals, gain their blessings, and ultimately obtain popular legitimacy among Belgian Catholics rather than actively obeying direct commands from the church hierarchy. Leo XIII sympathized with the League's mission and focus on labor rights. The conservative turn with Pius X in the Vatican's stance on labor movements and Christian Democracy meant that the League faced significant pushback to its political activism: "From about 1900 to 1911, especially under the papacy of Pius X, a group of conservative Catholics throughout Europe, led especially by Monsignor Benigni and Cardinal Merry du Val in Rome, waged a campaign to repress what they considered heterodoxy ... Although not interconfessional, the Belgian Catholic unions [i.e., Belgian Democratic League] were vulnerable. They organized strikes, cooperated at times with Socialists, and, at least from the point of view of the conservatives, accepted material solutions to social problems."[344] Personal appeals by Verhaegen to the pope in the Vatican, such as the October 29, 1903 meeting between Pope Pius X and Verhaegen,[345] were to no avail.

Nonetheless, under Verhaegen's leadership the Christian Democrats continued battling the Federation and Woeste for a greater role within the Catholic Party in the face of attacks by the conservative flank of the party. The reduction in the Catholic Party's parliamentary majority following the 1906 elections created an opening for a change in the party. Christian Democrats seized the opportunity to affect legislation on various social policy issues such as old-age pensions, accidents in industrial workplaces, and the recognition of Sunday as a mandatory rest day. Christian Democrats' influence within the party and the government substantially increased in the years that followed.[346] In an effort to gain greater power within the cabinet, the Christian Democrats pushed out the de Naeyer government, leading to a government led by de Trooz on May 2, 1907. The new government included Christian Democrats Jules Renkin and Joris Helleputte. Simultaneously, Woeste faced increasing resistance within the ranks of the Federation to his leadership, gradually weakening until after World War I.[347] Christian Democrats found some success in their pursuit of societal support to challenge the Federation when Bishop Désiré-Joseph Mercier of Malines facilitated the convention of a Catholic Congress in Malines in 1909. Following World War I, the Catholic Party came under greater control of the

---

[343] Strikwerda 1997, 243.
[344] Strikwerda 1997, 343.
[345] "Christian Democracy in Belgium," *The Tablet*, November 14, 1903. Available at: https://books.google.com/books?id=5bqKct7ChQYC&dq (accessed August 2, 2020)
[346] Witte, Craeybeckx, and Meynen 2009, 119.
[347] Defossez 1972, 325.

Christian Democratic wing. The Belgian Democratic League gradually dissolved in this period to be replaced by Algemeen Christelijk Werkersverbond in 1921 to serve as the umbrella organization for the Catholic workers' organizations. While remaining grounded in the Catholic identity, the Belgian Catholic Party prioritized social and economic policy issues, in a way similar to other Catholic parties in Europe.

Politicization of Catholicism in Belgium and the rise of the Belgian Catholic Party followed a different path than the Catholic parties in Italy and Germany. The close and favorable relationship between the Catholic Church and Conservative (Catholic) politicians for much of the nineteenth century came to define the early years of the Catholic Party – as an outgrowth of the Conservative Party – and resulted in the slow emergence of a Christian Democratic movement. The primary axis of conflict among Belgian Catholics was between the Christian Democrats and the ultramontane wing of the Catholic activists. Overpowered by ultramontane activists and the Federation, the Christian Democratic Belgian Democratic League sought to find its footing and acquire greater power within the party at the expense of the Federation. With the expansion of suffrage, the League and the Christian Democrats fought the Federation and ultimately won over the Catholic Party. Despite the delay in taking control of the party, as compared to other Catholic parties, the Belgian Catholic Party charted an independent course once it was free of ultramontane control within the party.

Conclusion

Looking Ahead – The Challenge of Islamist Organizational Reform

Informed by the historically divergent trajectories of Sunni Islamist parties in the Middle East and Catholic parties in Western Europe, this book examined the impact of religious institutions on religious party change. Despite the many similarities in their early trajectories, Catholic and Islamist parties pursued different paths in modern politics. In answering the question "Why do religious parties become less anti-system?," I examined the institutional context in which religious parties operate and underscored the centrality of religious institutions and religious competition to the process of religious party change. Religious parties are embedded in distinct *religious* institutional structures that shape their actions as they navigate electoral politics. In particular, the level of institutionalization and the party-movement hybrid organization are decisive factors influencing religious parties' stance vis-à-vis the existing governing system. The level of institutionalization in a religion – centralization and hierarchical organization of religious authority – negatively correlates with the level of religious competition, thereby undermining the utility of religion as a political resource for religious parties. Likewise, a religious party's organizational structure outlines the limits of the party's ideological flexibility and target audience. These religious institutional features collectively mediate the conflict between religious actors over religious authority and political power and impact religious party evolution in critical ways.

My answer to the question of why religious parties become less anti-system underscores competition over political and religious power. This religious competition is embedded within two distinct institutional structures. First, the extent of centralization, or decentralization, of religious authority in a religion shapes the strategies used by religious parties to vie for such authority. In cases where a centralized, hierarchically organized, and autonomous religious institution such as the Vatican defines the parameters of the religious sphere, religious parties have greater difficulty breaking free from the monopoly of such an institution, ultimately weakening their claim on religious and moral authority. In cases such as Sunni Islam where a centralized religious institution does not exist, religious political parties are able to assert religious authority because they are not competing with a powerful central religious institution. Religiopolitical movements tend to justify their political legitimacy on religious grounds by claiming religious authority and authenticity in the absence of a centralized religious institution. Religious authority is so central to religious parties' identity because it defines the limits of political discourse in which religious parties can engage. Second, the nature of the relationship between the religious party and the religious movement from which the party hails constitutes a key element of the institutional environment that religious parties operate within and shapes the incentive structure that they face. This relationship fundamentally alters the political landscape and the meaning of electoral politics for religious parties, with crucial implications for ideological rigidity. Religious parties typically evolve out of mass religious movements; when they do, the party-movement hybrid structure – where the religious party maintains some form of an organic and subservient relationship to the religious movement – tends to be the parties' preferred organizational structure. Hybrid structures, in turn, entrench ideological rigidity and reinforce the confessional dilemma for religious parties.

My analysis began with an overview of the creation of Sunni Muslim and Catholic political identities in the early modernization periods of the Middle East and Western Europe, respectively. This historical episode highlighted the significance of religious institutions in shaping future divergence in the evolutionary trajectories of religious parties within two different contexts. At the time of their emergence, Islamist and Catholic parties embraced nearly identical religious visions for the state and society. They sought to eliminate the democratic political system and secular conceptions of the state and religion relationship and institute a state based on their religious visions and overseen by men of religion. Islamist and Catholic parties, however, gradually experienced divergent paths as they encountered distinct religious institutional environments. Only one was able to overcome its confessional dilemma.

Islamist parties faced an open field insofar as the religious sector is concerned; there was no dominant religious actor who could challenge or undermine these religious parties in their formative years. The Egyptian Muslim Brotherhood's launch in the late 1920s came about in a period of major political, social, and economic turbulence. When Hassan Al-Banna formed the Brotherhood, he faced little competition from other religious actors in Egypt. His organization was broad and encompassing, acting both as a religious movement and a political organization. The Brotherhood adopted a hybrid party-movement structure with a deeply anti-system rhetoric that sought to transform the very fabric of the state and society in their Islamic vision. The absence of a centralized religious authority structure that commanded the religious field meant the Brotherhood faced no pressure to change its organization

Conclusion 263

or ideology. When the Brotherhood had an opportunity for a fresh start following Mubarak's removal from power in 2011, the religious faction saw no reason to establish a true separation between the movement and the newly formed Freedom and Justice Party. Ennahdha's emergence in the late 1960s corresponds to the heydays of secular modernization in the postindependence Tunisia. Rachid Ghannouchi and his colleagues accurately identified the void in the religious field and formed Ennahdha as a hybrid organization. Unlike the Egyptian Brotherhood, Ennahdha's political faction was able to push back against its religious faction and create a definitive break between the political party and religious movement by implementing the Specialization Policy. The National Outlook Movement's formation in the late 1960s stands as a testament to the draw of the hybrid party-movement structure for religious parties. Despite being able to form a purely political party, Necmettin Erbakan opted for a hybrid structure because of its advantages in recruitment, grassroots mobilization, and resources. When the hybrid structure proved to be a burden rather than an asset to the party's political aspirations, the Reformists broke away from the movement and formed the AKP under Recep Tayyip Erdogan's leadership in 2001. Like in Ennahdha, winning power was a critical motivation for the party leaders. Importantly, both Ennahdha and the AKP adopted ideologies far removed from anti-system discourses.

Catholic parties forged a different path in their formative periods as they faced the Catholic Church: a formidable religious actor wielding near universal control of the Catholic faith. A new endeavor that claimed to speak for or represent Catholicism such as the Catholic political parties had to confront the Church as they fought to create a religiopolitical identity. In Germany, the Center Party's origins lay in waves of anticlerical attacks in the nineteenth century. Middle-class German Catholics' calls for a more direct and political response to the anticlericalism in Germany through a Catholic political party did not resonate with the Catholic Church because of the Church's concern about losing the power over the Catholic faithful. The Center Party's eventual emergence in the 1870s came about as a secular party divorced from the Catholic Church and the broader Catholic mass movement. The Italian Popular Party (PPI) was subject to most pressure by the Catholic Church because of its proximity to the Vatican. Rooted in the activism of Opera dei Congressi and Catholic Action movements, Don Luigi Sturzo formed the PPI in 1919. Sturzo's efforts to convince the Church to form a Catholic party eventually pushed him to pursue his political plans entirely outside of the Catholic structure in Italy, including the mass movement. The Church's strict control over the organizational structure of Catholic mass movement activism in Italy left no room for Sturzo to integrate his nascent party into the Catholic movement. The PPI's short-lived existence as a secular party came to an end in part because of the Vatican's pressure on party leadership. In Belgium, the Catholic Party's path to formation was notably different from other Catholic parties despite similar beginnings. Catholic religiopolitical organization and activism emerged in response to the Belgian government's anticlerical policies that started in the 1850s. By appealing to various socioeconomic segments of the Belgian Catholics, The Federation, the Boerenbond, and the Belgian Democratic League formed a formidable Catholic mass movement that forged a political Catholic identity. Despite being under ultramontane influence early on, the Belgian Democratic League gradually assumed the party's control following the expansion of suffrage in Belgium in the 1890s.

A comparative analysis of Sunni Islamist parties of the Middle East and the Catholic parties of Western Europe is not merely an interesting methodological exercise, but an analytically imperative endeavor to better understand religious party evolution. The perception largely remains that these are two inherently different kinds of political parties, thereby subject to different causal dynamics. One obvious drawback of this assumption is that it compartmentalizes the religion-politics relationship in differing religious contexts and essentializes religious parties. Consequently, it undermines our ability to account for longitudinal change in either set of religious parties. In contrast to past efforts, this book engaged in a rare case of comparative cross-national empirical research into religious parties' evolution across time and space. It focused on the nearly identical anti-system characters of both sets of religious parties in their formative stages, the differences in religious institutional structures, and the differential effects of religious institutions on the evolution of religious parties.

The role of religion in government and public policy constitutes a major challenge to governance in modern times. Religious parties especially tend to play the role of spoiler to democratization and democratic governance around the world. In Muslim-majority countries, this issue is compounded by the permissive religious institutional environment that religious parties operate within; Islamist parties capitalize on the absence of a centralized hierarchical religious authority and take on hybrid party-movement structures to claim to represent the faith. Governments, as a result, struggle to contain Islamist parties to the political sphere. On July 15, 2020, Jordan's Court of Cassation ruled that the Jordanian Muslim Brotherhood failed to "rectify its legal status" and dissolved the group.[1] This is another step in the long history of conflict between Islamist groups and state authorities, both in Jordan and beyond. What distinguishes this episode from previous bouts of confrontation is the emphasis on separating political and religious activism. As Oraib Rintawi observes, the Jordanian government aimed to send "a strong message to the Brotherhood that they must seriously look into separating their charitable, social and educational activities from politics."[2] The Islamic Action Front (IAF) – the Jordanian Muslim Brotherhood's political

---

[1] "Jordan Dissolves Muslim Brotherhood, Moves Closer to Saudi-UAE Camp," *The Arab Weekly*, July 17, 2020. Available at: https://thearabweekly.com/jordan-dissolves-muslim-brotherhood-moves-closer-saudi-uae-camp

[2] "Jordan Top Court Dissolves Country's Muslim Brotherhood," *Yahoo News*, July 16, 2020. Available at: https://news.yahoo.com/jordan-top-court-dissolves-countrys-muslim-brotherhood-103952921.html

Conclusion

arm – is already in the Jordanian parliament, so a formal and complete separation would allow the IAF to fully dedicate itself to political activism. The expectation is that such a formal separation would facilitate a political distinction between the party and the movement and temper the party's sharp anti-system discourse by incentivizing the political over the religious.

The ideological orientation of Islamist parties has historically garnered notable interest across various religious contexts. Islamist parties often face high levels of scrutiny because of their nontransparent organizational structures and the multiplicity of voices emanating from distinct parts of their organization. Most contemporary analyses, especially of Islamist parties, disproportionately focus on the factors behind their ideological change, social activism, and intraparty conflicts at the expense of their organizational structures, despite the latter's great political and policy relevance. Until recently, Islamist parties were almost uniformly organized as hybrid party-movements. The opening of and ensuing variation in the political space across the region contributed to the process of organizational divergence among Islamist parties. Islamist movements are mass organizations that draw support on the grounds of religious identity as well as ethnicity, clientelism, social services, and anti-elite backlash, depending on the specific context.

This lack of focus on Islamist organizational structures, however, is troubling and might reflect one of two ways of thinking on this issue. First, the ultimate goal of Islamist parties remains the same with or without organizational change. Islamist parties want to Islamize the state and the society; therefore, focus on the organizational structures of these parties is inconsequential. If anything, such organization can only make these parties more effective in their pursuit of Islamization. Second, Islamist parties might be insincere in their attempts at reorganization. Organizational change might serve to mislead others into believing that there has been real change when there has not. In other words, change is merely a façade and reflects the duplicity used by Islamists to achieve their goals.

While both perspectives might have some truth to them, they obscure critical information regarding the significance of the broader context in which these organizational reforms arise and their implications for the future of these parties. First, as rational actors, Islamists spend time on how to effectively organize, reach out to their audiences, and achieve their policy and political goals. Organizational changes of Islamist groups are a product of serious deliberation and reflect factional conflict resulting from the divisions created by their hybrid movement-party structures. The resultant changes are, indeed, consequential for the direction of the party. Therefore, their preferred organizational structure conveys a great deal of information about how these parties deliberate and operate as rational actors. Second, the organizational structure of Islamist parties has important implications for their discourse and ideologies. It is no coincidence that organizational change in the Moroccan Party for Justice and Development, Tunisian Ennahdha, and Turkish Justice and Development Party is accompanied by ideological change. Religious parties do not remain faithful to the same organizational structure during their lifetime; instead, they adopt changes pro-actively in their political journeys. Lastly, Islamist parties' organizational structures are intimately tied to the way they use religion. Religious parties value religion because of its utility as a political resource for boosting political identification, legitimizing their discourse, and mobilizing voters.

Islamist parties do not make their decisions about their organizational structures in a vacuum. Decisions to reform – or not – are strategic choices that reflect Islamist movements' evaluation of their environments and the ways to respond to them in order to achieve their policy and political objectives. Therefore, it is important to identify the dynamics behind their thinking and decision-making on organizational structures. As I examined in this book, organizational reform in Islamist parties represents the underlying conflict between the political and religious factions of these parties. And this conflict is not an insignificant one – it can potentially determine the identity, audience, and policy platform of the party. Despite the appearance of unity in the goals that different factions pursue, whichever faction – religious or political – wins the conflict over the organizational structure of the party shapes the future direction of the party: Who is the audience? What kinds of policies will be pursued? Who will assume the party's leadership? What is the religion's role? The cost of engaging in organizational reform can be high; parties that engage in these reform efforts are usually locked into certain paths that are difficult to break from.

Multiple policy options exist for incentivizing organizational reform within Islamist parties, with the end goal of facilitating a process of ideological reform. However, ideological change should be a result of these policies, not a direct subject of them. Past attempts to directly compel Islamist parties to change their ideologies have largely been ineffective beyond tempering their violent tinge. Therefore, policies must aim to anchor ideological change in Islamist parties in their organizational restructuring. Organizational change is typically less confrontational; it offers the opportunity to frame legal political participation as a carrot in exchange for organizational reform. This strategy should be pursued for good reason. Islamist parties' hybrid organizational structures afford these parties an advantage over non-Islamist parties by enabling them to draw on their movements for recruitment, mobilization, and resources, which their non-Islamist peers lack. It is impossible to overstate the importance of such hybrid organizational structures for Islamists; one of the key reasons why many governments across the Muslim world are wary of installing democratization reforms is the prospect of an Islamist landslide victory should they open up the political system. Many non-Islamist parties lack the resources and grassroots mobilization to offer them a chance at competing with Islamist parties. In this regard, the policies to push Islamist parties toward organizational reform can serve to level the playing field for other political parties in the system. Islamist parties and their hybrid organizational structures command an inherent advantage over others. These regulations can create the conditions for fair political competition.

One question that requires an answer is, why would Islamists agree to an organizational change? Islamists likely believe that the organizational structure

Conclusion

that served them well for so long will continue doing so in the future; therefore, convincing them of the necessity of change can prove difficult. The question, however, rests on the assumption that Islamists are homogenous and act in unison. Yet, the division between religious and political factions among Islamists can prove to be crucial. Policies that seek Islamist organizational reform need to take advantage of this existing cleavage between the two factions. The prospect of legal political participation can empower the political faction, which tends to be weaker vis-à-vis the religious faction. This policy has a chance of success only insofar as the political faction pushes for and embraces organizational reform policy, which in turn is incentivized by an avenue for legal political participation.

Three policy options stand out for reforming Islamist party organizations: organizational, personnel, and financial separation. These policy options are not mutually exclusive and can work in complementary ways. Organizational separation refers to the idea that the explicitly political activism of social movements should be formally separated from their nonpolitical activism. The policy should apply to Islamist and non-Islamist groups alike. This policy aims to discontinue the hybrid organizational structure of Islamist parties and formalize the divide between their political and nonpolitical activism. For Islamist groups, their political activities should be conducted under the banner of a formal political party while the rest of the movement's social and religious activism falls outside the scope of the party. Islamists should have formally separate organizational entities – one of which is a political party – with clear delineation of objectives and scopes of activity. The objective of this policy proposal is to give the government the ability to hold political parties accountable and establish a mechanism to check on party compliance. In cases where the political party fails to uphold the formal separation between the party and the movement, the political party may face sanctions that would temporarily constrain the party's space in the formal political arena.

Another policy option is to limit the extent to which political party officials can take leadership roles in civil society organizations. Islamist parties tend to share leaders between their political and religious wings; some leaders can assume leadership positions in both wings simultaneously. The problem with shared leadership is that it facilitates coordination and collaboration between the party and the religious movement. More importantly, it enables the religious faction to rein in the political faction, undermining the latter's ability to pursue independent political action that prioritizes the preferences and interests of the party rather than the movement. Therefore, this personnel separation policy should aim to uphold the party's independence from the influence and direction of the Islamist movement. This policy would facilitate an independent trajectory for the political party by requiring the party to respond to political and electoral dynamics rather than the demands of the movement, whose primary allegiance is to its own base rather than the broader electorate. Leaders in violation of this policy may face temporary suspensions from political activity.

Lastly, a financial separation policy could mandate Islamist parties to clearly distinguish their finances from the religious movement they hail from. Such funding separation must encompass routine operation of the party, grassroots mobilization, electoral campaigns, and personnel compensation. The policy should extend to all systematic in-kind contributions and support the party might receive from the movement. The intended objective of this policy is to compel Islamist parties to develop greater dependence on the broader electorate rather than the religious movement. Continued reliance on the religious movement they hail from would suggest limited independence on the part of the party and should be a cause of concern.

Islamist organizational change can be incentivized in directions that facilitate ideological change away from anti-system positions and anchor broader democratization processes around these parties. In doing so, an existing division among Islamists between the political and religious factions should be the departure point. In particular, the political faction's primary interest lies in carrying out its policy preferences through political means. Therefore, conditioning their political participation on the government's rules of political engagement can provide them with a structure and incentive to push for official separation within Islamist parties between the party and the movement. This, however, requires clarity in policy expectations, commitment to regulations, and the formal space for Islamists to participate in politics. Uncertainty and obscurity only serve to undermine the incentives for the political faction.

Future research can take one of two directions on this topic. Expanding the scope of the research into geographies beyond the Middle East and Western Europe or religions beyond Sunni Islam and Catholicism is the logical next step. Such an expansion of scope can help assess how far the theory travels and whether the variation observed across Islamist and Catholic parties is context specific. Testing the theory in different contexts – in particular, varying religious contexts – is crucial to assessing the robustness of the effect of religious institutions on religious parties. Comparative analyses of religious parties in Latin America, Eastern Europe, Africa, and Israel can offer critical tests of the theory developed in this book. Religion's increased political significance and recent ascendance of religious political parties in contexts where they did not exist previously offer a unique occasion to examine institutional constraints and opportunities facing religious parties.

Further research into the organizational structures of religious parties is one of the most important avenues of research that remains largely unexplored despite a rich body of work on religious parties. As more religious parties make their way into the political space by competing in elections or taking part in governments, concern about religious parties' potential effect on the future of democratic politics has gained renewed significance. In this regard, future research should focus on the intraparty organizational dynamics of religious parties. Factional conflict, party–movement relations, and leadership and personnel decisions are all areas where more research can identify patterns that will help better illuminate dynamics of change in religious parties.

Bibliography

"The Closing Statement of the 21st Session of Ennahdha Movement Shura Council." 2018. www.ennahdha.tn/البيان-الختامي-للدورة-21-لمجلس-شورى-حركة-النهضة.

"Christian Democracy in Belgium." 1903. The Tablet. https://books.google.com/books?id=5bqKct7ChQYC&dq.

"Program of the Catholic Center Party's Reichstag Caucus (Late March 1871)." 1871. http://ghdi.ghi-dc.org/sub_document.cfm?document_id=683.

"Milli Nizam Partisi Kuruluş Beyannamesi." 1970. https://acikerisim.tbmm.gov.tr/xmlui/handle/11543/798.

A Catholic Priest. 1907. "Three Years and a Half of Pius X." *The North American Review* 184 (606): 35–45.

Abduh, Muhammad. 2000. "The Necessity of Religious Reform." In *Contemporary Debates in Islam: An Anthology of Modernist and Fundamentalist Thought*, edited by Mansoor Moaddel and Kamran Talattof, 45–52. New York: St. Martin's Press.

Abduljaber, Malek. 2018. "The Determinants of Political Cleavages in Jordan, Tunisia, and Yemen: An Analysis of Political Attitudes Structure in the Arab World." *Digest of Middle East Studies* 27 (1): 97–120.

Abedi, Amir, and Thomas Carl Lundberg. 2009. "Doomed to Failure? UKIP and the Organisational Challenges Facing Right-Wing Populist Anti-Political Establishment Parties." *Parliamentary Affairs* 62 (1): 72–87.

Abou El Fadl, Khaled. 2007. "Islam and the Challenge of Democratic Commitment." *Oriente Moderno* 87 (2): 247–300.

Abou El Fadl, Khaled. 2001. *Speaking in God's Name: Islamic Law, Authority and Women*. Oxford: Oneworld Publications.

Abu-Rabi, Ibrahim. 1997. "Facing Modernity: Ideological Origins of Islamic Revivalism." *Harvard International Review* 19 (2): 12–13, 15.

AbuKhalil, As'ad. 1994. "The Incoherence of Islamic Fundamentalism: Arab Islamic Thought at the End of the 20th Century." *Middle East Journal* 48 (4): 677–94.

Accetti, Carlo Invernizzi. 2019. *What Is Christian Democracy? Politics, Religion, and Ideology*. Cambridge: Cambridge University Press.

Achilov, Dilshod, and Renat Shaykhutdinov. 2014. "State Regulation of Religion and Radicalism in the Post-Communist Muslim Republics." *Problems of Post-Communism* 60 (5): 17–33.

Bibliography

Affan, Mohammad. 2016. "The Ennahda Movement … A Secular Party?" AlSharq Forum. https://research.sharqforum.org/2016/06/14/the-ennahda-movement-a-secular-party/.

Affan, Mohammad. 2017. "Rise and Alleged Fall of Islamism: The Case of Ennahda Movement Party." https://research.sharqforum.org/2017/08/23/rise-and-alleged-fall-of-islamism-the-case-of-ennahda-movement-party/.

Afsaruddin, Asma. 2006. "The 'Islamic State': Genealogy, Facts and Myths." *Journal of Church and State* 48 (1): 153–73.

Agócs, Sándor. 1973. "Christian Democracy and Social Modernism in Italy during the Papacy of Pius X." *Church History* 42 (1): 73–88.

Agócs, Sándor. 1975. "'Germania Doceat!' The 'Volksverein,' the Model for Italian Catholic Action, 1905–1914." *The Catholic Historical Review* 61 (1): 31–47.

Ahmadov, Ramin. 2008. "Counter Transformations in the Center and Periphery of Turkish Society and the Rise of the Justice and Development Party." *Turkish Journal of International Relations* 7 (2 & 3): 15–36.

Ahmed, Shahab. 2016. *What Is Islam? The Importance of Being Islamic.* Princeton: Princeton University Press.

Akdoğan, Yalçın. 2004. *AK Parti ve Muhafazakar Demokrasi. [AK Party and Conservative Democracy].* Istanbul: Alfa Publishing.

Akinci, Ugur. 1999. "The Welfare Party's Municipal Track Record: Evaluating Islamist Municipal Activism in Turkey." *Middle East Journal* 53 (1): 75–94.

Al-Anani, Khalil. 2011. "Egypt's Freedom & Justice Party: To Be or Not to Be Independent." https://carnegieendowment.org/sada/44324.

Al-Anani, Khalil. 2016. *Inside the Muslim Brotherhood: Religion, Identity, and Politics.* New York: Oxford University Press.

Al-Arian, Abdullah. 2014. *Answering the Call: Popular Islamic Activism in Sadat's Egypt.* Oxford: Oxford University Press.

Al-Banna, Hassan. 2009. "Toward the Light." In *Princeton Readings in Islamist Thought: Texts and Contexts from Al-Banna to Bin Laden,* edited by Roxanne L. Euben and Muhammad Qasim Zaman, 56–78. Princeton: Princeton University Press.

Al-Banna, Hassan. 1978a. "Between Yesterday and Today." In *Five Tracts of Hassan Al-Banna,* edited by Charles Wendell, 13–39. Berkeley: University of California Press.

Al-Banna, Hassan. 1978b. "On Jihad." In *Five Tracts of Hassan Al-Banna,* edited by Charles Wendell, 133–61. Berkeley: University of California Press.

Al-Banna, Hassan. 1978c. "Our Mission." In *Five Tracts of Hassan Al-Banna,* edited by Charles Wendell, 40–68. Berkeley: University of California Press.

Al-Banna, Hassan. 1978d. "Toward the Light." In *Five Tracts of Hassan Al-Banna,* edited by Charles Wendell, 103–32. Berkeley: University of California Press.

Al-Banna, Hassan. 1978e. "To What Do We Summon Mankind?" In *Five Tracts of Hassan Al-Banna,* edited by Charles Wendell, 69–102. Berkeley: University of California Press.

Al-Turabi, Hassan. 1983. "The Islamic State." In *Voices of Resurgent Islam,* edited by John L. Esposito, 241–51. New York: Oxford University Press.

Alam, Anwar. 2009. "Islam and Post-Modernism: Locating the Rise of Islamism in Turkey." *Journal of Islamic Studies* 20 (3): 352–75.

Alam, Mohammad Shahid. 2016. *Poverty from the Wealth of Nations: Integration and Polarization in the Global Economy Since 1760.* New York: Palgrave.

Alaoudh, Abdullah. 2018. "Ulama in Islamic Law-Making and Adjudication in Contemporary Egypt." *Digest of Middle East Studies* 27 (1): 121–43.

Bibliography

Alexander, Anne. 2011. "Brothers-in-Arms? The Egyptian Military, the Ikhwan and the Revolutions of 1952 and 2011." *The Journal of North African Studies* 16 (4): 533–54.

Alexander, Edgar. 1953. "Political Catholicism." In *Church and Society: Catholic Social and Political Thought and Movements 1789–1950*, edited by Joseph N. Moody. New York: Arts Inc.

Allani, Alaya. 2009. "The Islamists in Tunisia between Confrontation and Participation: 1980–2008." *The Journal of North African Studies* 14 (2): 257–72.

Almond, Gabriel A. 1948. "The Political Ideas of Christian Democracy." *The Journal of Politics* 4 (4): 734–63.

Altholz, Josef L. 1962. *The Liberal Catholic Movement in England: The "Rambler" and Its Contributors, 1848–1864*. Montreal: Palm Publishers.

Altinordu, Ateş. 2010. "The Politicization of Religion: Political Catholicism and Political Islam in Comparative Perspective." *Politics and Society* 38 (4): 517–51.

Altinordu, Ateş. 2016. "The Political Incorporation of Anti-System Religious Parties: The Case of Turkish Political Islam (1994–2011)." *Qualitative Sociology* 39 (2): 147–71.

Aly, Abd al-Monein Said, and Manfred W. Wenner. 1982. "Modern Islamic Reform Movements : The Muslim Brotherhood in Contemporary Egypt." *Middle East Journal* 36 (3): 336–61.

Anderson, Margaret Lavinia. 1981. *Windhorst: A Political Biography*. Oxford: Clarendon Press.

Anderson, Margaret Lavinia. 1986. "The Kulturkampf and the Course of German History." *Central European History* 19 (1): 82–115.

Anderson, Margaret Lavinia. 1988. "Interdenominationalism, Clericalism, Pluralism: The Zentrumsstreit and the Dilemma of Catholicism in Wilhelmine Germany." *Central European History* 21 (4): 350–78.

Anderson, Margaret Lavinia. 1995. "The Limits of Secularization: On the Problem of the Catholic Revival in Nineteenth-Century Germany." *The Historical Journal* 38 (3): 647–70.

Arango, Tim. 2013. "Turkish Liberals Turn Their Backs on Erdogan." *The New York Times*. www.nytimes.com/2013/06/20/world/europe/turkish-liberals-turn-their-backs-on-erdogan.html.

Ascoli, Max. 1935. "The Roman Church and Politics." *Foreign Affairs* 13 (3): 441–52.

Ataç, C. Akça. 2019. "Pax Ottomanica No More! The 'Peace' Discourse in Turkish Foreign Policy in the Post-Davutoğlu Era and the Prolonged Syrian Crisis." *Digest of Middle East Studies* 28 (1): 48–69.

Atacan, Fulya. 2005. "Explaining Religious Politics at the Crossroad: AKP-SP." *Turkish Studies* 6 (2): 187–99.

Atkin, Nicholas, and Frank Tallett. 2003. *Priests, Prelates and People: A History of European Catholicism since 1750*. Oxford: Oxford University Press.

Ayari, Farida. 2015. "Ennahda Movement in Power: A Long Path to Democracy." *Contemporary Review of the Middle East* 2 (1 & 2): 135–42.

Ayata, Sencer. 1996. "Patronage, Party, and State: The Politicization of Islam in Turkey." *Middle East Journal* 50 (1): 40–56.

Aydin, Senem, and Rusen Cakir. 2007. "Political Islam in Turkey." In *Political Islam and European Foreign Policy: Perspectives from Muslim Democrats of the Mediterranean*, edited by Michael Emerson and Richard Youngs, 113–35. Brussels: Centre for European Policy Studies.

Aydogan, Abdullah. 2020. "Party Systems and Ideological Cleavages in the Middle East and North Africa." *Party Politics* 27 (4): 814–26.

Ayoob, Mohammed. 2004. "Political Islam: Image and Reality." *World Policy Journal* 21 (3): 1–14.

Ayoob, Mohammed. 2008. *The Many Faces of Political Islam: Religion and Politics in the Muslim World*. Ann Arbor: University of Michigan.

Bacik, Gokhan, and Bulent Aras. 2002. "Exile: A Keyword in Understanding Turkish Politics." *The Muslim World* 92 (3–4): 387–406.

Badè, William Frederic. 1911. "Italian Modernism, Social and Religious." *The Harvard Theological Review* 4 (2): 147–74.

Badger, C. R. 1937. "Studies in Italian Nationalism, Romolo Murri." *The Australian Quarterly* 9 (4): 46–52.

Bano, Masooda. 2018. "At the Tipping Point? Al-Azhar's Growing Crisis of Moral Authority." *International Journal Middle East Studies* 50 (4): 715–34.

Banti, Alberto Mario. 2000. "Public Opinions and Associations in Nineteenth-Century Italy." In *Civil Society before Democracy: Lessons from Nineteenth-Century Europe*, edited by Nancy Bermeo and Philip Nord. Lanham: Rowman and Littlefield. pp. 43–59.

Baravelli, Andrea. 2015. "Post-War Societies (Italy)." *International Encyclopedia of the First World War*. https://encyclopedia.1914-1918-online.net/pdf/1914-1918-Online-post-war_societies_italy-2015-09-03.pdf.

Barnett, S. J. 1999. *Idol Temples and Crafty Priests: The Origins of Enlightenment Anticlericalism*. New York: Palgrave Macmillan.

Beach, Derek. 2017. "Process-Tracing Methods in Social Science." *Qualitative Political Methodology*. doi: 10.1093/acrefore/9780190228637.013.176.

Bein, Amit. 2007. "A 'Young Turk' Islamic Intellectual: Filibeli Ahmed Hilmi and the Diverse Intellectual Legacies of the Late Ottoman Empire." *International Journal Middle East Studies* 39: 607–25.

Bein, Amit. 2011. *Ottoman Ulama, Turkish Republic: Agents of Change and Guardians of Tradition*. Stanford: Stanford University Press.

Bellin, Eva. 2008. "Faith in Politics: New Trends in the Study of Religion and Politics." *World Politics* 60 (2): 315–47.

Benavot, Aaron, and Phyllis Riddle. 1988. "The Expansion of Primary Education, 1870-1940: Trends and Issues." *Sociology of Education* 61 (3): 191–210.

Benedikter, Roland. 2020. "Freemasonry in Turkey's Modern History of Ideas: A Factor of Liberalization and Individualization?" *Digest of Middle East Studies* 29 (1): 127–44.

Bennett, Andrew. 2010. "Process Tracing and Causal Inference." In *Rethinking Social Inquiry: Diverse Tools, Shared Standards*, edited by Henry E. Brady and David Collier, 2nd ed., 207–19. Lanham: Rowman and Littlefield.

Bennett, Gaymon. 2016. *Technicians of Human Dignity: Bodies, Souls, and the Making of Intrinsic Worth*. New York: Fordham University Press.

Bergin, Joseph. 1999. "The Counter-Reformation and Its Bishops." *Past & Present* 165: 30–73.

Berman, Sheri. 2008. "Taming Extremist Parties: Lessons from Europe." *Journal of Democracy* 19 (1): 5–18.

Bermeo, Nancy. 1997. "Myths of Moderation: Confrontation and Conflict during Democratic Transitions." *Comparative Politics* 29 (3): 305–22.

Bibliography

Betz, Hans-Georg, and Stefan Immerfall. 1998. *The New Politics of the Right: Neo-Populist Parties and Movements in Established Democracies*. New York: St. Martin's Press.

Bilinski, Adam. 2013. "Avoiding the 'Algerian Scenario': The Aborted Democratization of Algeria and Its Effect on Islamist Movements' Strategies in Tunisia and Egypt." Unpublished manuscript.

Binder, Leonard. 1998. "Exceptionalism and Authenticity: The Question of Islam and Democracy." *The Arab Studies Journal* 6 (1): 33–59.

Bireley, Robert. 2009. "Early-Modern Catholicism as a Response to the Changing World of the Long Sixteenth-Century." *The Catholic Historical Review* 95 (2): 219–39.

Black, Antony. 2001. *The History of Islamic Political Thought: From the Prophet to the Present*. New York: Routledge.

Blackbourn, David. 1975. "The Political Alignment of the Center Party in Wilhelmine Germany: A Study of the Party's Emergence in Nineteenth-Century Württemberg." *The Historical Journal* 18 (4): 821–50.

Blackbourn, David. 1980. *Class, Religion and Local Politics in Wilhelmine Germany: The Centre Party in Wurttemberg before 1914*. New Haven: Yale University Press.

Blancarte, Roberto J. 2000. "Popular Religion, Catholicism, and Socioreligous Dissent in Latin America." *International Sociology* 15 (4): 591–603.

Bonacina, Conrad. 1951. "The Catholic Church and Modern Democracy." *Cross Currents* 2 (1): 1–14.

Boswell, Jonathan. 1993. "Catholicism, Christian Democrats and Reformed Capitalism." In *Ethics and Markets: Cooperation and Competition within Capitalist Economies*, edited by Colin Crouch and David Marquand, 48–65. Oxford: Blackwell.

Bouscaren, Anthony Trawick. 1949. "The European Christian Democrats." *The Western Political Quarterly* 2 (1): 59–73.

Bowen, John R. 2004. "Does French Islam Have Borders? Dilemmas of Domestication in a Global Religious Field." *American Anthropologist* 106 (1): 43–55.

Brocker, Manfred, and Mirjam Kunkler. 2013. "Religious Parties: Revisiting the Inclusion-Moderation Hypothesis – Introduction." *Party Politics* 19 (2): 171–86.

Brooke, Steven. 2019. *Winning Hearts and Votes: Social Services and the Islamist Political Advantage*. Ithaca: Cornell University Press.

Brooke, Steven, and Neil Ketchley. 2018. "Social and Institutional Origins of Political Islam." *American Political Science Review* 112 (2): 376–94.

Brooks, Risa A. 2002. "Liberalization and Militancy in the Arab World." *Orbis* 46 (4): 611–21.

Brown, Nathan. 1997. "Sharia and State in the Modern Middle East." *International Journal Middle East Studies* 29 (3): 359–76.

Brown, Nathan J. 2011. "The Muslim Brotherhood as Helicopter Parent." May 27, 2011. https://carnegieendowment.org/2011/05/27/muslim-brotherhood-as-helicopter-parent-pub-44266.

Brown, Nathan J. 2012a. "Contention in Religion and State in Postrevolutionary Egypt." *Social Research: An International Quarterly* 79 (2): 531–50.

Brown, Nathan J. 2012b. "When Victory Becomes an Option: Egypt's Muslim Brotherhood Confronts Success," no. January.

Brown, Nathan J. 2012c. *When Victory Is Not an Option: Islamist Movements in Arab Politics*. Cornell: Cornell University Press.

Bibliography

Brown, Nathan, Amr Hamzawy, and Marina Ottaway. 2006. "Islamist Movements and the Democratic Process in the Arab World: Exploring the Gray Zones." Carnegie Papers No. 67.

Brubaker, Rogers, and Frederick Cooper. 2000. "Beyond 'Identity'." *Theory and Society* 29 (1): 1–47.

Brunner, Rainer. 2009. "Education, Politics, and the Struggle for Intellectual Leadership: Al-Azhar between 1927 and 1945." In *Guardians of Faith in Modern Times: 'Ulama' in the Middle East*, edited by Meir Hatina, 109–38. Leiden: Brill.

Buehler, Matt. 2013. "The Threat to 'Un-Moderate': Moroccan Islamists and the Arab Spring." *Middle East Law and Governance* 5 (3): 231–57.

Bugra, Ayse. 2002. "Political Islam in Turkey in Historical Context: Strengths and Weaknesses." In *the Politics of Permanent Crisis: Class, Ideology and State in Turkey*, edited by Neşecan Balkan and Sungur Savran, 107–45. New York: Nova Science Publishers.

Bulac, Ali. 2010. "The Most Recent Reviver in the 'Ulama Tradition: The Intellectual' Alim Fethullah Gulen." In *Muslim Citizens of the Globalized World: Contributions of the Gulen Movement*, edited by Robert A. Hunt and Yuksel A. Aslandogan, 101–20. Houston: Tughra Books.

Burns, Gene. 1990. "The Politics of Ideology: The Papal Struggle with Liberalism." *American Journal of Sociology* 95 (5): 1123–52.

Çaha, Ömer, and Ömer Baykal. 2017. "Milli Görüş Hareketinin Kuruluşu: Türk Siyasetinde Milli Nizam Partisi Deneyimi [The Establishment of National Outlook Movement: The Experiment of National Order Party in Turkish Politics]." *Gazi Üniversitesi İktisadi ve İdari Bilimler Fakültesi Dergisi* 19 (3): 788–806.

Calvin, John. 1536. "Institutes of the Christian Religion."

Campbell, Heidi. 2007. "Who's Got the Power? Religious Authority and the Internet." *Journal of Computer-Mediated Communication* 12 (3): 1043–62.

Capoccia, Giovanni. 2002 "Anti-System Parties: A Conceptual Reassessment." *Journal of Theoretical Politics* 14(1): 9–35.

Cary, Noel. 1996. *The Path to Christian Democracy*. Cambridge, MA: Harvard University Press.

Casanova, Jose. 2005. "Catholic and Muslim Politics in Comparative Perspective." *Taiwan Journal of Democracy* 1 (2): 89–108.

Casanova, Jose. 2008. "Public Religions Revisited." In *Religion: Beyond the Concept*, edited by Hent de Vries, 101–19. Fordham: Fordham University Press.

Cavatorta, Francesco. 2006. "Civil Society, Islamism and Democratisation: The Case of Morocco." *The Journal of Modern African Studies* 44 (2): 203–22.

Cavatorta, Francesco. 2012. *The Success of "Renaissance" in Tunisia and the Complexity of Tunisian Islamism*. Madrid: The International Political Science Association Conference.

Cavatorta, Francesco, and Fabio Merone. 2013. "Moderation through Exclusion? The Journey of the Tunisian Ennahda from Fundamentalist to Conservative Party." *Democratization* 20 (5): 857–75.

Cavatorta, Francesco, and Fabio Merone. 2015. "Post-Islamism, Ideological Evolution and 'La Tunisianité' of the Tunisian Islamist Party Al-Nahda." *Journal of Political Ideologies* 20 (1): 27–42.

Cerulo, Karen A. 1997. "Identity Construction: New Issues, New Directions." *Annual Review of Sociology* 23: 385–409.

Bibliography

Cerutti, Furio. 1999. "On the Political Identity of the Europeans." Working Paper.

Çevik, Salim. 2019. "Erdoğan's Comprehensive Religious Policy (Management of the Religious Realm in Turkey)." www.swp-berlin.org/en/publication/erdogans-comprehensive-religious-policy/.

Chadwick, Owen. 1990. *The Secularization of the European Mind in the Nineteenth Century*. New York: Cambridge University Press.

Chambers, Richard L. 1972. "The Ottoman Ulema and the Tanzimat." In *Scholars, Saints, and Sufis: Muslim Religious Institutions in the Middle East since 1500*, edited by Nikki R. Keddie, 33–46. Berkeley: University of California Press.

Chamkhi, Tarek. 2015. "Neo-Islamism after the Arab Spring: Case Study of the Tunisian Ennahda Party." Murdoch University.

Chaves, Mark. 1994. "Secularization as Declining Religious Authority." *Social Forces* 72 (3): 749–74.

Ciftci, Sabri. 2021. *Islam, Justice, and Democracy*. Philadelphia: Temple University Press.

Cizre, Umit. 2008. "The Justice and Development Party and the Military: Recreating the Past after Reforming It?" In *Secular and Islamic Politics in Turkey*, edited by Umit Cizre, 132–72. New York: Routledge.

Cizre, Umit. 2009. *Secular and Islamic Politics in Turkey: The Making of the Justice and Development Party*. Edited by Umit Cizre. New York: Routledge.

Cizre, Umit, and Menderes Cinar. 2003. "Turkey 2002: Kemalism, Islamism, and Politics in the Light of the February 28 Process." *The South Atlantic Quarterly* 102 (2/3): 309–32.

Clark, Janine Astrid 2004. *Islam, Charity and Activism: Middle-Class Networks and Social Welfare in Egypt, Jordan and Yemen*. Bloomington: Indiana University Press.

Clark, Janine Astrid. 2006. "The Conditions of Islamist Moderation: Unpacking Cross-Ideological Cooperation in Jordan." *International Journal of Middle East Studies* 38 (4): 539–60.

Clark, Janine Astrid. 2012. "Patronage, Prestige, and Power: The Islamic Center Charity Society's Political Role within the Muslim Brotherhood." In *Islamist Politics in the Middle East: Movements and Change*, edited by Samer Shehata, 68–87. New York: Routledge.

Cole, Juan Ricardo. 1999. *Colonialism and Revolution in the Middle East: Social and Cultural Origins of Egypt's Urabi Movement*. Cairo: American University of Cairo Press.

Collier, David. 2011. "Understanding Process Tracing." *PS: Political Science and Politics* 44 (4): 823–30.

Commins, David. 1986. "Religious Reformers and Arabists in Damascus, 1885–1914." *International Journal of Middle East Studies* 18 (4): 405–35.

Cook, Michael. 2014. *Ancient Religions, Modern Politics: The Islamic Case in Comparative Perspective*. Princeton: Princeton University Press.

Cowell-Meyers, Kimberly. 2002. *Religion and Politics in the Nineteenth-Century: The Party Faithful in Ireland and Germany*. London: Praeger.

Crecelius, Daniel. 1972. "Nonideological Responses of the Egyptian Ulama to Modernization." In *Scholars, Saints, and Sufis: Muslim Religious Institutions in the Middle East since 1500*, edited by Nikki R. Keddie, 167–210. Berkeley: University of California Press.

Crone, Patricia, and Martin Hinds. 1986. *God's Caliph: Religious Authority in the First Centuries of Islam*. New York: Cambridge University Press.

Cunsolo, Ronald S. 1993. "Nationalists and Catholics in Giolittian Italy: An Uneasy Collaboration." *The Catholic Historical Review* 79 (1): 22–53.

Curran, Charles. 2002. *Catholic Social Teaching, 1891–Present: A Historical, Theological, and Ethical Analysis.* Washington DC: Georgetown University Press.

Dabashi, Hamid. 1989a. *Authority in Islam: From the Rise of Muhammad to the Establishment of the Umayyads.* New Brunswick: Transaction Publishers.

Dabashi, Hamid. 1989b. "By What Authority? The Formation of Khomeini's Revolutionary Discourse, 1964–1977." *Social Compass* 36 (4): 511–538.

Dagi, Ihsan. 2005. "Transformation of Islamic Political Identity in Turkey: Rethinking the West and Westernization." *Turkish Studies* 6 (1): 21–37.

Dawes, Helena. 2011. "The Catholic Church and the Woman Question: Catholic Feminism in the Early 1900s." *The Catholic Historical Review* 97 (3): 484–526.

Day, Victor. 1932. "The Catholic Church in Belgium (1919–1931)." *The Catholic Historical Review* 18 (3): 297–327.

Defossez, Philippe. 1972. "Jeune Droite et Vieille Droite Avant Le Congrès Catholique de 1909." *Belgisch Tijdschrift Voor Nieuwste Geschiedenis* 3 (3–4): 285–332.

Diamant, Alfred. 1957. "Austrian Catholics and the First Republic, 1918–1934: A Study in Anti-Democratic Thought." *The Western Political Quarterly* 10 (3): 603–33.

Diotallevi, Luca. 2002. "Internal Competition in a National Religious Monopoly: The Catholic Effect and the Italian Case." *Sociology of Religion* 63 (2): 137–56.

Djupe, Paul, and J Tobin Grant. 2001. "Religious Institutions and Political Participation in America." *Journal for the Scientific Study of Religion* 40 (2): 303–14.

Doizy, Guillaume. 2006. "From Anticlerical Caricature to Biblical Farce." *Archives de sciences sociales des religions* 134 (2): 63–91.

Domenico, Roy P., and Mark Y. Hanley. 2006. *Encyclopedia of Modern Christian Politics: Volume 2: L-Z.* Edited by Roy P. Domenico and Mark Y. Hanley. London: Greenwood.

Donker, Teije Hidde, and Kasper Ly Netterstrøm. 2017. "The Tunisian Revolution & Governance of Religion." *Middle East Critique* 26 (2): 137–57.

Donno, Daniela, and Bruce Russett. 2004. "Islam, Authoritarianism, and Female Empowerment: What Are the Linkages?" *World Politics* 56 (4): 582–607.

Dorraj, Manochehr. 1998. "Tunisia's Troubled Path of Democratization." *Digest of Middle East Studies* 7 (4): 13–18.

Driessen, Michael D. 2013. "Religious Democracy and Civilizational Politics: Comparing Political Islam and Political Catholicism." *Center for International and Regional Studies: Georgetown University* Occasional.

Driessen, Michael D. 2014. *Religion and Democratization: Framing Religious and Political Identities in Muslim and Catholic Societies.* New York: Oxford University Press.

Drury, Marjule Anne. 2001. "Anti-Catholicism in Germany, Britain, and the United States: A Review and Critique of Recent Scholarship." *Church History* 70 (1): 98–131.

Durham, W. Cole Jr., and A. Dushku. 1993. "Traditionalism, Secularism, and the Transformative Dimension of Religious Institutions." *Brigham Young University Law Review* 2 (2): 165–421.

Eickelman, Dale, and James Piscatori. 1996. *Muslim Politics.* Princeton: Princeton University Press.

Eisenhart, Tess Lee. 2010. "Metamorphosis or Maturation: Organizational Continuity in Egypt's Muslim Brotherhood." Wesleyan University.

Eister, Allan W. 1957. "Religious Institutions in Complex Societies: Difficulties in the Theoretic Specification of Functions." *American Sociological Review* 22 (4): 387–91.

Bibliography

El-Ghobashy, Mona. 2005. "The Metamorphosis of the Egyptian Muslim Brothers." *International Journal of Middle East Studies* 37 (3): 373–95.

El-Khawas, Mohamed A. 2012. "Tunisia's Jasmine Revolution: Causes and Impact." *Mediterranean Quarterly* 23 (4): 1–24.

Emre, Suleyman Arif. 1990. *Siyasette 35 Yil – 1*. Istanbul: MGV Yayinlari.

Emre, Suleyman Arif. 2015. *Siyasette 35 Yil – 3*. Istanbul: MGV Yayinlari.

Ensminger, Jean. 1994. "The Political Economy of Religion: An Economic Anthropologist's Perspective." *Journal of Institutional and Theoretical Economics* 150 (4): 745–54.

Epstein, Klaus. 1959. *Matthias Erzberger and the Dilemma of German Democracy*. Princeton: Princeton University Press.

Ertman, Thomas. 2000. "Liberalization, Democratization, and the Origins of a 'Pillarized' Civil Society in Nineteenth-Century Belgium and the Netherlands." In *Civil Society before Democracy: Lessons from Nineteenth-Century Europe*, edited by Nancy Bermeo and Philip Nord, 155–78. Lanham: Rowman and Littlefield.

Esposito, John L. 1997. "Claiming the Center: Political Islam in Transition." *Harvard International Review* 19 (2): 8–11, 60–61.

Esposito, John L. 2002. *What Everyone Needs to Know about Islam*. New York: Oxford University Press.

Esposito, John L., and James P. Piscatori. 1991. "Democratization and Islam." *Middle East Journal* 45 (3): 427–40.

Esposito, John L., and Natana DeLong-Bas. 2001. *Women in Muslim Family Law*. 2nd ed. Syracuse: Syracuse University Press.

Euben, Roxanne L. 1997. "Premodern, Antimodern or Postmodern? Islamic and Western Critiques of Modernity." *The Review of Politics* 59 (3): 429–59.

Evans, Ellen Lovell 1984. "Catholic Political Movements in Germany, Switzerland, and the Netherlands: Notes for a Comparative Approach." *Central European History* 17 (2): 91–119.

Evans, Ellen Lovell. 1999. *The Cross and the Ballot: Catholic Political Parties in Germany, Switzerland, Austria, Belgium and The Netherlands, 1785–1985*. Boston: Brill Academic Publishers.

Fabbe, Kristin. 2019. *Disciples of the State? Religion and State-Building in the Former Ottoman World*. Cambridge: Cambridge University Press.

Farag, Mona. 2012. "Egypt's Muslim Brotherhood and the January 25 Revolution: New Political Party, New Circumstances." *Contemporary Arab Affairs* 5 (2): 214–29.

Farr, Ian. 1983. "From Anti-Catholicism to Anticlericalism: Catholic Politics and the Peasantry in Bavaria, 1860–1900." *European Studies Review* 13 (2): 249–69.

Feuer, Sarah J. 2017. *Regulating Islam: Religion and the State in Contemporary Morocco and Tunisia*. Cambridge: Cambridge University Press.

Fish, Stephen M. 2002. "Islam and Authoritarianism." *World Politics* 55 (1): 4–37.

Foot, John M. 1997. "'White Bolsheviks'? The Catholic Left and the Socialists in Italy-1919–1920." *The Historical Journal* 40 (2): 415–33.

Fox, Jonathan. 1999. "Do Religious Institutions Support Violence or the Status Quo?" *Studies in Conflict and Terrorism* 22 (2): 119–39.

Fox, Jonathan, and Shmuel Sandler. 2005. "Separation of Religion and State in the Twenty-First Century: Comparing the Middle East and Western Democracies." *Comparative Politics* 37 (3): 317–35.

Freer, Courtney. 2018. *Rentier Islamism: The Influence of the Muslim Brotherhood in Gulf Monarchies*. Oxford: Oxford University Press.

Freston, Paul. 2017. *Protestant Political Parties: A Global Survey. Protestant Political Parties: A Global Survey.* London: Routledge.

Gasiorowski, Mark J. 1992. "The Failure of Reform in Tunisia." *Journal of Democracy* 3 (4): 85–97.

Gedmin, Jeffrey. 2019. "Right-Wing Populism in Germany: Muslims and Minorities after the 2015 Refugee Crisis." *The One Percent Problem: Muslims in the West and the Rise of the New Populists.* www.brookings.edu/research/right-wing-populism-in-germany-muslims-and-minorities-after-the-2015-refugee-crisis/.

Gellott, Laura. 1988. "Defending Catholic Interests in the Christian State: The Role of Catholic Action in Austria, 1933–1938." *The Catholic Historical Review* 74 (4): 571–89.

George, Alexander L., and Andrew Bennett. 2005. *Case Studies and Theory Development in the Social Sciences.* Cambridge, MA: MIT Press.

Gerring, John. 2007. "Is There a (Viable) Crucial-Case Method?" *Comparative Political Studies* 40 (3): 231–53.

Gill, Anthony. 2008. *Rendering unto Caesar: The Catholic Church and the State in Latin America.* Chicago: Chicago University Press.

Gill, Anthony. 2001. "Religion and Comparative Politics." *Annual Review of Political Science* 4: 117–38.

Gill, Anthony. 2019. "A Great Re-Awakening: The Return to a Political Economy of Religion." In *Advances in the Economics of Religion,* edited by J. P. Carvalho, S. Iyer, and J. Rubin, 361–76. Cham: Palgrave Macmillan.

Gingeras, Ryan. 2019. *Eternal Dawn: Turkey in the Age of Ataturk.* Oxford: Oxford University Press.

Glenn, Gary D., and John Stack. 2000. "Is American Democracy Safe for Catholicism?" *The Review of Politics* 62 (1): 5–29.

Goldstone, Jack. 2003. "Introduction: Bridging Institutionalized and Noninstitutionalized Politics." In *States, Parties and Social Movements,* edited by Jack Goldstone, 1–26. Cambridge: Cambridge University Press.

Gontijo, Lorenzo C. B., and Roberson S. Barbosa. 2020. "Erdoğan's Pragmatism and the Ascension of AKP in Turkey: Islam and Neo-Ottomanism." *Digest of Middle East Studies* 29 (1): 76–91.

Goodstein, Laurie. 2012. "Religion: Priest Excommunicated for Ordaining a Woman." *The New York Times.*

Gorski, Philip S. 2000. "Historicizing the Secularization Debate: Church, State, and Society in Late Medieval and Early Modern Europe, ca. 1300 to 1700." *American Sociological Review* 65 (1): 138–67.

Gorski, Philip S., and Ateş *Altinordu.* 2008. "After Secularization?" *Annual Review of Sociology* 34: 55–85.

Greenhouse, Steven. 1988. "Rebel Archbishop Anoints 4 Bishops." *The New York Times.*

Greif, Avner, and David D. Laitin. 2004. "A Theory of Endogenous Institutional Change." *American Political Science Review* 98 (4): 633–52.

Grew, Raymond. 2003. "Suspended Bridges to Democracy." In *European Christian Democracy: Historical Legacies and Comparative Perspectives,* edited by Thomas Kselman and Joseph A. Buttigieg, 11–42. Notre Dame: Notre Dame University Press.

Grewal, Sharan. 2018. "Can Tunisia Find a Compromise on Equal Inheritance?" *Order from Chaos.* www.brookings.edu/blog/order-from-chaos/2018/09/25/can-tunisia-find-a-compromise-on-equal-inheritance/.

Bibliography

Grewal, Sharan. 2020. "From Islamists to Muslim Democrats: The Case of Tunisia's Ennahda." *American Political Science Review* 114 (2): 519–35.

Grewal, Sharan, Amaney A. Jamal, Tarek Masoud, and Elizabeth R. Nugent. 2019. "Poverty and Divine Rewards: The Electoral Advantage of Islamist Political Parties." *American Journal of Political Science* 63 (4): 859–74.

Gross, Michael B. 2004. *The War against Catholicism: Liberalism and the Anti-Catholic Imagination in Nineteenth-Century Germany*. Ann Arbor: University of Michigan Press.

Grzymala-Busse, Anna. 2012. "Why Comparative Politics Should Take Religion (More) Seriously." *Annual Review of Political Science* 15 (1): 421–42.

Grzymala-Busse, Anna. 2015. *Nations under God: How Churches Use Moral Authority to Influence Policy*. Princeton: Princeton University Press.

Guerlac, Othon. 1908. "The Separation of Church and State in France." *Political Science Quarterly* 23 (2): 259–96.

Guiler, Kimberly G. 2020. "From Prison to Parliament: Victimhood, Identity, and Electoral Support." *Mediterranean Politics* 26 (2): 168–97.

Gulalp, Haldun. 1999. "Political Islam in Turkey: The Rise and Fall of the Refah Party." *The Muslim World* 89 (1): 22–41.

Gulalp, Haldun. 2001. "Globalization and Political Islam: The Social Bases of Turkey's Welfare Party." *International Journal of Middle East Studies* 33 (3): 433–48.

Gumuscu, Sebnem, and Deniz Sert. 2009. "The Power of the Devout Bourgeoisie: The Case of the Justice and Development Party in Turkey." *Middle Eastern Studies* 45 (6): 953–68.

Gunes-Ayata, Ayse. 2003. "From Euro-Scepticism to Turkey Scepticism: Changing Political Attitudes on the European Union in Turkey." *Journal of Southern Europe and the Balkans* 5 (2): 205–22.

Gunther, Richard, and Larry Diamond. 2003. "Species of Political Parties: A New Typology." *Party Politics* 9 (2): 167–199.

Gurbuz, Mustafa. 2014. *The Long Winter: Turkish Politics after the Corruption Scandal*. Rethink Paper 15.

Gurses, Mehmet. 2014. "Islamists, Democracy and Turkey: A Test of the Inclusion-Moderation Hypothesis." *Party Politics* 20 (4): 646–53.

Hafen, Bruce. 1992. "Disciplinary Procedures." In *Encyclopedia of Mormonism*. Macmillan Publishing Company.

Haider, Aliya. 2002. "The Rhetoric of Resistance: Islamism, Modernity, and Globalization." *Harvard Blackletter Law Journal* 18: 91–128.

Hall, Thomas. 1913. "Christianity and Politics: IV. Politics and the Reformation." *The Biblical World* 41 (4): 229–35.

Hallaq, Wael. 1999. *A History of Islamic Legal Theories: An Introduction to Sunni Usul Al Fiqh*. New York: Cambridge University Press.

Hallaq, Wael. 2009. *An Introduction to Islamic Law*. New York: Cambridge University Press.

Hallaq, Wael. 2012. *The Impossible State: Islam, Politics, and Modernity's Moral Predicament*. Columbia, NY: Columbia University Press.

Hallaq, Wael B. 1999. "The Authenticity of Prophetic Hadith: A Pseudo-Problem." *Studia Islamica* 89: 75–90.

Hallaq, Wael B. 2003. "Juristic Authority vs. State Power: The Legal Crises of Modern Islam." *Journal of Law and Religion* 19 (2): 243–58.

Halperin, S. William. 1947. "Italian Anticlericalism, 1871–1914." *The Journal of Modern History* 19 (1): 18–34.

Halperin, S. William. 1974. "Catholic Journalism in Italy and the Italo-Papal Conflict of the 1870's." *The Catholic Historical Review* 59 (4): 587–601.

Hamid, Eltigani A. 2004. *The Qur'an Politics: A Study of the Origins of Political Thought in the Makkan Qur'an.* 1st ed. Herndon: International Institute of Islamic Thought.

Hamid, Shadi. 2014. *Temptations of Power: Islamists and Illiberal Democracy in a New Middle East.* Oxford: Oxford University Press.

Hamid, Shadi. 2017. "Islamists on Islamism Today: An Interview with Amr Darrag, Leading Muslim Brotherhood Figure." www.brookings.edu/blog/markaz/2017/02/09/islamists-on-islamism-today-an-interview-with-amr-darrag-prominent-egyptian-muslim-brotherhood-figure/.

Hamil-Luker, Jenifer, and Christian Smith. 1998. "Religious Authority and Public Opinion on the Right to Die." *Sociology of Religion* 59 (4): 373–91.

Hamzawy, Amr, and Nathan J. Brown. 2008. "Islamist Parties and Democracy: A Boon or a Bane for Democracy?" *Journal of Democracy* 19 (3): 49–54.

Hanley, David. 1994. "Introduction: Christian Democracy as a Political Phenomenon." In *Christian Democracy in Europe: A Comparative Perspective*, edited by David Hanley, 1–14. London: Pinter.

Harik, Palmer. 1996. "Between Islam and the System: Sources and Implications of Popular Support for Lebanon's Hizballah." *Journal of Conflict Resolution* 40 (1): 41–67.

Hashemi, Nader. 2009. *Islam, Secularism, and Liberal Democracy: Toward a Democratic Theory for Muslim Societies.* New York: Oxford University Press.

Hastings, Adrian, ed. 1990. *Modern Catholicism: Vatican II and after.* Oxford: Oxford University Press.

Hatina, Meir. 2009a. "Introduction." In *Guardians of Faith in Modern Times: 'Ulama' in the Middle East*, edited by Meir Hatina, 1–17. Leiden: Brill.

Hatina, Meir. 2009b. "The Clerics' Betrayal? Islamists, 'Ulama' and the Polity." In *Guardians of Faith in Modern Times: 'Ulama' in the Middle East*, edited by Meir Hatina, 247–62. Berkeley: University of California Press.

Herbermann, Charles. 1910. *The Catholic Encyclopedia: An International Work of Reference on the Constitution, Doctrine, Discipline, and History of the Catholic Church.* Robert Appleton.

Hefner, Robert W. 2001. "Public Islam and the Problem of Democratization." *Sociology of Religion* 62 (4): 491–514.

Heilbronner, Oded. 2006. "The Age of Catholic Revival." In *A Companion to Nineteenth-Century Europe, 1789–1914*, edited by Stefan Berger, 236–47. Malden: Blackwell Publishing.

Helmy, Khaled. 2006. "The Contrasting Fates of Middle Eastern Politicized Islam and European Politicized Christianity." Religion and Democracy Seminar, Columbia University.

Hennesey, James. 1988. "Leo XIII: Intellectualizing the Combat with Modernity." *U.S. Catholic Historian* 7 (4): 393–400.

Heper, Metin. 2013. "Islam, Conservatism, and Democracy in Turkey: Comparing Turgut Özal and Recep Tayyip Erdoğan." *Insight Turkey* 15 (2): 141–56.

Herzog, Michael. 2006. "Can Hamas Be Tamed?" *Foreign Affairs* 85 (2): 83–94.

Heyworth-Dunne, James. 1950. *Religious and Political Trends in Modern Egypt.* Washington.

Hill, Edmund. 1989. "Who Does the Teaching in the Church?" *New Blackfriars* 70 (824): 67–73.

Bibliography

Hintz, Lisel. 2018. *Identity Politics Inside Out: National Identity Contestation and Foreign Policy in Turkey*. Oxford: Oxford University Press.

Hoebink, Michel. 1999. "Thinking about Renewal in Islam: Towards a History of Islamic Ideas on Modernization and Secularization." *Arabica* 46 (1): 29–62.

Hughes, Aaron W. 2013. *Muslim Identities: An Introduction to Islam*. New York: Columbia University Press.

Huntington, Samuel P. 1993. *The Third Wave: Democratization in the Late Twentieth Century*. Norman: University of Oklahoma Press.

Huntington, Samuel P. 1996. "The West: Unique, Not Universal." *Foreign Affairs*, 75 (Nov/Dec): 28–46.

Iannaccone, Laurence R. 1998. "Introduction to the Economics of Religion." *Journal of Economic Literature* 36 (3): 1465–95.

Iannaccone, Laurence R., and Eli Berman. 2006. "Religious Extremism: The Good, the Bad, and the Deadly." *Public Choice* 128 (1/2): 109–29.

Inglehart, Ronald, and Pippa Norris. 2003. *Rising Tide: Gender Equality and Cultural Change Around the World*. New York: Cambridge University Press.

Insel, Ahmet. 2003. "The AKP and Normalizing Democracy in Turkey." *The South Atlantic Quarterly* 102 (2/3): 293–308.

Ismail, Salwa. 2001. "The Paradox of Islamist Politics." *Middle East Report*, 221: 34–39.

Issawi, Charles. 1982. *An Economic History of the Middle East and North Africa*. New York: Columbia University Press.

Issawi, Charles. 1988. *The Fertile Crescent, 1800–1914: A Documentary Economic History*. Oxford: Oxford University Press.

Jamal, Amaney. 2013. *Of Empires and Citizens: Pro-American Democracy or No Democracy at All?* Princeton: Princeton University Press.

Jelen, Ted. 2003. *Sacred Market, Sacred Canopies: Essays on Religious Markets and Religious Pluralism*. New York: Rowman & Littlefield Publishers.

Jones, Linda G. 1988. "Portrait of Rachid Al Ghannouchi." *Middle East Research and Information Project*, no. 153.

Juergensmeyer, Mark. 2007. "The New Religious State." *Comparative Politics* 27 (4): 379–91.

Kalyvas, Stathis N. 1996. *The Rise of Christian Democracy in Europe*. Ithaca: Cornell University Press.

Kalyvas, Stathis N. 1998. "From Pulpit to Party: Party Formation and the Christian Democratic Phenomenon." *Comparative Politics* 30 (3): 293–312.

Kalyvas, Stathis N. 2000. "Commitment Problems in Emerging Democracies: The Case of Religious Parties." *Comparative Politics* 32 (4): 379–98.

Kalyvas, Stathis N. 2003. "Unsecular Politics and Religious Mobilization: Beyond Christian Democracy." In *European Christian Democracy*, 320–93.

Kalyvas, Stathis N., and Kees Van Kersbergen. 2010. "Christian Democracy." *Annual Review of Political Science* 13: 183–209.

Kamali, Masoud. 2001. "Civil Society and Islam: A Sociological Perspective." *European Journal of Sociology* 42 (3): 457–82.

Kaminski, Joseph. 2014. "Comparing Goals and Aspirations of National vs. Transnational Islamist Movements." In *Caliphates and Islamic Global Politics*, edited by Timothy Poirson and Robert L. Oprisko, 35–48. Bristol: E-International Relations.

Kandil, Hazem. 2015. "Inside the Brotherhood." *International Affairs* 91 (3): 658–60.

Karakaya, Suveyda, and A.Kadir Yildirim. 2013. "Islamist Moderation in Perspective: Comparative Analysis of the Moderation of Islamist and Western Communist Parties." *Democratization* 20 (7): 1322–49.

Karasipahi, Sena. 2009. "Comparing Islamic Resurgence Movements in Turkey and Iran." *Middle East Journal* 63 (1): 87–107.

Kardas, Tuncay, and Ali Balci. 2019. "Understanding the July 2016 Military Coup: The Contemporary Security Dilemma in Turkey." *Digest of Middle East Studies* 28 (1): 144–63.

Katznelson, Ira. 1986. "Working-Class Formation: Constructing Cases and Comparisons." In *Working-Class Formation: Nineteenth-Century Patterns in Western Europe and the United States*, edited by Ira Katznelson and Aristide R. Zolberg, 3–45. Princeton: Princeton University Press.

Kautzer, Kathleen. 2012. *The Underground Church: Nonviolent Resistance to the Vatican Empire*. Leiden: Brill.

Kaya, Serdar. 2009. "The Rise and Decline of the Turkish 'Deep State': The Ergenekon Case." *Insight Turkey* 11 (4): 99–113.

Keddie, Nikki R. 1972a. "Intellectuals in the Modern Middle East: A Brief Historical Consideration." *Daedalus* 101 (3): 39–57.

Keddie, Nikki R. 1972b. "Introduction." In *Scholars, Saints, and Sufis: Muslim Religious Institutions in the Middle East since 1500*, edited by Nikkie R. Keddie, 1–15. Berkeley: University of California Press.

Keddie, Nikki R, ed. 1972c. *Scholars, Saints, and Sufis: Muslim Religious Institutions in the Middle East Since 1500*. Berkeley: University of California Press.

Keddie, Nikki R. 2003. "Secularism and Its Discontents." *Daedalus* 132: 14–30.

Kedourie, Elie. 1992. *Politics in the Middle East*. Oxford: Oxford University Press.

Kersbergen, Kees Van. 1994. "The Distinctiveness of Christian Democracy." In *Christian Democracy in Europe: A Comparative Perspective*, edited by David Hanley, 31–62. New York: Continuum International Publishing.

Kersten, Carool, and Susanne Olsson. 2013. "Introduction: Alternative Islamic Discourses and Religious Authority." In *Alternative Islamic Discourses and Religious Authority*, edited by Carool Kersten and Susanne Olsson, 1–16. Burlington: Ashgate.

Khalid, Adeeb. 2015. "Conflict and Authority among Central Asian Muslims in the Era of the Russian Revolution." In *Jews and Muslims in the Russian Empire and Soviet Union*, edited by Martin Schulze Wessel and Michael Brenner. Göttingen: Vandenhoeck and Ruprecht.

Khomeini, Imam Ruhullah. 2000. "The Necessity of Islamic Government." In *Contemporary Debates in Islam: An Anthology of Modernist and Fundamentalist Thought*, edited by Mansoor Moaddel and Kamran Talattof, 251–62. New York: St. Martin's Press.

Kilinc, Ramazan. 2019. *Alien Citizens: The State and Religious Minorities in Turkey and France*. Omaha: University of Nebraska.

Kilinc, Ramazan, and Carolyn M. Warner. 2015. "Micro-Foundations of Religion and Public Goods Provision: Belief, Belonging, and Giving in Catholicism and Islam." *Politics and Religion* 8 (4): 718–44.

Kingston, Paul. 2001. "Reflection on Religion, Modernization, and Violence in the Islamic Middle East." *Method & Theory in the Study of Religion* 13 (3): 293–309.

Kirdiş, Esen. 2011. "Between Movement and Party: Islamic Political Party Formation in Morocco, Turkey, and Jordan."

Bibliography

Kirdiş, Esen. 2016. "Same Context, Different Political Paths: Two Islamic Movements in Turkey." *International Area Studies Review* 19 (3): 249–65.

Kirdiş, Esen. 2019. *The Rise of Islamic Political Movements and Parties: Morocco, Turkey and Jordan*. Edinburgh: Edinburgh University Press.

Kitschelt, Herbert. 1989. *The Logics of Party Formation: Ecological Politics in Belgium and West Germany*. Ithaca: Cornell University Press.

Kittell, Allan H. 1961. "Socialist vs Catholic in Belgium: The Role of Anticlericalism in the Development of the Belgian Left." *The Historian* 23 (4): 418–35.

Knapp, Thomas A. 1976. "*The Catholic Church and the Working Class in Imperial and Weimar Germany*." 9 (9): 9–11.

Knight, Kevin. 2017. "Tradition and Living Magisterium." *Catholic Encyclopedia*. www.catholicplanet.com/TSM/general-magisterium.htm.

Knippenberg, Hans. 2006. "The Political Geography of Religion: Historical State-Church Relations in Europe and Recent Challenges." *GeoJournal* 67 (4): 253–65.

Koesel, Karrie J. 2014. *Religion and Authoritarianism: Cooperation, Conflict, and the Consequences*. Cambridge: Cambridge University Press.

Kolçak, Hakan. 2020. "Consociationalism under Examination: Is Consociationalism the Optimal Multiculturalist Approach for Turkey?" *Digest of Middle East Studies* 19 (1): 26–52.

Kosebalaban, Hasan. 2005. "The Impact of Globalization on Islamic Political Identity: The Case of Turkey." *World Affairs* 168 (1): 27–37.

Krämer, Gudrun. 2006. "Drawing Boundaries: Yusuf Al-Qaradawi on Apostasy." In *Speaking for Islam: Religious Authorities in Muslim Societies*, edited by Gudrun Kramer and Sabine Schmidtke, 181–217. Boston: Brill.

Krämer, Gudrun. 2010. *Hasan Al-Banna (Makers of the Muslim World)*. Oxford: Oneworld Academic.

Krämer, Gudrun, and Sabine Schmidtke. 2006. "Introduction: Religious Authority and Religious Authorities in Muslim Societies. A Critical Review." In *Speaking for Islam: Religious Authorities in Muslim Societies*, edited by Gudrun Kramer and Sabine Schmidtke, 1–14. Boston: Brill.

Kuechler, Manfred, and Russell J. Dalton. 1990. "New Social Movements and the Political Order: Inducing Change for Long-Term Stability?" In *Challenging the Political Order: New Social and Political Movements in Western Democracies*, edited by Russell J. Dalton and Manfred Kuechler, 277–304. Cambridge, UK: Polity Press.

Kumbaracibasi, Arda Can. 2009. *Turkish Politics and the Rise of the AKP: Dilemma of Institutionalization and Leadership Strategy*. London: Routledge.

Kunkler, Mirjam, and Julia Leininger. 2009. "The Multi-Faceted Role of Religious Actors in Democratization Processes: Empirical Evidence from Five Young Democracies." *Democratization* 16 (6): 1058–92.

Kunz, Josef L. 1952. "The Status of the Holy See in International Law." *The American Journal of International Law* 46 (2): 308–14.

Kuran, Timur. 2001. "The Provision of Public Goods under Islamic Law: Origins, Impact, and Limitations of the Waqf System." *Law & Society Review* 35 (4): 841–98.

Kuran, Timur. 2016. "Legal Roots of Authoritarian Rule in the Middle East." *The American Journal of Comparative Law* 64 (2): 419–54.

Kurtz, Lester R. 1983. "The Politics of Heresy." *American Journal of Sociology* 88 (6): 1085–115.

Kuru, Ahmet T. 2005. "Globalization and Diversification of Islamic Movements: Three Turkish Cases." *Political Science Quarterly* 120 (2): 253–374.

Kuru, Ahmet T. 2006. "Reinterpretation of Secularism in Turkey: The Case of the Justice and Development Party." In *The Emergence of a New Turkey: Democracy and the AK Parti*, edited by M. Hakan Yavuz. Salt Lake City: The University of Utah Press.

Kuru, Ahmet T. 2007. "Passive and Assertive Secularism: Historical Conditions, Ideological Struggles, and State Policies toward Religion." *World Politics* 59 (4): 568–94.

Kuru, Ahmet T. 2009. *Secularism and State Policies toward Religion: The United States, France, and Turkey*. New York: Cambridge University Press.

Kuru, Ahmet T. 2012. "The Rise and Fall of Military Tutelage in Turkey: Fears of Islamism, Kurdism, and Communism." *Insight Turkey* 14 (2): 37–57.

Kuru, Ahmet. 2019. *Islam, Authoritarianism, and Underdevelopment: A Global and Historical Comparison*. Cambridge: Cambridge University Press.

Kurzman, Charles. 2003. "The Qum Protests and the Coming of the Iranian Revolution, 1975 and 1978." *Social Science History* 27 (3): 287–325.

Lakoff, George. 1995. "Metaphor, Morality, and Politics, or, Why Conservatives Have Left Liberals in the Dust." *Social Research* 62 (2): 1–22.

Landau, Jacob M. 1974. *Radical Politics in Modern Turkey*. Leiden: Brill.

Lapidus, Ira M. 1996. "State and Religion in Islamic Societies." *Past & Present* 151 (1): 3–27.

Lapidus, Ira M. 1997. "Islamic Revival and Modernity: The Contemporary Movements and the Historical Paradigms." *Journal of the Economic and Social History of the Orient* 40 (4): 444–60.

Lapidus, Ira M. 1992. "The Golden Age: The Political Concepts of Islam." *The Annals of the American Academy of Political and Social Science* 524 (1): 13–25.

Laurence, Jonathan. 2021. *Coping with Defeat: Sunni Islam, Roman Catholicism and the Modern State*. Princeton: Princeton University Press.

Lease, Gary. 2000. "Vatican Foreign Policy and the Origins of Modernism." In *Catholicism Contending with Modernity: Roman Catholic Modernism and Anti-Modernism in Historical Context*, edited by Darrell Jodock, 31–55. New York: Cambridge University Press.

Leininger, Julia. 2016. "It's Institutions, Not Theology! Muslim Actors' Influence on Democratization in Mali." *Politics and Religion* 9 (4): 815–42.

Lewis, Bernard. 1958. "Communism and Islam." In *The Middle East in Transition: Studies in Contemporary History*, edited by Walter Z. Laqueur, 311–25. London: Routledge.

Lewis, Bernard. 1988. *The Political Language of Islam*. Chicago: University of Chicago.

Lewis, Bernard. 1996. "A Historical Overview." *Journal of Democracy* 7 (2): 52–63.

Lia, Brynjar. 1998. *Society of the Muslim Brothers in Egypt: The Rise of an Islamic Mass Movement 1928–1942*. Reading: Ithaca Press.

Limage, Leslie. 2005. "The Growth of Literacy in Historic Perspective: Clarifying the Role of Formal Schooling and Adult Learning Opportunities." UNESCO. https://unesdoc.unesco.org/ark:/48223/pf0000146061.

Linden, H. Vander. 1920. *Belgium: The Making of a Nation*. Oxford: Oxford University Press.

Livny, Avital. 2020. *Trust and the Islamic Advantage Religious-Based Movements in Turkey and the Muslim World*. Cambridge: Cambridge University Press.

Bibliography

Lombardi, Ben. 1997. "Turkey – The Return of the Reluctant Generals?" *Political Science Quarterly* 112 (2): 191–215.

Lord, Robert H. 1923. "Belgium: A Study in Catholic Democracy." *The Catholic Historical Review* 9 (1): 30–47.

Lord, Ceren. 2018. *Religious Politics in Turkey: From the Birth of the Republic to the AKP*. Cambridge: Cambridge University Press.

Lord, Ceren. 2018. "The Story behind the Rise of Turkey's Ulema." *Middle East Report Online*.

Lyon, Margot. 1967. "Christian-Democratic Parties and Politics." *Journal of Contemporary History* 2 (4): 69–87.

Lyttelton, Adrian. 1983. "An Old Church and a New State: Italian Anticlericalism 1876–1915." *European Studies Review* 13 (2): 225–48.

Mackenzie, William James Millar. 1978. *Political Identity*. Manchester: Manchester University Press.

Mainwaring, Scott, and Anibal S. Perez-Linan. 2013. *Democracies and Dictatorships in Latin America: Emergence, Survival, and Fall*. Cambridge: Cambridge University Press.

Maio, Tiziana Di. 2004. "Between the Crisis of the Liberal State, Fascism and a Democratic Perspective: The Popular Party in Italy." In *Political Catholicism in Europe 1918–1945, Volume 1*, edited by Wolfram Kaiser and Helmut Wohnut. New York: Routledge.

Makdisi, George. 1981. *The Rise of Colleges: Institutions of Learning in Islam and the West*. Edinburgh: Edinburgh University Press.

Mandaville, Peter G. 2007. *Global Political Islam*. London: Routledge.

March, Andrew F. 2011 *Islam and Liberal Citizenship: The Search for an Overlapping Consensus*. Oxford: Oxford University Press.

March, James G., and Johan P. Olsen. 2005. "Elaborating the 'New Institutionalism'." 11. ARENA Working Papers.

March, James G., and Johan P. Olsen. 2008. "Elaborating the 'New Institutionalism'." In *The Oxford Handbook of Political Institutions*, edited by Sarah A. Binder, R. A. W. Rhodes, and Bert A. Rockman, 3–20. Oxford University Press.

Mardin, Serif. 1981. "Religion and Secularism in Turkey." In *Atatürk: Founder of a Modern State*, edited by Ali Kazacigil and Ergun Ozbudun, 213–17.

Mardin, Serif. 2005. "Turkish Islamic Exceptionalism Yesterday and Today: Continuity, Rupture, and Reconstruction in Operational Codes." *Turkish Studies* 6 (2): 145–65.

Marks, Monica. 2015. "Tunisia's Ennahda: Rethinking Islamism in the Context of ISIS and the Egyptian Coup."

Marschall, Melissa, Abdullah Aydogan, and Alper Bulut. 2016. "Does Housing Create Votes? Explaining the Electoral Success of the AKP in Turkey." *Electoral Studies* 42: 201–12.

Marsot, Afaf Lutfi Al-Sayyid. 1972. "The Ulama of Cairo in the Eighteenth and Nineteenth Centuries." In *Scholars, Saints, and Sufis: Muslim Religious Institutions in the Middle East since 1500*, edited by Nikki R. Keddie, 149–66. Berkeley: University of California Press.

Mason, Whit. 2000. "The Future of Political Islam in Turkey." *World Policy Journal* 17 (2): 56–67.

Masoud, Tarek. 2014. *Counting Islam: Religion, Class, and Elections in Egypt*. New York: Cambridge University Press.

Masud, Muhammad Khalid. 2005. "The Construction and Deconstruction of Secularism as an Ideology in Contemporary Muslim Thought." *Asian Journal of Social Science* 33 (3): 363–83.

Matera, Paulina. 2020. "Under Hegemonic Pressure: 2018 American Sanctions against Iran and Turkey's Response." *Digest of Middle East Studies* 29 (2): 183–99.

Matesan, Ioana Emy. 2020. "Grievances and Fears in Islamist Movements: Revisiting the Link between Exclusion, Insecurity, and Political Violence." *Journal of Global Security Studies* 5 (1): 44–62.

Maududi, Sayyid Abul A'la. 2000. "Fallacy of Rationalism." In *Contemporary Debates in Islam: An Anthology of Modernist and Fundamentalist Thought*, edited by Mansoor Moaddel and Kamran Talattof, 207–21. New York: St. Martin's Press.

McCarthy, Rory. 2018a. *Inside Tunisia's Al-Nahda: Between Politics and Preaching*. Cambridge: Cambridge University Press.

McCarthy, Rory. 2018b. "When Islamists Lose: The Politicization of Tunisia's Ennahda Movement." *The Middle East Journal* 72 (3): 365–84.

McNeill, John T. 1919. "Catholic Modernism and Catholic Dogma." *The Biblical World* 53 (5): 507–14.

Mecham, R. Quinn. 2004. "From the Ashes of Virtue, a Promise of Light: The Transformation of Political Islam in Turkey." *Third World Quarterly* 25 (2): 339–58.

Mecham, R. Quinn. 2017. *Institutional Origins of Islamist Political Mobilization*. Cambridge: Cambridge University Press.

Meddeb, Hamza. 2019. "Ennahda's Uneasy Exit from Political Islam."

Meijer, Roel. 1995. *The Quest for Modernity: Secular Liberal and Left-Wing Political Thought in Egypt, 1945–1958*. Amsterdam: University of Amsterdam.

Menchik, Jeremy. 2016. *Islam and Democracy in Indonesia: Tolerance without Liberalism*. Cambridge: Cambridge University Press.

Meral, Ziya. 2018. *How Violence Shapes Religion: Belief and Conflict in the Middle East and Africa*. Cambridge: Cambridge University Press.

Mergel, Thomas. 1996. "Ultramontanism, Liberalism, Moderation: Political Mentalities and Political Behavior of the German Catholic Bürgertum, 1848–1914." *Central European History* 29 (2): 151–74.

Merone, Fabio, Ester Sigillo, and Damiano De Facci. 2018. "Nahda and Tunisian Islamic Activism." In *New Opposition in the Middle East*, edited by Dara Conduit and Shahram Akbarzadeh, 177–201. Singapore: Palgrave Macmillan.

Misner, Paul. 1992. "Social Catholicism in Nineteenth-Century Europe: A Review of Recent Historiography." *The Catholic Historical Review* 78 (4): 581–600.

Misner, Paul. 2004. "Catholic Labor and Catholic Action: The Italian Context of 'Quadragesimo Anno.'" *The Catholic Historical Review* 90 (4): 650–74.

Mitchell, Richard P. 1993. *The Society of Muslim Brotherhood*. Oxford: Oxford University Press.

Mitchell, Timothy. 1988. *Colonising Egypt*. Cambridge: Cambridge University Press.

Mjaaland, Marius Timmann. 2013. "Apocalypse and the Spirit of Revolution: The Political Legacy of the Early Reformation." *Political Theology* 14 (2): 155–73.

Mohammed, Jihan, and Abdullah Alreth. 2020. "Iraqi Kurds: The Dream of Nation State." *Digest of Middle East Studies* 29 (2): 215–29.

Mohseni, Payam, and Clyde Wilcox. 2009. "Religion and Political Parties." In *Routledge Handbook of Religion and Politics*, edited by Jeffrey Haynes, 211–30. New York: Routledge.

Molony, John. 1977. *The Emergence of Political Catholicism in Italy: Partito Popolare, 1919–1926*. Totowa: Rowman and Littlefield.

Momayesi, Nasser. 2000. "Iran's Struggle for Democracy." *International Journal on World Peace* 17 (4): 41–70.

Bibliography

Moody, Joseph N. 1953. "From Old Regime to Democratic Society." In *Church and Society: Catholic Social and Political Thought and Movements 1789–1950*, edited by Joseph N. Moody, 95–174. New York: Arts, Inc.

Moody, Joseph N., ed. 1953. "Manifesto of the Belgian Democratic League." In *Church and Society: Catholic Social and Political Thought and Movements 1789–1950*. New York: Arts, Inc. p. 323.

Moos, Malcolm. 1945. "Don Luigi Sturzo – Christian Democrat." *The American Political Science Review* 39 (2): 269–92.

Moran, Gloria M. 1995. "The Spanish System of Church and State." *BYU Law Review* 1995 (2): 535–53.

Mork, Gordon R. 1971. "Bismarck and the 'Capitulation' of German Liberalism." *The Journal of Modern History* 43 (1): 59–75.

Mouline, Nabil. 2014. *The Clerics of Islam: Religious Authority and Political Power in Saudi Arabia*. New Haven: Yale University Press.

Moussalli, Ahmad S. 1993. "Hassan Al-Banna's Islamist Discourse on Constitutional Rule and Islamic State." *Journal of Islamic Studies* 4 (2): 161–74.

Moustafa, Tamir. 2000. "Conflict and Cooperation between the State and Religious Institutions in Contemporary Egypt." *International Journal Middle East Studies* 32 (1): 3–22.

Mozaffari, Mehdi. 2007. "What Is Islamism? History and Definition of a Concept." *Totalitarian Movements and Political Religions* 8 (1): 17–33.

Mozaffari, Mehdi. 2009. "The Rise of Islamism in the Light of European Totalitarianism." *Totalitarian Movements and Political Religions* 10 (1): 1–13.

Mozaffari, Mehdi, and Michel Vale. 1986. *Authority in Islam*. Vol. 16.

Munson, Ziad. 2001. "Islamic Mobilization: Social Movement Theory and the Egyptian Muslim Brotherhood." *The Sociological Quarterly* 42 (4): 487–510.

Napoleon, I., Gaspard Gourgaud, and Charles Jean Tristan. 1823. *Memoirs of the History of France during the Reign of Napoleon*. London: H. Colburn and Co.

Nasr, Vali. 2003. "Lessons from the Muslim World." *Daedalus* 132 (3): 67–72.

Nawas, John A. 2013. "The Ulama as Autonomous Bearers of Religious Authority: Explaining Western Europe's Current Identity Problem with Islam." In *Negotiating Autonomy and Authority in Muslim Contexts*, edited by Monique Bernards and Marjo Buitelaar, 15–28. Walpole: Peeters.

Neslihan, Cevik. 2016. *Muslimism in Turkey and Beyond: Religion in the Modern World*. New York: Palgrave Macmillan.

Nevo, Joseph. 1998. "Religion and National Identity in Saudi Arabia." *Middle Eastern Studies* 34 (3): 34–53.

Nexon, Daniel H. 2009. *The Struggle for Power in Early Modern Europe: Religious Conflict, Dynastic Empires, and International Change*. Princeton: Princeton University Press.

Nielsen, Richard A. 2016. "Case Selection via Matching." *Sociological Methods and Research* 45 (3): 569–97.

Nielsen, Richard A. 2017. *Deadly Clerics: Blocked Ambition and the Paths to Jihad*. Cambridge: Cambridge University Press.

Nielsen, Richard A. 2020. "Women's Authority in Patriarchal Social Movements: The Case of Female Salafi Preachers." *American Journal of Political Science* 64 (1): 52–66.

North, Douglass. 1990. *Institutions, Institutional Change and Economic Performance*. New York: Cambridge University Press.

Ochsenwald, William. 1981. "Saudi Arabia and the Islamic Revival." *International Journal of Middle East Studies* 13 (3): 271–86.

Offe, Claus. 1990. "Reflections on the Self-Transformation of Movement Politics: A Tentative Stage Model." In *Challenging the Political Order: New Social and Political Movements in Western Democracies*, edited by Russell J. Dalton and Manfred Kuechler, 232–50. Cambridge, UK: Polity Press.

Okumus, Muhammad Yasir. 2014. *Will Islamic Democracy Embrace All in Tunisia?*. Istanbul: Istanbul Sehir University.

Olson, Daniel V. A. 2003. "Competing Notions of Religious Competition and Conflict in Theories of Religious Economies." In *Sacred Markets, Sacred Canopies: Essays on Religious Markets and Religious Pluralism*, edited by Ted Jelen, 133–66. Lanham: Rowman and Littlefield.

Onis, Ziya. 2006. "Globalization and Party Transformation: Turkey's Justice and Development Party in Perspective." In *Globalizing Democracy: Party Politics in Emerging Democracies*, edited by Peter Burnell, 122–40. London: Routledge.

Ottaway, Marina. 2013. "Learning Politics in Tunisia."

Ounissi, Sayida. 2016. "Ennahda from within: Islamists or 'Muslim Democrats'?" www.brookings.edu/wp-content/uploads/2016/07/Ounissi-RPI-Response-FINAL_v2.pdf.

Ozbudun, Ergun. 2006. "From Political Islam to Conservative Democracy: The Case of the Justice and Development Party in Turkey." *South European Society and Politics* 11 (3–4): 543–57.

Ozel, Soli. 2003. "Turkey at the Polls: After the Tsunami." *Journal of Democracy* 14 (2): 80–94.

Ozzano, Luca. 2013. "The Many Faces of the Political God: A Typology of Religiously Oriented Parties." *Democratization* 20 (5): 807–30.

Ozzano, Luca, and Francesco Cavatorta. 2013. "Introduction: Religiously Oriented Parties and Democratization." *Democratization* 20 (5): 799–806.

Papadakis, Elim. 1984. *The Green Movement in West Germany*. London: Croom Helm.

Pargeter, Alison. 2013. *The Muslim Brotherhood: From Opposition to Power*. London: Saqi Books.

Parsons, Wilfrid. 1910. "The Coming Elections in Belgium." *The Month* 115: 503–14.

Pellicer, Miquel, and Eva Wegner. 2012. "Electoral Rules and Clientelistic Parties: A Regression Discontinuity Approach." *Quarterly Journal of Political Science* 8 (4): 339–71.

Pelz, William A. 2016. *A People's History of Modern Europe*. London: Pluto Press.

Peter, Frank. 2006. "Individualization and Religious Authority in Western European Islam." *Islam and Christian-Muslim Relations* 17 (1): 105–18.

Peters, Edward. 2014. *Excommunication and the Catholic Church: Straight Answers to Tough Questions*. West Chester: Ascension Press.

Pevná, Katarína. 2014. "Moderation of Islamist Movements. A Comparative Analysis of Moroccan PJD and Egyptian Muslim Brotherhood." In *ECPR Graduate Conference*.

Piana, Giorgio La. 1920. "The Roman Church and Modern Italian Democracy." *The Harvard Theological Review* 13 (2): 159–83.

Pius, XI. 1922. "Ubi Arcano Dei Consilio (On the Peace of Christ in the Kingdom of Christ)." https://w2.vatican.va/content/pius-xi/en/encyclicals/documents/hf_p-xi_enc_19221223_ubi-arcano-dei-consilio.html.

Poggi, Gianfranco. 1967. *Catholic Action in Italy: The Sociology of a Sponsored Organization*. Stanford: Stanford University Press.

Bibliography

Pope Pius IX. 1875. "Quod Nunquam (On the Church in Prussia)." *Papal Encyclicals Online.* www.papalencyclicals.net/Pius09/p9quodnu.htm.

Pope Pius X. 1905. "Il Fermo Proposito (On Catholic Action in Italy)." www.ewtn.com/library/ENCYC/P10FERMO.HTM.

Powell, Mike. 2009. *Papal Infallibility: A Protestant Evaluation of an Ecumenical Issue.* Grand Rapids: Eerdmans.

Probst, Peter. 1989. "The Letter and the Spirit: Literacy and Religious Authority in the History of the Aladura Movement in Western Nigeria." *Africa: Journal of the International African Institute* 59 (4): 478–95.

Przeworski, Adam, and John Sprague. 1986. *Paper Stones: A History of Electoral Socialism.* Chicago: University of Chicago Press.

Quataert, Donald. 2005. *The Ottoman Empire 1700–1922.* 2nd ed. Cambridge: Cambridge University Press.

Rabasa, Angel, Cheryl Bernard, Lowell H. Schwartz, and Peter Sickle. 2007. *Building Moderate Muslim Networks.* Santa Monica: RAND Corporation.

Rabasa, Angel, and F. Stephen Larrabee. 2018. *The Rise of Political Islam in Turkey.* Santa Monica: RAND Corporation.

Rahner, Karl. 1968. *Encyclopedia of Theology: A Concise Sacramentum Mundi.* London: A&C Black.

Reese, Thomas J. 1996. *Inside the Vatican: The Politics and Organization of the Catholic Church.* Cambridge, MA: Harvard University Press.

Reinhard, Wolfgang. 1989. "Reformation, Counter-Reformation, and the Early Modern State: A Reassessment." *The Catholic Historical Review* 75 (3): 383–404.

Remond, Rene. 1983. "Anticlericalism: Some Reflections by Way of Introduction." *European Studies Review* 13 (2): 121–26.

Repp, Richard. 1972. "Some Observations on the Development of the Ottoman Learned Hierarchy." In *Scholars, Saints, and Sufis: Muslim Religious Institutions in the Middle East since 1500,* edited by Nikki R. Keddie, 17–32. Berkeley: University of California Press.

Rhonheimer, Martin. 2013. *The Common Good of Constitutional Democracy: Essays in Political Philosophy and on Catholic Social Teaching.* Washington, DC: CUA Press.

Robilant, Irene De. 1930. "The Catholic Press in Italy." *Foreign Affairs* 8 (3): 465–69.

Robinson, Francis. 1993. "Technology and Religious Change: Islam and the Impact of Print." *Modern Asian Studies* 27 (1): 229–51.

Robinson, Francis. 2009. "Crisis of Authority: Crisis of Islam?" *Journal of the Royal Asiatic Society* 19 (3): 339–54.

Rodrigo, Rafael Ortega. 2014. "*The Muslim Brotherhood: Creation, Evolution, and Goals for the Future.*" *Islamic Movements of Europe: Public Religion and Islamophobia in the Modern World,* edited by Frank Peter and Rafael Ortega, 7–13. London: I.B. Tauris.

Rose, Dina R. 2000. "Social Disorganization and Parochial Control: Religious Institutions and Their Communities." *Sociological Forum* 15 (2): 339–58.

Rosenblum, Nancy L. 2003. "Religious Parties, Religious Political Identity, and the Cold Shoulder of Liberal Democratic Thought." *Ethical Theory and Moral Practice* 6 (1): 23–53.

Ross, Ronald J. 1976. *Beleaguered Tower.* Notre Dame: Notre Dame University Press.

Ross, Ronald J. 1998. *The Failure of Bismarck's Kulturkampf: Catholicism and State Power in Imperial Germany, 1871–1887.* Washington DC: The Catholic University of America Press.

Rowley, Charles K., and Nathanael Smith. 2009. "Islam's Democracy Paradox: Muslims Claim to Like Democracy, so Why Do They Have so Little?" *Public Choice* 139 (3/4): 273–99.

Roy, Olivier. 1998. "Tensions in Iran: The Future of the Islamic Revolution." *Middle East Report* (207): 38–41.

Rubin, Jared. 2017. *Rulers, Religion, and Riches: Why the West Got Rich and the Middle East Did Not*. Cambridge: Cambridge University Press.

Rubin, Jared. 2019. "The Political and Economic Consequences of Religious Legitimacy." In *Advances in the Economics of Religion*, edited by Jean-Paul Carvalho, Sriya Iyer, and Jared Rubin, 311–20. Cham: Palgrave Macmillan.

Ryad, Umar. 2009. *Islamic Reformism and Christianity: A Critical Reading of the Works of Muḥammad Rashīd Riḍā and His Associates (1898–1935)*. Leiden: Brill.

Sacher, Hermann. 1914. "The Centre." In *The Catholic Encyclopedia Vol. 16*, edited by Charles G. Herbermann. New York: The Encyclopedia Press.

Salama, Mohammad, and Rachel Friedman. 2012. "Locating the Secular in Sayyid Qutb." *The Arab Studies Journal* 20 (1): 104–31.

Salem, Maryam Ben. 2018. *The Reconfiguration of Ennahdha's Recruitment Strategy in Tunisia. Issue Brief No. 04.30.18*. Houston: Rice University's Baker Institute for Public Policy.

Salt, Jeremy. 2015. "Turkey's Counterrevolution: Notes from the Side." *Middle East Policy Council* 22 (1).

San Martín, Inés. 2014. "Pope Defrocks Argentine Priest on Sexual Abuse Charges." *Crux*.

Sanabria, Enrique. 2009. *Republicanism and Anticlerical Nationalism in Spain*. New York: Springer.

Sánchez-Cuenca, Ignacio. 2004. "Party Moderation and Politicians' Ideological Rigidity." *Party Politics* 10 (3): 325–42.

Sanchez, Jose. 1972. *Anticlericalism: A Brief History*. Notre Dame: University of Notre Dame Press.

Sandal, Nukhet. 2017. *Religious Leaders and Conflict Transformation: Northern Ireland and Beyond*. Cambridge: Cambridge University Press.

Sarfati, Yusuf. 2014. *Mobilizing Religion in Middle East Politics: A Comparative Study of Israel and Turkey*. New York: Routledge.

Sarıkoyuncu, Ali. 2002. *Atatürk, Din, ve Din Adamları*. Ankara: Turkiye Diyanet Vafi Yayinlari.

Sartori, Giovanni. 1976. *Parties and Party Systems: A Framework for Analysis*. New York: Cambridge University Press.

Sattar, Noman. 1995. "'Al Ikhwan Al Muslimin' (Society of Muslim Brotherhood) Aims and Ideology, Role and Impact." *Pakistan Horizon* 48 (2): 7–30.

Schmidt, Vivien A. 2010. "Taking Ideas and Discourse Seriously: Explaining Change through Discursive Institutionalism as the Fourth 'New Institutionalism'." *European Political Science Review* 2 (01): 1.

Schwedler, Jillian. 2006. *Faith in Moderation: Islamist Parties in Jordan and Yemen*. New York: Cambridge University Press.

Schwedler, Jillian. 2011. "Can Islamists Become Moderates?: Rethinking the Inclusion-Moderation Hypothesis." *World Politics* 63 (2): 347–76.

Scott, Rachel M. 2012. "What Might the Muslim Brotherhood Do with Al-Azhar? Religious Authority in Egypt." *Die Welt Des Islams* 52 (2): 131–65.

Bibliography

Sedgwick, Mark. 2012. "Salafism, the Social, and the Global Resurgence of Religion." *Comparative Islamic Studies* 8 (1): 57–69.

Seidler, John. 1986. "Contested Accommodation: The Catholic Church as a Special Case of Social Change." *Social Forces* 64 (4): 847–74.

Şen, Serdar. 1995. *Refah Partisi'nin Teori ve Pratiği: Refah Partisi, Adil Düzen ve Kapitalizm. [The Theory and Practice of the Welfare Party: Just Order and Capitalism.]*. Istanbul: Sarmal Publishing.

Şen, Serdar. 1995. *Refah Partisi'nin Teori ve Pratiği: Refah Partisi, Adil Düzen ve Kapitalizm.* Istanbul: Sarmal Yayinevi.

Seyit, Kuranda. 2006. "The Paradox of Islam and the Challenges of Modernity." In *Negotiating the Sacred: Blasphemy and Sacrilege in a Multicultural Society*, edited by Elizabeth Burns Coleman and Kevin White, 51–65. Canberra: ANU Press.

Sezgin, Ipek Genzel. 2011. "Political Engagement Patterns of Islamist Movements: The Case of the Nizam/Selamet Movement." Doctoral Dissertation. İhsan Doğramacı Bilkent University.

Sezgin, Yüksel, and Mirjam Künkler. 2014. "Regulation of 'Religion' and the 'Religious': The Politics of Judicialization and Bureaucratization in India and Indonesia." *Comparative Studies in Society and History* 56 (2): 448–78.

Shechter, Relli. 2003. "Press Advertising in Egypt: Business Realities and Local Meaning, 1882–1956." *Arab Studies Journal* 10 (2): 44–66.

Shehata, Mostafa. 2018. "Egypt's Political Actors Post-2011 Revolution: Incomplete Struggle for Democracy." *Digest of Middle East Studies* 27 (2): 205–26.

Sheline, Annelle R. 2019. "Constructing an Islamic Nation: National Mosque Building as a Form of Nation-Building." *Nationalities Papers* 47 (1): 104–20.

Sheline, Annelle R. 2020. "Shifting Reputations for 'Moderation': Evidence from Qatar, Jordan, and Morocco." *Middle East Law and Governance* 12 (1): 109–29.

Sherkat, Darren E., and Christopher G. Ellison. 1999. "Recent Developments and Current Controversies in the Sociology of Religion." *Annual Review of Sociology* 25: 363–94.

Sigmund, Paul E. 1987. "The Catholic Tradition and Modern Democracy." *The Review of Politics* 49 (4): 530–48.

Sigmund, Paul E. 2014. "Latin American Catholicism's Opening to the Left." *The Review of Politics* 35 (1): 61–76.

Silvestri, Sarah. 2007. "Muslim Institutions and Political Mobilisation." In *European Islam: Challenges for Public Policy and Society*, edited by Michael Emerson Samir Amghar and Amel Boubekeur, 169–71. Freibur: Center for European Policy Studies.

Skovgaard-Petersen, Jakob. 1997. *Defining Islam for the Egyptian State: Muftis and Fatwas of the Dar Al Ifta*. Leiden: Brill.

Smith, Rogers M. 2004. "Identities, Interests, and the Future of Political Science." *Perspectives on Politics* 2 (2): 301–12.

Smith, Wilfred Cantwell. 1957. *Islam in Modern History*. Princeton: Princeton University Press.

Soage, Ana Belén. 2008. "Rashid Rida's Legacy." *The Muslim World* 98 (1): 1–23.

Soage, Ana Belén, and Jorge Fuentelsaz Franganillo. 2010. "The Muslim Brothers in Egypt." In *The Muslim Brotherhood: The Organization and Policies of a Global Islamist Movement*, edited by Barry Rubin, 39–55. London: Palgrave Macmillan.

Somer, Murat. 2007. "Moderate Islam and Secularist Opposition in Turkey: Implications for the World, Muslims and Secular Democracy." *Third World Quarterly* 28 (7): 1271–89.

Sonn, Tamara. 1987. "Secularism and National Stability in Islam." *Arab Studies Quarterly* 9 (3): 284–305.

Soper, J. Christopher, and Joel S. Fetzer. 2007. "Religious Institutions, Church–State History and Muslim Mobilization in Britain, France and Germany." *Journal of Ethnic and Migration Studies* 33 (6): 933–44.

Southern, Gilbert E. 1977. "The Bavarian Kulturkampf: A Chapter in Government, Church, and Society in the Early Bismarckreich." University of Massachusetts Amherst.

Sperber, Jonathan. 1980. "Social Change, Religious Practice and Political Development in a Catholic Region of Central Europe: Rhineland-Westphalia, 1830–1880." University of Chicago.

Sperber, Jonathan. 1982. "Roman Catholic Religious Identity in Rhineland-Westphalia, 1800–70: Quantitative Examples and Some Political Implications." *Social History* 7 (3): 305–18.

Sperber, Jonathan. 1984. *Popular Catholicism in Nineteenth-Century Germany.* Princeton: Princeton University Press.

Sperber, Jonathan. 1986. "Competing Counterrevolutions: Prussian State and Catholic Church in Westphalia during the 1850s." *Central European History* 19 (1): 45–62.

Spiegel, Avi. 2015. *No Young Islam: The New Politics of Religion in Morocco and the Arab World.* Princeton: Princeton University Press.

Spiegel, Avi. 2015. "Succeeding by Surviving: Examining the Durability of Political Islam in Morocco." *Rethinking Political Islam Series.* The Brookings Institution.

Stacher, Joshua A. 2002. "Post-Islamist Rumblings in Egypt: The Emergence of the Wasat Party." *Middle East Journal* 56 (3): 415–32.

Stark, Rodney, and William Sims Bainbridge. 1979. "Of Churches, Sects, and Cults: Preliminary Concepts for a Theory of Religious Movements." *Journal for the Scientific Study of Religion* 18 (2): 117–31.

Stark, Rodney, and William Sims Bainbridge. 1985. *The Future of Religion: Secularization, Revival and Cult Formation.* Berkeley: University of California Press.

Stark, Rodney, and Roger Finke. 2000. *Acts of Faith: Explaining the Human Side of Religion.* Berkeley: University of California Press.

Starrett, Gregory. 1998. *Putting Islam to Work: Education, Politics, and Religious Transformation in Egypt.* Berkeley: University of California Press.

Steinmetz, David C. 2010. *Calvin in Context.* 2nd ed. Oxford: Oxford University Press.

Steinmo, Sven. 2001. "The New Institutionalism." In *The Encyclopedia of Democratic Thought,* edited by Barry Clark and Joe Foweraker, 560–65. London: Routledge.

Stepan, Alfred. 2012. "Tunisia's Transition and the Twin Tolerations." *Journal of Democracy* 23 (2): 89–103.

Stoop, John J. de. 1931. "Farmers' League in Belgium, or 'Boerenbond'." *Journal of Farm Economics* 13 (2): 325–28.

Storm, Lise. 2020. "Exploring Post-Rebel Parties in Power: Political Space and Implications for Islamist Exclusion and Moderation." *Open Journal of Political Science* 10(4): 638–67.

Strikwerda, Carl. 1988. "The Divided Class: Catholics vs. Socialists in Belgium, 1880–1914." *Comparative Studies in Society and History* 30 (2): 333–59.

Strikwerda, Carl. 1997. *A House Divided: Catholics, Socialists, and Flemish Nationalists in Nineteenth-Century Belgium.* Lanham: Rowman and Littlefield.

Strindberg, Anders, and Mats Wärn. 2011. *Islamism: Religion, Radicalization, and Resistance.* Cambridge: Polity.

Bibliography

Sturzo, Don Luigi. 1944. "The Catholic Church and Christian Democracy." *Social Action* 10(5): 3–43.

Tabaar, Mohammad Ayatollahi. 2018. *Religious Statecraft: The Politics of Islam in Iran*. New York: Columbia University Press.

Tabaar, Mohammad Ayatollahi, and A.Kadir Yildirim. 2020. "Religious Parties and Ideological Change: A Comparison of Iran and Turkey." *Political Science Quarterly* 135 (4): 697–723.

Tadros, Mariz. 2012. *The Muslim Brotherhood in Contemporary Egypt: Democracy Redefined or Confined?* London: Routledge.

Tarhan, Gulce. 2011. "Roots of the Headscarf Debate: Laicism and Secularism in France and Turkey." *Journal of Political Inquiry* 4: 1–32.

Tarrow, Sidney. 1994. *Power in Movement: Social Movement, Collective Action and Protest*. Cambridge: Cambridge University Press.

Tas, Hakki. 2014. "Turkey's Ergenekon Imbroglio and Academia's Apathy." *Insight Turkey* 16 (1): 163–79.

Tas, Hakki. 2015. "Turkey – From Tutelary to Delegative Democracy." *Third World Quarterly* 36 (4): 776–91.

Tas, Hakki. 2018. "A History of Turkey's AKP-Gülen Conflict." *Mediterranean Politics* 23 (3): 395–402.

Taylor, Verta. 1989. "Social Movement Continuity: The Women's Movement in Abeyance." *American Sociological Review* 54 (5): 761–75.

Tepe, Sultan. 2005. "Turkey's AKP: A Model 'Muslim-Democratic' Party?" *Journal of Democracy* 16 (3): 69–82.

Tepe, Sultan. 2012. "Moderation of Religious Parties: Electoral Constraints, Ideological Commitments, and the Democratic Capacities of Religious Parties in Israel and Turkey." *Political Research Quarterly* 65 (3): 467–85.

Tessler, Mark. 1997. "The Origins of Popular Support for Islamist Movements: A Political Economy Analysis." In *Islam, Democracy, and the State in North Africa*, edited by John P. Entelis, 93–126. Bloomington: Indiana University Press.

Thomas, Samuel. 1980. "The American Press and the Church-State Pronouncements of Pope Leo XIII." *U.S. Catholic Historian* 1 (1): 17–36.

Tibi, Bassam. 1980. "Islam and Secularization: Religion and the Functional Differentiation of the Social System." *Archives for Philosophy of Law and Social Philosophy* 66 (2): 207–22.

Tierney, Brian. 1972. *Origins of Papal Infallibility, 1150–1350: A Study on the Concepts of Infallibility, Sovereignty and Tradition in the Middle Ages*. Boston: E.J. Brill.

Tilly, Charles. 1964. *The Vendee*. Cambridge: Harvard University Press.

Tissier de Mallerais, Bernard. 2004. *The Biography of Marcel Lefebvre*. Saint Marys: Angelus Press.

Toft, Monica, Daniel Philpott, and Timothy Shah. 2011. *God's Century: Resurgent Religion and Global Politics*. New York: Norton.

Torelli, Stefano Maria. 2012. "The 'AKP Model' and Tunisia's Al-Nahda: From Convergence to Competition?" *Insight Turkey* 14 (3): 65–83.

Trager, Eric. 2016. *Arab Fall: How the Muslim Brotherhood Won and Lost Egypt in 891 Days*. Washington, DC: Georgetown University Press.

Türkmen, Gülay. 2021. *Under the Banner of Islam? Turks, Kurds, and the Limits of Religious Unity*. Oxford: Oxford University Press.

Turner, Bryan S. 2007. "Religious Authority and the New Media." *Theory, Culture & Society* 24 (2): 117–34.

Ugur, Etga. 2019. *Faith and Politics in the Public Sphere: The Gülen Movement and the Mormon Church*. Syracuse: Syracuse University Press.

UNESCO. 1957. "World Literacy at Mid-Century: A Statistical Study."

Unver, Akin. 2009. "Turkey's 'Deep-State' and the Ergenekon Conundrum."

US Department of Labor Bureau of Labor Statistics. 1929. "Cooperation." *Monthly Labor Review* 28 (3): 141–45.

Vaillancourt, Jean-Guy. 1980. *Papal Power: A Study of Vatican Control over Lay Catholic Elites*. Berkeley: University of California Press.

Vallier, Ivan. 1971. "The Roman Catholic Church: A Transnational Actor." *International Organization* 25 (3): 479–502.

Vauthier, Maurice. 1894. "The Revision of the Belgian Constitution in 1893." *Political Science Quarterly* 9 (4): 704–29.

Viaene, Vincent. 2001. *Belgium and the Holy See from Gregory XVI to Pius IX (1831–1859): Catholic Revival, Society and Politics in 19th-Century Europe*. Leuven, Belgium: Universitaire Pers Leuven.

Waltz, Susan. 1986. "Islamist Appeal in Tunisia." *Middle East Journal* 40 (4): 651–70.

Warner, Carolyn M. 2012. "Christian Democracy in Italy: An Alternative Path to Religious Party Moderation." *Party Politics* 19 (2): 256–76.

Warner, Carolyn M. 2000. *Confessions of an Interest Group: The Catholic Church and Political Parties in Europe*. Princeton: Princeton University Press.

Warner, Carolyn M., Ramazan Kilinc, Christopher Hale, Adam Cohen, and Kathryn Johnson. 2015. "Religion and Public Goods Provision: Experimental and Interview Evidence from Catholicism and Islam in Europe." *Comparative Politics* 47 (2): 189–209.

Webster, Richard A. 1960. *The Cross and the Fasces: Christian Democracy and Fascism in Italy*. Stanford: Stanford University Press.

Wegner, Eva. 2011. *Islamist Opposition in Authoritarian Regimes: The Party of Justice and Development in Morocco*. Syracuse: Syracuse University Press.

Wegner, Eva, and Francesco Cavatorta. 2019. "Revisiting the Islamist–Secular Divide: Parties and Voters in the Arab World." *International Political Science Review* 40 (4): 558–75.

Weichlein, Siegfried. 2011. "Nation State, Conflict Resolution, and Culture War, 1850–1878." In *The Oxford Handbook of Modern German History*, edited by Helmut Walser Smith, 281–306. Oxford: Oxford University Press.

Wendell, Charles (tr.). 1978. *Five Tracts of Hasan Al-Banna (1906–1949): A Selection from the Majmu'at Rasa'il Al-Imam Al-Shahid Hasan Al-Banna*. Berkeley: University of California Press.

Wetenschappelijke Raad Vor het Regeringsbeleid. 2006. *Dynamism in Islamic Activism: Reference Points for Democratization and Human Right*. Amsterdam: Amsterdam University Press.

White, Jenny B. 2012. "Islamist Social Networks and Social Welfare Services in Turkey." In *Islamist Politics in the Middle East: Movements and Change*, edited by Samer Shehata, 59–67. New York: Routledge.

White, Jenny B. 2014. "Milli Gorus." In *Islamic Movements of Europe*, edited by Frank Peter and Rafael Ortega, 14–22. London: I.B. Tauris.

Whyte, John Henry. 1981. *Catholics in Western Democracies: A Study in Political Behaviour*. New York: Gill and Macmillan.

Bibliography

Wickham, Carrie Rosefsky. 2002. *Mobilizing Islam*. New York: Columbia University Press.

Wickham, Carrie Rosefsky. 2004. "The Path to Moderation: Strategy and Learning in the Formation of Egypt's Wasat Party." *Comparative Politics* 36 (2): 205–28.

Wickham, Carrie Rosefsky. 2015. *The Muslim Brotherhood: Evolution of an Islamist Movement*. Princeton: Princeton University Press.

Willis, Michael J. 2004. "Morocco's Islamists and the Legislative Elections of 2002: The Strange Case of the Party That Did Not Want to Win." *Mediterranean Politics* 9 (1): 53–81.

Willis, Michael J. 2012. *Politics and Power in the Maghreb*. London: Hurst and Company.

Windell, George G. 1954. *The Catholics and German Unity, 1866–1871*. Minneapolis: University of Minnesota Press.

Winter, Michael. 2009. "'Ulama' between the State and the Society in Pre-Modern Sunni Islam." In *Guardians of Faith in Modern Times: 'Ulama' in the Middle East*, edited by Meir Hatina, 21–45. Leiden: Brill.

Witham, Larry. 2010. *Marketplace of the Gods: How Economics Explains Religion*. Oxford: Oxford University Press.

Witte, Els, Jan Craeybeckx, and Alain Meynen. 2009. *Political History of Belgium: From 1830 Onwards*. Brussels: ASP.

Wolf, Anne. 2013. "An Islamist 'Renaissance'? Religion and Politics in Post-Revolutionary Tunisia." *The Journal of North African Studies* 18 (4): 560–73.

Wolf, Anne. 2017. *Political Islam in Tunisia: The History of Ennahda*. Oxford: Oxford University Press.

Woltering, Robbert A. F. L. 2002. "The Roots of Islamist Popularity." *Third World Quarterly* 23 (6): 1133–43.

Woods, Joseph M. 1921. "The Rise of the Papal States up to Charlemagne's Coronation." *The Catholic Historical Review* 7 (1): 44–54.

Wright, Robin. 1996. "Islam and Liberal Democracy: Two Visions of Reformation." *Journal of Democracy* 7 (2): 64–75.

Wright, Robin. 1988. "The Islamist Resurgence: A New Phase?" *Current History* 87 (526): 53–56, 85–86.

Wuthrich, F. Michael, and Sabri Ciftci. 2020. "Islamist Parties, Intraparty Organizational Dynamics, and Moderation as Strategic Behaviour." *Mediterranean Politics* 27 (3): 321–43.

Yadav, Stacey Philbrick. 2010. "Understanding 'What Islamists Want': Public Debates and Contestation in Lebanon and Yemen." *Middle East Journal* 64 (2): 199–213.

Yates, Miranda, and James Youniss. 1998. "Community Service and Political Identity Development in Adolescence." *Journal of Social Issues* 54 (3): 495–512.

Yavuz, M. Hakan 1997. "Political Islam and the Welfare (Refah) Party in Turkey." *Comparative Politics* 30 (1): 63–82.

Yavuz, M. Hakan. 2000. "Cleansing Islam from the Public Sphere." *Journal of International Affairs* 54 (1): 21–42.

Yavuz, M. Hakan. 2003. *Islamic Political Identity in Turkey*. Oxford: Oxford University Press.

Yavuz, M. Hakan. 2003. *Islamic Political Identity in Turkey*. New York: Oxford University Press.

Yavuz, M. Hakan. 2009. *Secularism and Muslim Democracy in Turkey*. New York: Cambridge University Press.

Yerkes, Sarah. 2018. "Too Strategic for the Base: How the Nidaa-Ennahdha Alliance Has Done More Harm than Good."

Yildirim, A.Kadir. 2013. "New Democrats: Religious Actors, Social Change and Democratic Consolidation in Turkey." *Contemporary Islam* 7 (3): 311–31.

Yildirim, A.Kadir. 2016. *Muslim Democratic Parties in the Middle East: Economy and Politics of Islamist Moderation.* Bloomington: Indiana University Press.

Yildirim, A.Kadir, and C. M. Lancaster. 2015. "Bending with the Wind: Revisiting Islamist Parties' Electoral Dilemma." *Politics and Religion* 8 (3): 588–613.

Yildiz, Ahmet. 2003. "Discourse of Political Islam in Turkey: The Parties of National Outlook." *The Muslim World* 93 (2): 187–209.

Yilmaz, Ihsan. 2005. "State, Law, Civil Society and Islam in Contemporary Turkey." *The Muslim World* 95 (3): 385–411.

Yilmaz, Ihsan. 2011. "Beyond Post-Islamism: Transformation of Turkish Islamism toward 'Civil Islam' and Its Potential Influence in the Muslim World." *European Journal of Economic and Political Studies* 4 (1): 245–80.

Yilmaz, Ihsan. 2021. *Creating the Desired Citizen: Ideology, State and Islam in Turkey.* Cambridge: Cambridge University Press.

Yilmaz, Muzaffer Ercan. 2012. "The Rise of Political Islam in Turkey: The Case of the Welfare Party." *Turkish Studies* 13 (3): 363–78.

Yonke, Eric E. 1990. "The Emergence of a Roman Catholic Middle Class in Nineteenth Century Germany: Catholic Associations in the Prussian Rhine Province, 1837–1876." *ProQuest Dissertations and Theses*, 1–271.

Yonke, Eric E. 2005. "Catholic Association of Germany." *Encyclopedia of 1848 Revolutions.*

Zaman, Muhammad Qasim. 2009. "The Ulama and Contestations on Religious Authority." In *Islam and Modernity: Key Issues and Debates*, edited by Muhammad Khalid Masud, Armando Salvatore, and Martin van Bruinessen, 206–36. Edinburgh: Edinburgh University Press.

Zaman, Mohammad Qasim. 2012. *Modern Islamic Thought in a Radical Age: Religious Authority and Internal Criticism.* New York: Cambridge University Press.

Zeender, John K. 1984. "Review: Recent Literature on the German Center Party." *The Catholic Historical Review* 70 (3): 428–41.

Zeghal, Malika. 1999. "Religion and Politics in Egypt: The Ulema of Al-Azhar, Radical Islam and the State (1952–94)." *International Journal of Middle East Studies* 31 (3): 371–99.

Zohny, Ahmed Y. 2019. "The Balancing Act in a Military-Dominated Transition to Democracy in Egypt after the Arab Spring." *Digest of Middle East Studies* 28 (1): 89–106.

Zollner, Barbara. 2019. "The Metamorphosis of Social Movements into Political Parties. The Egyptian Muslim Brotherhood and the Tunisian Al-Nahda as Cases for a Reflection on Party Institutionalisation Theory." *British Journal of Middle Eastern Studies* 48 (3): 370–87.

Zollner, Barbara. 2009. *The Muslim Brotherhood: Hasan Al-Hudaybi and Ideology.* London: Routledge.

Zouaghi, Sabrina, and Francesco Cavatorta. 2018. "A Doomed Relationship: Ennahdha and Salafism."

Zubaida, Sami. 2005. "Islam and Secularization." *Asian Journal of Social Science* 33 (3): 438–48.

Zulianello, Mattia. 2017. "Anti-System Parties Revisited: Concept Formation and Guidelines for Empirical Research." *Government and Opposition* 53 (4): 653–81.

List of Interviews

- AbdelHamed Al-Ghazali, MB advisor, and professor, Cairo University, November 11, 2008, Cairo, Egypt
- Abdul Mawgoud Dardery, former Freedom and Justice Party parliamentarian, April 16, 2017, Minneapolis, MN
- Sameh El-Essawy, former Member of President Mohammed Morsi's Communications Office, April 18, 2017, Tampa, FL
- Amany Aboul Fadl Farag, Muslim Brotherhood regional official, November 23, 2008, Cairo, Egypt
- Wael Haddara, former Senior Advisor to President Mohamed Morsi, April 24, 2017, Toronto, Canada
- Gamal Heshmat, Muslim Brotherhood Shura Council member and former Freedom and Justice Party parliamentarian, April 25, 2017, Montreal, Canada
- Ibrahim Mounir, Muslim Brotherhood Deputy Supreme Guide and Acting General Guide, May 3, 2017, London, England
- Hussein Rabee, Muslim Brotherhood local official in Alexandria, April 28, 2017, Liverpool, England
- Mohamed Soudan, Muslim Brotherhood's Arbitration Committee member and former Foreign Affairs Committee Secretary of the Freedom and Justice Party, May 1, 2017, London, England
- Aziz Babuscu, former AKP Istanbul province chairman and current parliamentarian, September 11, 2008, Istanbul, Turkey
- Reha Denemec, former AKP deputy party chairman, September 3, 2008, Ankara, Turkey
- Dengir Mir Mehmet Firat, former AKP parliamentarian and former deputy chairman, September 3, 2008, Ankara, Turkey
- Halide Incekara, former AKP parliamentarian, September 11, 2008, Istanbul, Turkey

298   *List of Interviews*

- Feyzullah Kiyiklik, former AKP parliamentarian, September 11, 2008, Istanbul, Turkey
- Mustafa Ozbayrak, former AKP parliamentarian, October 14, 2008, Ankara, Turkey
- Yasar Yakis, AKP founding member and former parliamentarian, August 29, 2008, Ankara, Turkey
- Rafik Abdesalam, Ennahdha Executive Bureau member and Former Minister of Foreign Affairs, February 10, 2018, Tunis, Tunisia
- Mohamed Akrout, Ennahdha Shura Council member, March 27, 2017, Tunis, Tunisia
- Mohamed Akrout, Ennahdha Shura Council member, February 9, 2018, Tunis, Tunisia
- Nawfal Al-Jamali, Ennahdha parliamentarian, March 17, 2017, Tunis, Tunisia
- Ossama Al Saghir, Ennahdha parliamentarian, March 28, 2017, Tunis, Tunisia
- Fathi Ayedi, Ennahdha parliamentarian, March 29, 2017, Tunis, Tunisia
- Dalila Babba, Ennahdha parliamentarian, March 29, 2017, Tunis, Tunisia
- Mohamed Ben Salem, Ennahdha Shura Council member, former Ennahdha Executive Council member, March 27, 2017, Tunis, Tunisia
- Pacha Bouasida, Ennahdha regional official March 24, 2017, Sfax, Tunisia
- Mohammad Chiha, Ennahdha local official, March 24, 2017, Sfax, Tunisia
- Sadok Chourou, former Ennahdha leader (1988–91), March 22, 2017, Tunis, Tunisia
- Nisaf Chrif, Ennahdha regional official, March 24, 2017, Sfax, Tunisia
- Habib Ellouze, Ennahdha Shura Council member, March 22, 2017, Tunis, Tunisia
- Habib Ellouze, Ennahdha Shura Council member, February 9, 2018, Tunis, Tunisia
- Rachid Ghannouchi, Ennahdha founder and current leader, February 8, 2018, Tunis, Tunisia
- Toumi Hamrouni, Ennahdha regional official, March 20, 2017, Nabeul, Tunisia
- Hbib Idriss, Ennahdha local official, March 24, 2017, Sfax, Tunisia
- Abdelhamid Jlassi, former Ennahdha Shura Council member, March 29, 2017, Tunis, Tunisia
- Abdelhamid Jlassi, former Ennahdha Shura Council member, February 12, 2018, Tunis, Tunisia
- Imed Khmiri, Ennahdha parliamentarian, March 22, 2017, Tunis, Tunisia
- Najib Krifi, Ennahdha local official, March 19, 2017, Tunis, Tunisia
- Mehrziya Laabidi, Ennahdha parliamentarian, March 21, 2017, Tunis, Tunisia
- Ahmad Laamari, Ennahdha parliamentarian, March 17, 2017, Tunis, Tunisia

List of Interviews

- Hicham Larayedh, Ennahdha Shura Council Member, March 17, 2017, Tunis, Tunisia
- Rabeh Mahdoui, Ennahdha local official, March 24, 2017, Sfax, Tunisia
- Ahmed Mechergui, former Ennahdha parliamentarian, March 28, 2017, Tunis, Tunisia
- Hassan Meddeb, Ennahdha regional official March 20, 2017, Nabeul, Tunisia
- Abdellatif Mekki, former Minister of Health from Ennahdha, March 28, 2017, Tunis, Tunisia
- Yousef Nouri, Ennahdha Party Committee for Civil Society Relations, March 17, 2017, Tunis, Tunisia
- Lotfi Zitoun, Advisor to Rachid Ghannouchi, March 21, 2017, Tunis, Tunisia

Index

2011 Revolution

ACI. *See* Catholic Action
ad-Dijwi, Yusuf, 78
Adil Düzen (Just Order), 143, 151
agency, 13, 17, 20, 27, 28, 30, 41, 47, 48, 62, 63, 232
Akef, Mohammed, 197, 203
AKP, 11, 14–16, 20, 43, 44, 112, 138, 150, 191, 209, 222, 224–233, 243, 263, *See also* Justice and Development Party
  debating joining the European Union, 227
Al-Azhar, 37, 70, 71, 75, 84, 122
al-Banna, Hassan, 3, 15, 71, 72, 75, 78, 106, 109, 112, 114–17, 119–129, 136, 140, 193, 194, 203, 262
al-Hudaybi, Hassan Ismail, 129, 130
al-Jamaa al-Islamiyya, 133, *See also* Islamic Group
al-Ma'mun, 63, 64
al-Manar, 78, 119
al-Maraghi, Mustafa, 75, 122
al-Nizam al-Islami, 128
al-Nour Party, 195
al-Shater, Khairat, 197, 199–201
al-Sisi, Abdel-Fatah, 122, 195, 218
al-Tilmisani, Umar, 131
al-Turabi, Hasan, 76
anti-Catholic, 16, 92, 98, 113, 153, 155, 165, 234, 235, 241, 242, 245, 246, 248
  legislation, 92
anticlericalism, 16, 89, 90, 92, 93, 96–98, 153, 155, 177–79, 181, 183, 186, 189, 234, 255, 263

anticlerical attacks, 19, 47, 87, 89, 91, 95, 96, 98, 104, 113, 114, 152, 155, 164, 174, 179, 180, 183, 252, 253, 263
  defined, 89
anti-religion, 19, 73, 87, 89, 98, 102–104, 106, 108
anti-religion attacks, 19, 88, 89, 103, 104, 106, 109
antireligious ideas, 73
anti-system, 2–13, 21, 22, 24, 25, 27, 31, 41, 43, 45, 47, 112, 113, 137, 138, 141, 151, 191, 196, 204, 225–27, 232, 233, 242, 250, 254, 261–65, 268
  defined, 9
anti-Westernism, 134
  anti-Western sentiment, 150, 223
AP, 145, *See also* Justice Party
Association Constitutionelle Conservatrice, 97, 179
Atatürk, Mustafa Kemal, 100, 107, 139, 149, 152
authority, 103, 121, 122, 162, 172, 176, 177, 194–96, 224, 230, 234, 240, 251, 253

Badie, Mohammed, 197, 199, 201, 202
Belgian Democratic League, 17, 114, 184–88, 193, 256–260, 264
Ben Ali, Zine el Abedine, 112, 134, 135, 191, 207, 211, 216, 222
black Turks, 143
Boerenbond, 17, 114, 184, 185, 187, 188, 257, 264
  Helleputte, Joris, 184, 186, 187, 189, 257, 259

301

Bonn Statement, 163
Bourguiba, Habib, 132–34, 139, 207, 211, 222
Bread Riots of 1978, 133

caliphate, 36, 68
Calvinism, 53, *See also* Reformed Protestantism
Catholic Action, 16, 114, 164–171, 174, 176, 185, 192, 247, 249, 250, 252, 253, 263
Catholic associations, 155–57, 181, 182, 253
Catholic Church, 1, 13, 16, 18, 19, 36, 44, 51–57, 60, 61, 87, 90–92, 95, 101, 103–105, 111, 113, 145, 153–55, 157, 158, 160, 161, 164, 167, 170, 174, 175, 177–79, 181–83, 186, 191, 192, 195, 203, 233–242, 244, 246, 251, 253, 256, 260, 263
  Belgian Church, 96, 97
  national church, 43, 44, 46, 48, 59, 62, 234
Catholic dogma, 3, 91, 98
Catholic identity, 46, 154, 164, 246, 260, 264
Catholic mass movements, 19, 20, 46, 47, 88, 112, 116, 118, 119, 138, 142, 145, 164, 167, 171, 190
  Belgian, 114, 181, 184, 186, 189, 254, 264
  Belgium, 114
  German, 152, 155, 156, 163, 165, 181, 238
  Italian, 164, 166, 192, 253, 263
Catholic orders, 104
Catholic parliamentarians, 47, 233, 237, 243
Catholic parties, 6
Catholic party, 113, 159
  in Belgium, 183, 189
  in Germany, 1, 163, 192, 234, 238
Catholic Party of Belgium, 17, 28, 114, 187–89, 193, 253–260, 263
Catholic political identity, 105, 113, 182
Catholic schools, 256
Catholic social teaching, 23, 236
Catholic state, 180, 242
Catholicism, 13
Catholicization, 173
CDU, 1, 2, 7, 209, *See also* Christian Democratic Union
Center Party, 14, 16, 113, 192, 233, 234, 236–246, 248, 249, 263
  Soest Program, 236, 237
Centrum conflict, 239
Centrum Party, 233
cercles littéraires, 181
CHP, 229, *See also* Republican People's Party

Christian Democracy, 167, 173, 175, 185, 186, 192, 259
  Belgian Christian Democrats, 193
  Christian Democrats, 1, 166, 172–74, 187, 192, 193, 247, 253, 256–260
Christian Democratic Union, 1
Christian missionaries, 125
  Christian missionary activism, 126
Christian society. *See* societas christiana
Church punishments, 60
church–state separation, 90
clergy, 16, 33, 36, 45, 52, 57, 59–63, 66, 73, 75, 89–91, 93–95, 98, 99, 105, 120, 154, 160, 162, 163, 165, 167, 169, 174, 178, 180, 185, 188, 192, 234, 236, 237, 241, 249, 252, 259
  Shiite clergy, 50
clericalism, 89, 90, 242, 245, 249
clericalization, 47
clerics, 60, 63, 91, 169, 183, 196, 238
Cologne Troubles, 153, 154
colonialism, 70, 105, 120, 132
  British colonialism, 115
colonization, 67, 72, 107, 127
  anti-colonial, 72, 123
Committee for the Promotion of Virtue and the Prevention of Vice, 37
confessional dilemma, 3, 4, 31, 262
confessional parties, 4, 13, 27, 46, 47, 49
Conservative Catholic politicians, 17, 193, 254
Conservative Catholics, 253
Conservative Party in Belgium, 4, 14
conservatives, 1, 82, 95–97, 103, 132, 139, 143, 157, 171, 176, 177, 187, 188, 243, 259
Cosan, Mahmud Esad, 147
Council of Trent, 52, 53
Crispi, Francesco, 94

Daens, Adolf, 188
Dar al-Ifta, 78
dawah, 111, 204, 209, 211, 213, 218, 222
Dechamps, Victor Augustin Isidore, 183
de-Christianization, 152
Demirel, Suleyman, 145, 148, 149
democracy, 3, 6–9, 11, 23, 24, 27–29, 32, 49, 95, 104, 105, 117, 130, 131, 137, 138, 151, 175, 182, 186, 188, 196, 214, 223, 225, 227, 228
democratic politics, 7, 10, 22, 25, 27, 28, 268
democratization, 7, 8, 15, 16, 20, 21, 27–29, 32, 205, 216, 264, 266, 268

Index

303

Directorate of Religious Affairs, 100, 232, *See also* Diyanet
divided loyalties, 43
Diyanet, 70, 84, 232
Droste-Vischering, 153, 155

Economic-Social Union, 169
Efendi, Musa Kazim, 73, 83
electoral politics, 4, 5, 13, 17, 24, 27, 31, 48, 204, 261, 262
Electoral Union, 169, 171
Unione Elettorale Cattolica (Catholic Electoral Union), 171
el-Erian, Essam, 198, 199, 201, 202
Ellouze, Habib, 209, 217–19, 221
Emre, Süleyman Arif, 140, 145
Ennahdha, 2, 4, 11, 15, 20, 44, 112, 209, 212, 233
Islamic Tendency Movement (MTI), 134–37
Shura Council, 2, 208, 217
specialization policy, 191, 204–207, 209–211, 215, 216, 218, 219, 221, 222
Erasmus, Desiderius, 57
Erbakan, Necmettin, 112, 142, 143, 145–152, 223–26, 263
Erdogan, Recep Tayyip, 148, 152, 224, 226, 228–232, 263
Ergenekon Case, 228
essentialism, 13, 23, 24, 30, 32, 50
estremisti, 251
EU, 151, 223, 227, *See also* European Union
European Union, 223, 226
excommunication, 57, 58, 60, 61, 163
Ezzat, Mahmoud, 197, 201

Farmers' League. *See* Boerenbond
fatwa, 37, 77, 78, 119, 124
February 28, 152, 223, 224
the Federation, 17, 114, 188, 254–260, 264
Federation of Catholic Circles, 183, 184, 189
Federation of Catholic Clubs, 183, 254
Federation of Catholic Clubs and Conservative Associations, 114, 181, 184, 188, 254, 258
financial separation, 267
FIS, 28, 131
FJP, 195–204, *See also* Freedom and Justice Party
control by the Muslim Brotherhood, 198–201
Fotouh, Abdel Moneim Aboul, 122, 123, 193, 198, 199
FP, 223, 224, *See also* Virtue Party

Frankfurt Assembly, 159
Free Officers, 129
Freedom and Justice Party, 15, 115, 191, 195, 196, 198, 199, 263
control by the Muslim Brotherhood, 196
Freemasons, 95, 96, 142, 178
as an anticlerical group, 90

Gafsa events, 134
German theology, 161
Ghannouchi, Rachid, 133–38, 205, 207–209, 212, 214, 215, 219, 220, 263
Golden Age of Islam, 75, 77, 143
Guardians of Religion, 48, 63
Gül, Abdullah, 224
Gulen Movement, 231, 232

hadith, 62–64, 69, 72, 74, 77
HDP, 229, 230, *See also* Peoples' Democratic Party
heterodoxy, 32, 160, 259
hierarchical organization, 4, 31, 39, 113, 261
Holy See, 54, 93, 94, 164, 165, 170, 174, 249, *See also* Vatican
hybrid organizational structures, 5, 15, 16, 20, 31, 42, 48, 111, 139, 152, 190, 204–206, 209–211, 218, 261, 263, 266, 267

IAF. *See* Islamic Action Front
identification
party, 41
political, 41, 88, 266
ideological flexibility, 39, 43, 261
ideological rigidity, 5, 47, 204, 262
Ijtihad, 74–76, 81, 220
defined, 74
Ikhwan al-Muslimun. *See* Muslim Brotherhood
Il fermo Proposito, 176, 168–170
Imam-Hatip schools, 139
imperialism, 103, *See also* colonialism
inclusion-moderation, 25, 196
exclusion, 9, 25, 217, 218
ideological moderation, 17, 25
institutional separation, 47
institutionalization, 4, 13, 18, 31, 36, 39, 51, 62, 85, 152, 261
institutions, 35
defined, 35
features of institutions, 35
interpretation of religion, 45
interpretations of the Qur'an, 63
religious interpretation, 24

interpretative authority, 74, 77, 83, 91
intra-party conflicts, 43, 265
Iranian Revolution, 133
Iskenderpasa lodge, 146
Islamic Action Front, 43, 264
Islamic Alliance, 131
Islamic doctrine, 22, 210
Islamic Group, 133
Islamic jurisprudence, 119
  Fiqh, 64
  jurisprudence, 75, 100, 101
Islamic law, 2, 22, 26, 64, 65, 67–69, 77, 101,
  102, 108, 132
Islamic modernism, 106
  Islamic reformist activism, 116
Islamic political identity, 103, 109
Islamic state, 4, 108, 109, 117, 118, 130, 134,
  136, 143, 180, 196
Islamist movements, 3, 8, 13, 15, 19, 20, 42,
  48, 84, 88, 106, 109, 111, 116, 118, 119,
  138, 147, 168, 170, 190, 209, 230, 231,
  265, 266
Islamist party, 6, 205, 267
  in Egypt, 195
  in Turkey, 226
Islamization, 144, 197, 265

jahiliya, 130
Jesus, 23
juridisation, 65
Justice and Development Party, 4, 16, 112,
  191, 209, 221, 224, 265
Justice Party, 139, 140, 143, 145, 146, 148,
  149

Katholischer Verein Deutschlands, 158
Kemalism/Kemalist ideology, 139
  Kemalist, 139, 140, 143, 144, 150
Khomeini, Ayatollah, 50, 72
Koblenz Laity Address, 161, 162
Kölner Wirren. *See* Cologne Troubles
Königswinter Protest, 163
Kotku, Mehmed Zahid, 141, 144–48, 150,
  151
Kültürkampf, 16, 90, 92, 93, 104, 153, 160,
  164, 192, 246
Kutan, Recai, 223, 224, 226
KVD, 158, 159, *See also Katholischer Verein
  Deutschlands*

Laabidi, Mehrziya, 208, 211, 217, 219
laïcité, 139, 212, 227

laiklik, 139
Lateran Pacts, 253
Lateran Treaty, 23, 95
The League, 173, *See also* National
  Democratic League
Lefebvre, 57, 58, 61
legitimacy, 14, 18, 19, 22, 34, 37, 41, 45, 51,
  52, 66, 71, 74, 76, 84, 85, 103, 106, 119,
  123, 172, 220, 241, 259
  political, 5, 66, 262
  religious, 6, 16, 31, 44, 45, 70, 84, 125
  state legitimation, 37
Leo XIII, 24, 94, 95, 97, 165, 168, 170, 172,
  185, 239, 241, 245, 255, 259
liberalism, 90, 92, 93, 96, 97, 104, 105, 108,
  156, 157, 171, 173, 174, 177, 178, 180,
  181, 187, 233, 248, 249, 255
liberals, 24, 91, 92, 95–98, 172, 177, 179,
  181, 182, 241, 244
L'Osservatore Cattolico, 165
lower class, 131, 154, 186, 188, 241
Lumen gentium, 55
Lutheranism, 52, 53, 57

madrasas, 65, 66, 68
Mady, Aboul Ela, 193, 194
magisterium, 23, 55–57
  magisterial authority, 56, 57
Mainz Association, 235, 236
Majalla, 68
Makki, Abdellatif, 208
Malines Congresses, 182, 258
Malou, Jules, 255
Maududi, Abu-l-A'la, 77
middle class, 17, 26, 113, 131, 154, 156, 184,
  188
middle-class German Catholics, 16, 157, 160,
  163, 166, 192, 238, 263
mihna, 63–65
  defined, 64
Milli Gorus Hareketi, 140, 146
Mirari vos, 177
MNP, 147–49, *See also* National Order Party
mobilization, 2, 38, 96, 115, 137, 181, 266
  electoral/political, 26, 29, 31, 41, 123, 150,
  240, 244
  grassroots, 45, 142, 146, 147, 152, 201,
  233, 237, 240, 263, 266, 267
  religio-political, 111, 114, 178, 254, 257
  religious, 3, 104, 114, 123, 181, 239, 254
moderation, 8, 25–27, 205
  moderateness, 138

Index

305

modernity, 3, 10, 15, 16, 19, 23, 71, 74, 76, 87, 104–106, 108–110, 121, 137, 142, 154, 157, 160, 163, 165, 192, 247

modernization, 4, 37, 38, 59, 67, 68, 70, 79, 84, 87, 89, 99, 104–107, 110, 111, 139, 141, 154, 160, 212, 262, 263

Montalembert, Charles, 182

moral authority, 5, 6, 14, 19, 31, 34, 38, 40, 41, 47, 48, 107, 109, 262

moral education, 82, 158

moral norms, 37

morality, 37, 40, 41, 72, 98, 104, 108, 116, 156, 170, 212, 220

public, 37, 104

Morsi, Mohamed, 195, 199–201

as Egyptian president, 201, 202

as leader within the FJP, 198, 201

most similar systems design, 6, 12

Mourou, Abdulfattah, 133

Movement for Unity and Reform, 147, 209

movement-party relationship/party-movement relationship, 6, 14, 20, 46, 205, 268

MSP, 148–150, *See also* National Salvation Party

Mubarak, Hosni, 131, 191, 194–97, 199, 204, 263

Muhammad's Youth, 128

MUR. *See* Movement for Unity and Reform

Murri, Romolo, 114, 166, 172–76, 192, 253

Muslim Brotherhood, 3, 4, 7, 14, 15, 20, 26, 38, 43, 71, 72, 76, 78, 82, 102, 112, 114, 115, 121, 124, 125, 127, 129, 130, 136, 137, 141, 144, 194–96, 199, 203, 204, 209, 211, 218, 262, 264

General Guidance Bureau, 127, 194, 197

Shura Council, 196, 197, 199, 202, 203

Muslim democracy, 205

Muslim parliamentarians, 48

Naksibendi Order, 141, 146, 231

Nasser, Gamal Abdel, 37, 129, 130, 139, 195

National Democratic League, 173

National Order Party, 147

National Outlook Movement, 16, 112, 117, 124, 138, 140–49, 151, 152, 191, 222–25, 232, 243, 263

Reformists, 191, 224, 225

Traditionalists, 224, 225

National Salvation Party, 148

nation-building, 37, 234

neo-Ottomanism, 230

NOM, 112, 144, 147, *See also* National Outlook Movement

non expedit, 94, 165, 175, 176, 247, 248

objectification of Islam, 71, 114

occultation, 50

the Opera, 114, 164–69, 172, 174, 192, 253, *See also* Opera dei Congressi

Opera dei Congressi, 16, 113, 164, 166, 170, 172, 263

Order of the Text, 82

organizational change, 42–44, 112, 205–208, 222, 265, 266, 268

organizational reform, 11, 207–209, 211, 265–67

organizational separation, 267

organizational structure, 5, 7, 11, 20, 43, 44, 46, 49, 54, 115, 123, 124, 164, 167, 169, 171, 180, 185, 187, 191, 193–95, 203, 206, 211, 219, 222, 233, 249, 261–63, 265, 266

organizational hierarchy, 42, 115

organizational independence, 42

orthodoxy, 36, 51, 58, 59, 61, 63, 72, 85, 157, 167

orthopraxy, 36, 51, 61, 63

Osservatore Romano, 252

Ottoman Empire, 36, 67, 68, 70, 76, 79, 80, 82, 83, 99, 143, 229

Ottomans, 36, 37, 72, 99, 102

Ottomanism, 143

Ozal, Turgut, 150

Pan-Islamism, 106, 132, 137

papacy, 53, 59, 91, 94, 175, 176, 247, 258, 259

papal orthodoxy, 153, 154

Papal State, 54, 93

parliamentary Catholics, 47, 243

parliamentary Muslims, 48

Partito Popolare Italiano. *See* Popular Party

Party for Justice and Development, 25, 265

party-movement hybrids, 6, 7, 15, 20, 31, 43, 49, 111, 112, 191, 204, 205, 221, 224, 230, 232, 262–65

Pascendi Dominici Gregis, 173

Paul VI, 58

Peoples' Democratic Party, 229

Perin, Charles, 181

personnel separation, 267

Pieni l'animo, 173

Pius Association, 157, 158, 235, 236, *See also* Piusverein
Pius IX, 92–94, 97, 154, 160, 161, 165, 171, 178, 181, 238, 241, 255
Pius X, 58, 114, 166–68, 170–75, 247, 259
Pius XI, 247, 250, 252, 253
PJD, 42, 44, *See also* Party for Justice and Development
political activism, 3, 11, 15, 16, 18, 20, 41, 44, 45, 48, 93, 113, 114, 123–25, 128, 140, 146, 152, 154, 157–161, 172, 174–76, 180, 183, 190, 191, 194, 195, 202, 204, 206, 209, 211, 217, 222, 234, 235, 238, 247, 253, 259, 265, 267
political authority, 39, 50, 53, 105, 153, 162
political behavior, 30, 32, 35, 37, 39, 202
political Catholicism, 2, 96, 163, 193, 233, 234, 240, 244, 253
political economic perspective, 27, 30, 33
political economy of religion, 33
political factions, 5, 15, 16, 20, 31, 94, 112, 114, 159, 164, 166, 179, 191, 206, 207, 211, 212, 216, 219, 222, 232, 233, 263, 267, 268
political identity, 3, 18, 87–89, 145, 147 formation, 18, 87–89
political Islam, 2, 22, 47, 49, 70, 76, 138, 191, 205, 224
pope, 52–56, 59, 62, 91, 93–95, 153, 156, 161–63, 165–68, 172–76, 180, 187, 192, 244, 245, 252, 253, 259
papal infallibility, 54–56, 92, 154, 161, 163
Popular Party, 4, 14, 16, 249, 250, 263
Popular Union, 169, 173, 176, 247, 249, 252
Pottier, Abbé, 186
PPI, 17, 175, 193, 237, 247–253, *See also* Popular Party
process tracing, 11, 12
Prophet Muhammad, 77, 143
Prophetic traditions, 62, *See also* hadith
pro-system, 5, 7, 9, 13, 24, 31, 41, 49, 193, 233
Protestantism, 40, 50, 52, 53, 55–57, 61
Augsburg Confession of 1530, 53
biblical inerrancy, 55
Protestant parties, 50
Protestant Reformation, 52, 53, 57, 105
proto-Islamists, 70, 71, 99
Abduh, Muhammad, 71–77, 106, 108, 116, 137
Ahmad, Sayyid, 71
al-Afghani, Jamal ad-Din, 71, 72, 74, 76

Quanta cura, 182
Quod Nunquam, 238
Qur'an, 2, 62–64, 69, 74, 76, 77, 86, 118, 119, 127, 229, 230
Koran, 75
Qutb, Sayyid, 77, 129, 130, 136, 140, 144

rational actors, 30, 43, 265
rational choice theory, 33
Reformed Protestantism, 52, 53
Reichensperger, Peter, 236, 237, 242
religion-secular divide
secular-Islamic conflict, 211
religion-secularism divide, 41
religious-secular conflict, 132
religiopolitical activism, 6, 7, 14, 15, 110, 111, 113, 115, 118, 119, 122, 148, 191, 204, 209, 217, 218, 224, 230, 264
religiopolitical authority, 18, 51, 85
religiopolitical identity, 19, 138, 263
religiopolitical movements, 2, 5, 6, 115, 137, 138, 145, 146, 150, 164, 204, 262
religiosity, 102, 104, 111, 118, 138, 139, 142, 212, 232
religious activism, 14, 15, 18, 48, 113, 116, 122, 125, 139, 147, 191, 195, 205, 206, 209, 215, 232, 264, 267
religious advice, 77
religious authority, 4, 11, 14, 16, 18, 19, 29, 31, 34, 38–40, 44–48, 50–54, 59, 61–67, 69–71, 73–79, 82–85, 98, 99, 103, 104, 106, 112, 114, 120, 121, 124, 133, 137, 153, 164, 166, 170, 190, 203–205, 232, 261, 262, 264
bureaucratization, 101
centralized, 5, 7, 13, 18, 46, 54, 56, 157, 162, 163, 251
claim religious authority, 5, 14, 19, 48, 202, 203, 206, 213, 215, 262
decentralized, 13, 14, 18, 28, 36, 44, 45, 50
defined, 39
existing holders of, 19, 44, 45
fragmentation of, 69, 71, 76
fragmented religious field, 47
monopolized, 5, 31, 33, 39, 44, 59, 61, 64, 66, 74, 76, 78, 82, 100, 102, 135, 176
new challengers, 29, 44, 69, 70, 74, 77, 78
online preachers, 40
religious texts, 40, 62, 63, 231
structures of, 4, 5, 10, 20, 28, 39, 50, 51
transnational religious authorities, 39
vacuum of, 48, 69, 102, 112

Index

religious competition, 4, 17, 30, 31, 33, 34, 39, 40, 44, 45, 62, 77, 82, 84, 190, 196, 250, 261
defined, 34
religious conflict, 32, 38, 57, 63, 139, 190
religious doctrine, 17, 18, 21–23, 32, 41, 43, 45, 51, 62, 85, 86, 91, 100, 107, 120
religious education, 2, 37, 44, 70, 76–78, 83, 84, 100, 111, 123, 142, 231
Christian, 164
Islamic, 99
religious establishment, 37, 68, 71–73, 82–84, 89, 98–101, 105, 106, 120, 122, 123, 132
religious factions, 5, 15, 31, 112, 164, 191, 206, 207, 209–211, 216, 217, 219, 221, 222, 232, 237, 263, 266–68
religious hierarchy, 28
religious identity, 4, 19, 41, 109, 154, 156, 191, 210, 212, 227, 231, 265
religious institutional structures, 4–6, 10–12, 14, 17, 18, 28, 33, 36, 47, 51, 54, 56, 62, 85, 101, 111, 204, 253, 261, 264
religious institutions, 2, 4, 6, 10, 12, 13, 17, 18, 27–33, 35–39, 51–53, 62, 84, 85, 92, 96, 100, 103, 139, 177, 196, 214, 261, 262, 264
defined, 7
religious instruction, 3, 94, 96, 178, 256
religious law, 2, 3, 67
religious market, 18, 31, 33, 44
religious mass movements, 15, 19, 42, 46, 110, 114, 139
Catholic, 3, 13, 16, 17
religious movements, 3, 5, 19, 20, 45, 49, 109–111, 140, 190, 204, 262
religious parties, 3, 4, 5, 6, 7, 8–21, 23, 25, 27–31, 33, 34, 39, 41–47, 49–51, 110, 137, 190, 206, 208, 261, 262, 264, 268
defined, 46
evolution of, 9, 10, 12, 264
religious party change, 4, 6, 7, 12, 13, 15, 17, 21, 27, 29, 30, 261
religious political identity, 18, 19, 31, 48, 87–89, 92, 109, 110, 112, 114, 132
religious politicization, 21
of Islam, 86
religious revival, 45, 92, 103–105, 112
Catholic, 103, 153
Catholic Revival, 103
Islamic, 103, 106, 108, 132, 134, 148
religious vision, 4, 10, 46, 110, 162, 262

Republican People's Party, 149, 229
Rerum Novarum, 168, 184, 186, 188
Egyptian, 15, 115, 191, 194–97, 207, 210, 218, 222
Tunisian, 191, 212, 213
Rida, Rashid, 71, 74–78, 108, 119, 120
risorgimento, 93, 165
Rogier Law, 178
Roman question, 93–95, 253
RP, 149–152, 223, *See also* Welfare Party

Sadat, Anwar, 130, 131, 194
Salafism, 70, 101
Salafists, 195, 196, 218
Salafiyya, 77
Salafi, 40, 77, 78, 82, 99, 101, 103, 216
School Wars, 179
secularism, 3, 6, 7, 9, 19, 23, 24, 36, 38, 49, 73, 83, 86, 87, 99, 103, 106, 107, 109, 116, 119, 139, 152, 157, 165, 180, 223, 226, 227, 232
Anglo-American model of, 139, 227
assertive, 108, 139
secular education, 97, 139, 179
secular governance, 10, 107, 139
secular society, 3, 10
secularization, 2, 15, 25, 27, 34, 73, 84, 87, 102, 105, 110–12, 125, 132, 139, 160, 240
secular reforms, 19, 37, 59, 98, 101, 110
secularization paradigm, 7
secularization thesis, 34
septennate, 245
shari'a, 22, 108, 130, 131, 136, 196
shariah, 68, 76, 216, 217
Shiite Islam, 50
Shiites, 70
Twelve Imams, 50
Twelver, 50
Shiites, 50
shumuliya, 118, 194
social justice, 108, 126, 134, 137, 186, 213, 248
social movement, 5, 6, 38, 44, 45, 125, 166, 168, 174, 184, 196, 204, 267
Social Question, 152, 158–160, 168, 192
societas christiana, 4, *See also* Christian society
Society of Italian Catholic Youth, 164, 169
Special Order, 128, 129
Specialization Policy, 15, 20, 112, 263
Sterckx, 179, 182

Sturzo, Don Luigi, 16, 17, 23, 167, 172, 175, 176, 192, 247–251, 253, 263
suffrage
  expansion of, 17, 187, 188, 192, 193, 256–58, 260, 264
  universal, 92, 187, 247
Sufism, 36, 68, 69, 112, 124, 126, 144, 146, 147
  Naksibendi Sufi, 141, 146, 147
Sunnah, 74
  sunna, 75
Sunni Islam, 5, 13, 18, 36, 39, 44, 47, 50–52, 62, 85, 111, 122, 203, 262, 268
Syllabus of Errors, 93, 161

Tanzimat reforms, 68, 101, 102
taqlid, 74, 75
territorial churches, 54
theology, 24, 32, 58, 83, 94, 153, 175
traditionalism, 71, 73, 99, 102
"true" Islam, 112, 121, 123
TURGEV, 231

Ubi Arcano Dei Consilio, 252
ulama, 13, 18, 22, 36, 38, 48, 52, 63–79, 81–85, 99–103, 120, 122, 124, 132
  anti-ulama, 19, 98, 101, 102, 106, 109
  anti-ulama attacks, 98
  decline, 18
  pact between the ulama and the ruling elite, 66
  state-ulama alliance, 48
ultramontanes, 16, 17, 97, 113, 114, 153, 154, 156–59, 161–64, 174, 178, 180, 182, 187, 188, 192, 193, 253–56, 260, 264
ultramontanism, 153, 156, 157, 159–161, 181, 255
Unione Donne, 169
Unione Popolare, 170, *See also* Popular Union

Van Humbeck Law, 97, 179, 183
vanguard, 144, 197, 215

Vatican, 5, 16, 23, 24, 36, 39, 43, 44, 48, 52, 54, 58, 59, 61, 91, 94, 97, 163, 165, 166, 169, 171, 172, 175, 176, 180, 184, 188, 237, 239, 241, 244, 245, 247–250, 252, 253, 255, 259, 261, 263
Vatican Council I, 54, 55, 161
Vatican Council II, 55, 56, 58
velayat-e faqih, 50
Vereine, 113, 155, 156, 161
  Katholikvereine, 163
  Leoverein, 240
  Piusverein, 157
  Protestantverein, 234
  Volksverein, 156, 170, 171, 235, 240, 241, 244
Verhaegen, Arthur, 186, 189, 257–59
Virtue Party, 223, 224
von Bismarck, Otto, 92, 233–35, 239, 241, 242, 245
von Ketteler, Wilhelm Emmanuel, 236
von Mallinckrodt, Herman, 236, 242

Wafd Party, 129, 131
Wahhabi clergy, 70
waqfs, 66–68, 101
  defined, 66
Wasat Party, 194, 195
Welfare Party, 143, 149, 150, 225, 226
white Turks, 143
Windthorst, Ludwig, 239, 241, 245, 246
Woeste, Charles, 188, 189, 254–56, 258, 259

Young Men's Muslim Association (YMMA), 124, 125
Young Turks, 80, 99

Zaytouna, 84, 85, 132, 133
Zentrum Party, 237, 240, *See also* Center Party
Zentrumfraktion, 233

Printed in the United States
by Baker & Taylor Publisher Services